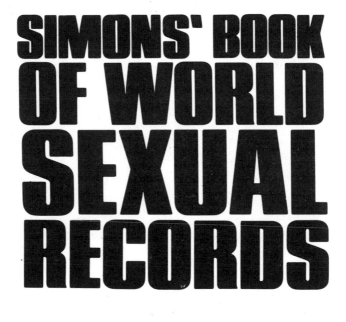

SIMONS' BOOK OF WORLD SEXUAL RECORDS

G. L. Simons

BELL PUBLISHING COMPANY
NEW YORK

INTRODUCTION

"In her abnormalities nature reveals her secrets"—
GOETHE

Records, rareties, firsts . . . the famous, the bizarre, the exceptional . . . prodigies, freaks, anomalies—all such things arouse curiosity and wonder. In a related way, the English philosopher David Hume talked of man's "usual propensity towards the marvellous", a propensity which, in history, has cast the blind woman in the role of seer and turned albino children into gods.

Sex too has its perennial fascination for mankind. As sexual creatures, men and women are seldom indifferent to the promptings of libido. And yet the natural impulse can be distorted into personal bitterness and moral outrage: the wholesome preoccupation with sex has been represented as *deviant, misguided* and *unhealthy*. One thing emerges—sex is a potent force, too ingrained in the biology of life to be ignored. In simple indulgence, the power symbols, the urge to mate, sex makes its demands. It will not go away.

The idea of sexual "records" or "superlatives" links the evocative realms of the *exceptional* and the *erotic:* the sexual superlative has a double potency . . .

Of the hundreds of items set forth in the present volume three basic types may be identified—

(1) matters of fact, well attested
(2) matters of fact, poorly attested
(3) matters of subjective evaluation

5

In the first class are the research findings of the best sexologists, the historical items scarcely open to doubt, and the simple truths laid up in common knowledge. In the second class are the factual claims made on a basis of poor documentation, anecdotal reference, and unsupported testimony. And to the third class belong the personal assessments as to fame, pre-eminence, and what is bizarre, vicious, important, etc. I leave the reader to judge to which class any particular item belongs . . .

The superlatives have been selected partly on the basis of their inherent interest. In giving brief background details to many of the items it is also hoped that the reader will find "mini-profiles" of many areas impinging on sexual and erotic matters—animal and human physiology, evolution, psychology, deviancy, law, history, anthropology, custom, religion, superstition, contraception, fertility, sexology, art, literature, sculpture, photography, etc. In any event it is hoped that this catalogue of extremes, firsts, excesses, and the like will inform, entertain, titillate, or simply amuse . . .

Chapter One

ANIMALS AND PLANTS

1. Plants—first to reproduce bisexually

It is surprising how many people are not aware, even to-day, that plants reproduce bisexually in many species. In fact the plants have been at it a long time. Algae first began to reproduce bisexually around 1,000,000,000 years ago. Considering that man has been copulating for a million years or so, the various species of algae score high on persistence. A freshwater algae (*Ulothrix*) is often used to illustrate the origin of gametes, i.e. the origin of sex-cells (1). The elongated filament-body of the algae generates a number of small spores which have lost the capacity to germinate (as they do in asexual reproduction): the spores come together and fuse to form a new individual—one of the simplest instances of the sex act.

2. Conjugation—in simplest plants

As a precursor to more complex forms of bisexual reproduction a number of simple plant and animal species learned to "conjugate", i.e. to exchange genetic material between the individuals within a species in such a way that the offspring could be distinct from either parent. The classic example among plants is *Pandorina,* a 16-cell species: the cells are loosely attached and each has a pair of flagella, or protoplasmic whips, for the purpose of locomotion through the water. To reproduce, the cells separate and fuse with the similar cells from another floating colony (2). The common bread mould represents another instance of primitive plan conjugation. The mould grows in the form of a mass of microscopic threads collectively known as a mycelium. Threads of two different kinds come together to form a special type of spore in which a blending of genetic material has taken place (3). It may be fanciful to call the two kinds of threads, respectively, *male* and *female,* but this is a clear instance of early bisexual reproduction.

3. Sexual functional differentiation—in simplest plants

In *Pandorina* (above) all the cells in the individual plant are capable of fusion with other cells for the purpose of reproduction. In more complex species however only some of the cells are involved in the reproductive process: the other cells remain in the colony and may function solely to push the plant through the water. The plant *Pleodorina* has 64 or 128 cells, only some of which take part in reproduction (4). This functional differentiation is immensely important for the evolution of living species: without it the emergence of higher life-forms would never have been possible.

4. Sex cells—first medium of transmission

One of the main problems in bisexual reproduction is how to get the sex cells together. Or—looked at another way—the whole business of sex is so pleasurable for human beings that the main problem is to keep the sex cells apart, i.e. to achieve effective contraception. In its earliest stages biological evolution managed to contrive a variety of means whereby the "male" and "female" components could come together for reproduction: the penis and vagina arrangement was "late" in the evolutionary scale. The earliest species lived in water and simply released their sex cells—the earliest equivalents of "sperm" and "egg"—to float about. Some of the cells had cilia, moving hairs, to propel them along.

5. Conjugation—in simplest animals

The tiny single-celled creature, Paramecium, is often instanced as representing the simplest form of animal conjugation. In general the *paramecium,* an inhabitant of freshwater pools, reproduces by binary fission, i.e. the single-cell simply splits in two to form a pair of identical individuals (infusoria). On occasions, however—and this is the really fascinating bit—if *paramecia* of different strains are brought into contact they adhere together by means of their primitive mouths and part of the genetic material of each individual moves slowly through the contiguous body-walls into the other. The whole process takes about a quarter of an hour to achieve, the couple having sunk in an apparently dormant state to the bottom of the water. When the genetic material from the individual nucleus has fused with its counterpart in the other individual the two *paramecia* separate and—now with a new genetic profile—continue reproducing by binary fission (5). Bisexual reproduction has also been demonstrated, on a basis of conjugation, in simple bacteria. In one experiment two mutants of one strain of *E. coli* were incubated and it was found that a few of the progeny had features of both mutants: the new cells could only be explained on the basis of an exchange of genetic material, i.e. a form of bisexual reproduction had taken place (6).

6. Sexual functional differentiation—in simplest animals

Volvox, an intriguing single-celled animal, incorporated a number of important evolutionary advances. In the words of one writer (7), it "invented the separation between body plasm and germ plasm", or—put another way—part of each individual *volvox* is concerned with reproduction and another part is concerned with feeding, movement and response to stimuli. Volvox is regarded as generating both sperm and egg (8): the sperm are flagellated and swim around until they find an egg or die. As with the higher forms of fertilization only one sperm penetrates the egg (there are some species where this is not so). The fertilized egg of *volvox* secretes a hard spiny shell which protects the inside in adverse environmental conditions such as drying or freezing.

7. Male animals—most types in a species

We are accustomed to thinking of sexually reproducing species having two sexes—one male and one female. Even in the simplest animals this is generally the case. The *Vorticella* protozoa, for instance—one of the simplest animals—have two discernable sexes, one "male" and the other "female". In some species, however, there can be *more* than two sexes. The nineteenth-century naturalist Fritz Muller described *Tanais,* a remarkable species of crustacean (9), in which the male is represented by two distinct forms. In the one form the male carries numerous smelling threads; and in the other more powerful pincers which serve to hold the female in copulation. Thus one type of male finds many females but cannot secure them as easily; the other type finds fewer females but hangs on to a bigger proportion. The upshot is the same for each male type—they both reproduce approximately the same number of offspring.

8. Sexes—most number in a species

Each sex in a species has a particular role in reproduction: it is by virtue of the role that the sex is identified. In the higher animals, "sexing" is generally a simple matter, achieved simply by a brief inspection of primary or secondary sexual features. There are sometimes confusing instances of intersexuality or hermaphroditism but such cases are usually regarded as anomalous since the reproductive capacity has been lost. The higher animals are thus regarded as having two sexes; we have seen that Tanais, the crustacean, has three; perhaps we will not be surprised now to learn that some primitive species have an even greater number of sexes. For instance, the single-celled *Paramecium amelia* is regarded as having eight different sexes, and the simple *Chlamydomonas* has no less than ten (10)—though to regard these as five "male" and five "female" seems rather fanciful.

9. Sexes—least number in a species

The least number of sexes in any species is none, one or two. It's all a matter of semantics. Some writers are only prepared to talk about *sexual* reproduction when primitive conjugation or the more highly developed forms of copulation occur in a species. In such a view *vorticella* and *paramecium* are capable of sexual reproduction, and the least number of sexes in a species is—by definition—two. If however we regard a sex as any animal or plant form capable of reproduction then clearly the least number of sexes in a species is one. The protozoa that reproduce, as paramecium sometimes does, by simple binary fission without the preceding exchange of genetic material may be regarded as having *one* sex. Or, on the earlier view, there are *no* sexes in a species that reproduces by binary fission alone.

10. Sexual dimorphism (animal)—least apparent

It is generally the case that the external genitals of the higher animals are sufficiently distinct to allow an animal to be sexed at a glance. This is not so with, for instance, some insects—where dissection is necessary before the creature's sex can be ascertained. There is also an interesting case among the mammals where the male and female genitals are surprisingly similar in appearance—thus one authority (11) comments that this species, the spotted hyaena (*Hyaenidae crocuta*) "is of unusual interest owing to the almost complete lack of external sexual dimorphism". The external genitals of the female, particularly when young, closely resemble those of the male: the clitoris has the unusual feature of being perforated by the urogenital canal and resembles in shape and position the penis of the male. And, remarkably enough, the female has scrotal pouches beneath the clitoris!

11. Sexual deviation (animal)—most frequent form

It is a common cry that variation in human sexual behavior is "unnatural," and in the same spirit a wide range of sexual acts have been condemned in law as "crimes against nature." In fact the bulk of *deviant* or *perverted* sexual behavior is commonplace throughout the animal kingdom from one species to another. Animals are quite capable of enjoying oral sex, rape, cross-species copulation (the equivalent of bestiality in humans), sadism, exhibitionism, etc. Ford and Beach, in a classic work (12), have instanced many such examples among the animals. Desmond Morris has gone to some lengths to investigate homosexuality among sticklebacks (13), and it is quite possible that this form of deviant sexual activity is the most common from one species to another. Kinsey has drawn our attention (14) to homosexual behavior in monkeys, dogs, bulls, cows, rats, porcupines, guinea pigs, rams, antelopes, stallions, donkeys, elephants, hyaenas, bats, mice, martens, hamsters, raccoons, and other species.

12. Hermaphrodite Siamese twins—most primitive species

This remarkable creature is a worm (*Diplozoon paradoxum*—the "paradoxical double animal"). It lives on the gills of carplike fish and as a hermaphrodite it is theoretically capable of mating with itself. In the course of maturing two of these parasitic worms grow together in the middle of their bodies and become effective Siamese twins joined together until death. The vagina of each half of the hermaphrodite becomes permanently linked to the spermduct of the other half. William Bolsche termed the beast "a love monstrosity, an errotic Briareus with four sexual organs mating crosswise in a double marriage (15)." There is more to the sex-life of worms than some of us realize!

13. Hermaphrodite tapeworm—longest

One species of worm, the fish tapeworm investigated by Max Braun, is a veritable giant. For a start it passes through no less than five stages before it achieves sexual maturity—egg, water worm, parasite of a crab, fish parasite, and parasite of a warm-blooded animal. This worm can actually attain a length of up to thirty feet and can live to the age of 35 years. In the course of its life it is capable of generating some four thousand segments, each of which is hermaphroditic. After copulation each segment is likely to contain an average of fifty thousand fertilized eggs. On this basis it would be theoretically possible for this enormous creature to produce two hundred million offspring. Perhaps we should be thankful that predators and other hostile environmental conditions greatly reduce the number of surviving offspring!

14. Hermaphroditism (hormonic) in mammals—best known form
When heterosexual twins develop side-by-side in cattle it is
common for the placentas to fuse, permitting an exchange
of blood: in such circumstances the ovaries of the female
twin are sterilized, and the sterile heifer which results is
called a free-martin. As long ago as 1916 Frank R. Lillie
interpreted them as resulting from the influence of the
foetal testicular hormone of the male twin (16). And in
100 B.C. and A.D. 100, Varro and Columella respectively
noted that the sterile cow is often a co-twin of a normal
bull. The body-build of a free-martin tends to resemble
that of a castrate. The clitoris is often enlarged and the
vagina is abnormally short; the gonads are more like testes
than ovaries. The condition has been described for sheep,
goats, pigs, etc. (references are given in Crew (17).

15. Sex change (birds)—commonest instances
Birds start off with two embryological ovaries but in general only one—the left—develops to maturity and the
right one remains rudimentary. If however the left ovary
is destroyed by disease or deliberate experimental technique then the right ovary will develop, not into a mature
ovary, but into a functional testis! In this way a complete
sex reversal can occur in some species of domestic fowl.
An erstwhile female may acquire cock plumage and tread
and fertilize hens. There are instances on record where
one individual started off by laying eggs and finished up
fertilizing females. Sex reversal very rarely occurs in the
opposite direction, i.e. from male to female.

16. Sex change (animal)—most primitive
Worms have a number of sexual tricks. In addition to exhibiting a range of hermaphroditic abilities they can also
undergo a complete sex reversal. Thus in one type of *Syllis*
the female will change into a male once it has laid its
eggs, and will then seek out a group of females to mate
with. Females can be artificially converted into males by
the simple expedient of cutting off half of the posterior
ring of their bodies. (The ancient question that troubled

the Greeks as to whether males or females enjoyed sex most could presumably be answered by worm individuals that have tried it both ways!) The oyster (*Ostrea edulis*) also has the habit of changing sex, but with a frequency dependent upon temperature. In one study at 20-22° C., an individual became female once a year, where as at 14-16° C., once every three to four years!

17. Sex change (fish)—best known example

The wrasse—or Cleaner fish as it is known because of its habit of eating parasites from the skin, gills, and mouths of other fishes—is a brightly colored fish living on Indo-Pacific coral reefs. In the words of one modern zoologist—"The ultimate ambition of female Cleaner fish is to become male (18)." A male generally dominates a group of females: if however he abandons his harem the most dominant of the remaining females begin to change sex within a few hours. The tendency in females towards sex change can be accounted for on the basis of an inspection of their gonads—the females are actually hermaphrodites as they all have small amounts of active (but walled-off) testicular material scattered through their ovaries. This peculiar situation among the wrasse is said to afford a number of ecological advantages.

18. Sex role reversal (animal)—only instances

The feminists derive little comfort from a glance at the animal world, where male and female roles are well defined and where the sexes conform to traditional modes of activity, i.e. males tend to be aggressive and dominant and females more interested in rearing the young. There are of course exceptions to this pattern. Female insects are often larger and more vicious than their husbands, and even among higher animals the "expected" sex roles do not always obtain. The female sea-horses actually possess a type of "penis", a prolonged genital papilla introduced into an opening in the male's abdominal sac. By this means the female introduces her eggs into a brood pouch in the male. Under this stimulation the male releases sperm into the pouch. The fertilized eggs develop, causing the abdomen of the "pregnant" father to swell enormously, until it is time for the male to give birth! Among birds the best known example of sex role reversal is the phalarope—the male sits on the eggs while the female goes out looking for food.

19. Sex organs (animal)—most numerous in a species

As human beings we are accustomed to thinking of males having one penis and two testes and females having one vagina and two ovaries (as we shall see, there are exceptions to this among men and women). However, a number of animals—generally quite primitive species—boast a greater quantity of sex organs. For instance the medusa of the water-living obelia, which looks like a tiny bell-shaped piece of clear jelly, has no less than four testes in the male and four ovaries in the female. Eggs and sperm are simply shed into the sea-water where fertilization takes place. But the most prolific number of sex organs can be found in our friend the tapeworm. It has been suggested that the tapeworm is "nothing but a bag of reproductive organs (19)." In every segment there are bunches of testes and bunches of ovaries—which means that an individual adult can finish up with hundreds of gonads.

20. Sex organs (animal)—most insecure

It hardly needs to be said that the sex organs are pretty important in any animal species. This being so, it is surprising that these organs are so insecure in many species. Many observers have suggested that a boy's testes seem vulnerable to kicks, stones, and sticks. But a number of animals have an ever harder time of it. When the male bee introduces his penis into the vagina of the queen the penis immediately breaks off and he bleeds to death (20). The sex organs of the bristle worm *Platynereis megalops* are eaten by a pursuing female to facilitate fertilization (21). In some species of squid the male copulatory arm breaks off as soon as it has penetrated the female's mantle cavity (22). And in the male opossum the prepenile scrotum is attached to the body by nothing more than a slender stalk (23).

21. Penis (animal)—largest

It is appropriate that large animals should have large genital organs. The penis of the hippopotamus and elephant can be several feet in length, and uses have sometimes been found for such weighty organs other than simple reproduction—the pizzle, for instance, formerly used for flogging, was in fact a bull's penis. One authority notes (24) that the elephant penis is around 150 cm. in length, a third of which is formed by the pendulous portion. The biggest of all animal penises are to be found among the cetaceans, which include dolphins and whales. In large Rorqual whales the penis can be 10 ft. long with a diameter of up to 1 ft (25). The whale penis, at its base, consists of two arms attached to the pelvic bones; the arms fuse into the rope-like organ. The penis in cetaceans can generally be retracted into a penile slit.

22. Penis (animal)—smallest

Almost certainly we have not yet discovered the animal species that carries the smallest penis. The reason for this is that the smallest penis will be fastened on to some tiny species of insect, and we are still discovering hundreds of such animals every year. Already we know of something like a million species of insect, with, for example, 350,000 known species of beetles. It is also open to debate as to what constitutes a penis: will a simple tube count or must there be some erectile capacity? As one example the penis on the mosquito is less than one hundredth of an inch long and there are thousands of smaller species of insects than this. The smallest insect penis in the world is certainly a fraction of a hundredth of an inch.

23. Penis (animal)—most

Most males in a relatively sophisticated species come equipped with one penis. This is not always the case. In reptiles, for instance, the genital apparatus is often paired: of the two penises on the normal male only one can be inserted into the vagina at any one time. Sometimes the paired penises are referred to as "hemi-penes"—with the suggestion that a single penis is arranged in two halves. It is also possible for each hemipenis to be split into two, resulting in four effective protruberances. Snakes exhibit such genital features as do a wide variety of other creatures. Sometimes a double penis (*diphallus*) occurs as a congenital abnormality. There are a number of well-attested cases for many mammalian species. As one example (26), a Wistar rat was noted to have an ectopic penis (possessing its own urethra) in addition to normal genital organs.

24. Penis (animal)—oddest

There is startling variation in the character of penises (penes) throughout the animal kingdom. Apart from size variation, already noted, shapes and coloring vary enormously. Insect and reptilian penises are often equipped with spines, corrugations, knobs, hooks, etc., to secure the female once insertion has taken place. If a copulating pair of insects or snakes are forcibly separated then either the male or the female may be irreparably damaged. The genital organs of the male may be torn off or the female may be terribly lacerated. Disengagement, following coitus, often needs to be a delicate business. The spines and hooks on certain animal penises are normal for the species and are often useful for purposes of classification. Sometimes however the penis may have congenital peculiarities that render coitus difficult if not impossible. One such instance is the "Corkscrew Penis" in bulls. Here the penis springs into a spiral just prior to coitus, preventing access to the cow. Veterinary experts do not seem at all clear as to why this condition occurs.

25. Penis (primate)—most unusual

Barbed penises, as we have seen, are common in many animal species. They are most uncommon among primates, so it is worth remarking on such an organ when we find one. In fact the spider monkey (*Ateles*) has a barbed penis, consisting of "a stout cylindrical organ, some 4cm X 1.5cm in size, which is remarkable for the presence of numerous small, intensely black barbs of cornified epithelium." The spider monkey is also unusual in that—unlike most other monkeys and apes—there is no bone in the penis. Part of the purpose of the barbed penis is to secure it, when erect, in the female's vagina.

26. Penis/clitoris—least size difference within species

The clitoris, as a rudimentary penis in whatever species, is generally much smaller than the male organ. Some women, for instance, even have trouble locating their clitoris but few men have difficulty finding where their penis is. In some species however the penis and clitoris are pretty well the same size, though the clitoris is thinner. Some primates, e.g. the gibbon and the spider monkey, have penis and clitoris in male and female respectively approximately the same length. It is not uncommon for the clitoris to be longer than the penis, a peculiarity which may make sexing difficult to the non-expert. Presumably male and female gibbons do not have this problem.

27. Penile thrusts in coitus (howler monkeys)—most number

Why howler monkeys, you may well ask? I have no excuse except that when I came across the superlative it seemed quite intriguing. Doubtless some monkeys have achieved a greater number of penile thrusts, but if they have I do not know of them. In one set of observations a male howler monkey managed no less than twenty-eight penile thrusts in a single intromission, after which period we may deduce that climax occurred or the fellow got bored.

28. Penile thrusts in coitus (howler monkeys)—least number

In the same set of observations as those mentioned above the minimum number of thrusts was also noted—and turned out to be eight. I rather suspect that human records would be more impressive, with possibly several hundred thrusts before climax in certain instances and only one or two in others. But in fairness it must be admitted that the performance of the various primates has hardly been examined in any detail in this respect. There may well be sturdier howler monkeys than the ones observed!

29. Testes (animal)—largest

It will hardly come as a surprise that elephants and whales have big testes: these creatures are after all weighty fellows. In one adult elephant the two testes weighted 1.8 kg. and 2.2 kg. respectively, and the left one measured 175 mm. X 150 mm. X 115 mm. in length, width, and thickness. It has been noted that bladder urine collected as much as twelve hours after death contained a large number of motile sperm. The really massive testes however belong to whales. On the whale the testes are only visible when the abdominal cavity has been opened and the intestines removed or pushed aside: the testes are two fairly elongated cylindrical organs with a white, smooth, and shiny surface. As has been pointed out, even when the whale testes have been located they are hard to handle since they weigh 60, 15, and 25 lb. in Fin, Sei, and Sperm whales respectively. In Blue Whales the testes may be more than two feet six inches long and weigh up to 100 lb. each (27)!

30. Testes (animal)—fewest

Prejudiced as we are by more or less close contact with human testes, we tend to think of these worthy organs as coming in pairs. This is usually—but not always—the case in men. In some species, as we have noted, there are more than two testes in an adult male or hermaphrodite (in some lower animals, for instance). In some species there is only one testis, this reproductive organ asymmetry being common in both sexes of the lower vertebrates. As one example, the adult male cyclostome or lamprey has only one testis; and in selachians the two testes are fused at their caudal extremities.

31. Testes (animal)—most mobile

Those of us who have read *Portnoy's Complaint* will know that human testes move about. Who, in this enlightened age, has not heard of an undescended testicle? What is perhaps more remarkable is that some animal testes move up and down according to the time of year: in one group of mammals, the testis sits happily in the abdomen for the greater part of the year but descends into the scrotum during the breeding or rutting season. Such animals include ground squirrels and bats. Yet other species have the remarkable, but sensible, ability to draw up the testes into the abdomen at moments of fright and excitement— "through the action of the cremaster muscle, within the patent processus vaginalis towards the peritoneal cavity (28)."

32. Testes (animal)—least mobile

The testes on some animals cannot be bothered making a descent into a scrotum or perineal cavity. In such creatures the internal body temperature is evidently not too high to allow effective spermatogenesis, as it would be, for instance, in primates. Animals that manage to reproduce with lazy testes include the monotremata (duckbill, spiny anteater), xenartha (sloth, armadillo), sirenia (dugong), proboscidea (elephant), cetacea (whale, dolphin), and certain insectivora (such as the golden mole). In view of all this it is strange that nature allowed *any* testes to descend. If sperm can be generated well within the abdomen it would seem to be a much safer site for such manufacture than in a pendulous exposed scrotum—and the mere process of descent is not always free from hazard.

33. Testicular follicles (insects)—greatest number

The testes of insects have a number of subdivisions— called follicles—each of which is a sperm factory. The sperm are generated in a number of stages, from spermatogonia through spermatocytes and spermatids to mature sperm ready for the task in hand. Each follicle is in a sense equivalent to the whole testis in, say, mammals. And the number of follicles varies widely from one insect species to another. *Prionoplus,* for example, has 15 follicles per testis; and *acridinae* holds the record with around one hundred. Each follicle, varying slightly in generative ability, may be considered to have a number of production zones or, looked at another way, a single production line.

34. Testicular follicles (insects)—least number

Now we all know what testicular follicles are in insects (if not then see above). Some species manage to be adequately productive with relatively few such testicular subdivisions. Lice, for example, only have two follicles per testis, and *Coleoptera adephaga* have one. In this latter case the testis more closely resembles that of mammals and, in contrast to the multiple-follicle *acridinae*, only one testicular tube is linked to the vas deferens.

35. Erection speed (animal)—fastest

In many mammalian males the speed of erection is remarkably fast. A period of three or four seconds from a fully flaccid state to full erection is commonplace and in many species the time is even less than this. Kinsey has remarked that "stallions, bulls, rams, rats, guinea pigs, porcupines, cats, dogs, apes, and males of other species may come to full erection almost instantaneously upon contact with a sexual object." As we may expect, the youngest men get the speediest erections in humans.

36. Ejaculate (animal)—largest

Whales, as may be expected, generate the greatest volume of seminal discharge—and the substance is sometimes discernable in the sea after a male has ejaculated. Among domesticated mammals the boar is usually cited as producing the greatest volume of ejaculate. The volume of fluid averages around 200 ml, but the range is from 100 ml to 500 ml (the upper limit representing a generous cupful). The volume of ejaculate in domestic animals has been monitored for purposes of artificial insemination. The artificial vagina for A.I. practices began development in the early thirties and is associated with the names of Milovanov (1932) and Rodolfo (1934).

37. Sex cell emission method—least expected

We are used to the idea of sex cells—eggs and sperm—being generated in such things as testes and ovaries and fed via penis or other genital tubes to a convenient site for fertilization. Many animals however, equally concerned that eggs and sperm should get together, have developed altogether different means of sex cell emission. One of the most surprising means is that adopted by the anemone: some such creatures reproduce asexually, by simply pulling themselves in two; while in *sexual* reproduction the eggs or sperms form on the partitions of the gastrovascular cavity and are ejected through the mouth! (Sperm don't last long in the human mouth with its complex of digestive juices.)

38. Sex cells—most number of types in a species

We already met volvox in a different context (see superlative 6). Here it is again. Unlike the bulk of other bisexual species, volvox boasts three types of sex cells—*agametes* (which propagate by simple division), *macrogametes* (which function like ova), and *microgametes* of other volvox spheres). This is really combining the best of both worlds—asexual and sexual reproduction. Simple plants and animals often do this, preferring one mode of generation in some environmental conditions and another mode in other conditions. The facility is of course helpful in allowing the species to survive if otherwise hostile fluctuations in environment.

39. Sex cells—largest male/female size difference

Sperm and egg are not only different sizes but *vastly* different sizes in most species. Eggs tend to be sluggish, relatively few and relatively large; sperm are mobile, numerous and tiny. In many species the eggs are visible to the naked eye; but in the vast bulk of species the sperm cannot be so easily detected. The word "egg" is often taken as synonymous with "ovum," yet confusion sometimes arises through such usage. Birds' eggs, for instance, often comprise much than the ovum: there are a variety of membranes and the voluminous yolk. It is in fact in bird species that there is the biggest size difference between sperm and egg—the typical egg is many millions of times greater in size, weight and volume than the individual sperm.

40. Sex cells—smallest male/female size difference

Sometimes in a species the male and female germ cells approach each other in physical dimensions. This sometimes occurs in the more primitive animals and plants. In *Actinophrys* and *Spirogyra,* for example, there is little size difference between the "eggs" and "sperm." Where this is the case there also tends to be less disparity in the number of germ cells generated in each sex.

41. Sperm (animal)—longest

Sperm come in a wide variety of shapes but in general tend to be elongated, to resemble simple filaments. The sperm of crayfish are star-shaped, while some have undulating membranes, explosive capsules, etc. It has been said that sperm never exceed 50 microns (1 micron=1 thousandth of a millimetre) in diameter, but there are a number of species in which the sperm attain remarkable lengths. In amphibia of the family *Discoglossidae* sperm can sometimes be as much as 2 mm. in length, and in the aquatic *Notonecta* the staggering length of 12 mm. is attained! Perhaps even more remarkable is the fact that in the ostracods, minute crustaceans, the sperm are six times as long as the entire body of the animal! When they are generated they are curled up in compact form (29).

42. Sperm (mammal)—longest

It is an interesting fact that the size of germ cells in a species is not related to the size of the individual within that species. In other words, the largest animals do not have the largest sperm and ova. In fact the longest mammalian sperm are to be found in the Chinese hamster, one of the most diminutive of mammals. In this species sperm are generally around 250 microns in length (30) considerably longer than in the bulk of other highly developed species.

43. Sperm (insect)—longest

Long filamentous sperm are common among insect species. As with mammals the insect sperm generally comprise a head (carrying the basic genetic material) and a tail (for purposes of locomotion). With insects however the head and tail are often very similar in cross-section and length, and in a number of species it is not always easy to tell where head ends and tail starts. What is particularly interesting is that many insect eggs have a protective waterproof *chorion* around them—which keeps out the smallest water globules but which allows the sperm to penetrate to the egg interior. In fact the sperm, immensely thin, find their way through tiny holes (*micropyles*) in the chorion. Despite their slender nature insect sperm are often extremely long. Perhaps the longest are the germ cells of *Rhodnius*—around 300 microns (31).

44. Sperm (mammal)—shortest

It is an interesting paradox that the animal with the largest genitals should generate the shortest sperm among mammals. The male Sperm Whale, with a vast penis and gigantic testicles, produces sperm about a seventh the length of those in *Rhodnius*. Whale sperm are generally around 41 microns in length. As with all mammals they are generated in vast numbers (32).

45. Sperm (animal)—least number produced

Those of us with a nodding acquaintance with the ways of sperm are accustomed to thinking of such fellows being generated in the hundreds of millions. One mammalian ejaculate can contain anything up to a thousand million germ cells! However the manufacturing abilities of many reproductively successful animals are much less impressive. The parasitic dipteran, *Miastor*—equipped with the statutory pair of testes—produces 512 sperm per testis, i.e. only 1024 sperm in all! If any mammal produced as many as ten times this quantity it would be considered sterile. The female *Miastor* lays a mere 56 eggs. Such a modest generation of germ cells has managed to keep the species viable for many millions of years (33).

46. Sperm (animal)—longest lived

In general sperm don't live long after they have been emitted from the male glands. In some species—e.g. in many insects and reptiles—there are facilities for keeping the sperm alive somewhere in the genital system of the female. Following coitus a female in some species may produce viable eggs or offspring months or even years later. The reptiles are most impressive in this field. Female lizards can store received sperm for up to six months; the African night adder manages a similar period; and the common grass snake can achieve no less than one and a half years. Turtles can store sperm for up to four years, and the brown snake can manage four and a half. The record for a female reptile storing viable sperm stands at six years: the species is Opisthoglypic colubrid snake (*leptodeira annulata polysticta*) (34). The six-year record was established by a snake in captivity—the female reproduced successfully six years after she had had access to a male partner.

47. Sperm (insect)—longest lived

Like reptiles a variety of insect females can store sperm successfully for a number of years. The desert locust (*schistocerca gregaria*) can lay fertile eggs ten weeks after the last coitus—not all that impressive by insect and reptile standards but very much longer than most mammals could manage. The honey bee loses its sexual receptivity at around 4 weeks old. The insect's *spermatheca* are used to store the sperm (between four million and 200 million) received already. A few days after the last mating the female starts to lay eggs for 24 hours a day: in a single day she can lay up to 2000 eggs (100,000 in a season). With 250,000 eggs fertilized it may be estimated that something like 1 in 30 sperm is successful. What is interesting in this context is that the female honey bee can store viable sperm for two years or even longer (35, 36).

48. Sperm (fish)—shortest lived

It is a paradox that sea-water—the medium in which many germ cells come into contact—is relatively hostile to

some types of emitted sperm and eggs. The lamprey drags
stones to make a depression in shallow, swift water. The
male is nicely equipped with a sucker by which, at appropriate times, he fastens himself onto the female. In such a
manner the two become entwined and a number of rapid
contortions ensue, whereupon eggs and sperm are emitted
into the water. After mating, the fish are soon exhausted
and quickly die. The sperm in the water have only a very
short time to make contact with the eggs. It is estimated
that the vast bulk of sperm are dead after only one minute!

49. Sperm (mammal)—longest lived

Female bats are remarkable among mammals in their capacity to store sperm for long periods. The reproductive
activity of bats and many other species is governed by a
cyclic breeding season. There is an interesting similarity
between the reproductive organs of man and the male
bat: the most important difference is that, owing to the
cyclical activity of bat reproduction the bat penis and
scrotum are seasonally either shrivelled or hugely expanded. In certain hibernating bats the process of fertilization
has been deferred in a certain stage of its progression. In
the species *Myotis, Eptesicus, Vespertilio,* and *Plecotus* the
received semen is stored in the uterus; but in the *Rhino-
lophids* the semen is stored in an outpocket of the vagina
in a viscous matrix. In the female bat the semen remains
alive throughout all the winter months: in the spring the
sperm recommence their journey towards the egg and fertilization follows (37). It has been estimated that live semen is stored in the female bat for periods of around five
months (38, 39).

50. Sperm—most elaborate

We all know that human sperm look like rather emaciated
tadpoles—and in fact most mammalian sperm have the
same sort of general configuration. Some sperm however—in both the plant and animal kingdoms—are most
elaborate affairs. For instance the sperm of a liverwort
has a couple of tails, and a lobster sperm has three. The
sperm of *macrura* is most complex, with three tails and a

translucent head; the cycad sperm look like a hairy onion; and the sperm of a fern has a curly head with numerous hairs extending from it. The maja sperm looks like a starfish. Biologically the various forms have evolved as suitable for their individual purpose in a given species. It is odd however that the basic task of fertilization—functionally similar in all animals and plants—is achieved throughout the living world by such a variously shaped range of sex cells.

51. Sperm (paired)—only mammals

Most sperm come as "one-off" jobs, i.e. they function as discrete individuals. Sometimes, i.e. in insects, they are neatly packaged in little parcels and handed over like a Christmas present. In only very few species do sperm ever appear as a couple, as a paired combination. This happens in the marsupials. The sperm, as with other mammals, exhibit the orthodox tail and head (the latter carrying the DNA responsible for conveying genetic features). What is odd however about marsupial sperm is that the heads are effectively linked, joined contiguously to a hemispherical form called the acrosome. Sometimes congenitally inferior sperm appear in isolation but "sperm couples" are the rule.

52. Sperm transfer (insect)—longest time

As we have seen, insects sometimes transfer sperm to females in a number of bundles. In general the female will hold the live sperm in her spermatheca prior to using them for the essential purpose of fertilization. The period taken for the sperm to reach the spermatheca after being deposited in the female varies from one species of insect to another. In some it is a matter of seconds. In others, hours. The longest time is taken by *Zygaena* (lepidoptera). In this species the sperm take around 15 hours to reach the spermatheca, though a period of 18 hours is not unknown.

53. Spermatoblasts (immature sperm)—first discovered

In all species, including man, a number of stages accompany the process of spermatogenesis. In insects the testicular follicles, as we have seen, have a number of sections to aid the development of mature sperm. One early stage in the production of sperm is concerned with the formulation of the spermatoblast, a spermatoid form prior to the maturation of the functional sperm. Spermatoblasts were discovered for various species in the nineteenth century. Notable among researchers was Von Siebold whose first significant work in this area dates to 1836.

54. Semen (animal) transportation—first

Semen for various animals can be kept alive for several days and in some cases for much longer in artificial conditions. It can therefore be transported over greater distances and males can reproduce, via artificial insemination, at a great distance. As one example, the semen of a ram has been collected in Cambridge, put in a thermos flask and sent to Poland by air. A Polish ewe subsequently bore healthy lambs. Other "long range" inseminations have taken place between the U.S. and the Argentine, North America and Italy, etc. The first instance of this form of *telegenesis* was achieved in 1880 by the anthropologist Vacher de Lapouge. He wrote (in his book *Social Selections*)—"Semen can be transported: in one of those idiotic experiments which Darwin recommends I obtained in Montpelier the fertilization of a rabbit with semen sent from Beziers by post."

55. Vagina (animal)—most primitive form

In most species needing a vagina a permanent channel exists beneath the abdomen. In a few animals however the vagina is a temporary affair, appearing when the young are about to be born and being virtually non-existent at other times. In marsupials the vaginal duct is blind until the young are about to be born, whereupon an opening is formed through the tissues. This primitive channel has been termed a "pseudo-vagina." It is likely to close, after the birth, until needed again. In evolutionary terms this is a primitive arrangement. Nevertheless, it works.

56. Vagina (animal)—longest

The vagina in the largest species is, by the standards of mere mortals, an extraordinarily capacious device. Elephants do not have the biggest vaginas but they are quite impressive in the magnitude of their genital apparatus. In the female elephant the vagina is a "simple, capacious tube which measures nearly 50 cm. in length (39A)." We may expect this channel to expand considerably upon insertion of the male organ. It is of some interest that the female genital channel comes equipped with a large transversely placed hymen. The largest vagina in the animal kingdom is unquestionably that of the whale. This need hardly suprise us as the female whale has to accommodate the largest animal penis. In the words of one writer (Marshall's *Physiology of Reproduction, 1,* 1, p. 99) "the vulva is a long elliptical groove which lies immediately cranial to the anus." The longest whale vagina is in the order of 6 to 8 ft. in length, capable of further elongation if necessary upon penile insertion.

57. Vagina (animal)—most number

Most animals needing a vagina make do with one. Some animals—by accident or intention—finish up with two. In the duckbill, the spiny anteater (i.e. in the *monotremes*), and in the marsupials the vaginas are paired, as are various other bits and pieces in the female genital arrangement. In the embryo the uterine tube, uterus and vagina exist as paired and entirely separate structures—and so they remain in adults of the species mentioned. This "paired" feature—common to some animals can appear as an abnormality, prohibiting reproduction, in others. Where there is a congenital fault a female may be born with a double vagina and inadequate channels to a double or single vagina. In humans surgery can be attempted.

58. Vagina (mammalian)—most unusual

Most mammalian vaginas are more or less the same in overall configuration: they basically comprise a smoothish, lubricated channel to allow penile insertion and subsequent parturition. Some vaginas are however exceptional. One such is the vagina in the female hippopotamus, coming equipped as it does with 10 to 19 transverse interlocking fibrous ridges. The ridges at the upper end of the vagina are the most pronounced, resembling heavy corrugations. Similar, though less pronounced, corrugations are discernible in the vagina of pig and warthog. In all cases the function of the ridges is a mystery.

59. Clitoris (animal)—longest

The clitoris of the female whale is about 8 cm long. Its apex is said to be "triloped" and is directed backwards. The whale clitoris, in common with the other sex organs of the largest cetaceans, are the biggest of any animal. Many other species have organs large for their body size, and in a number of species there is a long clitoris. We have already noted the large clitoris in the hyaena and the spider monkey. It is also surprisingly long in the mole (in the non-breeding season it is as long as the penis). In cats and civets the clitoris is a complicated structure reinforced with bone, and the organ is particularly prominent. Considering the absence of any functional role for the clitoris in most species it is a surprisingly impressive device in many species (40, 41).

60. Clitoris (animal)—most number

In common with the genital features of a wide range of species the clitoris is sometimes paired in a female animal. Or, put another way, the clitoris appears in two halves. Sometimes only part of the clitoris is paired, i.e. it branches towards the upper end. In marsupials the *glans clitoridis* frequently appears as a paired organ. In some reptiles a similar phenomenon can be observed in the penis but female reptiles possess no clitoris whatsoever—this does not seem to detract from enjoyment of coitus!

61. Clitoris—first developed by testicular grafts

It is possible to induce the clitoris to grow into a penis-like structure by treating a female animal with testicular grafts. Insight was gained into the significance of hormonal secretions by carrying out a number of such experiments early in the nineteenth-century (in 1849 Berthold grafted the testis of a cockerel beneath the skin of a capon and the animal assumed the normal appearance of a cockerel). In 1916 Steinach inserted testicular grafts into spayed guinea-pigs (females without ovaries): he described the growth and development of the clitoris into an organ resembling the penis.

62. Uterus—most primitive form
One of the most intriguing things about biology is how any of the sophisticated organs in living creatures can be related to more primitive organs in creatures lower down in the evolutionary tree. This is as true of the sex organs as of any other organs. In certain species of fish, e.g. the *elasmobranches*, there is an immensely primitive uterus. In fact is is hardly a uterus at all, consisting of a slight modification of the oviduct. This may well give a pointer to how the first well-defined uterus evolved (42). There are *missing links* between organs in different species just as there are between species.

63. Uterus—most number in species
If any hardy reader is ploughing through these items one-by-one he will know that various organs can be "paired," i.e. a species can have a double vagina or a double clitoris, etc. The *double* uterus is not uncommon in animal species, nor are *multi*-uteri. Our hardy reader will remember a few remarks about the tapeworm: it will not come as a surprise therefore to learn that the uterus in each segment of the tapeworm develops a number of branches, in any or all of which an embryo can develop. There is thus a *double* plurality of uteri in the tapeworm: each individual segment, of which there are many, develops a multitude of uteri (or, in an alternative jargon, many uterine branches). The uterus in a segment starts off single but after the completed eggs have been deposited the uterine branches begin to form. The tapeworm gives birth in an unusual way: "ripe" uterine sections detach from the worm and pass out with faeces.

64. Mammals—only ones egg-laying

There are very few animals that lay eggs and also suckle their young. It is an almost universal feature of mammals that they give birth to live young, i.e. they are viviparous. The *monotremata* constitute the lowest order of mammals and comprise two species—the duck-billed platypus (*Ornithorhynchus paradoxus*) and the spiny anteater (*Echidna aculeata*). These mammals are distinguished from all others in being egg-laying, i.e. oviparous. Their eggs are incubated either in a special brood-pouch. (*Echidna*) or in a nest (*Ornithorhynchus*). It is a general feature of mammals that they have evolved beyond the egg-laying stage. The monotremes are the only mammalian exception to this (43). Echidna generally lays only one egg (where two eggs appear one is degenerate); the platypus usually lays two eggs, but sometimes one or three.

65. Ova—largest

Ova, though bigger than sperm in general, are usually microscopic. In a few species they are comparatively large and can easily be detected by the naked eye. In the ostrich and the mackerel shark, for instance, the ovum may be as much as 80 mm. in diameter. This scale of magnitude constitutes a record, not just for sex cells, but for any single cells. Thus such ova are the largest single cells in the existing animal kingdom (44).

66. Ova (mammal)—smallest

The field vole (*microtus agrestis*) generates the smallest of all the mammalian ova. The typical sex cell of this creature is around 40 microns in diameter (remember 1 micron = a thousandth of a millimetre). The sperm, as usual for a mammal, are somewhat smaller. It is also of some significance that the field vole is one of the most primitive of mammals (45).

67. Eggs (insect)—largest

The size of insect eggs varies with the number laid. Moths of the family *Citheroniidae* lay large eggs: for instance the eggs of *Polyphemus* have a diameter of about one eighth of an inch, and some *Orthoptera* and *Hymenoptera* have eggs whose long axis may measure about the same(46). Probably the biggest of all insect eggs are those of *Acrididae* which can measure 8 mm. in length though only 1 mm. in diameter (47).

68. Eggs (insect)s—smallest

Termites and mayflies lay many eggs and they are very small, generally less than 1/25 in. in diameter. Females of some chalcids have eggs less than 1/100 in. long, and those of the gall midge (*Dasyneura leguminicola*) measure 1/75 by 1/250 in. (48). In *Mymaridae* the eggs range from 60 to 250 microns in length, and those of *Platygasteridae*—parasitic on the *cecidomyd* larvae—range from 20 to 100 microns in length (49). In the *Guinness Books of Records* we find reference to the tiny parasitic wasp *Caraphractus cinctus* with eggs weighing about 0.0002 mg, or 141,750,000 to the ounce.

69. Eggs (reptile)—largest

Reptilian eggs are often larger than birds' eggs. The largest egg produced by a reptile comes from the great snake, *python molurus*. Such an egg may measure 120 mm. in length: it is however only about half this dimension in width, around 60 mm.

70. Eggs (reptile)—smallest

The smallest reptilian egg comes from the lizard, *Leiolopisma laterale*. The egg from this creature measures about 5 mm. by 7 mm., i.e. considerably more circular than the great python egg (50).

71. Eggs (birds)—largest

Anyone who has seen an ostrich egg will not be surprised that it is the biggest among birds. The typical ostrich egg measures around 155 mm. by 130 mm. Even this monstrosity is unimpressive next to the egg of the long-extinct *Aepyornis* (known to us only through fossil remains). The

egg of this ancient bird often reached the size of 37.5 cm.
by 24 cm.; the egg weighed something like 120,000 gm.
and enjoyed a two-gallon capacity.

72. Eggs (birds)—smallest
Of all birds the humming-bird produces the smallest
egg—about 14 mm. by 9.5 mm. The ovum of the humming-bird is usually about 6 mm. in diameter.

73. Eggs (fish)—most number produced
The common sun-fish (*Mola mola*) generates up to 300,-
000,000 eggs $\frac{1}{10}$ in. long and $\frac{1}{20}$ in. in diameter. The
ling only manages a mere 28 million; the turbot 10 million;
and cod 7 million. Fish eggs are said to be *pelagic* (if they
float) and *demersal* (if they sink in the water). As a general rule the more eggs produced by a fish the less the
amount of attention given to the young (51).

74. Ova—fewest produced annually
The majority of mammals only produce a few ova every
year—women, as most of us suspect, generate about thirteen. In cases of cyclic sexuality a mammal may only produce one ovum in a year: some monoestrous sheep fall
into this category. Other sheep, with more than one sexually active period within twelve months may ovulate
several times in the year.

75. Eggs (rabbit)—first identified
In 1797 Cruickshank detected tubal rabbit eggs as early as
the third day after coitus, but he was not able to find eggs
nearer to the ovaries. Another thirty years passed before
the ovarian egg was discovered. Cruickshank declared—
"Experiments in which, on the third day after impregnation, the ova of rabbits were found in the Fallopian tubes;
and on the fourth day after impregnation in the uterus itself, with the first appearance of the foetus."

76. Ovum implantation (animal)—longest delay

Detailed accounts have been given of reproduction and early development in the nine-banded armadillo (*Dasypus novemcinctus*). One of the most interesting aspects of the sexual cycle is the long interval which occurs between fertilization and the attachment of the blastocyst to the uterus. Delay in implantation occurs in a variety of mammals (e.g. mustelids and deer), but *Dasypous* was one of the first to be studied in this context. In Texas the armadillo breeds during July. Following fertilization the ovum reaches the uterus but progress then ceases and the ovum does not become attached inside the uterus. This "free vesicle" stage lasts for 3½ to 4 months. In November implantation takes place, after which the blastocyst develops at a normal rate. Thus only half of the eight-month pregnancy is concerned with the development of the intra-uterine young.

77. Ovaries—most primitive form

In frogs the ovaries exist in a very primitive form. In fact they are little more than "mere folds of the peritoneum, having no solid stroma as is found in mammals." Follicle cells surround each egg, many of which degenerate before they have a chance of fertilization. The brain pituitary gland causes the eggs to ripen at the right time of the year; and ripening can be caused at any time of the year by means of mammalian anterior pituitary extract injections. The "prolans" excreted in the urine of pregnant women has a similar effect on frogs' eggs: thus the production of ovulation in *Xenopus* is used to ascertain the existence of human pregnancy.

78. Ovaries—largest

Whales have the largest ovaries of any animal species. In one estimate (52) they vary between 20 and 40 cm. in length, and in the humped-back whale (*Megaptera nodosa*) a single ovary may weigh as much as 1.4 kg. The organs are convoluted and have a very irregular surface. In a pregnant Rorqual whale one of the ovaries was seen to have a spherical mass with the dimensions of a small football—the "so-called corpeus luteum (53)." In one paper (54) a description is given of ovaries taken from non-pregnant mature blue whales: the heaviest ovary was found to weigh 15 lb. The greatest recorded weight of ovaries from a pregnant female is 35 lb. (55). The usual weight of ovaries of a large pregnant blue whale is between 22 and 24 lb. During the 1953-4 Antarctic whaling season, an 83-ft female blue whale was found to have ovaries and foetus with a combined weight of 131 lb., more than three times heavier of the pair of ovaries, containing a large corpus luteum of pregnancy, weighed 73 lb.

79. Ovaries—fewest in animal

A number of species, though equipping their embryological females with two ovaries, only exhibit one ovary in the mature female. Thus the duckbill platypus generally has atrophy of the right ovary, leading to a condition of ovarian asymmetry: the left ovary is functional but the right is diminutive and rudimentary. The same is true of birds in which, as a rule, only the left oviduct and ovary develop, the right gonad and oviduct remaining in a useless rudimentary condition. Surprisingly enough, predatory birds differ from other birds in possessing paired ovaries. The single gonad in the brook lamprey arises from paired organs which subsequently fuse. In some species, e.g. the monotremes, there is ovarian asymmetry without the smaller ovary being entirely useless (56). Bats too only have a single functional ovary.

80. Ovarioles (ovary sub-sections)—most number (insect)

The ovarioles are the female equivalent of the testicular follicles, i.e. they are gonad sub-sections responsible for the generation of sex cells. Usually they are only few such ovarioles in an insect species but in some *Diptera* and *Hymenoptera* there can be up to 200. And the queen of the higher termites, greatly concerned with vast egg production, may have as many as 2000: with this facility it becomes possible for queens to lay between 1000 and 2000 eggs a day, or about one a minute.

81. Ovarioles (ovary sub-sections)—least number (insect)

The usual number of ovarioles in insect ovaries is 4, 6 or 8. However the females of the aphis *Phylloxera*, and those of the "woolly aphids," have only a single ovariole which produces a single egg filling the whole body cavity. These are the eggs produced in the winter. Aphids are thus among the least prolific of insect egg-producers.

82. Mammary glands—largest

Back to whales again! In general, cetaceans have no protruding udders like cows. Whale mammaries are two long and fairly flat organs inclined to each other at a slight angle. Their tips are not far from the umbilicus, and the average dimensions in "resting" Rorqual cows are about 7 ft. by 2 ft. 6 in. by 2¼ in. In lactation, as with all other mammals, there are discernable changes in the size of the mammary glands. During lactation, the thickness of the glands can increase from as little as the 2¼ in. mentioned to a maximum of 1 ft: and the color changes from pink to golden brown. If the glands are strongly distended, the nipples can be detected from the outside. Jets of milk have been seen to shoot from the nipples of whale carcasses, when whalers call them "milk-filled"—a sure sign that the animal was lactating (57).

83. Nipples (animal)—largest number

It is estimated that breast-feeding began more than 200 million years ago, the time of the first mammals (which laid eggs and hatched them). Subsequently no less than 18,000 different species of mammals evolved. The kangaroo has the unique ability to produce two types of milk from two teats for young of different ages. It is curious that the number of teats or nipples varies throughout the mammalian world. The horse and elephant, for instance, have only two nipples; and though the cow has only one udder the single massive gland empties into four teats. The dog has five paired glands. The hog can have as many as eighteen mammae (58). Supernumerary nipples are common in many species, e.g. primates, rodents, ruminants.

The largest number of nipples is present in *Centetes*, a primitive insectivore with twenty-two to twenty-four nipples and as many as thirty-six young at birth (59).

84. Heat without ovulation—only animal

According to one authority the mare is the only "spontaneously ovulating" species in which the common occurrence of heat without ovulation has been established. Ovulation has also been detected in the absence of heat, and it can be artificially provoked by various methods. In some species coitus is necessary to stimulate ovulation: where this is *not* necessary a species is said to ovulate "spontaneously." A connection between ovulation and heat (sexual receptivity and excitement) is also biologically common. In the apparent absence of such a connection the mare may be regarded as exceptional. There is a myth that heavy mares have a longer oestrus cycle than lighter ones: there are no facts to support this notion.

85. Sexual activity (sheep)—highest degree

Many species of sheep only breed once a year. Hampshire Down sheep are traditionally given access to rams in the summer and do not, as a rule, breed more than once. Many foreign breeds of sheep, however, lamb twice a year, e.g. the horned sheep which run half-wild in Patani in the Malay Peninsula. Indigenous sheep of India are said to produce lambs three times in two years, and there is no definite season for lambing. In Argentina the merinos have two annual breeding seasons within the year, but it has been suggested that this may only represent a single, though extensive, breeding season. The highest degree of sexual activity experienced by any sheep is shown by certain Australian merinos, which can breed through the year—which implies, in the absence of gestation, an unbroken series of oestrous cycles. A report of the Chief Inspector of Stock for New South Wales (1891) has been quoted as dividing the time of lambing into six periods which embrace the entire year.

86. Coitus via anus—only animal species

The proximity of the human genital organs to those of elimination has upset many fastidious people and those with a religious bent (witness Augustine's cry: *"Inter faeces et urinam nascimur"*—"We are born between faeces and urine"). Such folk would surely be disturbed if they knew of the reproductive habits of certain primitive amphibians. In some land salamanders the male anus inverts over the female's to ensure that the sperm are deposited in exactly the right place. In yet other amphibians the male actually thrusts his anus *into* that of the female, a mode adopted by the primitive wormlike caecilians. Bolsche has been quoted—"Since this anus is at the same time a genuine gateway of love, our blind burrowing friend pushes out the wall of its anus in the form of a long pointed cone, till the anus itself looks like a genuine copulatory member. And this it now thrusts deep into the anus of the female burrower, as a really ingenious pederast . . ."

87. Coitus (animal)—longest

As in all other matters sexual there is immense variation throughout the animal kingdom in the actual duration of the coital act. In fact intercourse can range from a few seconds to many hours. Copulating snakes typically remain in union for one or two hours or for much longer periods—there is a suggestion that six to twelve hours is average. The record is held by a pair of rattle-snakes who remained in copulatory connection for no less than 22¾ hours (60). Such long periods may in part be explained by the difficulty the male has, on account of his spiked penis, in getting away! The fluke, *Schistosoma heamatobium*—with the female eternally living within a fissure in the male's body—has been said to exist in a state of "permanent copulation."

88. Coitus (chimpanzee)—longest

Sexual intercourse in most anthropoid apes is over very quickly, with the period of penetration measured in seconds rather than minutes. The great researcher Yerkes published the results of 95 timed matings involving three adult male chimpanzees and six different females (the data has been reproduced by Ford and Beach). The most protracted intromissions barely exceeded 15 seconds and the average duration of insertion was less than 10 seconds. The average number of copulatory thrusts shown by the different males ranged from 12.4 to 19.7. A quick coitus, implying rapid ejaculation, is represented as good from a survival point of view. Even if a female soon decides to reject a male, he has probably already had time to deposit his semen.

89. Coitus (mink and sable)—longest

Coitus of the longest duration in mammals occurs in mink and sable. Unlike coitus in other species, there is no "locking" of the genitals, but when intromission has once been achieved it is maintained for very long periods: several ejaculations can occur with rests between them. Timed matings of the sable have lasted for as long as 8 hours from the moment of original insertion until the time of withdrawal (61). One authority (62) gives coitus in the mink, as in the ferret, as "prolonged" and usually lasting for 30 to 40 minutes—with a range of 20 minutes to 2 hours. Ovulation follows after a period of about 40 hours: if conception does not occur, the animal experiences a state of "pseudopregnancy."

90. Coitus (insect)—longest

Certain species of insect are capable of coitus lasting for hours or even days, thus rivaling snakes but perhaps not the fluke. The insect *Oncopeltus* manages a coitus lasting around 5 hours, *Locusta* up to 10 hours, and *Anacridium* (*Orthoptera*) up to a magnificent 60 hours! Some insect copulations are prolonged by the difficulty of separation: insect penises, as with the organs of some reptiles, actually lock within the female vagina and withdrawal is sometimes difficult if not quite impossible. Where the male organ cannot be withdrawn it often breaks off. The unfortunate male quickly dies but his penis acts as a handy plug to stop the seminal fluid running away (63). Insect copulations, as well as being lengthy in certain species, are immensely varied in position, frequency and general character from one type of insect to another.

91. Coitus (mammal)—shortest

We have already seen that chimps do not take very long over coitus; a number of other mammals are even swifter. Slijper has noted that bulls, rams, and stags copulate "with astonishing rapidity" and that the whole process lasts no more than a few seconds (64). Horses manage a few minutes. Whales too are said to copulate very rapidly, a circumstance no doubt conditioned by their ungainly mass. In some descriptions of whale coitus the great beasts are said to dive, then to swim towards each other at great speed, "then to surface vertically and to copulate belly to belly." In this act it is often the case that the entire thorax and part of the abdomen protrudes out of the water. Slijper reports eye-witness accounts of such whale copulations. Horizontal copulation in whales is also described, a mode allowing coitus to last up to 30 seconds.

92. Coitus (insect)—shortest

Insects, we noted, achieve the longest genital coitus. They are versatile enough, in other species, to manage the shortest also. Many insects mate on the wing, allowing only a second or two of contact. As one example, various types of mosquitoes perform a sex act that lasts only 2 or 3 seconds (65).

93. Coitus (ape and monkey)—most frequent

Captive chimpanzees have been observed to achieve two or three orgasms within one hour, but it is thought unlikely that more than three or four matings would occur in a day, despite constant access to a cooperative partner. Yerkes has pointed out that the oestrous female will copulate repeatedly until her mate is quite exhausted. Carpenter has suggested that in free-ranging rhesus monkeys three or four ejaculations per day represents the greatest amount of copulatory activity, and after three or four days of sexual contact most males become unresponsive to the female. The female, in contrast, cohabits with several males in succession and may copulate fifty or sixty times during an oestrous that lasts about nine days. In howler monkeys also the female tires much less quickly than the male; and as the male becomes less interested the female will behave in an increasingly provocative fashion. In observations by Bingham it was found that a male "black ape" managed to copulate and ejaculate three times in the space of twenty minutes, but thereafter his potency soon declined. Erection was lost after a single ejaculation whereas earlier it has been maintained during the intercopulatory periods.

94. Coitus (cat)—most frequent

In laboratory experiments it has been found that cats will copulate four or five times and then be unresponsive to the female. In some rare cases male cats will regularly mate nine or ten times in a one hour test. As with the apes and monkeys the sexual responsiveness of the receptive female cat is thought to greatly exceed that of the male.

95. Coitus (rat)—most frequent

In many rodents ejaculation is produced by a series of very brief intromissions. Male rats, for example, incline to mount the female, penetrate her, and dismount several times before orgasm takes place. Each ejaculation is followed by a period of low sexual responsiveness in the male. In one series of observations, over a period of fifteen minutes some male rats achieved intromission as many as twenty or twenty-five times and had three or four ejaculations. If male rats were left with receptive females for three hours, as many as ten ejaculations took place; but in many cases three or four climaxes appeared to represent the maximal degree of activity. Again the female remains permanently receptive during oestrous and is quite capable of exhausting a sequence of males.

96. Coitus (insect)—most frequent

As we have seen, insects have already chalked up a few records in the coital stakes. In frequency of coitus they are also the champions. Many insects copulate rapidly over and over again. Thus in experimental conditions a male *Mormoniella* mated 154 times in 4½ hours; a male *Aedes aegypti* mated 30 times in 30 minutes. Often the coitus is not successful in the sense that sperm is deposited: the quantity of semen is quickly used up and a male may copulate repeatedly to no reproductive purpose (66). Thus of seven copulations by Aedes only four resulted in actual insemination of the female (67). Also the material for the bag (spermatophore) in which the sperm are conveyed to the female may be limited. *Galleria* males which copulated within 3 hours of previous copulation produced only small spermatophores often devoid of sperm. The production of spermatophores can take up to 12 hours in many insect species (68).

97. Coitus (insect)—least frequent

Some insects, not equipped for copulation, do not mate at all. Others, e.g. the females of *Callitroga* (Diptera) mate only once in a life-time, the female becoming immediately non-receptive after the initial mating. In these circumstances the normal sexual response is inhibited by nervous stimuli received from the spermatheca containing the spermatophore: this happens in, for example, the female of *Gomphocerus*. Thus some insects mate hundreds or even thousands of times, while others mate only once or not at all (69).

98. Coital positions (animal)—class with most variation

It is a feature of most copulating species that they copulate the same way each time. A few diligent researchers have observed monkeys and apes copulating face-to-face, an uncommon position for non-human primates—but in general there is little or no variation in basic coital position. Insects of different species, however, mate in many different ways. The male may effectively lie along the female, or the female may be uppermost. In some insect copulations one partner may be above but the genitals may curve under and make contact from *beneath* the other partner. In yet other instances the two insects may lie in opposite directions with only the genital region in contact.

99. Reproductive behavior (arthropods)—most varied

Those nervous folk who see "perversion" in all variation in human sexual behaviour should take a glance at the arthropods. Here all manner of sexual activity is practiced. In the words of Wendt—". . . the members of this phylum of the animal kingdom enjoy virtually every method of sexual union conceivable . . . rape, cannibalism, vampirism, abuse of children, murder of spouses, and the wildest acrobatic tricks in copulation. Also to be found are marital fidelity, tenderness, touching child care and a number of other traits to make up for the erotic chamber of horrors." There is more to animal sexuality than many of us realize!

100. Coital clasping (insect)—most unusual technique

The mating of dragonflies is remarkably complex. The male first grasps the female thorax with his second and third pair of legs, while the first pair touch the basal segments of her antennae. He then flexes his abdomen forward and fits two pairs of claspers into position on the female. Then he lets go with his legs and the two fly off "in tandem." The claspers consist of superior and inferior pairs: in *Anisoptera* the superior claspers fit round the neck of the female while the inferior claspers press down on the top of her head. In some species a sticky secretion secures the claspers: this happens in, for example, the *Coenagriidae*.

101. Coitus (insect)—oddest anatomical preliminary

One of the strangest things about all *Diptera* (two-winged insects) is that when the male emerges in the initial winged state its genitals are the wrong way round for copulation, i.e. in order to propagate, the rear end of the male has to undergo a full turn of 180 degrees to finish up upside down from its original position. The mosquito (one species of *Diptera*), for instance, has to undergo this modification. The last two segments of the male abdomen, pivoting on the membrane between the seventh and eight segment, begin to rotate. In the first three hours this end portion has turned through 90 degrees; by the twentieth hour it has made a full turn of 180 degrees. The twist—clearly visible, upon dissection, in the tracheae (air tubes), the nerve cord, and sperm ducts—is permanent (70).

102. Coitus (insect)—most vicious
A number of female insects eat their husbands during the coital act. It has been aruged that in the praying mantis, for example, the male can only copulate successfully when half his head has been eaten away—something to do with releasing nervous inhibitions! It has been pointed out that mantises will mate satisfactorily in the terrarium if the female's terrible forelimbs are tied before she is introduced to the male—so perhaps cannibalism is not essential to coitus (71). The females among many insect-eating *Diptera* are also apt to gnaw away at their husbands, and a variety of other fates may await the amorous male. In the fly *Serromyia femorata,* of the family *Ceratopogonidae,* mating takes place with the two ventral surfaces together and the mouthparts touching. At the end of mating, the female sucks out the body content of the male through the mouth. In the *Asilidae,* the male sometimes eats the female during or after mating (72).

103. Coitus (insect)—most remarkable
We have already noted some rather surprising preliminaries or accompaniments to insect coitus, but the mechanics of the coital act itself is sometimes equally remarkable. In bed bug copulation the sperm is placed in a pocket in the cuticle on the ventral surface of the female abdomen, whereupon the sperm actually makes its way through the body wall and reaches the ovaries via the blood stream. In many species—some bed bugs (as well as leeches, planarians, etc.)—the penis actually penetrates the body wall, resulting in a form of hypodermic insemination.

104. Birth immaturity—most apparent in animal species
Of all young the offspring of marsupials are the least developed at birth. The embryos of the opossum, for instance, leave the womb in an almost larval state: they can be born as little as twelve days after conception, emerging

as tiny helpless bits of flesh. They seek out their mother's milk glands, attach their mouths firmly to them, and hang on at all costs. Weeks pass before the creature's limbs and sense organs have developed sufficiently for the embryo to break this intimate contact. If a baby kangaroo is accidently dislodged from its mother's pouch it will hang by the mouth from the nipple.

105. Gestation period (animal)—longest

In most species of mammals there is a definite relation between the duration of the gestation period and the size of the young at birth, since the rate of foetal growth is the same in all of them. Thus horses carry their young for eleven months, camels for twelve months, giraffes for fourteen months, rhinoceroses for eighteen months, and elephants for as long as twenty-two months. Surprisingly (and exceptionally) every cetacean species has its own rate of foetal growth: a 4,000-lb. Blue Whale baby develops in exactly the same time (about ten months) as a twelve-lb. baby porpoise. The reason for this odd cetacean feature is thought to rest in the food situation.

106. Gestation period (animal)—shortest

The golden hamster has a gestation period of 16 days and intervals between litters as short as eighteen days: the *Guinness Book of Records* remarks that a female hamster could theoretically produce 100,000 descendants in a year. The duckbill platypus has an *even shorter gestation period* —between 7 and 10 days.

107. Litter—largest

The largest mammalian litter ever recorded at a single birth is 36, in the case of the common tenrec (*Centetes ecaudatus*) found in Madagascar and the Comoro Islands. Most litters number about 14. (We met this creature in another connection—see superlative 83).

108. Reproduction—fastest rate

However short the gestation period of mammals or the incubation period of birds the reproductive rate of such creatures is no match for that in the simplest animals. The protozoa, for instance, reproduce by binary fission—they simply split up into two parts. *Glaucoma* can undergo fission as frequently as every three hours.

109. Reproduction—simplest method
It has already been suggested that binary fission is the simplest means of reproduction. The *amoeba*—a single-celled blob of animate jelly (always instanced in biology books)—reproduces by binary fission, as do the bulk of other protozoa. Bolsche called such creatures "immortal dwarfs," because they multiply and continue to live instead of begetting children and then dying. The simplicty of the protozoa mode of reproduction does render such species immune to various sorts of reproductive hazard. Individuals are self-contained reproductive units—like hermaphrodites but without their internal complexity. It is interesting that the fertilized egg, in the higher animal species, undergoes a form of binary fission with the various resulting parts remaining joined in ever-increasing complexity.

110. Reproduction (bird)—most famous 16th Century legend
Man has always created legends about the animal world. One of the most engaging and well-known in the 16th C was devised by Konrad Gesner, the zoologist, on the love-life of birds of paradise. He decided that this creature mated in the air and raised their offspring there also. The male, it was imagined, had a concave back and the female a concave belly. After mating, the female—still flying— laid its eggs in the male's hollow back, and sat on them for incubation purposes. To secure the two birds together while they hovered in the air the male wound his two long thin tail feathers around the female's body.

111. Virgin birth (vertebrate)—first achieved in domestic fowl
Birds and mammals are not known to have produced parthenogenetic populations in the wild. But, oddly enough, experimenters working with turkeys have had considerable success in producing parthenogenetic strains. Using more than 42,000 eggs American scientists were able to increase the number of eggs "which started to develop" from 16.7

per cent in 1952 to 41.7 per cent in 1959. This improvement was a result of selective breeding. Birds producing a high proportion of eggs with parthenogenetic tendencies were mated from males descended from other such birds. Towards the end of the experiment 67 embryos were reared to hatching, a few survived to maturity, three produced sperm, and one actually produced offspring. More recently, Patricia Sarvella of the US Department of Agriculture reported the birth of four male parthenogenetic chickens, hatched from 8532 eggs: all four reached maturity (*Nature,* vol. 243, p.171).

112. Reproduction (insect)—most common form

One of the many fascinating things about insects is the wide range of reproductive modes adopted from one species to another. The most common technique is internal fertilization afer coitus, followed by oviposition (egg-laying by ovipositor), followed in turn by external development of the embryo and then hatching. Less common modes of perpetuating a species include parthenogenesis, which can be of three basic types—thelytokous (female-producing), arrhenotokous (male-producing), and amphitokous (either-producing); and viviparity, in which an insect female gives birth to active live young. It is interesting that in some viviparous insects use is made of an elementary type of placenta.

113. Masturbatory organ (animal)—least expected

Most of us tend to associate masturbatory activities with the genitals, though a few of us may also think of such bodily parts as the nipples or anus. It is curious that the antlers of deer are also an extremely effective masturbatory tool. It appears that during the rutting season—generally between September and October—the hardened antlers apparently constitute a highly sensitive erotic zone. Darling has been quoted (73)—masturbation "is accomplished by lowering the head and gently drawing the tips of the antlers to and fro through the herbage. Erection and extrusion of the penis from the sheath follow in five to seven seconds . . . Ejaculation follows about five seconds after the penis is erected . . . These antlers, used now so delicately, may within a few minutes be used with all the body's force behind them to slash with the antlers of another stag."

114. Female orgasm (animal)—most convincing evidence

There has been considerable debate as to whether female animals experience orgasm. Bronowski, for instance, has been prepared to declare that the human female is the only animal to experience orgasm. There is some inconclusive evidence that hermaphrodite snails can experience orgasm (e.g. rising curves of electrical excitement followed by discharge), and some evidence also that female rabbits experience orgasm. This question intrigued Kinsey and he wrote to various researchers who were supposed to know all about rabbits (74). Klein, for instance, wrote to Kinsey—". . . I have very often observed a quite definite peak of response with climax, from which the female falls back abruptly into a quiet state . . ." Hammond too believed there was orgasm in female rabbits and female ferrets (with regard to the latter he wrote—"A film of copulation in the ferret would, I think, show you by the expression on the face of the female that an orgasm did occur.")

115. Group Sex—largest animals

It will come as no surprise to those interested in the animal world as a whole that human beings did not invent the idea of group sexual activity. Arthropods, for example, frequently engage in such practices, as do various more highly developed species. Cetaceans—porpoises, for example—are particularly keen on various group sex activities, and so are their larger brothers and sisters, the whales. Of Grey Whales it has been noted (75)—"Another interesting habit is that mating is done in threes one female and two males. The role of the second male is not well understood but it has something to do with mutual assistance." When we think of the size of these creatures perhaps we begin to appreciate why some "mutual assistance" in mating is required.

116. Kiss—in most primitive species

Roman snails are very keen on sex play prior to copulation. The preliminary courting can include extensive rocking and to and fro, rearing up, and rhythmic oscillations. The sex play can also include what one author has termed "smacking kisses" (75). After all these happy preliminaries the actual copulation itself may last for several minutes.

117. Kiss (animal)—longest

Many fish appear to take pleasure in kissing: this is particularly the case with "ornamental" fish. Wendt remarks that "The couples use their lips in the ceremonies of courtship in a surprisingly human manner." One particular type of labyrinth fish is known as the "kissing gurani." In this species the enthusiasm for the kiss is such that one such act may last as much as twenty-five minutes. Doubtless human kisses can exceed this in duration but such achievements must be rare.

118. Love-songs (animal)—first

Many animals produce mating-calls and more complex sequences of sounds that may be termed "love-songs." Insects, for instance, generate involved musical sequences and many water-living creatures produce sounds, some of which are outside the range of human hearing. Amphibians first produced love-songs that could have been heard by human beings—had there been any alive at the time. Amphibians first started singing to each other on dry land, somewhere between two hundred and three hundred and fifty million years ago, in the Carboniferous Period. Thus Wendt—". . . we can scarcely imagine that the as yet unknown ancestors of frogs who lived in the earlier Paleozoic Era did not jump and croak. How otherwise would they have met for mating?" Perhaps the argument is not conclusive but it is oddly romantic to think of animals first beginning to communicate by sound.

119. Love-songs (animal)—longest

Many animals communicate to each other, generally for purposes of mating, with long complex sound sequences. Each sound sequence—in birds, insect, etc.—may legitimately be termed a song, and what is surprising is the complexity of some of these compositions. Whales, for example, can "sing" to each other over vast distances—up to a hundred miles, the water carrying the great booming sounds. And a single sound-sequence, i.e. a song, can last for as long as thirty minutes without repetition. We are accustomed to whales breaking anatomical records in the animal kingdom. Perhaps we would less quickly think of them as proficient songsters.

120. Love-songs (insect)—most complex

Among grasshoppers the *Saltatoria* emit "complex and highly specific songs." The hind legs are rubbed against the wings and the sounds produced are perceived by tympanal organs on the legs. Such activity is a clear mating display. Above a certain temperature the males of the species may sing spontaneously, sounding a number of notes followed by a pause. A receptive female answers with a softer call. The male and female then call alternately, the male now with a newly modified song. In threat displays two males may sing *at* each other. Perdeck has shown (76) that grasshopper songs are sexually stimulating to both sexes. In fact females get so excited that they even try to mate with silent males of the wrong species; and males speed up their locomotion and their efforts to copulate.

Chapter Two

HUMAN PHYSIOLOGY

121. Penis (human)—largest (fact)

We all know that men are supposed to worry endlessly about penis size. In popular mythology a small organ is still thought to signal a totally inadequate lover. All the best books tell us that this idea is absurd but nonetheless the notion persists. What can we say of penis size? How big is the biggest? One problem is who is to do the measuring. If men measure their own organs they are likely to exaggerate the results: it is not an area in which there are abundant objective surveys. And women too may exaggerate the size of a particular penis in their acquaintance. Walter (of *My Secret Life*) demonstrated this clearly enough: a woman spoke of a penis as being 7 in. long or even more—yet the "very large penis" measured by Walter turned out to be significantly less than 7 in. (77). According to Wardell B. Pomeroy, the Kinsey co-worker, the longest penis encountered was ten inches (78). This figure accords quite well with the results of the special *Forum* survey into penis size (79). In this careful and detailed survey, published in 1970, the largest penis was found to be 9½ in. in erection, hardly able to compete with the vast organs of pornographic fiction. In an earlier inter-racial survey, carried out about forty years ago, larger dimensions were recorded (80). In this survey, organs nearly 12 in. in length are reported. Of all penis sizes quoted in the literature the largest is unquestionably the 14 in. erect organ mentioned by Dr. David Reuben (81). But as no source is quoted perhaps we should not take too much no-

53

tice of this figure. The largest well-attested penises would seem to be between ten and twelve inches in the erect state. (See also superlatives 123, 125 and 126).

122. Penis (human)—smallest

Vast numbers of men—in one estimate the great majority—think that they have a penis much below the average in size. Perhaps they should console themselves with the thought that many men have extremely diminutive organs. Pomeroy states that the smallest penis encountered in the Kinsey surveys was 1 in. long (78). In the *Forum* study the smallest erect penis was found to be 4.75 in. in length, quite large compared with many of the specimens that do exist. There are instances reported in the medical literature of penises that do not exceed 1 cm. in full erection: such organs are sometimes labeled with the appropriate term "micropenis." And even 1 cm. is not the smallest-sized penis known to medical researchers. There is a condition known as *congenital hypoplasia,* where the body of the penis is totally absent and the glans is attached to the pubic region. In one such reported case (82), with an effective penis of much less than 1 cm. in length, the testes and secondary sexual characteristics were found to be quite normal. (See also superlatives 124 and 125).

123. Penis (human)—largest by race

In the Dr. Jacobus survey (80) definite penis size differences on a basis of race were detected. The largest Arab penises were found to be between eight and ten inches; but it was among the Muslim Sudanese that Jacobus found "the most developed phallus"—notably "one of the maximum dimensions, being nearly 12 in. in length, by a diameter of 2¼ in." The hardy researcher remarked that this was "a terrific machine"—"more likely the penis of a donkey than of a man." He concluded that the "Sudanese Negro possesses the largest genital organ of all the races of mankind." In a less extensive survey, but equally interesting, Dr. Robert Chartham measured erect penises for groups of men of various nationalities. The largest organs

for each nationality were as follows: *English—10½ in.;
West German—8½ in; Negro—7½ in.; French—7¾ in.;
Danish—8 in.; American—7¾ in.; and Swedish—7¾ in.
The groups were small, ranging from only 9 to 121 indi-
viduals; nevertheless the data acquired are not without sig-
nificance.

124. Penis (human)—smallest by race

In the Jacobus survey the Hindu man was reckoned to
have a penis that only averaged around 4 inches, a much
smaller figure than for the other races investigated. In the
Chartham survey (see also superlative (78) the smallest
organs in the various nationality groups were are follows:*
English—2¾ in.; West German—3½ in.; Negro—4 in.;
French—3½ in.; Danish—5 in.; American—3½ in.; and
Swedish—5 in. As we have already suggested, with the
groups being rather small no racial conclusions can be
drawn.

125. Penis (human)—largest by sex offender class

The Kinsey group compiled data on penis size for the detailed report on sex offenders. Various classes of offenders
were asked to estimate their penis length on the ventral
surface from the abdomen to the tip of the penis. Penis
lengths for various groups were found to average 6.3 to
6.5 in. It was found that only one group—the "aggressors
v. minors"—reported an above-average length penis
(around 6.75 in.). It was pointed out that contrary to expectation the estimated penis length of the exhibitionists
was not unusual (83). These efforts represent one of the
few attempts to discover correlations between penis size
and types of sex offender. Some writers have seen fit, however, to remark on the penile characteristics of offenders.
For instance it has been pointed out, by Colin Wilson (84)
and others, that the penis of the sexual murderer DeWitt
Clinton Cook was "so tiny that he and his wife were
forced to satisfy one another orally."

*I am indebted to Dr. Robert Chartham for permission
to quote these figures.

126. Penis (human)—largest through disease
There can be little doubt that the largest of all human penises result through the various effects of penile and scrotal elephantisasis. In the medical literature the penis in this condition is sometimes depicted as a vast sphere, as much as two feet across with the penile aperture still visible in the centre. In such unpleasant circumstances the penile skin is rough and dry on account of the destruction of the sweat glands, and varicose veins in the scrotum can sometimes burst and bleed profusely. In one picture before me a vastly inflated penis is shown reaching as low as the knees (85).

127. Penis (human)—most
There are many cases on record of a boy being born with two penises (86). Depending upon the nature of the condition surgery may or may not achieve the establishment of a normal state of affairs. I have not yet come across three penises being recorded.

128. Penis (human)—oddest
"Oddest"—like beauty—is a subjective matter. There are various penile conditions that most of us would think odd, but anyone suffering from such a state of affairs may incline to disagree. If one has to live with a condition it may come to seem quite normal, though it is hard to think of some conditions being accepted with equanimity. There is, for instance, Peyronies Disease—in which the penis bends sharply one way or the other: this can be caused by wasting of the tissue on one side of the penile stem. In Reuben's words "sexual intercourse becomes, if not impossible, very confusing." Then there is hypospadias, often associated with forms of hermaphroditism. In this condition the penile aperture may be only half way along the body of the penis, not at the end as nature presumably intended. And as one other condition worth mentioning, the penis and scrotum may be transposed, i.e. the scrotum may actually be in front and on top of the penis. This latter condition is the norm in certain animal species but

hardly so in man. In all these instances there are numerous medical references.

129. Castration (human)—least likely consequences

Castration—in the context of law, physiology, etc.—yields a number of superlatives (some of these are dealt with in Chapter 7). Here we may remark that castration, as interfering quite drastically with human physiology, may have remarkable consequences. For instance, one case has been quoted of sexual zeal actually being argumented after castration (87). A fifty-three year-old patient had been *gonadectomized*, i.e. castrated, because of tuberculosis at the age of twenty-four. Before the operation he had a coital frequency of once a month. But after the operation he noted a return of sexual interest while still at the hospital. And "later he had intercourse several times a week not only with his wife but with other women as well." There is abundant evidence that sexual interest and capacity can survive castration.

130. Phalli amputated in battle—most detailed record in ancient world

In 1300 B.C. King Menephta returned to Karnak in Egypt after defeating the Libyans. As a mark of his success he brought with him more than 13,000 phalli taken from his defeated adversaries. On an ancient monument at Karnak details of his success are given:

Phalluses of Libyan generals	6
Phalluses cut off Libyans	6359
Sirculians killed, phalluses cut off	222
Etruscans killed, phalluses cut off	542
Greeks killed, phalluses presented to the king	6111

131. Foreskins—most famous biblical tribute

The most famous biblical tribute of this sort is certainly the "dowry" reported in 1 Samuel xviii, 25-27. It is clear from the text that the foreskins of the Philistines were to serve in the stead of a conventional dowry. Thus—"And Saul said, Thus shall ye say to David, The king desireth not any dowry, but an hundred foreskins of the Philistines ... Wherefore David arose and went, he and his men, and slew some of the Philistines two hundred men; and David brought their foreskins, and they gave them in full tale to the king, that he might be the king's son-in-law. And Saul gave him Michal his daughter to wife."

132. Circumcision—first biblical reference

It is in Genesis xvii, 10-14 that God first introduces the idea of circumcision—although the rite was almost certainly practiced in pre-biblical peoples. God is said to have claimed as his convenant that every man-child be circumcised—"And he that is eight days old shall be circumcised among you, every man-child in your generations . . . and the uncircumcised man-child, whose flesh of his foreskin is not circumcised, that soul shall be cut off from his people; he hath broken my covenant."

133. Circumcision—most severe

To most of us circumcision may seem a simple enough matter: the foreskin is brought forward over the glans penis and then severed. In fact there are many variants on the simple procedure. Man has always been imaginative in ways of mutilating himself. The most extreme form of circumcision is where all *the* penile skin is removed. A procedure in which the penis of a boy was stripped of skin along its entire length was frequently performed in front of Arab fathers and the victim's intended bride (88). It has been stated that a fifth of all boys died as a result of this operation: if a boy cried out his father would kill him as a coward and unworthy of manhood. In some primitive ceremonies the penis was slit along its length as deep as the urethra: this bizarre form of mutilation was practiced among a number of Australian people.

134. Circumcision—least severe

Without doubt the mildest form of male circumcision occurred in the Americas. In some Indian tribes of South America it was the custom to make a tiny slit in the prepuce (89). Often this simple operation involved removing no skin at all and the wound would heal in a short time. The ceremony, leaving no permanent damage in the majority of cases, had a largely symbolic significance.

135. Testicle (human)—largest

Testicles are much of a muchness, varying in dimensions very little from man to man. One authority puts the "mature testicle" at from 4 to 4½ cm. long, and from 2 to 2⅖ cm. broad. It is suggested that "at the utmost" the testicle does not exceed 5 cm. in length (90). This is probably true for healthy men, though venereal and other diseases can produce staggering results. In some maladies a testicle the size of a football is not unknown. One can only try to imagine the agony caused by elephantiasis and other conditions in which the testicles can swell to proportions vastly larger than the victim's head.

136. Testicular travel (human)—most extreme in coitus

It is an interesting fact about many animal species that the testes move about from time to time. In man and some other mammals it is normal for the testes to descend into the scrotum and stay there. Kinsey has pointed out (91) that at the time of maximum sexual tension the testes are usually pulled up by their supporting cremaster muscles— "in many males the testes are pulled tight against the shaft of the penis, against the perineal surfaces, or into the groins." In a few unusual cases the testes may be pulled high enough to enter the (pathologically open) inguinal canals or even the abdomen—it is such an occurrence that accounts for "the near (or more rarely complete) disappearance of the testes of some human males when they are engaged in sexual activity." Kinsey points out that this phenomenon was noted by Aristotle in the fourth century B.C.

137. Testes (fully developed)—youngest boy

There is a rapid increase in testicular development around the age of puberty. In a few isolated cases this development takes place prematurely and may or may not be accompanied by a variety of other sexual manifestations. In one extreme case (92) a boy of only seven was found to have adult-sized testicles: in this particular instance the boy "died from an astrocytoma arising from the floor of the third ventricle." It is suggested that the discernible sexual maturity occurs in forms of precocity of cerebral origin only.

138. Vas deferens (human)—most

Most men have two vas deferens, the tubes that carry the sperm to the urethra. Occasionally in the medical literature there is a report of a man having a third vas. This possibility sometimes makes the operation of vasectomy a hazardous contraceptive measure: the surgeon may diligently cut two vas and not notice the anomalous presence of a third—in which case the vasectomised male is emphatically not sterile!

139. Sex chromosomes—first identified in sperm

The suggestion that there might be two types of sperm—one responsible for males and the other for females—was first made in 1890. It was as late as 1902 that C. E. McClung suggested that a seemingly mismatched pair of chromosomes were sex chromosomes. This idea laid the basis for the bulk of later work into the character of sexual determination in simple and complex species.

140. Sex chromosome abnormalities—rarest cases

Since 1956 workers at many medical research centers, using clever new chromosome-visualization techniques, have greatly enlarged the new science of chromosome study known as cytogenetics. It is only in the last twenty years, for example, that we have known that some girl babies are born with three X chromosomes (XXX) instead of the usual two; other girls may be born with one X chromosome missing. Similarly boys are sometimes born with an extra X chromosome (XXY), with two extra, or with an extra Y chromosome. Immensely rare cases of XXXXY and XXYY have also been reported.

141. Spermatogenesis—oldest man

In the average human ejaculate there are several hundred million live and motile sperm. The older a man gets the fewer sperm he manages to manufacture: by the age of eighty or ninety most men are infertile, though they often have enjoyable sex-lives. In a few relatively isolated communities old men appear to sire offspring with great success, a facility that appears to be associated with great longevity—as, for instance, in Georgia in the USSR and in the valley of Vilcabamba in Ecuador (93). I have yet to see studies of fertility in old men in these communities. The oldest man I have seen quoted as still producing live sperm is mentioned by Havelock Ellis—"the sperm-secreting function has no necessary final term and may be continued to advanced old age, even in one reported case to the age of 103 (94)."

142. Spermatogenesis—first shown to continue after vasectomy

The general area of vasectomy yields a number of superlatives (some of which are dealt with in Chapter 7). Here it may be remarked that the biological function of spermatogenesis continues after severing of the *vas deferens*. Of course we may expect this—the factory can function even when the channels of distribution are not operating! It was in 1830 that Cooper first showed that spermatogenesis continued after a vasectomy had been performed, though strictly speaking the experiment only demonstrated spermatogenesis some years after the operation—leaving open the possibility that spermatogenesis had stopped for a time and then restarted (95).

143. Sperm (human)—most

Writers are notoriously vague about the number of human sperm produced. It doesn't matter too much—when you are dealing in hundreds of millions of the little fellows the odd few million are not all that important. One writers suggests that the number of human sperm can vary from zero to 700 million or more per millilitre. The zero bit needn't surprise us: after all we know that some men are sterile. The upper extreme, however, is quite remarkable. Considering the complexity of a single sperm the capabilities of the testes in generating such intricate machines by the hundreds of million are little short of miraculous.

144. Sperm (human) storage by freezing—longest period of viability

According to the American Public Health Association there is weighty evidence that the potency of sperm is retained up to sixteen months after initial freezing, but they are unwilling to commit themselves for longer periods. Dr. Behrman, of Michigan, has claimed pregnancies achieved after no less than ten years' storage of sperm. But, in the words of two co-authors, "not enough long-term attempts have been made for probabilities to be reliably assessed."

145. Sperm (human)—longest lived naturally

Compared with many animals, humans don't score well on sperm durability. In general human sperm die a few hours or at most a day after being deposited in the female vaginal tract. In a few cases the sperm may survive for days—making a nonsense of the pre-ovulation "safe period." One authority has commented that sperm survival up to fifty hours or more "is not unusual (96)." And he quotes one study in which survival up to three and a half weeks was claimed (97). In general, safe-period folk may be assured that sperm arriving in the female genital tract more than twenty-four hours before the release of a ripe ovum are unlikely to result in fertilization. It's small comfort. There are many reasons why safe-period contraception is ill-advised!

146. Sperm (human)—shortest lived naturally

Sperm usually have a rough time of it in any event. For one thing there just aren't enough eggs to go round; and for enough there are a variety of vaginal circumstances hostile to sperm mobility and survival. Some of the circumstances are artificially created—as with spermicidal creams and sprays. In some instances however the environment is deadly to sperm without artificial assistance. Some females seem intent upon emasculating a man's fertility by the simple expedient of killing off his sperm as soon as they get inside her. Some women worried by contraception may envy such a vaginal condition. Other women, keen on the idea of procreation, do not boast when they find they possess such a condition.

147. Sperm banks—first
The idea of an effective sperm bank has appealed to eugenically-minded individuals for a good few centuries. Such arrangements have only recently become practically feasible. The first two sperm banks, set up in Iowa City and Tokyo, both began life in 1964.

148. Sperm bank child—first
The first sperm-bank child was born in the U.S. in 1953—and, in the words of Gerald Leach, was "perfectly normal" Since then the numbers have swelled, with the sperm storage period being gradually lengthened. It seems that little ecological or eugenic thought has gone into this subject.

149. Ejaculate (human)—largest (fact)
Penis size has always worried human males more than ejaculate volume—though if more men read pornography they may enlarge their ambitions. Van de Velde suggests that human semen, in one ejaculation, can be as much as 10 ml (98). Though Swyer sets his sights higher—"volumes up to 15 ml. have been recorded" (99). Walter (again of *My Secret Life*) mentions a harlot who "knew a man who spent a dessert-spoonful" (100). It's not an area that men have tended to boast about, though in certain forms of literature a copious discharge is a definite point in the hero's favor (try Chapter 8). In pornography there is frequently talk of veritable "lakes of sperm," a state of affair that is not all that likely to arouse ordinary folk to efforts of emulation.

150. Ejaculate (human)—farthest projected
This, we may assume, is yet another one for a future Sex Olympics. Considering the amount of masturbation that goes on there must be considerable volume of semen discharged in the absence of a convenient vaginal receptacle.

The distances the seminal fluid achieves before being arrested in flight must surely vary. I have seen very little documentation on this. One writer notes that the "rhythmic spasms of ejaculation fling forth the semen from the external orifice with an impetus which may be perceived if the emission takes place *in vacuo*." He adds, with the air of the true scientist, that the "seminal stream usually covers a distance of from 15 to 20 cm., but has been known to exceed 1 m." (101).

151. Nocturnal emissions (human)—most frequent by age

Kinsey has pointed out that nocturnal emissions "follow the general picture in having their maximum range of variation in the youngest years, and narrower ranges in the older years." In the Kinsey sample it was found that boys under fifteen were achieving as many as twelve nocturnal emissions per week; and men in the fifty-six to sixty age-group were only managing one a fortnight (or, in the happy Kinsey table, 0.5 a week).

152. Nocturnal emissions (human)—most frequent by social class

It was one of the Kinsey findings that nocturnal emissions occur most often "in that segment of the population that goes to college." Thus among males of the college level the emissions begin at earlier ages than among males of lower educational levels—"About 70 per cent of the boys who will go to college have such experience by age 15, whereas only about 25 per cent of the grade school group has started by then. Between 16 and 20 years of age, 91 per cent of the single males of the college level experience nocturnal emissions, while only 56 per cent of the lower level boys have such experience in the same period." It is interesting that virtually all the better educated males have such experience, whereas the incidence is only 86 per cent for the high school group, and only 75 per cent for the grade school group.

153. Semen contact—most extreme female reaction

Most women don't mind semen too much, though some unduly fastidious ones complain about its smell or stickiness. Some females, however, have a quite extraordinary reaction to seminal fluid: they are happily rare. In one case reported in 1967 a girl had an acute allergic reaction to human sperm. She came from a family with a long history of various kinds of allergy, including eczema, asthma, and dermatitis. A short time after her first sexual experience she developed a rash and asthma; her lips, eyelids, tongue, and throat became swollen, she had violent pains in the pelvis and finally lost consciousness. Most of these symptoms appeared every time she had sexual intercourse: they began within half an hour and lasted well into the next day. When semen diluted one part per million was injected under her skin it left an angry weal, so intense was the girl's reaction (102).

154. Semen—most powerful attributed characteristics

Most of us know that semen has the remarkable ability to help start babies. But this is only one of the powers attributed to the mysterious substance. One idea is that semen has a "magnetic" effect—those who retain their semen, i.e. refrain from sexual activity, are able to draw both men and women to themselves. It has often been assumed that semen has mystical or religious powers. Thus a sub-sect of the Gnostics mixed the fluid with the sacramental draught in their religious ceremonies. And in the so-called Black Mass, semen has served as holy water. Aleister Crowley reckoned that art, literature and philosophy were all the outcome of sexual power, and that the whole of human psychology was a radiating miasama from the seminal stream: he is reported as saying that "Mind is a disease of semen."

155. Semen—largest contributing gland

In this enlightened age we all know that semen comprises more than sperm. In fact there are various component substances, secreted by a number of glands and all appearing in the seminal discharge. Most of the fluid of the ejaculate derives from the prostate gland situated at the base of the penis. Sperm only represent a small proportion of the total seminal volume—which is why the discharge before and after vasectomy appears the same. Some people claim there is a visual difference between fertile and infertile semen. I have seen no reliable documentation to this effect.

156. Mother—oldest

Most child-bearing is accomplished by women in their twenties. By the age of forty few women expect to be pregnant, though a fair number of surprises happen every year! Mothers giving birth over fifty are extremely rare, with the menopause, i.e. the ending of female fertility, generally happening in the mid-forties. The oldest mother I have seen reliably documented is aged 57: at this age the woman produced a daughter in the US.

157. Mother—youngest

Girls giving birth in their teens is of course a common-place in modern society; historically, despite fluctuations in the time of first menstruation, things were probably little different. A few isolated cases exist of girls of nine or ten having babies, though a number of the tales are fanciful rather than well documented. One writer notes that "In one extreme case a girl started her periods at one year old and was delivered of a baby at six." The astounded reader may reasonably assume this to be a record. He would be wrong. The youngest mother on record is a Chilean girl who was 5 years of age when delivered of a live child by Caesarian section.

158. Female characteristics—most popular by society

It is generally assumed that American adult males like their women to have big breasts, that Latins go for legs and rumps, and so on and so forth. One of the most thorough anthropological studies on preferences of this sort was carried out by Ford and Beach (103). In the range of primitive communities studied it was found that plump body build was the most popular female trait. Thirteen societies showed definite preference for a body build of this sort. By contrast only five peoples like slim body build. Large breasts and elongated *labia majora* also rated high (nine and eight societies expressing such preferences).

159. Female characteristics—least popular by society

Of all the female attributes studied in the Ford and Beach profile (103), narrow pelvis, slim hips, and a large clitoris were the least popular female traits. It is not easy to see why particular features should come in for admiration in one tribe and not another. Explanations have been attempted on the ground of biological survival. Without exception such theories and elucidations have been simplistic. The roots of cultural value-judgment have yet to be defined.

160. Breasts—heaviest

Many men, as we all know, are fascinated by massive breasts. Magazines cater specifically for such tastes and a number of strip-tease artists try hard to capitalize on their gigantic mammary apparatus (connoisseurs will recall the fifty-odd-inch busts of Big Julie and Big Bertha in the clubs). Zola wrote of Désire who kept a bar and a dance hall (was she based on fact?)—"she seemed so vast, with a pair of breasts each one of which required a man to embrace it. Rumour had it that nowadays she had to have two of her weekday lovers each night to cope with the job." (*Germinal*) In one recorded instance a girl of fourteen had breasts weighing sixteen pounds; and in another case a woman of thirty had breasts weighing fifty-two pounds (104). As with the male sexual organs breasts are sometimes grossly enlarged by disease or some other unwelcome cause. For instance some women have hypertrophied breasts, sagging vastly and of quite giant proportions. An Abyssinian woman with this condition is shown by Mantegazza (105).

161. Breasts—first reduced by surgery

In severe cases of overgrown breasts it is possible to cut away some of the unwanted tissue and achieve a much improved cosmetic result. A name for one of these types of operation is reduction mammaplasty. An early masectomy was reported by Durston in 1731 (106). The particular case described apparently happened 60 years previously.

Of the breasts in question it was noted that they were
nothing but "prodigious bigness." The next case to be reported was described by Velpean in 1857.

162. Breasts—oldest age to develop
The median age for breast development in the Kinsey
sample was 12.4 years for females. Of course in some
women, perhaps those with a peculiar chromosomal inheritance, there is virtually no breast development throughout
their life. In intersexual cases a nominal woman may have
little breast development though her genital features may
appear typically female. Of "normal" women who eventually develop breasts the latest age for such an occurrence
appears to be the mid-twenties. Kinsey remarks on some
women who did not "recall breast development until the
age of 25."

163. Breasts—youngest age to develop
In the Kinsey sample there were a number of women who
claimed discernible breast development by the age of
eight, so it is quite possible that breasts could be starting
to swell, in extreme cases, by the age of six or seven. Even
earlier ages than this have been noted for breast development: such cases are often instances of a pathological
condition, real sexual precocity often resulting in totally
inadequate adult sexuality. One writer (107) notes that
premature enlargement of the breasts can be accompanied
with no increase in height, weight, or bone age. In five
cases studied "the breast enlargement was present at birth
. . ." This particular condition is distinguished from
"constitutional precocity." One explanation is an increased
sensitivity of the breast tissue to the normal low concentration of circulating aestrogens. (As with other superlatives,
records exist at the extremes of the normality spread, with
"freaks," and on account of disease.)

164. Breasts—most pendulous according to race
Breasts come in all shapes and sizes and hues. We have already noted some massive specimens (see superlative
100): there are other ways in which breasts can be excessively dimensioned. They can, for instance, be extremely

long, dangling like strips of skin. This occurs in a number of African tribes and can be common in both young and old women. It is not unknown for women to toss their breasts over this shoulders to keep them out of the way while working.

165. Breasts—least pendulous according to race
The smallest and least pendulous breasts are usually attributed to the Mongoloids. Among such people the women often appear with an almost boyish slimness—and the vast mammaries favored in other parts of the world would be regarded as monstrous deformities.

166. Vulva (human)—longest
Among the bush people of Africa—and in particular the Hottentots—the *labia minora* are long and pendant. This artificially enlarged bit of the female anatomy is generally referred to as the "Hottentot Apron" on account of its remarkable size. The labia can hang as much as 7 in. in length and often the clitoris also is enlarged (108). It has been reported that some Sinhalese women have similarly long inner lips. The explanation is much more in terms of manipulation than hereditary peculiarity. Women so endowed often find it necessary to push the long labia into the vaginal orifice to protect them during normal household chores. Felix Bryk observed (109) that "there is hardly a female to be found among the Swahili without a Hottentot apron since her youth ... women without a Hottentot apron are simply boycotted by men; marriage itself would be annulled if the woman decided to retain her natural clitoris and refused to elongate her *labia minora.*"

167. Vulva (human)—greatest distortion through disease
In one case the labia of a French girl formed a tumor which protruded a full 2 or 3 in. (110). In fact, as with other parts of the human anatomy, a variety of tumors can appear in the genital region. One such is lipoma, fortunately very rare. Another type is fibroma, less rare. Fibromas arise from the fibrous tissue of the vulva and are usu-

ally quite small growths. But in extreme cases the growth may hang between the legs like a pendulum. In one extraordinary case (111) a fibroma of the vulva weighed no less than 268 lb., the woman being quite incapable of normal locomotion and many other bodily activities.

168. Vagina (human)—most

As with many non-human animals it is possible for a female baby to be born with two vaginas. Oddly enough the condition is often not detected until the girl begins an active sex life or becomes pregnant. Such cases are extremely rare and are of immense interest to medical men when they are detected. The degree of "doubling up" can vary from one case to another. In some instances there may be two vaginal tracts but only one external orifice. In other cases two external orfices may both be fused onto a single, though often distorted genital tract. Sometimes a woman may have twice the number of oviducts as the normal female, and other organs may occur in unexpected profusion. The double vagina can come with a double uterus—when the two Mullerian ducts develop without communicating with each other, one fallopian tube attached to each (112).

169. Vagina (human)—most capacious (fact)

The human vagina, when not engaged in coitus, is often much smaller than the local penis. The vaginal tissue, happily enough, has the facility to expand to welcome the vistor and in such circumstances can quite easily double its volumetric capacity and become half as long again. It is not always realized, however, how capacious the human vagina can in fact be. There is a case (113) reported by Walter (a matter of fact if we are to believe the Kronhausens' interpretation of *My Secret Life*), in which a woman is encouraged to insert as many coins as possible into her vagina. Walter produced five English pounds—"all in shillings"—and attempted to insert as many coins as possible into the woman's capacious tract. "Shilling after shilling I put up her, until forty were embedded in the elastic gully . . ." On and on she went, until no less than seventy coins were inserted—"Triumphantly she walked up and down the room, none falling out of her vagina." In the event the woman, Nellie, managed to retain eighty-four shillings in this manner—"I wish someone would do this every day."

170. Vagina (human)—shortest

The shortest human vaginas are almost too small to measure, being only a dimple in the pubic area. Such useless vaginas—scarcely meriting the name—can occur in women who are otherwise sexually normal. Various measures can be taken to correct this condition, from surgical construction of a vaginal passage to the use of perineal dilators (this latter a technique developed in part by Masters and Johnson). Where a vagina is structurally normal, i.e. with mucous lining and appropriate connections to the uterus, then it may be as small as two or three centimetres in length (114). Such a condition can allow conception in the normal way but is hardly conducive to satisfactory sexual intercourse, unless the partner too has a diminutive organ. Hermaphrodites, also, may have tiny vaginas or none at all, though in other respects apparently female.

171. Vagina (human)—most remarkable tricks

The vagina, usually associated with sexual intercourse and childbirth, can be employed in a variety of other ways. In addition to serving as a money-box (see superlative 108) the vagina can also play the part of billiard table, a game seemingly favoured in parts of Scandinavia. Thus one writer (115) remarks "The ladies will lift up their skirts ... They will sit against the wall, their legs spread well apart. The gentlemen will take their places on the opposite side of the room ... Everyone has a try. The object is to flick the glass marbles into the hole of this delightful billiard table. One can guess at the winner's reward ..." But this is passive on the part of the woman. The vagina has other possibilities. It can, for instance, drink a glass of whisky or play a mouth organ (116).

172. Vagina (human)—most remarkable content

Medical men have been called upon to extract a wide variety of objects from the vagina and the urethra following masturbation or accident. Usually the woman knew that the object was inside her and requested medical assistance. Sometimes however a foreign body can lodge in the vagina, after an accident of some sort, and the woman can be totally unaware of its presence. A remarkable instance of this sort occurred when a woman fell down stairs (117). A broken-off handle of a broom entered the vagina through a buttock. This was not noticed by her or by the casualty officer who treated her. The broom handle remained undetected in the woman's vagina for three months. Eventuallly a vaginal discharge made her visit her own practitioner, where upon the offending object was detected and removed.

173. Vagina (human)—first transplant

A woman aged twenty-one in Salonica was reported as having a boyfriend, two years after receiving a vagina transplant from her mother aged fifty. A professor at the city's university was reported as saying there had been no signs of tissue rejection. The woman's previous deformity had led to the dissolution of her first marriage. The operation to equip her with a new genital tract was apparently successful (*Guardian*, 5/3/73).

174. Vagina (human)—most common method of reconstruction

Perhaps the most common method of building a new vagina is termed the free skin grafting method (118). In this method a vertical incision is made in the labia and a cavity is opened up "by blunt dissection." A graft from the thigh—about 8 in. X 3 in. is draped over an inserted mould which stays in situe for 3-6 months. One suggesttion is that the reconstruction of the vagina should always be timed "in relation to intended marriage." Presumably "intended sexual intercourse" would be a more up-to-date phrase.

175. "Semen" (female)—first postulated

The Greeks are associated with the idea that women, as well as men, generate a form of *semen*. Aristotle thought in such terms, as did a number of his learned contemporaries. Galen (AD 130-200) reckoned that a substance was separated from the blood stream by means of the ovaries and subsequently passed into the uterus through the fallopian tubes. The idea of female "semen" is of course absurd, as are a number of the Greek ideas on human sexual anatomy. At the same time it is fact that women "contribute" in the fertilization process, and the use of the concept of semen may simply have been a circumlocution for talking of *eggs* or *ova.*

176. Clitoris (human)—longest

Clitoris size has only rarely been of importance in human society. A few communities—Ford and Beach mention the Easter Islanders—have favored the large clitoris and some natives have tried with varying degrees of success to enlarge this organ in their girls. For the most part, however, with a prevailing indifference in the nineteenth-century and early part of the twentieth-century to sexual arousal in women, the clitoris has been neglected. Needless to say, it varies in size. How big are the largest? Theo Lang mentions one recorded instance of a woman having a clitoris 2 in. long, and 3 in. "when fully erect" (119). Pomeroy has remarked that clitorises measuring more than 1 in. are very rare in whites, but may occur in 2 or 3 per cent of blacks—"measurements of 3 in. and more were obtained from perhaps one out of 300 or 400 black women" (120). Another writer notes that Parent-Duchalet came across a clitoris that measured 3.14 in. (121). The eighteenth-century Swiss biologist, Albrecht von Haller, is said to have come across a woman with a monstrous clitoris no less than 7 in. long (122). But the record clitoris is almost certainly the 12 in. specimen mentioned by various writers (123).

177. Clitoris (human)—shortest

A significant proportion of women never locate their clitoris. There may be several reasons for this. One is that the clitoris can be "hooded" and an effective circumcision is necessary to release it. Another reason—assuming that there is a clitoris to locate—can be that the clitoris is extremely small. A clitoris size of 2 mm. diameter has been noted (124). Women with no discernible clitoris should not worry that this may interfere with their sexual arousal. The whole of the clitoral area is well supplied with nerve-endings, and the importance of the clitoris in sexual response is often over-stressed.

178. Ovaries (human)—most
Female ovaries usually come in pairs. In animals they may be more or less frequent than this (see superlatives 19 and 79). It is also the case that human females can have more or less than two ovaries. In some rare cases a woman is found to have three ovaries; and in even rarer cases four have been detected. If, for any reason, a woman has to have her ovaries removed she may think that after two have been extracted she will necessarily be sterile. This is not always the case.

179. Ovaries (human)—least
As already suggested, a girl may be born with only one ovary—or, indeed, with none at all. As one example, when an XY egg divides to form identical twins, each half normally receives the Y chromosome paired with an X, and develops into a boy. In exceptional instances the Y drops out from one of the halves and this twin develops into an abnormal girl of the XO *Turner syndrome* type. In such an event there can be many abnormalities—including rudimentary or totally absent ovaries.

180. Menarche—most recent evidence of arrest towards earlier age
We all know that girls are supposed to be menstruating for the first time ever younger with each new generation. Nice little graphs can be drawn to show the trends towards earlier menarche over a good few decades in this century and the last. There is, however, some evidence to suggest that a "levelling off" is taking place. The fall in menarche by about three or four months per decade over the past century is well established. In 1973 it was suggested that girls in America and Britain were no longer pushing down the age of menarche. For instance in a 12-year study of students entering the University of Swansea, Wales, it was found that the age of menarche has

plateaued at 12.5 years with girls born in 1946 and on-wards.

181. Menstruation—oldest woman

The onset and termination of menstruation is subject, like all other sexual phenomena, to immense variation. It has been known for a girl to start menstruating at three months old (125), and occasionally the menopause too occurs at a very early age: there are instances of girls reaching the menopause before the age of twenty. The menopause rarely occurs after the age of fifty-five but rare cases do occur. In one instance menstruation was continuing in a woman aged 104 (126). One writer has suggested that many of the patients with delayed menopause reported "in the older literature" were suffering from oestrogen-producing tumors of the ovary (127).

182. Menstruation—oldest age to start

Menstruation, commonly functioning in the vast bulk of teenage girls, may be delayed well past the teens. In a number of cases medical attention needs to be sought; in others the condition may exist in a "normal" but "slow" girl. In the Kinsey sample some girls did not start menstruating until they were in their twenties. The latest instance was a girl who started to menstruate when she was twenty-five years old.

183. Menstruation—youngest age to start

Kinsey came across some girls who started to menstruate when they were only nine years of age. This, as we have seen, is far from being a record. Cauthery and Cole mention a girl who started to menstruate at one year of age (128). And Parkes instance one case of a menstruation that began in a girl aged only eight months (129). The record for youthfulness at first menstruation is unquestionably the three months already cited (125). As we may expect, such cases of sexual precocity are extremely rare.

184. Menstruation—first "self-help" device

A year or two ago a variety of Women's Health Collectives and Medical Centers began to spring up all over America—mainly as a consequence of what was taken in feminist circles to be male chauvinism on the part of physicians confronted with female health problems. Two women in the forefront of "self-help through self-knowledge" are Carol Downer and Lorraine Rothman. One of the most significant innovations associated with the work of these women is a device called the Del-'Em, which incorporates the Karman plastic cannula (used for vacuum aspiration abortion) attached to a syringe and two airtight bottles. The device is used in the Self-Help Clinics for menstrual extractions. Margaret Mead has been quoted as saying that "the invention of the Del-'Em is the greatest thing since the development of the wheel(130)."

185. Menstruation—oddest place to advertise 19th-Century sanitary towels

Some places seem more likely than others to carry ads for sanitary towels. Sometimes advertisements have appeared in the least likely places. Thus no less than one third of the back cover of *The Antiquary* for July 1888 was taken by the principal manufacturers of sanitary towels, Southall Brothers and Barclay of Birmingham, to advertise their product. The ad was addressed to "Ladies traveling by Land or Sea" and the items were represented as "patented Articles of Underclothing, Indispensable to Ladies Traveling. Sold at Cost of Washing Only! To burn when done with. Of Drapers and Ladies' Outfitters Everywhere."

186. Menstrual blood—highest estimate of loss by weight

There have been efforts over the years to estimate the blood loss through menstruation. Often individuals have inclined to over-estimate the volume of fluid passed as menstrual flow. One suggestion is that the total loss does not exceed 50 gm. monthly, with a figure of 30 gm. not uncommon(131). Before careful measurements were carried out doctors tended to assume that the total blood loss was in the order of 100 to 200 gm. The largest—and quite erroneous medical estimate—was 600 gm.!

187. Menopause—commonest symptom
Many women fear the onset of menopause or "change of life" because of imagined symptoms that will accompany the event. In fact the symptoms are rarely very troublesome and in a healthy woman are likely to be short-lived. The commonest symptom of the menopause is the occurrence of hot flashes. This is hardly a cause for alarm.

188. Menopause—least common symptom
In a scale of conditions that might be expected in some women at menopause a statistical incidence can be attributed to each. In one such listing (*New Society*, 29/10/70) it was pointed out that sleeplessness and sweating were among the least likely symptoms in women undergoing the "change of Life."

189. Pubic hair (boy)—youngest
Pubic hair, normally a sign of the onset of puberty, can occur—as can menstruation (see superlative 117)—at a surprisingly early age. One writer(132) mentions a boy of only eighteen months who had both an enlarged penis and pubic hair. Often such conditions are associated with a number of other abnormalities. In the cited case the boy "presented with a right-sided abdominal mass." Autopsy showed the mass to be a primary hepatoblastoma.

190. Pubic hair (girl)—oldest age to develop
In some women there is little pubic hair growth at any time. Such a circumstance can occur in women sexually normal in every other respect. In yet other women pubic hair may eventually grow in a completely normal way but may commence growth at a surprisingly early or late age. In the Kinsey survey (133) some women did not have any pubic hair until they reached the age of eighteen. It is unlikely that this is a record. We may reasonably speculate that some women in their early twenties have not yet started to grow hair in the genital area.

191. Pubic hair (girl)—youngest

In the "normality spread," as shown, for example, in Kinsey (p. 123) some girls began growing pubic hair as early as eight years of age. This is very young to begin such growth yet cannot be considered "abnormal." The real records relate to instances of sexual precocity often, as we have seen, connected with (sometimes fatal) abnormalities. Hugh Jolly noted instances of pubic hair in babies: in one case a girl of only one month old had hair growth around the genitals (134).

192. Pubic hair (woman)—longest

Pubic hair, short and curly in most of us, sometimes grows to quite extraordinary lengths. Havelock Ellis worked as a midwife in his early days, and he notes that only in one case did long pubic hair hamper his efforts. In some remarkable cases recorded by a certain Dr. F. L. John (1778-1852) the pubic hair was longer than the woman's ordinary hair. Thus (Paulini): the pubic hair reached the knees. . . . (Bartholia): the pubic hair was plaited behind the woman's back. Ronald Pearsall, who nicely notes these instances, observes with appropriate insight that such cases "are unquestionably freakish(135)."

193. Pubic hair (woman)—most prolific

There is long pubic hair (see superlative 123) and there is pubic hair that is thick and expansive in the general abdominal area. Walter (of *My Secret Life*), an evident connoisseur in such matters, talks with clear delight of a fine bush of "Scots red" pubic hair—"The bush was long and thick, twisting and curling in masses half-way up to her navel, and it spread about 5 in. up her buttocks, gradually getting shorter there." In another part of his autobiography Walter remarks that he has seen those "bare of hair, those with but hairy stubble, those with bushes six inches long, covering them from bum bone to navel." And he adds reflectively—"there is not much that I have not seen, felt or tried, with respect to this supreme female article." In like vein, in the *Memoires of Dolly Morton*, an

American classic, the attributes of Miss Dean are noted with some surprise (she is stripped and beaten for helping runaway slaves)—her spot was covered with a "thick forest of glossy dark brown hair," with locks nearly two inches long. One man remarked, "By Gosh! I've never seen such a fleece between a woman's legs in my life. Darn me if she wouldn't have to be sheared before man could get into her."

194. Buttocks—largest

The largest buttocks occur in cases of steatopygy, generally associated with Hottentot, Bushman, and other African tribes. The condition is said to be rare in white-women. In its most developed state each buttock can be two or three feet across; and even the youngest members of the tribe can exhibit enormously inflated posteriors. Montegazza has included a number of pictures of women with posterior steatopygy (136).

195. Hermaphrodite (human)—rarest type

The rarest cases of human hermaphroditism are the instances of *true* or *gonadal hermaphrodite*. In this condition each gonad is an ovotestis—part ovary and part testis—or one is an ovary and the other a testis. Swyer, writing in 1954, remarks that only forty cases had been recorded in all the medical literature (137). The condition can be diagnosed only by microscopial examination of parts of the gonads. Among the outward signs in a "male" are hypospadias, undescended testicles and abnormal breast development; in the "female" with this condition there is abnormal development of the clitoris. Normal spermatogenesis may occur close to an ovary in which ovulation takes place (138).

196. Hermaphrodite (human)—best non-medical description

The medical literature abounds with descriptions of the various types of hermaphroditism. Sometimes a good *non*-medical description is produced. Perhaps the best is that in Henry Spender Ashbee's *Catena Librorum Tacendorum*. The "woman" was fairly attractive. Ashbee said—"She was about twenty years of age, rather pretty, and quite womanly, with beautiful eyes, a good complexion, and fair hair; her nose was rather masculine and her mouth rather rough and large, with bad teeth; her chest was expansive, and her breasts well developed; the lower part of the legs slightly bowed, and masculine. She possessed, in appearance at least, the organs of both sexes, but neither perfect: a small penis, as in a lad of twelve or fourteen years, and testicles apparently developed; the yard was, however, not perforated. Underneath the testicles was what seemed to be a perfect female vestibule, of which the opening was, however, only large enough to allow her to pass water, but not to receive a man, or even to admit the insertion of the end of a quill ... she had no monthly flow, but felt, nevertheless, a periodic indisposition; she experienced pleasures in the embraces of both sexes, and had even an erection when with a sympathetic female. She could not, of course, satisfy her desires."

197. Sex-change (human)—most famous court case

The most famous "sex-change" case to get to court was that of England's April Ashley. She had been born with male genitals but was psychologically female, i.e. she was a transsexual. She hated her penis and in 1960 underwent an operation to remove the visible signs of maleness: strictly speaking this was not a change of sex, since all she had accomplished was to remove the visible evidence of her genetic sex. In the eyes of the law she was still a man (and in fact had been brought up as George Jamieson). In February 1970 her marriage to Arthur Corbett was declared null on the ground that she was not really married. Mr. Justice Ormrod declared that "She is a biological male and has been so since birth." She had male chromosomes and male gonads. Lawyers supported the court ruling but medical opinion was divided. Dr. Benjamin, author of *The Transsexual Phenomenon*, noted that "April Ashley has a vagina, so she is a woman." For April Ashley herself the court ruling was a personal disaster (139).

198. Virgin birth (human)—most thoroughly investigated

There have been many claims of virgin birth in human history, strong in legend (Greek mythology, the Bible, etc.) and weak in the medical literature. In some rare cases a woman has carried part of her twin around inside her and subsequent "delivery" has created the elusion of virgin birth. In November 1955 the London *Sunday Pictorial* asked women to come forward who thought that there had been no father to their child. Nineteen claims were made to the newspaper and these were investigated. Eleven were negated in the initial enquiry because the mothers thought an intact hymen inevitably indicated a virgin conception. Finally the nineteen cases were reduced to one possible. Mrs. E. Jones and her daughter were subjected to further thorough investigation. Their blood, saliva and tasting powers were all examined, and attempts were made to graft skin from one to the other. Blood, saliva, and tasting powers were almost identical, but the grafts did not take. In June 1956 the *Sunday Pictorial* was prepared to state that, after six months of detailed medical investigation, the results were consistent with a case of virgin birth. Professor J. B. S. Haldane disagreed and argued that the evidence in fact led to the opposite conclusion— the child had a father.

199. Virgin—most famous (legend)

The most famous virgin in human history is Mary, of Christian fame. I was not hard-pressed in researching this superlative! Some readers may object to my putting a parenthetical "legend" on the title of this item. But I doubt that many folk *really* believe that the mother of Jesus *never* had carnal connection with a man. Alas, the *Sunday Pictorial* (see superlative 128) was not around at the time to test the religious claims!

Chapter Three

SEX TECHNIQUE, PERFORMANCE,
AND RESPONSE

200. Aphrodisiac—most effective (fact)

Man has always searched for ways to enhance his sexual
capacities. Special foods have been tried and a whole
range of drugs and medications. In superstitious communities magic is invoked and priests have been known to say
appropriate prayers for a small fee. Many current "sex
aid" products rely on the alleged aphrodisiac properties of
ancient concoctions—but, alas, there seems to be little evidence that a person's sexual prowess can be significantly
improved by such devices. The Kinsey investigators
summed up the situation nicely—"good health, sufficient
exercise, and plenty of sleep still remain the most effective
of the aphrodisiacs known to man."

201. Aphrodisiac—oldest

Some aphrodisiacs have been popular since the days of antiquity. The mandrake plant is mentioned in the Old
Testament and is still in use today. Mandrake (or mandragora, *mandragora officinarum*) is a member of the po-
tato family with a large dark-brown root and small red
fruit. It contains the alkaloids atropine and scopolomine:
in mild doses these are soporifics; in larger doses they can
kill! In antiquity there were magical rules for harvesting the
plant. Pliny noted that the plant roots were in the form of
human genitals—which explains, through the idea of sympathetic magic, the supposed aphrodisiac effect. Can-
tharides, another ancient aphrodisiac, was first mentioned

83

by Aristotle: its active principle, cantharidin, is extracted
from the dried and powdered bodies of the blister beetle,
a brown or bluish creature found in southern Europe. Yet
another old alleged aphrodisiac is Ginseng, the "mystic
plant of the Orient," made into tablets by modern sex aid
retailers and also into a wine. In the Far East today Ginseng wine is termed kaoliang (as strong as vodka), with
the roots of ginseng soaked in the cask for at least three
years. Users are recommended to take a small glass before
going to bed.

202. Aphrodisiac—most bizarre

An endless range of bizarre concoctions have been devised
with the aim of restoring failing sexual powers. Sometimes, as we have seen, plants were used because of their
physical resemblance to the human genital organs. Drugs
have always been popular. Perhaps the most bizarre types
of aphrodisiac are those involving an element of cannibalism. We all know of the use of parts of non-human animals to increase human potency (a Chinese Emperor, for
example, kept a herd of deer so he could drink their blood
to increase his virile powers); but often it was thought desirable also to consume parts of men and women for this
purpose. Menstrual blood, placenta, and genitals have all
been devoured to increase sexual prowess; semen was also
popular. ("The semen of virile young men should be
mixed with the excrement of hawks or eagles and taken in
pellet form.") Chinese eunuchs, seeking regeneration of
their lost sexual organs, would hopefully eat the warm
brains of newly decapitated criminals (140).

203. Aphrodisiac—most severe measure

The Amazons are reputed to have employed a quite extraordinary measure to enchance virility. Eustathius may
be quoted (141)—"The Amazons broke either a leg or an
arm of the captives they took in battle, and this they did,
not only to prevent their attempts at escape, or their plot-
ting, but also, and this more especially, to render them
more vigorous in the venereal conflict; for, as they themselves burnt away the right breast of their female children
in order that the right arm might become stronger from
receiving additional nutriment, so they imagined that, sim-

ilarly, the genital member would be strengthened by the
deprivation of one of the extremities, whether a leg or an
arm. Hence, when reproached by the Scythians with the
limping gait of her slaves, Queen Antianara replied: 'The
lame best perform the act of love.' "

204. Aphrodisiac—most famous Oriental drug

Despite the legendary nature of ginseng (see superlative
201) most of us in the West are more likely to have heard
of the various uses to which *opium* has been put. This
drug has in fact been employed optimistically as an aphrodisiac over the centuries. Even a mild dose of opium is
supposed by Orientals to provide about one hour of continuous genital stimulation—"assuring the desideratum of
at least three thousand phallic thrusts:" it is worth quoting
further the poetic mention of the opium pill at it appears
in *Chin P'ing Mei*—

> Take but a speck of this, set it upon you, then
> Rush like a whirlwind to the bridal chamber.
> The first engagement will leave you full of vig-
>   or;
> The second, even stronger than before.
> Though twelve exquisite beauties, all ar-
>   rayed in scarlet, wait your onset,
> You may enjoy each one, according to your
>   fancy . . .

And so on and so forth—"Ten women in one night will be
as one to you."

205. Aphrodisiac—most detailed concoctions in China

There are some immensely complicated formulae for ancient Chinese aphrodisiacs. A number of these, from the
Wang Tao *Collection of Secret Prescriptions,* are quoted
by Eric Chou. One example will suffice here (for use in
the spring) (1 fen = 0.36 grams)—

Fu ling (underground fungus) — 4 fen
Ch'ang p'u (Acorus calamus) — 4 fen
Shan chu yu (plant)   — 4 fen

K'u lou root (herb)	— 4 fen
T'u ssu tzu (herb seeds)	— 4 fen
Niu ch'i (herb)	— 4 fen
Dry ti huang (Rebmannia)	— 7 fen
Hsi hsin (wild ginger)	— 4 fen
Fan feng (herb)	— 4 fen
Shu yu (yam root)	— 4 fen
Hsu tuan (herb)	— 4 fen

The ingredients of this prescription, as with other concoctions, were to be ground down and made into pills.

206. Love-charm—most bizarre

In ancient Irish legend amorous girls were said to invade graveyards in the search for corpses buried nine days. When they found one they cut from the body a narrow strip of skin extending from the top of the head down to the extremity of one foot. They then tried to knot the length of dead skin round the arm or leg of a sleeping lover and to remove it before he awoke. If the girl kept the skin hidden from all eyes, and managed to perform her task every night—so long would the man love her! Canidia, the Witch of Horace's fifth *Epode,* got up to even worse tricks for aphrodisiac purposes. For example, she buried a kidnapped boy in the earth up to his chin and left him to starve with food placed on the ground in front of his face—so that she might use his bone marrow and liver in love potions once he was dead (142). (For another dash of the bizarre see also superlative 131.)

207. Frigidity cure—most complicated in China

As we have seen, some of the most complex remedies for lack of sexual capacity and interest are the various forms of aphrodisiac concoction. Perhaps equally complex are the rules governing collection of plant or animal ingredients. As a cure for frigidity it was often thought necessary, not only to mix a complex of herbs and animal parts together—often cemented into pills by means of honey— but also to perform a number of ritualistic moves over the compound. Magic was often thought to aid chemistry. In one cure for frigidity it was thought necessary to search out a particular species of red bat which rested in pairs amid the red flowers of banana trees. The bats were dried, ground into powder, and hopefully spread on a woman externally to make her feel sexy.

208. Sexual behavior—most inhibited species

Man, proud of his imagined superiority over the rest of the animal kingdom, can hardly be rated a winner in the sexual stakes. His sexual organs are neither the largest nor the most impressive performers; his copulatory capacities are out-stripped by many animal species; and he is hardly the most prolific reproductively. In addition man is much more likely to get sexual hang-ups than any other animal. If a snake fancies a bit of necrophilia, a marten a bit of rape, or a porpoise a bit of group sex, then such individuals are unlikely to experience inhibiting feelings of guilt at the thought. Man, however, is beset by anxiety, fear, guilt, and moral loathing with regard to many fancied sexual activities: few individuals indeed have come to terms with their sexuality. With all his psychosexual problems man is without doubt the most sexually inhibited among animal species.

209. Sexual response (human)—first detailed paper read

Throughout the nineteenth and twentieth-centuries a growing number of papers on human sexuality have been read at learned conferences. Many of these papers were psychological or statistical in nature and often suffered from a severe lack of hard empirical data. Perhaps the first really empirical paper was first read by Dr. William H. Masters in April 1959 at a two-day "Conference of the Vagina" held in New York under the auspices of the New York Academy of Sciences. For several prior years Dr. Masters and his colleagues had been studying how the human body actually responded to effective sexual stimulation. Earlier work had been carried out by other scientists: Dr. Masters was not the first, but his work was the most detailed, most broadly based, and the most influential in the field of empirical laboratory evaluation of human sexual response.

210. Sexual behavior—first use of antiandro genic drugs
In the early 1960s Neuman and his co-workers in West Berlin, researching with rats, discovered the capacity of cyproterone and cyproterone acetate to affect sexual behavior. Shortly afterwards the new drugs were experimented with in selected clinics in West Germany and Switzerland. Among the patients chosen for treatment were sex offenders, i.e. "men whose self-regulation of publicly and legally unacceptable sexual behavior was so severely impaired that their only alternative was long-term incarceration." In the United States and elsewhere the new drug was not released for behavioral research on human beings.

211. Infantile sexuality—first established
The idea that children have sex-lives—now hardly disputed—was first advanced in a detailed form by Sigmund Freud. Not without good cause has his *Three Essays on the Theory of Sexuality* (1905) been termed "revolutionary." Freud was not the first to put forward the idea that children were deeply involved with sexual phenomena at various psychological and physical levels: in fact thousands of observant mothers throughout history must have known as much. Freud, however, developed the notion and gave it some scientific respectability. In 1908 Moll published *The Sexual Life of the Child,* considered by Havelock Ellis to be "the earliest comprehensive study of the subject and . . . still among the most judicious."

212. Sexual response—youngest
Kinsey reported some infants who showed erotic responses *at birth* (143). This we may find remarkable but there may be more to come. I remember the impact in the popular press when babies were first shown to suck their thumbs, or try to do so, before they were born. It is not at all unlikely that the pre-birth child is capable of erotic responses. Even a new-born baby boy can have erections. It is certainly not too fanciful to imagine such an occurrence before he emerges from the womb. Of course the extent to which such an event could reasonably be called "erotic" is open to debate.

213. Orgasm—youngest boy

How, many readers may wonder, can a young boy experience orgasm? The question, reasonable enough, has yet to be answered but the fact remains—the *youngest* children experience orgasm. Kinsey observed orgasm in boys of five months! How do we know that a child of such a tender age in fact experienced anything that may reasonably be termed *orgasm?* Only by observing his behavior. The reasonable inference of orgasm in a boy of only four months of age (138) should put an end once and for all of speculation about infantile sexuality. The question now is—what is its nature, not—does it exist?

214. Orgasm—youngest girl

Human females, having the edge—in some circumstances—on men in the frequency of their orgasms, also have the edge on the youthfulness at which first orgasm is experienced. We expect girls to develop more quickly than boys in certain areas. For example, they are expected—by people who study such things—to be more precocious verbally. They also have the edge on youthfulness at first orgasm. In the Kinsey survey a girl was discovered who had first orgasm aged only four months! How do we know that orgasm existed in a girl so young? There is a description in Kinsey (145) of orgasm in a three-year-old girl, made by "an intelligent mother." It is worth quoting—"Lying face down on the bed, with her knees drawn up, she started rhythmic pelvic thrusts, about one second or less apart. The thrusts were primarily pelvic, with the legs tensed in a fixed position. The forward components of the thrusts were in a smooth and perfect rhythm which was unbroken for momentary pauses during which the genitalia were readjusted against the doll on which they were pressed; the return from each thrust was convulsive, jerky. There were 44 thrusts in unbroken rhythm, a slight momentary pause, 87 thrusts followed by a slight momentary pause, then 10 thrusts, and then a cessation of all movement. There was marked concentration and intense breathing with abrupt jerks as orgasm approached. She was completely oblivious to everything during these later stages of the activity. Her eyes were glassy and fixed in a vacant stare. There was noticeable relief and relaxation after orgasm. A second series of reactions began two minutes later with series of 48, 18, and 57 thrusts, with slight momentary pauses between each series. With the mounting tensions, there were audible gasps, but immediately following the cessation of pelvic thrusts there was complete relaxation and only desultory movements thereafter."

215. Sexual response—latest

The capacity for sexual response varies enormously throughout the population. As we have seen (superlatives 213 and 214) babies of only a few months are sometimes capable of the most extreme sexual responses. At the other end of the scale some people never experience erotic arousal—or scarcely recognize it when they do. In the Kinsey survey women were noted who experienced their first sexual response when they were over thirty years of age. There is something rather sad about such a circumstance. Sexual experience, so fructifying in human beings, is surely the birthright of us all. That it should occur so late in some people may reasonably be regarded as a cause for social concern.

216. Orgasm—latest

Kinsey also went to some lengths to ascertain the "age at first response to orgasm." We have already indicated the youngest orgams for both girls and boys. At the other extreme there are many women who reached the age of late forties without experiencing orgasm. In particular Kinsey notes three women who had not reached their first orgasm until they were between forty-eight and fifty years of age. It should be stressed however that lack of orgasm is not synonymous with lack of sexual response, and that a very satisfying sex-life coexist with lack of orgasm.

217. Orgasm—most extreme reactions

Orgasm, stressing the body in various ways, has been known to produce some dire consequences. Kinsey again—"At orgasm some individuals may remain unconscious for a matter of seconds or even for some minutes

(146)." Kinsey also notes more than a dozen authorities—from Roubaud (1876) to Brown and Kempton (1950)—who recorded "loss of sensory capacity or even of consciousness during extreme emotion or sexual arousal." And orgasm has been known to accompany a variety of forms of damage to the body—including lesions and ruptures of various organs. Death has also occurred from time to time! (See also superlative 264.)

218. Orgasm (men)—fastest

It is interesting to note how quickly the "preadolescent" can respond to sexual stimulation. Kinsey tabulated the percentage of the population who could respond to the point of orgasm in less than ten seconds of sexual stimulation. No less than 6.4 per cent of preadolescents could achieve orgasm in less than ten seconds of sexual stimulation. And a quarter of all those tested could manage orgasm in less than one minute (147). Kinsey notes that erection is much quicker in preadolescent boys than in adults; and some two-year-olds come to climax in less than ten seconds.

219. Orgasm (men)—most common types

Kinsey delineated six types of male orgasm. In part the types vary according to the intensity of the reaction exhibited. The most common type of male orgasm—supposedly characterising about 45 per cent of adult males—features some body tension. There may also be twitching or tension in one or both legs, of the mouth, of the arms, or of other particular parts of the body. There is gradual build-up to a climax which involves rigidity of the whole body and a degree of throbbing in the penis. There is orgasm with a few spasms but little after-effect. This is seen as the most common type of male orgasm (148).

220. Orgasm (men)—least common types

In the Kinsey delineation around 3 per cent of men experience an orgasm of a particularly severe kind (149). Here there can be extreme trembling, collapse, loss of color, and sometimes total loss of consciousness. This type of orgasm is said to occur sometimes with a boy's first sexual experience and not thereafter. In only very few cases do such extreme orgasmic reactions occur with every (or even a majority of) sexual encounters. Extreme sexual response of this sort is thought to be more common among females.

221. Orgasm (men)—most frequent (fact)

Frequency of orgasm has, like most other male sexual parameters, often been taken as defining sexual worth. The more orgasm the better, has been a general cry. It would not help the ego of most men to learn they can generally be beaten in this area by young boys. In the Kinsey data, in a series of 182 observed cases, 81 of the preadolescent boys achieved orgasm only once, 17 achieved it twice, 42 achieved it three, four, or five times in succession, 30 achieved it from six to ten times in succession, and 12 achieved it more than ten times in succession. The undisputed record was twenty-one orgasms in a row. One eleven-month-old baby boy managed fourteen orgasms in thirty-eight minutes; one eleven-year-old had eleven orgasms in an hour; a fourteen-year-old had eleven orgasms in four hours, and so on and so forth. It should be remembered that such startling multiorgasmic capabilities are generally lost at the time when orgasm is accompanied by the ejaculation of semen (150). At the same time there are some adult men who achieve high orgasmic performance over a long period. Kinsey records the case of one man who had three orgasms a day over a period of thirty years, and one who averaged 33.1 orgasms a week over a thirty-year period (151).

222. Orgasm (men)—least frequent

Some men are not so hot on orgasms. In cases of total impotence it is quite possible for a man never to have an orgasm throughout his life. Where orgasm does occur, but very infrequently, there may be no more than a single orgasm in many years. Kinsey records a case of one unfortunate man who experienced a single orgasm in a thirty-year period.

223. Orgasm correlates (women)—most ambitious studies

A number of sexological studies have attempted to relate the orgasmic capacities of women to a host of other factors, such as family background, attitudes towards parents, and personality structure. In recent times the most ambitious studies of this sort were carried out by L. M. Terman. The first (152) involved a large sample of married women (and their husbands), predominantly middle-or upper middle-class in California. The second study (153) was also based on a California sample and made use of wives who were either highly intelligent themselves or married to intelligent husbands. One intention was that the second study would provide an opportunity to cross-validate any findings that emerged from the first. These studies are discussed by Fisher (154).

224. Orgasm correlates (women)—priority study areas

Seymour Fisher (*The Female Orgasm*, 1973) in summing up aspects of female sexuality, as illuminated by his own and other studies, suggest that "high priority should be assigned to learning more about the conditions that facilitate or inhibit a woman's orgasmic potential." In particular, five areas are stressed—the importance of cross-cultural studies, of studying fathers of women with contrasting orgasm consistencies, the role of the partner in a woman's orgasmic capacity, the perceptual changes that occur in women as excitement builds up to orgasmic levels, and treatment procedures for increasing orgasmic consistency in women who have response difficulties.

225. Sexual responsiveness (women)—most important aiding factor

In the studies carried out by Fisher, women were asked questions about the conditions that facilitated their sexual responsiveness. Two factors—privacy, and good relationship with husband—were mentioned most frequently (by 18 per cent of the women) as aiding sexual responsiveness. Presumably we could infer that "good relationship with lover" was the operative phrase in the second instance: the importance of marriage *per se* as a contributing factor in sexual responsiveness has yet to be investigated in depth. It would also be of interest to see the extent to which "privacy and freedom from intrusion" was culturally biased: presumably Trobrianders would not rate this condition so highly.

226. Sexual responsiveness (women)—least important aiding factor

Fisher elicited a number of conditions that were not thought to contribute much to sexual arousal in women (see also superlative 225) (155). To have had a good meal prior to sexual activity was thought not to aid sexual responsiveness. And soft music and "to have had a few drinks" were rarely mentioned as factors aiding sexual responsiveness. This is not to say, of course, that a few drinks may not aid sexual *pliability*. As far as I know there have been no studies on the seductive value of alcohol! That sexual intercourse occur during the day was also very rarely mentioned as a factor aiding sexual responsivenesss. In fact in all these instances—food, music, drink, day-time sex—only 2 per cent of women advanced such factors as aiding sexual responsiveness.

227. Sexual passion (women)—highest estimate

Historically women have been seen as sexually rampant, as vamp and temptress—or as sexually dead (the proper state for moral wives). One index of sexual awareness and interest is the degree of masturbation in an individual (though of course masturbation may be infrequent or non-existent in highly sexed individuals when an adequacy of other outlets exists). Masturbation is said to be so widespread among both married and unmarried Muslim females throughout Africa and the East that "it is commonly regarded by the menfolk as customary and matter-of-fact"(156). "Rubbing" or "pounding" is considered a natural manifestation of feminine nature—for "women's passion is ten times greater than man's." In this spirit it has been suggested that since it taken ten men to satisfy one woman, it is only normal that a woman faithful to one man should masturbate from time to time to satisfy sexual needs. (French troops marching off to war were said to provide their wives with dildos to reduce the chances of adultery in their absence.)

228. Sexual passion (women)—lowest estimate

Moralists and men nervous of their virility have always been eager to suggest that sexual feelings are weak or non-existent in women. Perhaps the most famous physician to argue in such a way was Sir William Acton who wrote a number of sexological books in the nineteenth century—and who has been roundly condemned by liberals ever since. He wrote, for instance, that "the majority of women (happily for them) are not very much troubled with sexual feeling of any kind ... The best mothers, wives, and managers of households, know little or nothing of sexual indulgence. Love of home, children, and domestic duties, are the only passions they feel. As a general rule, a modest woman seldom desires any sexual gratification for herself. She submits to her husband, but ... would far rather be relieved from his attentions ... (157) Acton also declared, in stronger terms, that to impute sexual feeling to a woman is a "vile aspersion," though he conceded that women of the lower classes may have such emotions.

229. Frigidity—lowest estimate of incidence

Acton presumably thought that most women were frigid, and that such a condition was to be encouraged in the interest of propriety. At the other end of the extreme it has been suggested by many liberal sexologists that there is in fact no such thing as a frigid women, that women thinking themselves to be frigid either do not having a sexual partner whom they love or have been given wrong information about the nature of orgasm. Thus the Hegelers state that "In all the cases in which contended frigidity has been carefully examined it has been found that the woman in question certainly did have sexual feelings"(158).

230. Frigidity—highest estimate of incidence

There are the moralistic estimates of frigidity and there are also the medical (or pseudo-medical). Much of what is meant by frigidity in the specialist literature is open to question. Does, for instance, lack of orgasm equate with frigidity? Personally I do not believe it. Before any adequate evaluation can be made of the incidence of frigidity it is necessary to define one's terms—but this is hardly the place to embark upon any such semantic digression. (In any event the counterposing of superlatives 229 and the present one should say all that is necessary.) In the medical literature, it has been suggested that up to 70 per cent of all women are frigid. Bergler has suggested that frigidity is a problem that "concerns from 70 to 80 per cent of all women Knight wrote that "perhaps 75 per cent of all married women derive little or no pleasure from the sexual act." And a similar estimate is made by Kroger and Freed (159).

231. Orgasm (women)—fastest

We are all led to believe that women are slower to achieve orgasm than are men. This is a more complicated picture than it seems—not least because, as some have argued, coitus itself may not be the more effective way to arouse a woman. Be this as it may it is still true that many women respond very quickly to sexual stimulation. Fisher notes that in one series of surveys (160) the average woman seemed to require about 8 minutes to achieve orgasm—"but it should be emphasized that there was remarkable individual variation, with some women requiring as few as 1 minute and others requiring as much as 30 minutes to reach orgasm." If, in a relatively small research survey, women were found who could achieve orgasm in less than 1 minute it is reasonable to surmise that some would require only 40 or 50 seconds to achieve the same result. And doubtless there are some "freakish" folk requiring much less time than this; for instance, the women noted by Pomeroy who achieved orgasm 2-5 seconds after penile insertion!

232. Orgasm (women)—slowest

In the Fisher study some women required as much as 30 minutes stimulation to achieve orgasm. This is a relatively long time but perhaps such women are consoled at the thought that some of their sexually active sisters never have orgasm at all and are perfectly happy. As we have suggested before, it is a mistake to think that a sexually satisfactory life needs to be punctuated at regular intervals by well-defined orgasms. The tardy orgasm may or may not cause distress, but it should always be stressed that there is more to sex than orgasm.

233. Orgasm (women)—most frequent

If the feminists want evidence of female superiority to men in the sexual sphere they should look to female multiorgasmic capabilities. In a *Playboy* interview with Timothy Leary we learn of the effects of LSD on a woman's orgasmic capacities—

> Playboy: We've heard that some women who ordinarily have difficulty achieving orgasm find themselves capable of multiple orgasms under LSD. Is that true?
> Leary: In a carefully prepared, loving LSD session, a woman can have several hundred orgasms.
> Playboy: Several *hundred?*
> Leary: Yes. Several hundred (161).

That female orgasms can be reckoned in hundreds—in the most extreme cases—in a single session may seem absurd. There is a body of evidence however to suggest that such a possibility could obtain in fact. Brecher, for instance, quotes (161) the experience of a male participant in the Sexual Freedom Movement—"I would estimate that she experienced between 100 and 200 orgasms during the 4 hour period. Her orgasms were quite obviously physiological; there was no possibility of 'pretending.'" Pomeroy notes "one woman who was capable of from fifteen to twenty orgasms in twenty minutes" (162) (163). Cauthery and Cole declare that "the world's standing record is 100 in one hour," though they give no reference for this remarkable accomplishment.

234. Orgasm (women)—longest

The idea of orgasm as *climax* suggests that it is soon over, and this is indeed true. At the same time a single orgasm can sometimes roll on and on with the man—or more likely the woman—carried along on waves of bliss. According to Fisher (166) the typical female orgasm lasts from 6 to 10 seconds. In a few extreme cases in the various samples it was reported that orgasm lasts "more than 20 seconds." With the general spread of human ability we may expect a record orgasm to last for around half a minute!

235. Orgasm (women)—shortest

Some orgasms are so brief and inconsequential that there is considerable doubt as to whether they even happened at all. Clearly, in such circumstances, a just-discernable orgasm could last for only a fraction of a second. Fisher came across women who claimed that their orgasms lasted for a second or two.

236. Erogenous zone (women)—most sensitive

We are always being told these days that the clitoris, richly equipped as it is with nerves, is the most sexually sensitive part of a woman's anatomy. It is probably true, but the thing should not be got out of proportion. Sexual arousal is more "fancying" someone than having the right bits of flesh stimulated. The clitoris may be useful to know about but it is certainly not a magic switch. And handled carelessly or roughly it can certainly be counter-productive. In the Fisher survey, women rated sexual foreplay to produce greatest excitement in the clitoris (165). It is of some interest that women who have lost their clitoris—through accident or necessary operation—are still capable of immense sexual excitement by hand- or mouth-stimulation of the general clitoral area.

237. Erogenous zone (women)—least sensitive

Many men are keen to play with a woman's vulva: women are often relatively indifferent to such activity—particularly if the man focuses on the outer lips. The inside lips (*labia minora*) are usually highly sensitive, the outer lips (*labia majora*) much less so. The women surveyed by Fisher rated the sexual excitement areas in the following sequence—clitoris, vagina near clitoris, inside lips of vulva, inside vagina, and breasts. The outside lips of the vulva were rated the least excitable of all (165).

238. Coitus (human)—maximum pulse rate

Graphic analogies have been drawn between human coitus and other forms of energetic activity, such as riding a bicycle or running a sprint. In all such cases various physiological effects can be noted, one of which is the more rapid circulation of blood. In the 1950s Kinsey pointed out that "precise measurements on the increase in pulse rate during arousal are few," a circumstance which—to a degree—Masters and Johnson have rectified. Mendelsohn produced graphs showing maximum pulse rate for men and women before, during and after coitus: a maximum pulse rate of 150 was recorded. Boas and Goldschmidt recorded maximums of 146 in four consecutive orgasms in a woman. And Klumbies and Kleinsorge noted a maximum pulse rate of 142 in a man at orgasm. In violent exercise boys have been known to reach a rate of 200; and young men running to a treadmill have reached 208.

239. Sexual response—first compared with epileptic seizure

Sexual response has been compared with fainting, epileptic seizure and death! Some of the earliest sexological writers have compared sexual response with manifestations of epilepsy. Among the Greeks, for instance, Democritus (around 420 B.C.) has been quoted as saying that orgasm is like a small epileptic seizure. Clement of Alexandria said similar things, as did Aretaeus (2nd to 3rd century A.D.) in his "On the Cure of Chronic Diseases." It has been pointed out by Kinsey that in the modern medical literature erection and ejaculation are sometimes listed as epileptic sequelae.

240. Dreams without orgasm—most frequent types

The patterns of sexual dreaming are partly conditioned by whether the dreamer has had sexual experience in particular areas. Havelock Ellis, Moll, Kinsey and others have discussed the relation of dreams to actual experience. Kinsey found that thirty-six per cent of women without "overt experience" actually had dreams about coitus: this was the most frequent type of dream, the next most likely being about homosexual contact (16 per cent). It is curious that of those *with* experience prior to the interview only thirty per cent had dreams, without accompanying orgasm, about coital activity. In fact there is less connection than one might have expected between the content of sexual dreams and the actual experience of the dreamer.

241. Dreams without orgasm—least frequent types
The least frequent sexual dreams without orgasm are much the same whether the dreamer has "overt experience" or not. In the Kinsey survey two types of dreams without orgasm were experienced by only two per cent of people: these were dreams of sexual contact with animals and dreams having a clear sado-masochistic content. Dreams of rape were noted by four per cent of the women surveyed.

242. Dreams with orgasm—most frequent types
In general fewer people report dreams with orgasm than dreams without orgasm. Orgasmic dreams, in people without "overt experience," were most frequently connected with coitus in the Kinsey female survey—though here only 10 per cent of women reported orgasmic dreams of coitus. The next most frequent type of dream—reported by seven per cent of women—was homosexual in character. Thirty-nine per cent of women "with experience prior to interview" reported orgasmic dreams of coitus—and the same percentage also noted orgasmic dreams in a non-coital heterosexual situation.

243. Dreams with orgasm—least frequent types
Dreams of petting and dreams having sado-masochistic content were less frequently reported, as an orgasmic experience in those women without "overt experience," than any other category of sexual dreams. In fact both those types of dreams were reported by only one per cent of the women in the Kinsey survey. Dreams of pregnancy and childbirth were accompanied by orgasm in two per cent of the "inexperienced" women surveyed. Dreams of contact

with animals produced orgasms in twice this number of women—in four per cent of those surveyed. In "experienced" women the least frequent types of dreams producing orgasm were those connected with animal contacts, dreams having sado-masochistic content, and dreams relating to pregnancy or childbirth. All these types of dreams produced orgasms in one per cent of women surveyed.

244. Coitus reservatus—first recommended

Coitus reservatus, whereby a man puts his penis inside a woman's vagina but aims not to ejaculate, has been practiced for a variety of religious, moral, contraceptive and other reasons. According to one authority it was first advocated by Dr. Alice Stockham of Chicago at the end of the nineteenth century, and later by Dr. Marie Stopes. Stockham can be quoted—"Manifestations of tenderness are indulged in without physical or mental fatigue; the caresses lead up to connection (coupling) and the sexes unite quietly and closely. Once the necessary control has been acquired, the two beings are fused and reach sublime spiritual joy. This union can be accompanied by slow controlled motions, so that voluptuous thrills do not overbalance the desire for soft sensations. If there is no wish to procreate, the violence of the orgasm will thus be avoided. If love is mutual, and if orgasm is sufficiently prolonged, it affords complete satisfaction without emission or orgasm. After an hour the bodies relax, spiritual delight is increased, and new horizons are revealed with the renewal of strength." When Dr. Stockham's book first appeared it was condemned by medical men in Britain and America. In more recent times some sexologists approve the method espoused; others condemn it. For instance, Dr. Robert Chartham urges that "it is *not* a method of lovemaking to be recommended . . ."

245. Coitus interruptus—most famous biblical instance

This form of coital activity, involving withdrawal of the penis so that no semen is ejaculated into the vagina, has long been practiced as an optimistic contraceptive method. The famous biblical example is to be found in Genesis XXXVIII, 8-10—"And Judah said unto Onan, Go in unto thy brother's wife, and marry her, and raise up seed to thy brother. And Onan knew that the seed should not be his: and it came to pass, when he went in unto his brother's wife, that he spilled it on the ground, lest that he should give seed to his brother. And the thing which he did displeased the Lord; wherefore he slew him also." God's hasty action, seemingly commonplace in those days, has been taken by the Church as a justification for all manner of obscurantism in the fields of masturbation and contraception.

246. Sex play—oldest recorded

There is a rich ancient literature dealing with various aspects of non-coital sex technique. Kinsey cites dozens of references to "non-coital petting techniques." For instance, there are ancient Near Eastern documents dating back to the second millenium B.C.; and in Ezekiel XXIII, 3 it is recorded that as people committed 'whoredoms' in various places, "there were their breasts pressed, and there they bruised the teats of their virginity." There is very little new in the modern sex manuals. We may be new-fangled with invitations to try a variety of sex techniques but the ancients did it all, or nearly all, before us.

247. Sex play—most effective technique

What works with one person does not work with another. What is sexually provocative or exciting is in the eye of the beholder. Having said this we should also remark that people also have a great deal in common. It would be surprising if it were otherwise: people are, after all, physically and psychologically similar in a number of ways. This similarity allows us to generalize in particular ways, i.e. in connection with what turns people on. A consensus seems to be emerging that of all sex-play techniques the most sexually stimulating is often oral sex—in which one partner kisses, licks, or "tongue-teases" the genitals of the other. If they lie head-to-toe—the celebrated *soixante-neuf* or 69 position—they can of course do it to each other simultaneously. (See however the later part of superlative 248).

248. Sex play—most dangerous techniques

Some tricks that people get up to for sexual enjoyment are quite remarkable. Some bondage and sadistic practices are cruel and hardly to be encouraged: in extreme cases people have been whipped to death, crucified on wooden beams, and burned alive. In such instances it is hard to imagine that the participants, willing or not, are unaware of the extreme hazards they run. Sometimes, however, there can be dangers that people do not realize—as, for example, with a man performing oral sex on a woman (*cunnilingus*). If he blows into the vagina, accidently or on purpose, he is quite likely to kill his loved one—through air embolism! Such an event is not designed to prolong a happy relationship. Death in such circumstances can be remarkably rapid, a matter of seconds. There are some such instances in the medical literature.

249. Sex play—most famous advice to royalty

The Empress Maria Theresa consulted her physician Van Sweiten about her sterility. He thought that if she would only come to orgasm then she would be fertile. With this in mind he remarked—"I am of the opinion that the clitoris of your Most Sacred Majesty should be titillated for some length of time before coitus." Whether or not the Empress took the advice we do not know; we do of course know that orgasm has nothing to do with conception. The lady did subsequently bear no less than sixteen children—and perhaps she had an enjoyable sex life (166).

250. Petting to climax—most frequent by age

In data based on single unmarried males Kinsey found that the 21-25 year-old group "petted to climax" more frequently than the other ten age ranges surveyed. Even so their record is hardly impressive—a mere seven times a week. Perhaps we should be surprised that this figure is higher than that for the 16-20 year-old group (4.5 times a week as maximum)—but the younger men are perhaps too busy masturbating (15 times a week compared with twelve for the 21-25 year age group).

251. Coitus (boy)—youngest

The youngest boy in the Kinsey data to have had sexual intercourse was nine years of age. There is no debate as to what constitutes sexual intercourse. If penetration suffices then there is no reason in principle why very young boys—say five or six—should not manage to achieve coitus. But in such circumstances coitus would clearly not involve the discharge of semen. The 9-year-old in Kinsey (167) is almost certainly not a record. Ford and Beach have remarked (168) that in some cultures heterosexual intercourse begins as early as eight. Among the Chewa it was thought that the young will not mature properly unless they indulge in early coitus; the Lepcha believe that girls would be infertile unless they had intercourse before the time of puberty.

252. Coitus (girl)—youngest

There is an obvious sense in which coitus is easier for a girl at an early age than for a boy. For a boy to have intercourse he must be capable of erection. The girl need have no particular physical capacity. Clearly if she is very young she will be very small but this would hardly be an obstacle to a male with a small thin penis. In the anthropological literature there is abundant evidence of girls having sexual intercourse long before puberty (we have already mentioned Ford and Beach). It has been noted (169) that among the Marquesans 8 year-old girls indulged in public sexual intercourse. Kinsey recorded 29 cases of pre-adolescent females who had had coitus with older males "with whom there had been complete genital union (170)." He also cites a Russian survey (1924) in which three out of 338 female Russian students had coitus before the age of five. But the record for early female coitus—perhaps one of our most remarkable superlatives—is the *two*-year-old girl cited in a recent work (171).

253. Coitus (human)—oldest couple

All relevant surveys have shown men and women still having sexual intercourse when in their eighties or even nineties, though around three-quarters of all men are impotent by the time they reach their eighties. The oldest potent male in the Kinsey survey was an 88-year-old Negro, who continued to enjoy regular sexual intercourse (172) with his ninety-year-old wife! It should be said that some cases of impotence in old men are certainly due to the absence of adequate stimulation: though it is arguable that sudden stimulation to orgasm in an old man could prove fatal, as has happened.

254. Coitus (human)—most frequent (fast)

We have already noted the most frequent orgasms for men and women. Obviously orgasmic frequency is related to coitus but only partly: there are other ways in which a person can come to climax. Kinsey found that some married couples were having sexual intercourse as many as twenty-nine times a week, i.e. couples in the 21-25 year age group (173). By the age of fifty, "maximum frequency" had dropped to around 14 times a week. And it has also been noted that in some exceptional cases, from the youngest lovers to those around forty years of age— "there were some individuals who were having coitus in their marriages on an average of four times a day, every day in the week (176). By the age of fifty-five no couples in the Kinsey sample were having coitus more frequently than seven or eight times a week. During one family planning trial in Britain one woman logged on her specially provided record card that she had intercourse ninety-one times in one month—"a figure considered so extraordinary that it was left out of the final calculation in case it ruined the figures for average frequency of copulation (about once every fourth day)" (175). In their extensive cross-cultural study, Ford and Beach (176) noted that Thonga males copulate with 3 or 4 wives in a single night; and Chegga men are supposed to have intercourse as many as ten times in a night. But does orgasm occur in each copulation—"the data unfortunately permit no definitive statements."

255. Coitus (human)—longest

The act of putting the penis inside the vagina but deliberately holding back from orgasm has been termed *coitus reservatus*. It has also been denoted *Karezza* in Sanskrit and Hindu literature. In some instances it has been practiced by whole communities, as in the Oneida Colony in the nineteenth century in New York State. The "colony," founded by Noyes in Vermont in 1841, moved to Oneida in 1848. What Noyes called "male continence" meant the man putting his penis inside the woman's vagina for periods of well over an hour and then withdrawing, without ejaculation, after the woman had experienced several orgasms (177). The practice has been known throughout the world. It has been pointed out (178) that busy men in China, "in the habit of spending hours each day" with concubines, would still manage to see to their affairs—"There are many instances in both novels and court records, of papers being signed without the male member being withdrawn, and of urgent matters being discussed with callers to the accompaniment of occasional movements to ensure that the erection was not lost." Mohammed was said to have recommended prolonged coitus of this type.

256. Love-making—longest session

It all depends what you mean by love-making. Does it count if you knock off for a sandwich and a drink and then start again? No agreed ground-rules have been established. Anyway one figure that will do for a starter is the fifteen hours recorded by Mae West in her autobiography—a man called "Ted" apparently made love to her for this length of time. He later said that "he was both astounded and pleased at his own abilities." (See also superlative 255)

257. Kiss (human)—longest

Kisses between men and women usually last for a few seconds. Kisses lasting minutes are unusual; kisses lasting hours quite remarkable. There is a type of kiss called *"maraichinage"*—after the Maraichins or inhabitants of

the district Pays de Mont in the Vendée (Brittany)—
which quite literallly lasts for hours (179). In this type of
exchange the couple mutually explore and caress the inside
of each other's mouths with their tongues "as profoundly
as possible." Maraichinage has been recommended as a
"real antidote against depopulation."

258. Kiss (human)—society in which least practiced

Most people take the values and practices of their own society as absolute, those of other cultures as subjective and
misguided. For those human beings accustomed to kissing
it may seem odd that some peoples do not indulge in any
such practice. Most of us have heard that Eskimos rub
noses rather than kiss. Fewer of us have heard of the
Siriono, mentioned in the anthropological literature: this
tribe, living in South America, do not indulge in kissing
(nor is breast stimulation a usual part of foreplay). Nor
do the Thonga go much on kissing: when they first saw
Europeans kissing they remarked—"Look at them—they
eat each other's saliva and dirt." This is not so odd as it
sounds. There are more germs in the mouth than in the
anus!

259. Coitus—most frequent (extra-marital)

In Kinsey we find that extra-marital intercourse is most
frequent in the 21-25 years age group, i.e. a maximum
frequency of about eighteen times a week. Homosexual
activity, coitus with prostitutes, petting to climax, marital
intercourse are also high for this group. Younger people
seemingly do better at masturbation and nocturnal emissions.

260. Coitus—most frequent with prostitutes

I have not yet come across data on maximum frequency
of coitus by an individual with a prostitute or with prostitutes. The maximum frequency noted in Kinsey (and already referred to) is the seven a week for men in the 21-
25 years age group. This is not a high figure and there
seems no doubt that many men employ prostitutes more
frequently than this.

261. Coitus (human)—most frequent in Islamic records

There are many tales, some purportedly true, in which sturdy heroes achieve staggering coital feats. Islamic folklore is full of such instances of prodigious sexual achievement; and no doubt some of the writers liked to think that the stories were based on fact. Two authorities talk of "fifteen forays" being served or of much "thrashing and slashing" and "poking and stroking" all night long. It is said that to be known as *abū zeqqzeqq* (father of thrusts), one capable of "great strokes of the prickle," is a great honor. The Hindu *dhakēlā* (pusher) is a worthy male performer to whom no woman worth her salt would deny herself. And *abū hhimlāt* (father of assaults) is taken as a fitting name for one of those "hardy cocks" of Upper Egypt, who is equipped to "take on twenty hens one after the other (180)."

262. Coitus (human)—most frequent biblical

In the Bible and old Hebrew writings there is much about sex, but one has to learn to delve into euphemism and circumlocution to unravel the true meaning. The Talmudists have written that—"... we read (1 Kings 1, 15), *And Bathsheba went in unto the king into the chamber.* Rab Judah said in Rab's name: "On that occasion Bathsheba dried herself thirteen times." This has been taken as meaning that Bathsheba and David had sexual intercourse thirteen times in succession—and after each orgasm, according to Mosaic law and custom, Bathsheba was obliged to wash and/or dry her genitals. And the Talmud notes, in reference to 2 Samuel II: 2 ("and it came to pass, in the early evening, that David arose from off his bed"), that "he copulated by day instead of night so that he might be free from desire by night." During the day King David copulated with eighteen wives. He records the consequences—

"I am tired of my moaning; every night I flood my bed with tears [Heb. *dim'ath*, prostatic and/or seminal fluid]; I soak my couch with my weeping. My strength is exhausted through my groaning all the day long; my moisture [semen] is dried up like the drought of sum-

mer. I am poured out like water; my moisture is eva-
porated as by the heat of the hot season; I am weary of
my weeping [continual ejaculations] (181).

263. Coitus (human)—most frequent by race

In their cross-cultural study of sexual performance, Ford
and Beach noted (182) the lowest incidence of copulation
among the Keraki, who generally have (had) sexual intercourse only once a week. The Lesu do a little better with
once or twice a week. Two or three times a week is
thought to be typical among the Chiricahua and the
Trukese. More active still, the Hopi Indians were reckoned to copulate three or four times a week; and—"although the Crow Indians think it weaking to have intercourse every night, they find it difficult to do so less frequently." Among the Siriono, coitus usually occurs about
once a day. The Aranda of Australia were said to have
sexual intercourse as much as five times nightly, sleeping
between each sex act. And the Ifugao of the Philippines
were reckoned to admire men who had intercourse several
times in a single night. The African Thonga male may copulate with three or four of his wives in a single night, as
already noted; and Chagga males have surprising virility. I
have come across no records among whites to equal the
Chagga accomplishments.

264. Coitus (human)—most extreme consequence

The most extreme consequence for any type of human activity is death: and such an unfortunate event has often
occurred through coitus. Death during sexual activity was
noted by Pliny A.D. 23-79, Hirschfeld, Van de Velde, Havelock Ellis, etc. It has been suggested that some Oriental
copulations have been pursued with the very aim of totally
exhausting, or even killing, the woman—the Japanese
gokuraku-ojo or "sweet death" (183). According to
Muhammed, to die in the glorious battle abed with one's
belly on top is to die a matyr of love. The Caliph Harun
er-Reshid was reckoned a hero because he died of heart
failure during sexual intercourse. Christian sages have
viewed things differently, seeing death in coitus as a final

infamy. Attila the Hun was said to have died fornicating with a blonde.

265. Coitus (human)—least extreme consequence
This is an easy one. Coitus *can* result in—absolutely nothing at all. A man may achieve an erection, he may penetrate his woman happily enough, and there may even be some emission; but such event *can* occur without significant orgasm, without much change in heart beat, and without any of the stressing of the body which occurs in more consequential encounters. A placid coupling such as this can, of course, result in conception, a quite extreme consequence.

266. Ejaculation (human)—most frequent on one occasion
The majority of men manage one ejaculation when called upon. Some—mostly the younger ones—manage a second within a short space of time. A fewer number manage a third or a fourth. In a tiny minority of cases a man may achieve an even greater number of orgasms and accompanying ejaculations. The highest number of ejaculations I have seen reliably reported is the 6 to 8 accomplished by a 39-year-old Negro male on a single occasion (184). This hardly compares with the high numbers achieved for *orgasmic* frequency, but it should always be remembered that orgasm can occur without the discharge of seminal fluid.

267. Ejaculation (old man)—most frequent
Kinsey found men still making love about once a week at the age of sixty-five? (185). In one group 75-year-olds were having sex about once a month; and 80-year-olds were managing it once every nine or ten weeks. The record for such things lies with a white man who was having—at the age of seventy—more than seven ejaculations per week!

268. Ejaculation (boy)—youngest
The earliest ejaculation remembered by any of the "apparently normal males" surveyed by Kinsey was at the age of

eight: this age was noted by three males. The history was also taken of one unusual boy, a Negro interviewed when he was 12, who reckoned he first ejaculated at the age of six. A clinician had diagnosed the boy as "idiopathically precocious in development." In the literature—Kinsey quotes three cases (186)—there are clinical instances of still younger ages. Non-motile sperm have been detected in urine after prostate massage at four and a half years. Kinsey opts for eight as the earliest reliably recorded ejaculation.

269. Ejaculation (human)—rarest case

Various extremely unusual masturbatory techniques have been used by both men and women to achieve orgasm and, with men, ejaculation. It is a commonplace that fantasy, accompanied by digital manipulation of the penis, can produce ejaculation in the majority of men. A small number, however, can accomplish ejaculation by means of fantasy alone. In the Kinsey survey of more than 5000 men, three or four were found who could ejaculate by deliberately concentrating on sexual fantasies, without any genital manipulation—"In such a case the psychic stimulation is entirely responsible for the result." Two or three males in a thousand are able to suck their own penises to achieve orgasm and ejaculation.

270. Ejaculation (human)—latest to start

We have noted that unusual boys may ejaculate as early as eight years of age. As we may expect, there are surprisingly late upper extremes as well. There are of course sad cases of life-long ejaculatory impotence. But assuming that most men start ejaculating at some time in their lives what is the latest age for such a commencement? According to Kinsey the latest ages of first ejaculation reliably recorded "are 21 for two apparently healthy males, 24 for a religiously inhibited individual, and 22 and 24 for two males with hormonal deficiencies."

271. Ejaculatory spurts (human)—most number

This is another parameter relatively neglected in medical science. In ejaculation, muscles at the base of the penis contract in spasms to eject the semen from the urethra. With each spasm a spurt of semen is discharged from the penis. With most men five or six spasms are the rule, by which time the seminal store is exhausted and the sexual tension no longer exists. In rare cases there may be as many as a dozen ejaculatory spurts accompanying one orgasm.

272. Ejaculatory spurts (human)—least number

Assuming that ejaculation is achieved what is the least number of contractile spasms achieving seminal discharge? The answer is one or none, depending on how you look at it. In men who have very weak orgasms the semen may "dribble" from the penis and there may hardly be a spurt in sight. Or there may be a single indentifiable contraction resulting in a solitary—but real—spurt. The frequency of ejaculatory spurts, probably not a topic for drawing-room conversation, may or may not be relevant to such considerations as likelihood of conception.

273. Erection angle (human)—steepest

The average position of the erect penis, observed for all ages, is very slightly above the horizontal. At the same time there are approximately 15 to 20 per cent of cases where the angle is about 45 degrees above the horizontal. In general the angle of erection is higher for males in their early twenties, and lower in more advanced ages. "Average angles become definitely reduced in males past fifty." As many as 8 to 10 per cent of males surveyed carried the penis, when erect, more or less vertically, tightly set against the belly (187). I have seen no assessment as to how such a condition affected sexual intercourse.

274. Erection (human)—longest mantained

For some purposes (see superlative 165) it may be desirable to maintain an erection for a long time. It is clear that periods of up to an hour are not uncommon, and that if the penis is in the vagina for this time then maintaining an erection is not difficult for some individuals. Kinsey noted that the length of time over which the erection can be maintained under "continuous erotic arousal" drops from an average of nearly an hour in the late teens and early twenties to seven minutes in men in their late sixties. It is pointed out that under prolonged stimulation "many a teen-age male will maintain a continuous erection for several hours . . ." (188)

275. Erection speed (human)—fastest
Speed of erection varies enormously from one man to another—and in the same man from one sexual encounter to another. Factors such as alcohol and fatigue are highly relevant, as is the degree of erotic arousal. In a few exceptional males the erection of the penis may occur in as little as three seconds (189).

276. Sex aid—oldest
When we survey all the sex aid paraphernalia in the modern magazines we may be forgiven for thinking that such things are a product of modern "permissiveness." Clearly the ancient Romans did not have the opportunity to play around with electronic vibrators—but they had a variety of gadgets that have hardly been surpassed today. And even older peoples have used sex aid devices, e.g. dildoes. In sculptures from ancient Babylon the dildo (artificial penis) is clearly shown, and such implements were equally common in Ancient India, China, and elsewhere (190). And the elaborate dildoes mentioned in Ezekiel XVI, 17 ("Thou hast also taken thy fair jewels of my gold and of my silver, which I had given thee, and madest to thyself images of men, and didst commit whoredom with them") may surprise a few people acquainted only with Sunday School scripture.

277. Dildo—first historical account of origins
Several accounts of the origin of the dildo have been published in Britain and elsewhere. The earliest thoroughgoing attempt is taken by one writer to be the "Wonderful

and Edifying History of the Origin of the Godemiché or Dildo," printed at the end of an erotic work *The Schoolfellows*; or *Young Ladies Guide to Love* (London, 1830). The account is a translation from *L'Histoire merveilleuse et édifiante du Godemiché* in the second part of L'Aretin ou la Débauche de l'Esprit of Abbé Dulaurens (Rome, 1763 and 1768).

278. Dildo in action—first English description

According to one authority the earliest account of a dildo in action in the English language is to be found in *The Choise of Valentines or the Merie Ballad of Nash his Dildo*. Nashe lived from 1567-1601: a detailed account, from this period, of a "deviate" sexual act is very rare.

279. Sex aid—first recommended in China

The first explicit recommendation of sex aids—as opposed to their age-old use—in China was made by Buddhist monks who urged the use of sex instruments during the reign of Empress Wu Tse-t'ien (A.D. 1685-1704). Historical records show that the imperial physician, Ming Ch'ung-yen, presented the Empress with a sex aid called a "live limb" for her amusement in the royal bedchamber. The device, made of rubber, was brought to the imperial capital by a Buddhist monk from India via Tibet. A full description is found in a Chinese version of one of the Buddhist classics—a nun, having "the need," has a "live limb" manufactured for her use—"When it was ready, the nun took it with her into the inner room. She tied the rubber live limb to her ankle and pushed it inside her by bending her knee and moving her foot so that her carnal desire was satisfied (191)."

280. Sex aid ("happy ring")—first introduced in China

The "happy ring," also known as the "goat's eyelid," was first introduced to the Mongol Emperors by Tibetan lamas in the thirteenth century. After a goat was killed its eyelids were removed together with the eyelashes. First they were put in quick-lime to dry; then they were steamed in a bamboo basket for not less than twelve hours—this procedure was repeated several times. Once completed the process yielded a sex aid that could be tied round the penis (jade-stem) prior to coitus. The goat's eyelashes were supposed to give the woman a pleasant tickling sensation. Modern versions of the "goat's eyelid"—usually made of plastic—can be found in sex aid shops in this country and elsewhere.

281. Sex aid—most famous in China

The Orient was prolific in its sex aids. Perhaps the most famous of the Chinese love instruments was the silver clasp. Clamped about the base of the penis, its purpose was to prolong erection by preventing the blood from leaving the engorged organ. The Japanese "pleasure ring" has a similar purpose. Elastic bands can accomplish the same purpose.

282. Dildo—most popular type

Throughout history the most popular dildoes have always been those that occurred in nature, i.e. fruit and veg. Carrots, bananas etc. have always been employed by frustrated—and not so frustrated—women as substitute penises. Of artificial devices the candle is perhaps the most widely used. John Atkins quotes "execrable verse" by Suckling—

> There is a thing which in the light
> Is seldom us'd; but in the night
> It serves the female maiden crew,
> The ladies and the good-wives too:
> They use to take it in their hand,
> And then it will uprightly stand;
> And to a hole they it apply,
> Where by its goodwill it would die;
> It spends, goes out, and still within
> It leaves its moisture thick and thin.

There are candle episodes in various fictional works, e.g. in Apollinaire's *Memories of a Young Rakehell*, Miller's *Sexus*, etc.

283. Sex aid—most drastic

Dissatisfaction with the penis as a sexual tool has led men to a variety of measures for its improvement. Some of these would seem to be rather hazardous. The Malays of Borneo, for instance, are reported (192) as perforating the penis with brass wire spread out at the ends—solely to aid titillation of the vagina. Sometimes bamboo, ivory, or silver rods, with metal balls at the ends, can be used in the same way (193). Among the Malays the device is known as *ampallang, palang, untang,* or *campion.* The Bataks of Sumatra actually insert lumps of stone into wounds made in the penis. When the wounds heal, the penis is lumpy, thus supposedly giving more pleasure to the woman in coitus.

284. Sex aid—most expensive

A wide range of sex aids are retailed in the modern world. Electrical penile attachments can cost up to forty dollars and an electrical artificial vagina can retail at around seventy-five dollars. A number of life-sized "dolls" are also available, fully equipped with breasts, nipples, and a vagina surrounded with pubic hair. The most expensive of these costs around one hundred and fifty dollars. A wide range of accessories are also offered—from panties to lubricating cream.

285. Vibrators (use of)—most unexpected consequences

Plastic vibrators, generally used by women as a dildo device, can also be employed by men, e.g. by homosexuals—sometimes with strange results. In a letter to a medical journal (194) two writers from London's St. Bartholomew's Hospital bring to the attention of readers "a new physical sign." Within the space of a fortnight two patients were admitted through the accident and emergency department "with a painful virbrating umbilicus." Both the patients were young homosexuals, aged 19 and 25 years, who were accustomed to using battery-operated stimulators or vibrators. What had happened was that the vibrators had been lost into the rectum through the anus, apparently at the moment of orgasm. Apart from the vibrating umbilicus, a cylindrical mass could be felt arising from the pelvis and a gentle hum could be heard. The vibrator was removed from one patient easily enough but the other required a general anaesthetic.

286. Sex aid retailer—most famous in eighteenth-century
A certain Mrs. Phillips, in eighteenth century London, operated a sex aid shop "unique in the world"—"It consists of wares which are never sold publicly, which indeed can hardly be found at all in ordinary towns, and are only made and used in London and Paris. In Paris they are sold secretly in fancy shops; in London this woman has a shop near Leicester Square with them as her only wares."

287. Sex aid retailer—most famous in swinging London
The most famous sex aid shops in England are the Pellen centres, begun and operated by Mr. and Mrs. Paul Rimmer. The main Pellen establishment in London is in West Green Road, Tottenham: a wide range of products is available and cubicles are provided to facilitate personal consultation. It is not uncommon for doctors to refer patients to the Pellen organization in the treatment of psychosexual problems.

288. Coital positions (human)—earliest described
There can be little doubt that from the earliest times man has experimented with different coital positions—so, for that matter, have non-human animals. According to Havelock Ellis the oldest known work on coital positions is contained in an Egyptian papyrus of 1300 B.C. in the State Library at Turin (195). Chinese sex manuals are, however, even older.

289. Coital positions—most in sex manual
Most sex manuals, past and present, do not enumerate more than forty or fifty coital positions—and much depends upon semantics. Here again there are few ground rules. If, for example, you shift a leg a couple of inches does it count as a new position? In one nineteenth-century

work a sexologist, F. K. Forberg, claimed that there were no less than ninety positions for sexual intercourse. This has been claimed as one of the highest estimates ever made. As a note to *The Perfumed Garden* Walton remarks that Forberg restricts himself to the positions assumed in ancient Greece and Rome. Presumably if only *slight* variations in position qualified as a different kind we could think of literally hundreds of coital possibilities.

290. Coital positions—most in Chinese sex manual

In a famous Chinese sex manual, the *Art of the Bedchamber*, a Taoist named Tung Hsuan Tzu developed the theories and instructions left behind by earlier sex instructors —such as Lady Purity, Lady Mystery, the Yellow Emperor and Peng Tsu. He begins his work—"Of all creatures, man is the noblest and wisest. Of all human behavior, intercourse is most sublime . . ." He discusses thirty positions for sexual intercourse—based on the nine methods of Lady Mystery, though with more variety. The coital positions carry pleasant titles, such as The Cuddling Chat, The Passionate Narration, The Fish Exposes Its Gills, The Unicorn Shows Its Horn, The Silkworms Entwine, The Dragon Swings, etc. In addition to the named positions, he also discusses a further twenty-eight positions, making a grand total of fifty-eight coital possibilities.

291. Coital positions—least number in sex manual

In his best-selling book *Ideal Marriage* Van de Velde lists only ten "possible" positions. These range from the normal or habitual posture with the woman supine to the "equitation" method of Martial where the woman sits astride the man and faces him. Each position is described in detail with attention given to the stimulation afforded in each case.

292. Coital position (marital)—most frequent

In the Kinsey surveys it was shown, hardly surprisingly, that the commonest position for marital coitus was with the male above. All the females questioned gave this as the usual position.

293. Coital position (marital)—least frequent

Only four per cent of women surveyed by Kinsey employed a standing position for marital coitus; and only about one in ten tried sexual intercourse in a sitting position—about the same percentage that *only* had intercourse with the man above.

294. Coital position (pre-marital)—most frequent

As we may expect, pre-marital coitus usually happened with the man above the woman and the woman on her back. Marriage did not affect this situation in people surveyed by Kinsey. It did, however, affect the willingness to experiment. The male above/woman below was the *only* position for 21 per cent of unmarrieds but only nine per cent of marrieds.

295. Coital position (pre-marital)—least frequent

As with married couples, standing among pre-marrieds was the least likely position for sexual intercourse (four per cent). Rear entry coitus was only slightly more likely (six per cent) among pre-married couples, though marrieds rated fifteen per cent. Marriage does not, apparently, affect the eagerness with which sitting coitus is embarked upon (eight per cent pre-marrieds, nine per cent marrieds). The figures, inevitably, can be interpreted in many ways. Do married couples enjoy sex more and so learn to give their coitus a wide-ranging richness? Or do they simply experiment to hold off marital boredom as long as possible? Possibly any generalization is unwise.

296. Coitus at weddings—most extreme instances

The wedding ritual has been accompanied, from one society to another, by a wide range of coital activities. In various countries feudal lords were apparently entitled to deflower the young bride before releasing her to her husband. This "right of the first night" (*jus primae noctis*), known also in France as *jus cunni* and in England as *marchette*, appears to have been established on the historical evidence. Monks sometimes held the right: thus the monks of St. Thiodard enjoyed this right over the inhabitants of Mount Auriol. More extraordinarily, in some tradition, e.g. the Nasamonian custom, all the wedding guests are expected to copulate with the bride. The kiss given the bride by men present at an English wedding is a poor relation of this old custom.

297. Sex role reversal—most famous communities

The Arapesh and Mundugumor tribes, described by Margaret Mead, agree in making little differentiation on a sex role basis. Differences that occur between individuals are not "sex-linked." A third tribe studied by Mead offers an example of a clear case of sex role reversal between men and women. This occurred among the Tchambuli partly as a result of the imposition of the *Pax Britannica,* which outlawed tribal wars. The warriors lost their traditional role and became largely decorative in society. The economic support of the society still depended upon the women and their status, in consequence, improved. In the words of one commentator—". . . the woman emerges as the dominant, impersonal managing partner, secure and cooperative, while the man develops into a less responsible and emotionally dependant person, prone to petty bickering and misunderstandings." Sex role reversal, insofar as it affects parental function, has also been noted among the Manus.

298. Sex manual—oldest

The oldest sex manuals in the world can be traced to China, more than two and a half thousand years before the birth of Christ. Huang-Ti (2697-2598 B.C.), the legendary Yellow Emperor, has been regarded as the originator of the traditional sex practices and beliefs. The ancient *Handbooks of Sex,* composed nearly five thousand years ago, anticipate anything produced in the West by well over two thousand years.

299. Sex manual—most famous in Rome

Ovid wrote his *Ars Amatoria* (The Art of Love) about the time of Christ. One writer (196) has characterized the book as "an immoral book" representing the art of love as "the adulterer's art rather than the husband's art." Renaissance humanists praised the book. It begins with the words—"If anyone among this people know not the art of loving let him read my poem, and having read be skilled in love. By skill swift ships are sailed and rowed, by skill nimble chariots are driven: by skill must love be guided."

300. Sex manual—most prolific Chinese writers

In the Eastern Han Dynasty (A.D. 25-220), a group of Taoist philosophers created Yin Taoism, firmly rooted in the importance of human sexual expression. This school of Taoists wrote volume after volume of sex manuals including *Su Nu Ching* (Manual of Lady Purity), *Yu Fang Mi Chueh* (Secret Codes of the Jade Room), the *Art of the Bedchamber* and *Yu Fang Chih Yao* (Important Guidelines of the Jade Room). To give their works authority and to exert influence on the emperors the Yin Taoists attributed the key points in their manuals to Huang Ti (the Yellow Emperor, see superlative 298) and the ancient authority Peng Tsu who was said to have lived to 800 years of age.

301. Sex manual—oldest in India

The oldest and best known Indian sex manual is the *Kama Sutra of Vatsyayana,* written about 1500 years ago. It has been pointed out that this comprehensive volume summarized many earlier writings on sexual topics dating back as much as three thousand years. The first English edition of the *Kama Sutra* was privately printed in 1883; the Indian *Ananga-Ranga* (or The Stage of Love, also known as *Kamaled-hiplava* or A Boat in the Ocean of Love) was translated into English ten years before the *Kama Sutra*. This latter, more important work, is the first full manual from India devoted exclusively to the subject of human sexuality and in particular to the relationships between the sexes.

302. Sex manual—first Indian volume translated into English
The *Ananga-Ranga,* published three-quarters of the way
through the nineteenth-century (see superlative 301), was
to have appeared as *The Kama Shastra,* or The Hindoo Art
of Love. Alas, the printer, after reading the galleys, lost
his nerve and refused to go on with the job. A consequence is that the proof copies in existence are extremely
rare. Arbuthnot and Richard Burton translated the *Ananga-Ranga*—which was not written by a holy man (as was
the *Kama Sutra*) but by a poet named Kalyana Mall. It
has been published into many languages under a variety
of titles—*The Pleasures of Women, The Form of the
Bodiless One, The Scripture of Play, The Writ of Desire,*
etc.

303. Sex manual—most important in medieval India
In the words of one jacket blurb:(197), the *Koka Shastra*
and its associated tests are to medieval literature what the
Kama Sutra was to ancient. When Kokkoka turned in the
twelfth century to the themes of love and sex the move
was audacious: for a thousand years the *Kama Sutra,* representing the summed wisdom of earlier times, had been
supreme. What more was there to say? Medieval India
was different to the India of Vatsyayana. "A new approach was needed yet the early pages suggest that we are
reading a new abridgement of the classic work, a sibling
rather than a sequel." And Kokkoka frequently expresses
his debt to the earlier master. The abiding value of the
Sanskrit texts, as of many other ancient works, is the positive attitude to human sexuality.

**304. Sex manual—first to deduce female sexual attributes from
face**
According to *Yu Mi Chueh* (Secret Codes of the Jade
Room), a Taoist sex manual written not long after the
birth of Christ, it is possible to judge a woman's sexual
features by scrutinising her face—"A woman with a small
mouth and short fingers has a shallow porte feminine and
she is easy to please. You can be sure that a woman must
have big and thick labia if she has a big mouth and thick

lips. If she has deep-set eyes, her porte feminine is bound to be deep too ... if a woman has a pair of big, sparkling eyes, her porte feminine is narrow at its entrance, and yet roomy in the inner part ... A woman with two dimples is tight and narrow down below. ..," etc., etc. It is interesting to note that some of the superstitions of ancient Chinese are current in modern Western society.

305. Sex manual—highest circulation

In this permissive age it may come as a surprise to many that perhaps the best selling sex technique book of them all was first published in 1926. Written simultaneously in Dutch and German, and quickly translated into many languages, *Ideal Marriage* by Theodoor Hendrik van de Velde (1873-1937) went through forty-two printings in Germany alone between 1926 and 1932: it was suppressed in 1933 when Hitler came to power. By the 1970s the English translation, published by William Heinemann in 1930, had gone through forty-three printings totaling an estimated 700,000 copies. In America more than half-a-million hardcover copies had been sold between 1945 and 1970; a revised edition was published in 1965. One writer (198) has commented that the very *limitations* of the book made it important to an entire generation—"For van de Velde was able to speak to his contemporaries, the post-Victorian victims of Victorian repression, in a language which neither alarmed nor repelled them."

306. Sex manual—most comprehensive (modern)

The most comprehensive—and most expensive!—of modern sex manuals is *The Joy of Sex* by Alex Comfort. In a pre-publication (199) advertisement in *The Bookseller* (12/1/74) the publishers (in Britain) informed us that the price was only £6.50—a far cry from the paperbacks in this area that many of us are accustomed to seeing. A subtitle on the book is "A Gourmet Guide to Love Making." Thirty-two color prints are included and more than a hundred black and white illustrations. Already 630,000 copies have been sold in the U.S. In *The Washington Post* Anthony Storr rather pompously remarked that "... the illustrations, of which there are many, are frankly beautiful and entirely lack that kind of surreptitious, suggestive titillation that characterizes pornography."

307. Sex technique expert—foremost in the 1970s

This is probably Robert Chartham (not his real name)—a Ph. D. who turned to sex counselling and writing sex manuals with very considerable success. Total sales on his books—*Mainly for Wives, Sex Manners for Men, Sex Manners for Advanced Lovers,* etc.—are the highest for any modern writer in this area (see superlative 508); and his connection with the *Forum* magazine, frequent articles in other periodicals, his work with sex aids (and the Pellen organization), etc., make Dr. Chartham the most influential sex technique researcher so far in this decade.

308. Sex manuals—highest circulation (one author)

Dr. Chartham (superlative 307) has had a considerable impact on the English (and international) sex technique scene—so we'll give him another superlative! His books—I have eleven titles in front of me—have now sold around seven million copies in all! And they have been translated into a dozen or so languages. Minor aspects of his writing can be criticised (of whom can this *not* be said?): some liberals would discern an element of prudery in a few passages; and *Your Sexual Future* (Hanau, 1973) advocates one or two disturbingly "Big Brother" tactics. However these are minor points in the overall context of Chartham's work in the fields of sex technique and therapy. (I personally am grateful to Dr. Chartham for his ready and detailed answers to questions of mine.)

309. Sexual financial expenses—highest incurred

Louix XV of France, a man of prodigious sexual appetite, established a royal harem in the *Parc aux Cerfs*; the house was situated in the grounds of Versailles. The local garrison was charged with the task of preventing local young men penetrating the secrets of the harem. And a certain Mère Bompart served the king as procuress. The cost of maintaining this institution was high. Some of the major items—apart from board and lodging on a luxurious scale—were indemnities paid to families, dowries for those who were married off, the maintenance of illegitimate children, presents to the *élèves*, and the particular expense of Mère Bompart. It has been estimated that in the thirty-four years of its existence the Parc aux Cerfs cost nearly 20 million dollars, or around $600,000 a year—a lot to pay for the sexual pleasures of one man.

310. Call-girl—most famous in England (modern)

This is almost certainly Christine Keeler, born in 1942, the British call-girl at the centre of the "Profumo Affair" scandal of 1963. She left home at 16, met Stephen Ward (200), and later became involved in a wide range of sexual activities in the Ward circle—nude parties, group sex, flagellation, voyeurism, etc. Christine met John Profumo, then Secretary of State for War, at Cliveden: he was attracted to her after seeing her swimming nude in the pool of Lord Astor. After a security warning Profumo stopped seeing Christine, but later lied about the affair to the House of Commons. Ward, deserted by Christine and arrested for living off immoral earnings, committed suicide before he was convicted. Christine sold her story to the *News of the World* for $50,000.

311. Promiscuity (male)—most extreme (fact)

In a field where lovers incline to boast it is always difficult to ascertain the truth. Kinsey found very few men or women who had had more than one hundred sexual partners. Historically, however, a number of performers have notched up a much higher figure than this. Some tales are perhaps too legendary to believe. For example, Conchobar, the King of Ulster in the twelfth century, was said (in the ancient *Book of Leinster*) to have slept with all the marriageable girls in the kingdom. Perhaps more reliably, the nineteenth-century Walter is said to have slept with a thousand or two women: the Kronhausens remark that he admitted making love "to at least one thousand two hundred women (201); and Brecher talks of Walter having an "estimated two thousand women (202)." Perhaps Don Juan—with "his personal tally of 2065 conquests"—is the record holder (203).

312. Promiscuity (female)—most extreme

In the Kinsey survey (204) only 1 per cent of women had, for example, pre-marital coitus with as many as twenty-odd different partners. Yet the same percentage of men had pre-marital coitus with more than a hundred different partners. Kinsey accepts "the male's greater inclination to be promiscuous:" yet this belief is going beyond the data. Perhaps, for instance, women desire wide sexual relationships as much as men but are more inhibited or lack the opportunities, a consequence of male-oriented society. Anyway a number of historical performers—Cleopatra, Messalina, etc.—are quite as impressive as the men. The record is surely held by Madame de Saint-Ange, who argued that a woman can be ruined by lovers but that mere acts of libertinism are quickly forgotten—"That is the conduct I would always prescribe to all women who would follow in my steps. In the twelve years I have been married I have been had by perhaps ten or twelve thousand individuals" (205).

313. Sexual athletes—most accomplished in Arab lore

There is a view of lore that it is based on fact. Be that as it may it is certainly true that the Arabs traditionally admired great sexual prowess, esteeming highly the most prodigious performers. In "The Fabulous Feats of the Futtering Freebooters" the value of hemp is celebrated as causing the jade-stick to "become as hard as iron and hot as fire, fit for intercourse with a hundred girls." The penis of Abu'l-Haylukh remained in erection for thirty days; Abu'l-Hayjeh deflowered eighty virgins in one night; Felah the Negro "did jerk off his yard for all of a week; the Negro Maymun made "sixty days of coition his score. . . ," etc., etc. (206).

314. Sexual athletes—most famous in the West

We have already mentioned some prodigious Western performers. To their names may be added Casanova (*Memoires*) and Frank Harris (*My Life and Loves*). Guy de Maupassant was said to suffer from satyriasis or chronic hyper-excitability of the penis—sometimes taken as the male equivalent of nymphomania. Maupassant told Frank Harris that he could make love half a dozen times in a single hour; later he made the same boast to Flaubert and, to prove his point, went to a brothel with a witness and accomplished the trick. Maupassant claimed to be no more tired after making love twenty times than after two!

315. Sexual athletes—most famous in China

The Emperor Yang Ti of the Sui Dynasty (A.D. 581-617) was foremost in inventing and indulging sexual pleasures. After various military adventures he settled down to pursue amorous intrigue. He enjoyed one queen, two deputy queens, six royal consorts and seventy-two royal madames. There were also 3000 palace maidens, hand-picked by special envoys throughout the land; and he included two of his late father's concubines in his harem. In particular he attached importance to novel ways of making love. When he traveled, he took with him a caravan of ten special chariots: in each a naked beauty lay on heavily padded red satin, awaiting his favour (207).

316. Celibate (man)—most famous

It has been said of a number of famous people that they never experienced sexual intercourse. It is hard to establish such claims as the truth. It was said that Immanual Kant, the German philosopher, died a virgin at the age of eighty. And the allegation was made that Sir Isaac Newton never experienced sexual intercourse. "Although mathematical genius can hardly be attributed to this singular neglect on Sir Isaac's part, it might certainly explain why he suffered so severely from insomnia (208)."

317. Sexual athlete—most famous Czarina

This, we all know, was Catherine of Russia, a woman of inexhaustible sexual appetite. Foot-tickling and bottom-slapping gave her particular sexual delight, and people were employed for these purposes. Even late in life this doughty Czarina was persistently seeking out new thrills. When she was sixty she fancied a young lieutenant in the horseguards, named Plato Zubof aged twenty-five. He was duly inspected by the Empress's English physician, Mr. Rogerson, and by Miss Protas, the royal *éprouveuse*. The function of the latter was to test out the sexual abilities of potential favorites. All, apparently, was successful and Zubof was dully installed.

318. Sexual behavior—first recorded for Pharaoh

A papyrus dating from the twentieth Egyptian dynasty (about 1200-1100 B.C.) is preserved at Turin. Twelve drawings, occupying some two-thirds of the space on the roll, deal with the amorous adventures of the Pharaoh Ramases III—"and were obviously designed to excite not only concupiscence but also laughter." Some of the pictures show familiar coital positions. In one scene he is carried away to rest by his adult partner: a small girl supports his legs while another upholds his enormous but limp penis. In yet another picture he handles a woman's genitals; while in a later scene she pulls his penis towards her.

319. "Playboy King"—earliest in China

King Chou-hsin of the Shang Dynasty (1558-1302 B.C.) has been represented as the first "playboy king" in Chinese history. The was said to be more than eight feet in height, the tallest man in his kingdom; he was described by one historian as a man "with a back as strong as that of a tiger and a waist comparable to that of a bear." He was said to kill tigers and leopards with his bare hands. Night after night, so it is said, he would cope with "ten healthy and strong women in a row" without any sign of contentment. One trick was to order a naked woman to entwine her legs round his waist: virtually supporting her on his erect member he would then walk round the room. Clearly Chou-hsin is a competitor to Yang Ti (superlative 315).

320. Caesar—most sexually active

Various Roman Caesars indulged themselves in a wide range of sexual pursuits. Nero and Caligula, for instance, were known for their orgies, sexual appetites, and "perverted" pleasures. Tiberius, perhaps, has the edge over them all. Throughout his life he indulged in all manner of sexual behavior; and even in old age he contrived a private sporting-house in which all forms of sexual behavior would be performed in front of him. Young boys, whom he called his "minnows," would move between his legs while he was swimming, to lick and tease his penis. Sometimes he even used unweaned babies to suck him—"such a filthy old man he had become!" (209) He also collected erotica—pictures, sculpture, and erotic manuals from Elephantis in Egypt. One story is that when an acolyte and his brother, the sacred trumpeter, would not submit to his pleasure he assaulted them and then had their legs broken.

321. Popes—most sexually active

The Papacy has a startling sexual history. Pope Sergius III arranged, with the help of his mother, that his bastard should become Pope after him. John XII, deposed in A.D. 963, turned St. John Lateran into a brothel: he was accused of adultery and incest. Leo VIII, who replaced him, died stricken in paralysis in the act of adultery. Benedict IX, elected Pope at the age of ten, grew up "in unrestrained license, and shocked the sensibilities even of a dull and barbarous age." Balthasar Cossa, elected Pope to end the Great Schism, later admitted to incest, adultery, and other crimes ("two hundred maids, matrons and widows, including a few nuns, fell victims to his brutal lust)." In one famous occurrence at the court of Pope Alexander VI, prostitutes were called to dance naked before the assembly, after which prizes were offered to those men who, in the opinion of the spectators, managed to copulate with the most number of prostitutes (210).

322. Virginity—earliest age recorded lost by celebrity

We have already noted the earliest age for coitus in boys and girls (see superlatives 251 and 252). These records relate to relatively unknown people. Among "celebrities" virginity has also been lost at an early age. Perhaps the earliest age at which virginity was lost in such a person was seven—claimed by the notorious Marquise de Brinvilliers.

323. Virgins deflowered—most by one man in a year

We recorded the legendary Arab who deflowered eighty virgins in a single night (superlative 193), but we may suspect that real possibilities lie elsewhere. The upper classes in eighteenth-century England developed a veritable obsession for deflowering virgins, and men boasted of their virility by claiming many conquests of this sort. One man claimed to have debauched no less than seventy girls in a single year (211). One purpose of the notorious Hellfire Clubs—devoted to drunkenness, wenching, group sex, etc.—was to provide a ready supply of virgin girls.

324. Marriage unconsumated—most famous royal example

Louis XIII of France married Anne of Austria when both were only fourteen years old. On their wedding night they spent two hours together with nurses in attendance. Louis apparently *pretended* to satisfaction, saying that he had consumated twice. Then—despite the urgings of the entourage, the confessor and the cardinal—he refused to attempt the sex act again until three years alter. After a further three years the Queen miscarried. Some time later Louis XIV was born.

325. Virgin (use of)—most famous biblical instance

The most celebrated use of a biblical virgin was the effort to rejuvenate the senile King David (212). David was "old and stricken in years," and so his servants thought that a virgin might help—"let her cherish him, and let her lie in thy bosom, that my Lord the king may get heat." They sought for "a fair damsel thoughout all the coasts of Israel ... the damsel was very fair, and cherished the king, and ministered to him: but the king knew her not." Adonijah, the son of Haggith, was not sorry: he declared "I will be king."

326. Streaker—first photograph on front of any newspaper

Streaking—the 1974 fashion of running naked from one point to another—has been variously attributed to "dares," means of raising money for charity, simple exhibitionism, or the more complex motives beloved of psychiatrists. The press loved the streaking phenomenon since it provided an excuse, if any were needed, to supply pleasantly titillating copy and to print nude pictures. The *Daily Mirror* (18/3/74) had the happy distinction of being the first large-circulation newspaper internationally to show us an active streaker on its front page. An attractive blonde streaker called Sally is shown pinned against the wall by a London policeman.

327. Streaker—most number in one instance

The University of Maryland claimed to have mustered no less than 553 naked students to streak three miles one evening in March 1974. This beats the record claimed by the University of South Carolina of 508 a few nights earlier. These efforts, however, are paltry compared with the 1000 claimed by the students at Athens, Georgia, or the 1200 claimed in Boulder, Colorado (213). (Perhaps most remarkable about the streaking fashion is the hysteria with which it has been greeted in some judicial and press circles. Yet again we are led to believe that the human body is inherently obscene, a judgment that is reflected in some of the penalties on offending streakers. In one instance in Britain a streaker, harmless enough, was fined $300; in another instance, in Belfast, a streaker was sent to jail for three months!)

Chapter Four

DEVIANT SEXUALITY

328. Sexual deviation—most bizarre

Bizarre is a subjective word. If I mention one or two practices which to me seem bizarre I still appreciate that to those who enjoy them the practices are *not* bizarre. Some folk can only get an orgasm if they wade knee-deep in mud. Others require that someone defecate on them. Yet others need to drink human or animal urine before an orgasm is possible. Perhaps these practices are *bizarre* to the average person. And there are many more: for example, there are men and women in the world who can only reach a sexual climax through eating someone else's nasal mucous (you'll find lots of this sort of thing in Krafft—Ebing 214). In a similar spirit Ivan Bloch has referred to a youth who described with fervor "the joys of *cunnilingus, urinam bibendi, faeces devorandi, the delicias omnium corporis partium* of the loved woman (215)."

329. Sexual "perversion"—allegedly most dangerous

Considering the number of "perversions" that are possible in human sexual behavior it is amazing that *masturbation* should have been most condemned in history. One reason for this is undoubtedly that masturbation is common in any society whereas many other types of deviant sexuality (see superlative 328) are rare. It is hard to think of a disease or debilitating condition that has not been represented, at one time or another, as an effect of masturbation. The following are picked at random from quotes in Alex

Comfort as supposed consequences of "self-abuse"—impotence, tabes dorsalis, pulmonary consumption, dyspepsia, dimness of sight, vertigo, epilepsy, hyochondriasis, loss of memory, fatuity, hysteria, asthma, melancholia, mania, dementia, paralysis and death! What is surprising is that *medical men* believed that such conditions could be caused by masturbation, a practice which—as we are told *ad nauseum* in these enlightened times—is entirely harmless.

330. Sex play among children—most permissive societies
In developed societies we are accustomed to children being dissuaded from sexual experimentation by parents or other people in authority. In many communities in the world the reverse has been true: children have been encouraged to indulge in sex-play as a supposed requisite for mature development. The anthropological literature is full of such instances. Young Marquesans, for instance (216), used to gather in the bush for masturbation contests, the object being to see who can experience orgasm or ejaculate first. In some primitive societies the parents participate in the sexual behavior of their children. Ford and Beach cite (217) a number of societies in which this happens. As one example, "Hopi and Siriono parents masturbate their youngsters frequently."

331. Paedophilia—most famous men
Some older adults take sexual satisfaction in contact with children. Where such satisfaction is interpreted in general terms this is true of many parents, most of whom do not suspect that their affections are sexually based. In a more precise interpretation contact with children may be the only way in which some adults can experience orgasm. The following cases may fall into either of these categories. Lewis Carroll (C.L. Dodgson), the mathematical expert who created Alice, took immense pleasure (to what degree sexual?) in the company of little girls. His is perhaps the best-known example. Francis Kilvert, a clergyman who led a blameless life in the nineteenth century, wrote in his diary—"Shall I confess that I traveled ten miles today over the hills for a kiss, to kiss that child's sweet face? Ten miles for a kiss!" After failure to consum-

mate his marriage, John Ruskin became infatuated with a girl of ten (218).

332. Sexual activity—most misunderstood

Having already given masturbation a mention (superlative 329) we'll give it a dozen or so superlatives. Considering its prevalence—all surveys and studies record that the vast majority of people masturbate—it is extraordinary how misunderstood the behavior has been. We have seen the dire consequences that were supposed to follow masturbation. Such consequences at least make masturbation an imprudent self-indulgence. In addition it was held to be highly immoral. The Jews and the bulk of later clerics in the Judeo-Christian tradition regarded masturbation as the worst sin of all—worse even than murder. One authority declared that masturbation merited death! For fear of the possibility of penile excitement a Jew was urged not to lie on his back while sleeping, not to wear tight trousers, and not to touch his penis while urinating. In rabbinical tradition, one of the four hateful types of men is "one who holds his virile member when making water." Rabbi Simeon ben Yohai has declared that such a man is hated by the Holy One (blessed be He!)

333. Ejaculation (human)—most frequent cause of first

There are a number of possible ways in which a human male can first be caused to ejaculate. Masturbation is the most frequent cause and occurs with about two-thirds of all men. Nocturnal emissions account for around one eighth of all cases, heterosexpal coitus accounts for about one boy in eight also; and homosexual contact induces about one twentieth of boys to experience their first ejaculation. Much less frequent causes are spontaneous ejaculation, petting to climax, and intercourse with non-human animals. It is interesting that a correlation exists between the source of first ejaculatory experience and the educational level of the boy.

334. Masturbation—most likely source of first experience

"Self-discovery" has been found to be the most frequent source of first masturbatory experience. In 2675 cases surveyed Kinsey found that 57 per cent of women first masturbated as a result of "self-exploration" or "self-discovery"; 43 per cent found out how to masturbate from verbal and printed sources; 12 per cent learned from petting experience; 11 per cent from "observation"; and three per cent only from homosexual experience. Kinsey correlated the findings for age of first experience, educational level, and the decade of birth.

335. Masturbation—least likely source of first experience

There appears to be little doubt, following research of Kinsey (see superlative 334) and others, that very few youngsters are first induced to masturbate through homosexual contact. With only one in thirty-three of the Kinsey women first induced, or taught, to masturbate for the first time in a lesbian context this can hardly be regarded as a means of much juvenile "corruption."

336. Masturbation (human)—most frequent

According to Kinsey maximum masturbation rates were to be found in children under the age of fifteen. For this age group the maximum frequency of masturbation was in excess of twenty-three times a week. Some females surveyed had experienced orgasm from this source as many as thirty or more times in a week. Some energetic females had masturbated to orgasm as many as one hundred times in a single hour! But some women only tried it once a month. Kinsey concluded that "the range of variation in almost every type of sexual activity seems to be far greater among females."

337. Masturbation—in youngest children

There is copious evidence (219) of children masturbating at all ages from a few months old onwards. Kinsey mentions one record of a seven-month-old infant and records of five infants under one year of age who were observed in masturbation. Some of the cited evidence includes Townsend (five cases under one year of age); Talmey (one case of nine months); Spitz (rocking and genital play observed in over half of 248 children under one year of age), etc.

338. Masturbation—first recommended

Alex Comfort points out that masturbation concerned few medical writers prior to 1720—and at least one writer saw it as a desirable practice (220). An anonymous author of *Hippolytus Redivivus* (1644) represented masturbation as a remedy against the dangerous allurements of Woman. Perhaps such an argument would not be popular today: at least it was preferable to the hysteria that was to follow in the eighteenth and nineteenth-centuries!

339. Masturbation fantasy—most frequent

Among masturbating females sixty per cent, according to Kinsey, indulge in heterosexual fantasy. This is hardly surprising since most females are heterosexual; only ten per cent of women had homosexual fantasies while masturbating.

340. Masturbation fantasy—least frequent

Not many women fantasize about sexual contact with animals. In the Kinsey survey only one per cent of women masturbated while fantasizing about animals. Four times as many as this had sadomasochistic fantasies during "self-stimulation."

341. Masturbation—most frequent by social class

One of the curious things about sexual behavior is that it correlates—in frequency, variety, etc.—with social class. Kinsey found that masturbation was more common in educated classes than in those groups concerned with unskilled or manual labor. Of all classes the professional groups masturbate most.

342. Masturbation (male)—oddest consequences

In another context we noted a strange consequence of anal masturbation (see superlative 285). A variety of consequences, bizarre or simply amusing can attend both anal and genital masturbation. For example, as we have seen, it is possible to *lose* things—into the rectum, the urethra or the female genitals. Many doctors know of a wide range of implements that have been extracted from one bodily orifice or another. Chapman Pincher mentions the case of a large glue bottle lost into the anus.

343. Masturbation—most dangerous techniques

Men and women will go to great lengths to give themselves sexual satisfaction. Sometimes the results are not what was hoped for. One writer mentions the case of a man who tried to masturbate by putting his penis into the sucking end of a vacuum-clean (221). In this case—and in a second similar one—the result was that all the skin was sucked off the penis. This method of masturbation "is not therefore recommended." Mantegazza has instanced the cases of a penis caught in a bayonet tube and in the bath tub faucet (222). Many similar such cases are known to doctors and diligent researchers.

344. Masturbation—least dangerous techniques

Most of us have masturbated one way or another and come to no harm. Masturbation can be a pleasant diversion or an essential part of the sex-life of a lonely man or woman. It *can* do harm if carried out too vigorously or with a dangerous implement (see superlative 343); it also damps down the sex urge for a time. Most manual methods of masturbation are harmless, and the gentler one is the less chance there is of tissue damage, ruptured blood vessel, etc.

345. Illegitimacy rate—highest in pre-war Europe

Scandinavia has long boasted a liberal and progressive attitude to sexual morality—and this includes tolerant views on pre-marital coitus. One consequence, according to some writers, has been a high illegitimacy rate. It has been pointed out that the rate for Sweden in the late nineteen-thirties meant that one child in every eight was a bastard.

346. Adultery (in wives)—oddest means of detection

Men have always been keen to detect adultery in their wives—or, by means of chastity belts, etc., to prevent them the opportunity. Some odd ways of discovering the unfaithful wife have been invented. Some have relied on magic, e.g. the test which makes use of the supposed power of holy water. There is a nice description of such an "adultery test" in Numbers V. We will quote one bit— "And when he hath made her to drink the water, then it shall come to pass, that if she be defiled, and have done trespass against her husband, that the water that causeth the curse shall enter into her, and become bitter, and her belly shall swell, and her thigh shall rot: and the woman shall be a curse among her people. As one couple of writers remark—"God did not trouble to institute any similar test for unfaithful husbands."

347. Adultery—most snobbish, excuse

Adultery has not always been condemned in history. There are a number of mitigating circumstances. Sometimes it is even desirable, from an ethical point-of-view, that a couple commit adultery. Great love has often been taken as sanctifying sex outside marriage! Another excuse is that one is offering oneself to a high-born person. This argument would be hard to advance in the modern world, but there was a time when it had a certain vogue. In medieval times folk sometimes saw things in an odd way—"Gawain praises the good taste of his own lady-love, Orgueilleuse, for having offered her favors to be so valiant a warrior as the Red Knight." In a Provençal romance, a husband reproaches his wife for her infidelity. She replies: "My Lord, you have no dishonor on that account, for the man I love is a noble baron, expert in arms, namely Roland, the nephew of King Charles." The husband is reduced to silence by the explanation and is filled with confusion at his unseemly interference.

348. Cunnilingus—only royal example

There is no reason to suppose that royal personages do not enjoy their sex the same as the rest of us. Apart from the occasional scandal, however, we know very little of the sexual predilictions of reigning monarchs: sometimes, after the event, some information leaks out. There is one nice case on record—of royal oral sex. The T'ang Dynasty Empress Wu Hu, evidently a keen feminist, designed a sexual custom aimed at elevating the female and humbling the male. To her, *fellatio* represented supposed masculine supremacy: so she devised a means whereby "licking of the lotus stamen" could be exalted into prime extracoital importance and thus symbolize the advent of feminine domination. Wu Hu insisted that all governmental officials and visiting dignitaries pay homage to her Imperial Highness by performing cunnilingus upon her. Thus old paintings depict the empress holding her robe open while a dignitary kneels before her to lick her genitals (223).

349. Fellatrice—most famous in ancient world

A fellatrice is a woman—often a prostitute—who specializes in the art of *fellatio*, i.e. exciting the male genitals by means of mouth, lips, and tongue. It is not a speciality that many women boast of these days, though some do—and in print! Cleopatra of Egypt has been represented as the "most famous free-love fellatrice of the ancient world." Cleo is said (I do not know how reliable the authority) to have performed fellatio on, i.e. sucked, a thousand men. Perhaps this is why the Greeks chose to call her *Merichane* (Gaper)—"she who gapes wide for ten thousand men; the wide-mouthed one; the ten-thousand mouthed woman." Cleopatra was also known as *Cheilon* (Thick-Lipped). It was said that she fellated a hundred Roman noblemen in one night (224).

350. Fellatio—youngest girls

According to Jacobus(225), four-fifths of North African Muslim and Jewish women were coaxed or forced into *fel-*

latio by their older brothers and/or other boys, including cousins and male relatives. "Most of the girls between the ages of three and five at the time of their first oral experience. The oldest was six; none could remember below the age of three." (See also superlative 449)

351. Oral sex—most number of positions for cunnilingus

There are literally an infinite number of positions for any form of sexual activity. This means that there is no upper limit to the number of ways that, e.g. oral sex, can be performed. This rather liberal way of interpreting sexual postures leads to odd consequences. Legman, for instance, has suggested that there are 14,288,400 positions for cunnilingus alone! This strikes me as rather perplexing. Is he sure that there are not 14,288,401?

352. Fricatrices—most famous

We have already met the fellatrice (superlative 349): the fricatrice, her younger sister, concentrates on *rubbing* the male genitals—which can be nice. The Jewesses of North Africa are supposed to have enjoyed a reputation for this sort of thing. Such females were also found among the inhabitants of Lesbos and were described by Catullus as standing at crossways and in alleys "to jerk off the high-souled sons of Rome." In eighteenth-century France the skilled fricatrice was well-known. In the United States, by contrast, "the fricatrice has never enjoyed any vogue. Practical Americans, if they want to masturbate, do it themselves . . ."

353. Group sex—most number of participants

Group sex, seemingly in fashion at the moment, has always had its adherents. In sex, as in most other things, there's nothing new under the sun. The largest number of group-sex participants almost certainly figured in religious orgies—where literally hundreds of half-crazed individuals could desport themselves in abandoned fashion. In the words of John Atkins, "Mass copulation has always had its devotees, sometimes for the most admirable of reasons (226)." The Bogomils and Fraticelli used to practice sexual promiscuity for the greater glory of God: they probably enjoyed it themselves as well.

354. Group sex—most men with one woman

One woman can be the target of several men at the same time: she does, after all, possess more than one bodily orifice. The tale told by Sade, in which Justine accommodated four men simultaneously, must have happened many times in reality. In the story, the Superior played with Justine's rear section, while Antonin "made an offering to the contrary God." Jerôme made use of her mouth and Clément fitted himself between her hands. The priestesses, as auxiliaries, stood around offering stimulation to any one who needed it. But four men to one woman would have seemed a distinctly modest number to Princess Shan-yin of the Sung Dynasty in China. On one occasion she ordered an enormous bed to me made so that she could roll over the naked bodies of thirty young men at the same time! (227)

355. Group sex—most women with one man

In Sade it is explained quite graphically how six women may minister to one man at the same time. This is a matter of geometry and it would be pointless to wade through the description. The central problem seems to be for each woman to contact the man in some intimate fashion, at the same time leaving some of him free to get at another body. Some men, doubtless through male chauvinism, like to dwell on such possibilities. Such fellows must regret that—unlike reptiles, some demons and a few congenital oddities—they have only one penis!

356. Martial partners—greatest number

In polygamous societies some high-ranking fellows can have, at any one time, as many as several hundred wives. This is partly a matter of definition. A man may have legal access to hundreds of women, though many would be classes as *concubines*, not enjoying the legal or social status of a spouse but still expected to live in their master's house and stay faithful to him. Where *serial* polygamy is practiced—as in parts of the United States—it is not uncommon for a man to have half a dozen wives one after the other. In other countries more impressive numbers may be achieved through what is, in many respects, an identical marital approach. In North Africa, for example, many men and women may be regarded as marrying as many as ten times before the age of thirty: and some Sudanis have been known to boast about a succession of from forty to fifty or more spouses(228). The late King Ibn Saud of Arabia contracted more than 400 marriages in his life, but claimed that he had never seen the faces of his brides. He would, for instance, contract a marriage with a daughter of a nomad tribe, sleep with her the same night, and then divorce her honorably the next morning! (229)

357. Wife-swapping—first scientifically studied

Considering the supposed prevalence of wife-swapping we may expect that it goes back a long way. Be this as it may, there has been a dearth of scientific investigation of the phenomenon: indeed it was only in the mid-sixties that any attempt was first made to assess such behavior in a rational way. The first "reliably researched book on the subject" was published in 1964(230). And according to one authority (231), "a few interpid behavioral scientists began to explore the swinging scene about 1965."

358. Wife-swapping—first magazine article

It was as late as 1957 that a magazine first decided to publish an article on wife-swapping. An issue of a men's magazine called Mr., published in New York and largely concerned with "seminude photos of bosomy females," carried a short article on this subject. In Brecher's words—wife-swapping is now a familiar term, "but it was fresh and attention-seizing back in 1957." The editor of Mr. Claimed it was this article that touched off the spate of similar articles in other magazines. Mr. followed up the original article with a correspondence section, and many unforeseen aspects of the phenomenon emerged, e.g. sex club devoted to trios, foursomes, or even larger groups. Soon magazines were carrying advertisements from people trying to contact other couples with a view to wife-swapping.

359. "Queer"—word first used to denote homosexual

The word was first employed in 1925 in the American theatrical periodical called *Variety*. Other words soon followed, e.g. "gay," "camp" (from the Italian *campeggiare*, meaning to stand out from a background), "minny," "fairy" "queen," etc.

360. Homosexual contacts in US—fewest by educational class

Kinsey found that college groups were least likely to have homosexual experience. Homosexual behavior was most common in group making high-school. This is another instance of the peculiar circumstance that types of sexual behavior can be correlated—at least for the American scene—with social class (see also superlative 341)

361. Homosexual love—most famous speech in its defence

Oscar Wilde, during his trial in 1895, declared—" 'The love that dare not speak its name" in this country, is such a great affection of an elder for a younger man as there was between David and Jonathan, such as Plato made the very basis of his philosophy, and such as you will find in the sonnets of Michelangelo and Shakespeare. It is that deep, spiritual affection that is as pure as it is perfect ... It is in this century misunderstood that it may be described as 'the love that dare not speak its name,' and on account of it I am placed where I am now. It is beautiful, it is fine, it is the noblest form of affection. There is nothing unnatural about it, and it repeatedly exists between an elder and a younger man, when the elder has intellect, and the younger man has all the joy, hope and glamour of life before him. That it should be so the world does not understand. The world mocks at it and sometimes puts one in the pillory for it." This has been described (232) as a "brilliant impromptu speech."

362. Homosexual marriage—first introduced in Holland

If marriage is desirable in any way that does not hinge upon procreation then there can be no reason in logic why the homosexual marriage should not exist as a social counterpart to the more frequent heterosexual equivalent. Some groups have urged such a course, and some societies have been prepared to tolerate such an arrangement. California has recently seen a homosexual marriage between two men, and not long ago—in 1969—a priest in a Rotterdam church conducted a marriage service for two homosexuals.

363. Sodomy—first recorded in China

Sodomy is one of those ambiguous words. In American law, for instance, it can mean anything—from oral sex to anal intercourse. Generally *sodomy* is a synonym for *homosexuality*, implying the commonplace homosexual act of anal intercourse. The first recorded instance of sodomy in Chinese history, figuratively described by the literati as "sharing the peach" occurred in the State of Wei. Thus Duke Ling committed sodomy with a young court official, Mi Tzu-hsia, who had a face "as pretty as that of a blooming maiden."

364. Sodomite—most famous pharaoh

The word *sodomite* has an old-fashioned ring. Like *sodomy* it is ambiguous: it can mean anything from a single deviant sexual propensity to a general debauched condition. All societies have thrown up *sodomites*, a circumstance taken by the pious to signal Original Sin or something equally blameworthy, but which in reality shows nothing more than variation in human sexual psychology. There is evidence of homosexual (sodomite) behavior amongst the ancient Egyptians, as among all other ancient peoples. The best known example of such a propensity is the case of Aknaton (or Akhnaton), 1372-1354 B.C., who apparently abandoned his queen Nefertiti in favor of his son-in-law.

365. Buggery—first detailed treatment in law

Buggery is another of those words, ambiguous but necessarily loaded with moral overtone. Its earliest treatment in law, i.e. the earliest legal assessment of the significance "Of Buggery, or Sodomy" occurs in the Third Part of Coke's *Institutes*, which was completed in 1628. In the circumstance where *buggery* meant sodomy with a human being or sexual contact with an animal there were of course legal rules in antiquity and beyond; but we have to wait until the seventeenth century to see a full legal disquisition. The reasoning in the *Institutes* is not such as would appeal to modern ears. There are remarks, for example, about the ancient sodomites being burnt by Almighty God: modern law tends to have a more secular base.

366. Lesbian—most famous

The most famous lesbian in history is without doubt Sappho of Lesbos, born in the seventh century B.C. Praised by the Greeks for her sublime poetry she was variously depicted the "the tenth Muse," "the marvel among women (233)," etc. There is still debate as to whether she was truly an exclusive homosexual or really bisexual, enjoying passionate relationships with both men and women. The life and poetry of Sappho—or Psappha, as she called herself in a local dialect—are filled with the love of women. She gathered a circle of girls around her; and with them she explored poetry, music, and love. Inevitably the early Christians thought her highly immoral. Thus Saint Gregory of Nazianzus, Bishop of Constantinople, ordered her books to be burned wherever they were found, and he termed her *gynaeon pornikon erotomanes* ("lewd nymphomaniac"). In 1072 Pope Gregory destroyed more of her surviving works. The poems of Sappho that are still known today are said to represent about 5 percent of her total output, the rest having been destroyed by the bigots. (234).

367. Lesbian activity—most famous site in Ancient Greece

Lesbos, home of Sappho (superlative 366), deserves another mention. So renowned was it, through the influence of its greatest poet, that its name came to symbolize the woman who has sexual love for another—*lesbian*. Lesbos was also the birthplace of Megilla, the heroine of the famous tribadic conversations in Lucian's collection of the *Dialogues of Courtesans*. Plutarch records that love between women was also very common in Sparta. But, as Licht points out, "female homosexual love in Greek antiquity was obviously as little tied to time and place as in modern times."

368. Lesbianism—only biblical reference

The various writers of the biblical texts were keen to condemn all sorts of sexual behavior. Homosexuality is condemned and punishments are laid down for homosexual offenders. But this is generally taken to apply to. *male* homosexuality. The only apparent reference to lesbianism in the Bible appears in Romans 1, 26—"For this cause God gave them up unto vile affections; for even their women did change the natural use into that which is against nature."

369. Lesbian—most famous Egyptian queen

The sexual inclination of the queen Hatshepsut (1520-1484 B.C.) is open to question. It has been suggested, however, that "in her ámatory amusements she may well have preferred girls to men (235)." In any event she used masculine names to refer to herself, was represented in pictures complete with a beard, and apparently quarrelled with all her husbands. Egyptian women, if high-born, had considerable personal freedom, so their amatory propensities are likely to have been expressed fully and without guilt.

370. Lesbian organizations—first in English-speaking world

The first open and avowed organization to cater exclusively for lesbian interests was in Britain. Established at the beginning of 1964 under the title, Minorities Research Group (M.R.G.). It followed an article, "A quick look at lesbians," by a journalist Dilys Rowe, which appeared in *Twentieth Century* (winter 1962-3, pp. 67-72). A lesbian was quoted as saying that "the thing that hurts a homosexual woman most is that the heterosexual does not recognize the spiritual quality of her love." Another lesbian replied in a subsequent issue of the magazine to the effect that what was resented was not that the spirituality of her life was doubted by the heterosexual, but its *authenticity*. The heterosexual does not realize how hard the homosexual woman finds it to imagine what it is to be in love with a man. (236)

371. Lesbians—most famous in Eighteenth-Century

Two Irishwomen, Lady Eleanor Butler, whose brother was Earl of Ormonde, and Miss Sarah Ponsonby, a cousin of the Earl of Bessborough, pioneered a type of lesbian relationship in the eighteenth century. After becoming close friends at school they eloped but were brought back in disgrace and forbidden to communicate with each other in any way. Eventually, however, their relatives allowed them to live together and even made provision for a small allowance. They settled in a cottage in the Vale of Llangollen in North Wales—and, in consequence, became known as "The Ladies of Llangollen." Sometimes also called "The Platonists," they became the two most celebrated virgins in Europe and were visited by a host of famous people, including Sir Walter Scott and the Duke of Wellington. (237)

372. "Intersex"—word first used

This word, used to denote biological oddities in both the human and non-human worlds, was first used by Goldschmidt in 1925 to describe sexually aberrant types encountered in 1911: these were peculiar offspring of the matings of European females of the Gipsy moth *Lymantria* dispar with *Lymantria japonica* males.

373. Transvestite—most famous in history

The most famous example of transvestism in history was that of Chevalier d'Eon de Beaumont, a distinguished diplomat in the service of Louis XV. He was born in 1728 and died at the ripe old age of eighty-three, having spent forty-nine years as a man and thirty-four as a woman (238). Many people thought him to be an hermaphrodite. At least one writer (239) considers this to be a possibility—"though we have no conclusive evidence." *Eonism* is sometimes taken as a synonym for *transvestism*.

374. Incest—highest incidence

Incest, evoking a variety of taboo responses, is condemned equally in primitive and advanced societies. International incidences have been reported as high as five per million population per year, and isolated pockets within a nation have been even higher, e.g. seven per million in the State of Washington. New Zealand holds the record with a figure of nine per million population per year. (240)

375. Incest—lowest incidence

The lowest international incidence of incest is one per million per year. In the United States, Weinberg has reported (240) incidences ranging from 1.2 cases per million in 1910 to 1.1 per million in 1930. It has been shown that incest frequency diminishes during war and increases during postwar periods. The crime is infrequent in all types of societies—some communities (e.g. the Mormons) and some primitive races have permitted incestuous unions. It has also prevailed historically in the social elites of many countries. (See superlative 228)

376. Incest—most famous biblical instance

In *Genesis* XX, 12, we learn that Abraham married his father's daughter—"And yet indeed she is my sister; she is the daughter of my father, but not the daughter of my mother, and she became my wife."

377. Incest—most famous unpunished case

In ancient Rome the laws against incest, like many Roman laws, were harsh. In the early years of the Republic, people who had committed incest were forced to kill themselves. And in the first century B.C., offenders were thrown from the cliffs at Tarpei. Constantine's sons also imposed the death penalty, and Theodosius (A.D. 379-395), who made Christianity the state religion, used death by burning. Perhaps the most famous *un*punished case of incest in ancient Rome is that of Caligula (A.D. 37-47), who married his sister Agrippina, who, as the wife of Claudius and Dowager Empress also had sexual relations with her own son by an earlier marriage, the future Emperor Nero.

378. Incest—most tolerant societies

Sumner (241) has cited a whole series of primitive cultures and groups from various societies in which incest is allowed or tolerated, and ones in which there is not even a concept of incest. As one example, certain hill-tribes in Cambodia allow brothers and sisters to marry; as another, the Indian, Kukis look favorably on all incestuous relations except those between mother and son.(242)

379. "Fetishism"—term first devised

According to Havelock Ellis, the term *erotic fetishism* was devised by Binet in 1888. Ellis had some interest in sexual terminology. He himself, for example, claimed to have invented the term "Eonism" for transvestism (see superlative 373).

380. Fetishism (rubber)—most famous English-language magazine

Rubber News was sold in England not long ago at $1 a copy. Gillian Freeman describes it on pp 165-166 of *The Undergrowth of Literature*. Alas, by page 179 the magazine no longer exists. *Rubber News* was represented as "infinitely more comprehensive and interesting" then "even the best homosexual magazines." It even included its own

Book Club—"Large publishers find that assured sales from a Book Club help to stabilize their costs and to give a reasonable guarantee of quantities. So why shouldn't a small publisher start a Book Club?" In June 1967 the Editor of *Rubber News* was fined £1000 for corrupting the innocent.

381. Urolagnia—most famous biblical justification

In 1949 John George Haigh admitted that he had murdered nine people, three of them complete strangers. In each case he opened a vein with a penknife, tapped off a glassful of blood, and drank it. He also liked the idea of drinking his own urine on account of the biblical text (John VII, 38)—"He that believeth in me, the Scripture hath said, out of his belly shall flow rivers of living water." It is well known that the drinking of urine can have a proudly erotic significance for some people. Havelock Ellis suffered (if that is the word) from urolagnia, as do a few writers to modern magazines such as *Forum*.

382. Coprolagnia—most famous religious instances

Contemplation of, or contact with, dirt—in its various forms—can have a great sexual significance for some people (see superlative 381). (It would be illuminating to investigate the psychologies of people who insist on calling erotica "dirt"!) Some people have been known to dwell on spittle, vomit, and faeces in order to promote orgasm. In the diaries of the saintly Alacoque, for instance, there is a constant contemplation of dirty and unpleasant things. Once, when she wished to clean up the vomit of a sick patient, she "could not resist" doing so with her tongue, an action which caused her so much pleasure that she wished she could do the same every day. Mme. Guyon described a similar experience and St. John of the Cross licked out the sores of lepers, which he described as "pleasurable." (243)

383. "Necrophilia, 'necrophagy,' necrosadism"—words first coined

Necrophilia was a word coined in 1860 by Dr. Guislain to define a category of "insane destroyers." In 1901 Epaulard suggested that anyone who loved corpses, platonically or not, should be called a "necrophile." The word *necrophagy* was invented in 1875 by W.A.F. Browne who reckoned it an instance of cannibalism without any erotic connotations. Epaulard was sure however that it had erotic significance. The necrophage is taken as different from the cannibal inasmuch as the latter choses the man he is going to eat while the victim is still alive. *Necrosadism* was a term invented by Epaulard in 1901 to designate those who mutilated corpses. The sadism in a case of this sort is only apparent as the victim can experience no pain. The corpse fulfills the purpose of a fetish. (244)

384. Necrophilia—most famous cases
There are many historical instances of men and women in love with corpses. Thus the tyrant Periandrus lived a year with the dead Melissa. Herod was said to have slept for seven years next to his dead wife Mariamne. And as Charlemagne grew older he would not be parted from the remains of his German mistress. Queen Juana of Castile kept the corpse of her husband Philip the Handsome near her from 1506 to 1509. The ancient Egyptians, knowing full well the sexual attractiveness of a dead boy to some folk, never let the embalmers near a corpse until several days after the death. (245)

385. Necrophilia—most famous instance in Greek history
There has been speculation about the possibility of necrophiliac rites in various societies in antiquity. We may lend credence to such a thing in view of the tale of Achilles: he was said to have had intercourse with the corpse of the Amazon queen Penthesilia after he had killed her. Even if the tale is mythical it is quite possible it reflects some custom or event in the ancient world.

386. Necrophilia—only instances in Greek antiquity
Licht "can only quote three passages from Grecian antiquity;" Dimœtes had sexual intercourse with a drowned girl; Herodotus relates how an Egyptian embalmer "misused the dead body of a beautiful woman;" and he

also tells us how Periander (Periandrus ?, superlative 384) committed an offense on the dead body of his wife Melissa after he had—perhaps accidentally—killed her.

387. Sexual cannibalism—most famous cases
This form of cannibalism (see superlative 383) has featured in a number of court cases. Ornella Volta gives us a number of graphic cases in which cannibalism has been linked to sexual pleasure. Gilles Garnier killed a young girl with his hands and teeth, and took a piece of her flesh home to his wife. A certain Andrea Bichel murdered little girls and was recorded as saying, "as I tore open their chests I was so excited that I wanted to tear off a piece of flesh and eat it." Tirsch boiled human flesh before eating it, and Antoine Leger ate it raw. The following court dialogue has been quoted—

> Judge: But what did you want to do with this little girl?
> Leger: Eat her up, your Honor.
> Judge: And why did you drink her blood?
> Leger: I was thirsty, your honor. (246)

388. Exhibitionism—most famous biblical instance
The Bible, replete with sexual material, has given us a number of superlatives. A famous exhibitionist case occurs with Noah who gets drunk and exposes himself (Genesis, IX, 21-25). Ham, Shem, and Japheth were horrified and tried to cover him up—"and their faces were backward, and they saw not their father's nakedness." It much have been a close thing!

389. Exhibitionism—most famous royal example
Sexual display or exposure has not always been an oddity, a type of "perverted" or "deviant" sexuality. It used to be common and was even indulged in as a sign of respect to a visitor—as with the famous ladies of Ireland. The Queen of Ulster and all the ladies of the Court, to the number of 610, came to meet Cuchulainn, naked above the waist, and raising their skirts "so as to expose their

private parts," by which they showed how greatly he was respected in the Court.

390. Ejaculation (human)—least frequent cause of first

In the Kinsey survey only six men had experienced their first ejaculation as a result of coitus with a non-human animal, i.e. only six out of a sample of 3588—which represents 0.2 percent of the sample. Needless to say, rural areas have a larger instance of bestiality than the towns.

391. Bestiality—most frequent

Kinsey found that the most frequent incidence of animal coitus, i.e. human/animal sexual intercourse, was in excess of eight times a week—and this for the age-group of under fifteen years!

392. Bestiality—least likely animals

Men and women have tried to have sexual relations with a wide variety of non-human animals. Some of the creatures are common domestic pets. Some are less common—and it says something for human imagination and ingenuity that sex was ever thought of in connection with them! Roman women uses the heads of live snakes. Herzog tells us of women who used the tails of live fishes for insertion in the vagina. Some women have smeared honey on the vulva to attract flies. Thus in Stekel we find—"The flies thus attracted by the honey would tickle her until her sexual appetite was appeased." Men also have used flies for sexual titillation. (247)

393. Bestiality—best documented case among Trobrianders

The Trobrianders of North-West Melanesia gained lasting fame through the anthropoligical researches of Bronislaw Malinowski. (248) It is quite possible that we know more about the sexual propensities and beliefs of a number of primitive communities than we do about our own complex but confused society. The Trobrianders yielded up their secrets to Malinowski. At least one well-documented case of bestiality is on record. In this instance a man copulated with a dog: the names of both man and dog were household words in the villages. The culprit, Moniyala, apparpently lived down his shame. "The subject of his past lapse, however, must never be mentioned in his presence, for, the natives say, if he heard anyone speaking about it he would commit *lo'u* (suicide by jumping from a tree)."

394. Bestiality—most famous Oriental type

Chinese lovers—in pre-Mao days—were said to be fond of fowl. Mantegazza has remarked that "The Chinese are famous for their love affairs with geese . . ." This would be remarkable enough: the actual *way* the Orientals used such a creature for sexual purposes is even more extraordinary. At the moment of ejaculation the man would pull the head off the live animal to get "the pleasurable benefit of the anal sphincter's last spasms in the victim." (249) De Sade has commented that a turkey was used in the same way in Parisian brothels, where the act was termed *avisodomy*. As well as causing desirable anal spasms in the poor bird, its body temperature was thought to rise as a consequence of losing a head, thus giving further titillation. Of a number of famous practitioners of this form of bestiality, one was Tipoo Sahib, the Sultan and "Tiger" of Mysore, for years the scourge of the British.

395. Bestiality—most famous instances in Greek mythology

Bestiality has often been noted in Greek mythology. Licht notes (250) the following cases—"Zeus approaches Leda as a swan, Persephone as a snake; Pasiphaë falls in love with a bull and has intercourse with it, and the fruit of this passion was the Minotaur, 'An ox that was half man, a man that was half an ox', as Ovid calls him" (*Ars am.*, ii, 24).

396. Bestiality—most famous religious instances

Men and women have copulated with a wide variety of animals to demonstrate piety and religious devotion. A popular expression in El-Islam was "The Pilgrimage to Mecca is not perfected save by copulation with the camel!" The Arab is said to hold bestiality to be "at its

worst a mere peccadillo". (251) Hindoos were similarly
keen to practice bestiality with a number of sacred animals, e.g. cattle and monkeys. This was recommended for
lay worshippers—"and the priests collected handsomely
for arranging the matter." The devout, keen to worship
Hunoomaun the Monkey-God, naturally thought it proper
to come as close as possible to their deity. White-bearded
apes (known as Lord Baboons) were kept in temples for
the benefit of the pious: copulation with the baboon sig-
nalled worship of the god. In Herodotus there is mention
of religious bestiality: women copulated with goats in
Egypt. (Voltaire also declared this and cited Plutarch and
Pindar as sources.)

397. Bestiality—most celebrated medieval tale

A famous tale is told by Peter Damain in his *De bono re-
ligiosi status et variorum animatium tropologia*. The elev-
enth-century story concerns a Count Gulielmus who had
both a pet ape and a wanton wife. In due course the ape
became her lover. One day the ape became so mad with
jealousy on seeing the count lying with his wife that it attacked him, wounding him so badly that he died. Damain
had been told about this incident by Pope Alexander II
who had also shown him a monster which was supposed to
be the offspring of the countess sired by the ape. The
monster, an ape-like boy, had been called Maimo after his
simian father.

398. Bestiality—first organized as public entertainment

Bestiality was a common form of entertainment in the
Roman arena—in the words of one writer (252) mass
bestiality, as public display in Rome, was "a phenomenon
unique in all of history." Beasts were specially trained to
copulate with women: if the girls or women were unwilling
then the animal would attempt rape. A surprising range of
creatures was used for such purposes—bulls, giraffes, leopards, cheetahs, wild boar, zebras, stallions, jack-asses,
huge dogs, apes, etc. The beasts were taught how to copulate with a human being, either via the vagina or via the
anus. In the modern world occasional shows are staged
where an animal copulates with a woman but there has

never been anything comparable to what was seen in the Roman arena.

399. Bestiality—most bizarre births in consequence (legend)

Dubois-Desaulle has quoted many alleged monstrosities following carnal relations between women and beast. He also cites the Catholic inquisitor Martin Del Rio who declared that women have 'have been seen to give birth to a doormouse, another to a savage rat, and another to a monster resembling a bear. Torquemada thinks these are punishments God sends to women who give themselves to disordered and abominable couplings. Among other examples: Alcipe gave birth to an elephant. In Switzerland, in 1278, a woman was delivered of a lion. In 1471, at Pavia, a woman gave birth to a dog. Finally, in 1531, another woman gave birth, from the same womb: first, to a male head enveloped in a film; secondly to a serpent with two feet; thirdly, to a whole pig.'

400. Bestiality—most experienced man (legend)

This—devout Christians may be surprised to learn—was Adam! According to certain rabbinical interpreters of the Old Testament Adam had sexual relations with any and every creature in the Garden of Eden before God finally hit upon the idea of creating Eve. (253)

401. Bestiality—most tolerant society

We are all supposed to condemn bestiality, though only rarely are sound medical or psychological factors advanced (254). Some societies, however, have not been quick to condemn sexual intercourse with animals. Ford and Beach mention the Copper Eskimoes who used to live on the Arctic Coast of North America. These people apparently had no aversion to intercourse with live or dead animals. Bestiality was also common among the Hopi Indians, the Masai, etc. Among the Fez there was a magic so powerful that it allowed a man to "deflower seventy-two virgin cows" in one night (255). Rasmussen has recorded a tale of the Eskimoes (256). "There was once a woman who would not have a husband. Her family let dogs copulate with her. They took her out to an island, where the dogs then made her pregnant. After that she gave birth to white men. Before that there had been no white men." The fishermen of the East African coast from the Red Sea to the Indian Ocean have regular coitus with the carcasses of the female dugong, an herbivorous aquatic mammal about eight feet in length. The vagina of the female is said to resemble anatomically that of a woman. Coitus with the carcass is thought to be necessary to "lay the ghost" of the creature: otherwise it might pursue the hunter (257). It was for this sort of reason that the ancient Egyptians and various other peoples committed sodomy on the bodies of fallen enemies.

402. Seduction of humans by animals—most prevalent tales

A variety of animals have supposedly made sexual advances to human beings. A few of the accounts—e.g. those of Kohler and Desmond Morris, are worth believing. But some are clearly fictitious. The baboon has often been represented as a seducer of women. Perhaps the most famous tale in this context is that entitled The King's Daughter and the Ape, from the Arabian classic *The Thousand Nights and a Night*. In his translation, Sir Richard Burton mentions that in his opinion the ape referred to is probably the *cynocephalus* (baboon), a beast "with a natural penchant for women."

403. Masochist—most famous

Leopold von Sacher-Masoch, born in 1836, was not the *first* masochist, despite the title of the book by Cleugh (258). Centuries before the arrival of Sacher-Masoch men and women would surely have discovered that in certain cases apparent suffering had the power to generate sexual delight. Count Leopold did however give his name to the phenomenon, and it is on this circumstance that his fame largely rests. This is, perhaps, a pity. He was after all a successful novelist—with over ninety titles to his credit. He was also said to be fond of children and cats.

404. Masochism—most extreme religious instances

Religious devotees have sometimes been known for their extreme masochism, as if sexually induced suffering was a mark of piety. A few examples will suffice. St. Mary Marie Alacoque cut the name of Jesus into her chest and, because the scars did not last long enough, burnt the words into the flesh. St. Mary Magdalene dei Pazzi rushed into the convent garden to roll on thorns, after which she would return to the building to whip herself. She also delighted in dropping hot wax on her skin and on one occasion arranged for a novice to stand on her mouth and whip her (259).

405. Flagellation—country in which most practiced

England has long been represented as the natural home of flagellation. Thus "Perhaps it was the cold climate which originally aroused in Englishmen a desire for whipping." "Nowhere in the world do we find such a deep affection for the rod.(259)." And again—"Flagellation-mania (the desire to beat and flog) and preference for the use of the rod may be described as a specifically English abuse; it was so widespread among all ranks and ages that it formed one of the most interesting features of their sexual life (260)." Many writers have suggested that flagellation is common in England as nowhere else. There has yet, I feel, a need for a cross-culteral study in rigorous empirical terms.

406. Flagellation—first mass incidence

The Flagellant movement, which began in Germany in the year of the Black Death, 1349, was a Christian effort to introduce self-scourging on a grand scale. Henriques quotes one contemporary report telling of "giganic women from Hungary" coming into Germany, tearing off their clothes, and beating themselves with rods and scourges (261). In the hysterical distress caused by the great plague, thousands joined in the movement—"and Europe was criss-crossed from end to end by hordes of desperate men, women, and children scourging themselves for the glory of God."

407. Flagellation processions—first organized by churchmen

By the eleventh century the Franciscans were extolling self-flagellation as a penance. And the Italian Benedictine St. Pietro Damian organized group flaggelation for laymen. Two hundred years later a procession of fanatical flagellants—closely linked to the Flagellant sect (superlative 406)—set out under the auspices of St. Anthony of Padua. This austere saint, theologian and preacher—keen to combat manifest sexuality—was in fact adding to the sexual ferment. In 1260 unofficial processions of voluntary scourgers, each member heartily whipping the man in front of him, started streaming through Italy and out into northern and central Europe. The participants, all male, carried banners and candles, and they sang as they marched.

408. Flagellation for laymen—first organized by churchmen

Towards the end of the eleventh century the church was exhorting ordinary men and women to chastise themselves as a form of penance. Whipping or scourging was becoming increasingly popular, and the clerics were keen that such practices should not remain the prerogative of the inmates of nunneries and monasteries. As we have seen, it was St. Pietro Damian who first organized group flagellation for laymen. In the superstitious and fearful atmosphere of the times we may suppose that many volunteers came forward, a substantial number of whom would have derived sexual satisfaction from a mode of chastisement meant to cure them of carnal thoughts.

409. Flagellation—most curious seventeenth-century account

In 1671 a small publication appeared entitled *Whipping Tom Brought to light, and exposed to capital Views: In an account of several late Adventures of the pretended Whipping Spirit.* It seems that the streets of London had been haunted by a phantom spanker, who had been nicknamed "Whipping Tom." He would lurk in dark corners and, grabbing a passing wench, he would toss up her petticoats and spank her vigorously until she cried for help. Then he would run off like a thief into the night. Until finally captured he was assumed to have supernatural powers.

410. Flagellation—most sadistic nineteenth-century book

One of the most sadistic books of the nineteenth century was entitled, *Experimental Lecture, By Colonel Spanker, on the Exciting and Voluptuous Pleasures to be derived from crushing and humiliating the spirit of a beautiful and modest young lady; as delivered by him in the assembly room of the Society of Aristocratic Flagellants.* The book recounts the experiences of Colonel Spanker and his cronies. According to Spanker's philosophy there can be no true enjoyment in whipping lower-class women, prostitutes, or any other victims who willingly submit themselves. Accordingly, Spanker and his band capture a beautiful seventeen-year-old blonde and lock her up in a house in Mayfair. There she is subjected to all forms of brutal torture and sexual maltreatment. A contemporary critic called the book "the most coldly cruel and unblushingly indecent of any we have ever read ... in the English language."

411. Flagellation—most typical nineteenth-century book

The eighteenth and nineteenth centuries saw the production or a wide range of flagellant material in England. A book held by one writer to be "the most typical" of all the late nineteenth century English flagellant novels was a book called *The Mysteries of Verbena House: or, Miss Bellasis birched for thieving.* The author signed himself simply Etonensis. A critic remarked—"After wading through so many dull, insipid, if not absolutely repulsive books on the subject, it is a relief to alight at last upon one which tact and clever writing render almost readable." The plot of the book is described by Hurwood.

412. Flagellation practitioner—most famous woman

There were many high-class brothels in the nineteenth century. One of the most famous of these was run by a Mrs.

Theresa Berkley (or Berkeley) of 28 Charlotte Street. She was a "governess", i.e. she specialized in chastisement, whipping, flagellation, and the like. She was even credited with the invention of the *Berkely horse,* an ingenious flogging machine that earned her a fortune. One writer said of her—"She possessed the first requisite of a courtezan, viz., lewdness; for without a woman is positively lecherous she cannot keep up the affectation of it, and it will soon be perceived that she moves her hands or her buttocks to the tune of pounds, shillings, and pence" (262).

413. Sadistic invention—most bizarre

There have been many sadistic inventions: the medieval torture chambers were full of them. We need not give a list here. Suffice it to mention that the inquisitors, with full theological sanction, thought it proper to introduce a clamp specially devised for the torture of pregnant women. In more recent times, electrical generators have been used on all parts of the bodies of men and women. And Chapman Pincher mentions (in *Sex in Our Time*) a pair of binoculars in the Black Museum of Scotland Yard—"These were sent anonymously through the post to a girl, and by chance her father turned the adjusting screw before she put them to her eyes. A pair of spring-loaded penknife blades shot out of the eyepieces."

414. Sadist—most famous man

Just as Sacher-Masoch (superlative 403) gave his name to masochism so the Marquis de Sade gave his name to sadism. There is controversy as to the extent to which de Sade was a practicing sadist. Did he in reality act out his fantasies or were his novels the main vehicles for his sexual imaginings? De Sade, like Sacher-Masoch, wrote books of merit; yet he is not remembered for these. The world inevitably associates him with sexual "perversion," but such a thing only touches part of the man—in addition to whatever sexual propensities he had he also possessed considerable political and philosophical stature. His life is a depressing catalogue of frustration, thwarted ambition, and imprisonment.

415. Sadist—most famous woman

Our woman sadist, unlike de Sade, was a practicing person, i.e. she wrote no books but killed and tortured to her heart's content. In 1611, aged fifty, the Hungarian noblewoman Erzsebet Bathory was walled up alive in her castle in the Minor Carpathians for having killed some six hundred young girls in various ways. The judge at her trial appears to have been particularly concerned that she murdered noblewomen as well as mere servant-girls. Bathory used a number of ingenious devices. For instance, she put a terrified naked girl in a narrow iron cage equipped with inward-pointing spikes to pierce the victim: then Bathory would hoist the cage to the ceiling and sit beneath to enjoy the rain of blood that came down. Another device was a robot—wearing real teeth torn from a servant—designed to clasp a victim in a tight embrace, whereupon sharp spikes would shoot out from the robot: the blood of the victim ran down a channel, was warmed over a fire, and collected for the countess's bath (263).

416. Necrosadism—most famous case

Mutilation of corpses has the capacity to generate sexual excitement in some people. There are many such cases on record, one of the most famous of which is that of Sergeant Bertrand in nineteenth-century France. He declared —"I would never have taken the risk of violating a corpse if I had not had the possibility of cutting it up afterwards." He also added by way of explanation—"If I have sometimes cut some male corpses into pieces it was only out of rage at not finding one of the female sex! Some nights I have had to dig up as many as a dozen men before finding a single woman in the common grave at Montparnasse!" He was particularly keen to open the stomachs of his dead victims with a knife, making the bowls come out like the stuffing of a child's doll, whereupon he would squeeze them convulsively in his hands. Of one corpse he remarked, "I squeezed her so strongly against me I nearly broke her in two" (264).

417. Raping chair—first introduced in China

In Chinese eighteenth- and nineteenth-century novels one often reads of a "romantic and comfortable chair." This device appears to have been much in use by outlaws and licentious landlords. It appears that the contraption was in the form of a collapsible chair, with automatic clasps fixed to its arms and legs. When a woman was put in the chair, the clasps would spring to hold her arms and legs and then the chair would collapse to form a miniature bed. It appears that such chairs were much employed for raping purposes: the possession of them was made illegal under the Manchu rule. In 1949 peasants are said to have found such a chair in a land-lord's mansion in Szechuan. The chair, possibly the last of its kind, was burned to ashes (265).

418. Rape—most ancient Oriental technique

Tirad el-kebsh (the ram's attack) is the oldest known form of rape in the Orient. The Mongols were notorious for it, and there are numerous Chinese and Rajput prints showing Moghul warriors raping women and girls in this attitude. The female is thrown on her side, the assailant lifts her upper leg and squats between her thighs. Bernhard Stern, who observed this method among the Turks and Bosnian Muslims, notes that the rapist sometimes shifts position by lifting the girl's legs upon his shoulders *like a yoke;* whereupon he holds her thighs tight in his arms with all his might and, kneeling, "drives his sex organ into her, throwing himself upon her with all his weight, untroubled by her sighs and groans (266)."

419. Rape—most likely site

Where are women most likely to be raped? Mythology has it that they will be violated on a dark street late at night, on the way home from a party or other entertainment. It happens. However, a majority of rapes—at least according to one American survey occur at the homes of one of the participants. A national report found for 17 cities, in 1967, that 33.2 per cent of rapes were committed in the bedroom, while 51.5 per cent of rapes were committed at the home of one of the participants; 14 per cent were committed in other inside locations. In Amir's study in Philadelphia 56 per cent of the victims were raped indoors, at one of the participant's residences. And a study by Reiss in Chicago showed that nearly half the rape cases investigated took place at the residence of one of the people involved. Similar results were found by Eralson in Chicago in 1946.

420. Rape—most likely time of year

Various researchers have found that rape is more likely to occur in the warmer months of the year. Amir found that the number of forcible rapes in the U.S. tended to increase during the hot summer months. Summer was also noted as the time when multiple rapes are most likely to occur. *Uniform Crime Reports* also show a higher incidence of rape in the warmer spring and summer months. A study of rape in Denmark—by Svalastoga, covering 1946-56—reached similar conclusions (268).

421. Rape—least likely time of year

You are least likely to be raped around the December/ January period, according to the various studies cited (268). This doesn't mean you won't be raped as part of the Christmas festivities, just that it is less likely than on an equally festive occasion in the middle of the summer. Efforts have been made to draw conclusions about a correlation between revealed sexual behavior (rape being one type) and the biological tide at any season of the year. Such ideas are not all that successful.

422. Rape—first recorded in Bible

It all depends what you mean by "rape:" it wasn't one of the words commonly used in the Bible. Quite a few women were "known" or "ravished"—so perhaps this latter counts. There is a ravishing as early as Genesis XXXIV; in the second verse Shechem saw Dinah—"he took her, and lay with her, and defiled her." This simple affair is taken to be a *ravishing*.

423. Group rape—most famous biblical instances

The "gang-bang" was not invented in the twentieth century. There are a few in the Bible and doubtless they weren't the first. In Genesis XIX, 1-8, Lot offers his daughters to a mob of "Sodomites." Thus—"... I have two daughters which have not known man; let me, I pray you, bring them out unto you, and do ye to them as is good in your eyes . . ." And this was not the only such incident recorded in the Old Testament.

424. "Impotence"—word first used

The word is derived from the Latin *impotentia* (lit: lack of power). In 1420 the word was used in a poem *de regimine Principum* by Thomas Hoccleve (c. 1370-1454) to mean "want of strength" or "helplessness:" "Hir impotence, Strecchith naght so fer as his influence." In another poem, *La male regle*, of the same period, the word is used in the sense of "want of physical power or feebleness:" "As I said, reeve on impotence that likely am to serve yit or eeue." But the use of the word to mean loss of sexual power first occurred in 1655 in *Church History of Britain* by Thomas Fuller (1608-61): "Whilest Papists crie up this, his incredible Incontinency; others uneasily unwonder the same by imputing it partly to Impotence, afflicted by an infirmitie (269)."

425. Impotence—first clinical definition

The first clinical definition appears in Copland's *Dictionary of Practical Medicine* in editions between 1833 and 1858. Later Strauss (1950) defines it as "the inability to perform the sexual act." Ernest Jones (1918) declares it is "the complete or incomplete inability satisfactorily to carry out heterosexual coitus per vaginam. Satisfactorily means adequate erection, time and control of epaculation (270)."

426. Impotence—most common type

There is dispute as to whether premature ejaculation should be counted an instance of impotence. It is evidently a sign of male inadequacy and is commoner than, say, erectile impotence. Kinsey however refused to recognize premature ejaculation as a problem for the male, though it evidently caused distress to a woman. Kinsey noted, in justification, that many mammals ejaculate very rapidly. Some sexologists have retorted that premature ejaculation is definitely a problem for the man. Thus Brecher remarks that "It seems to me very clear that on this point Kinsey was quite wrong. The later Masters-Johnson studies of premature ejaculation reveal in precisely what respects he was wrong."

427. Impotence—least common type
Men suffering from ejaculatory impotence are unable to ejaculate during coitus despite erotic arousal and a steady erection. Often they are able to achieve ejaculation, accompanied by orgasm, by masturbation after coitus. Masters and Johnson have described this unusual condition in detail; Kinsey found only six such cases in his survey of 4,108 respondents.

428. Impotence treatment—most famous charlatan
There is always money to be made out of the fears and anxieties of gullible men. Dr. John R. Brinkley was most successful in cheating impotent men by means of gland therapy. This entrepreneur collected over twelve million dollars in twenty years for transplanting goat glands into sixteen thousand men worried about their sexual prowess; he also sold Special Gland Emulsion. He held many fraudulent degrees from bogus schools that sold diplomas; he began his career in Greenville, South Carolina, with an advertisement in the Greenville *Daily News*—"Are You a Manly Man Full of Vigor?" Men who felt they were not could have an injection of colored distilled water into hip or arm for a mere twenty-five dollars (271).

429. Nymphomaniac—most famous in antiquity
Valeria Messalina of ancient Rome almost certainly wins this one; indeed her name (the "Messalina complex") has been used as a synonym for nymphomania. With her insa-

tiable sexual appetites she acted as prostitute and seducer. She married Claudius when only sixteen; it has been speculated that she started an active sex life when she was thirteen or fourteen. If she fancied a man, Claudius would order him to submit to her whims: it was useful being married to an emperor. Dio Cassius has declared that she kept her lustful husband well supplied with housemaids for bedbellows. She often enjoyed herself in the local brothel (272).

430. Nymphomania—most frequent psychological cause

According to Ellis and Sagarin, (273) *one outstanding reason* why a woman becomes a nymphomaniac in our society is through "an overwhelming need to be loved, a hunger that generally seems to be greater in women than in men." Thus—in her efforts to seek out affection, security, and acceptance—she comes to have many sexual experiences that she might otherwise not welcome. There is a clear sense in which this is a patriarchal interpretation of female sexuality. Not all male writers are ready to come to the conclusion that a fair number of women can simply enjoy sex and see it as worth experiencing for its own sake.

431. Nymphomania—most frequent physiological cause

The authors mentioned in superlative 430 represent the failure in a woman—through *physiological* rather than *psychological* reasons—to achieve orgasm as the "most frequent *physiological* cause of nymphomania" (p. 95). This is a highly contentious subject. Not much work has been done on it, and it is extremely difficult to say what is a *physiological*, and what a *psychological*, block to experience of orgasm.

432. Brothels—most modern

There is some agitation in France and other parts of Europe to introduce sanitary, well-equipped brothels where such do not already exist (see *Guardian* 9/8/73). Mme Martle Richard, responsible for the closing of French brothels after the last war, has long regretted her action:

now prostitution has not disappeared but is simply harder to control. A former boxer, Herr Kurt Kohls, in West Germany is already running six highly profitable "hotels." The Kohl organization provides the hotels, plus a canteen and other facilities, and the girls rent a room in it, Hygiene is said to be *scrupulous.* Mme Richard wants to see similar establishments started in France.

433. Brothels—first introduced in England
Again it all depends what you mean by ... Henry II organized the "stews" (bath-houses with opportunity for sex) in 1161. And the famous "seraglios" were introduced in 1750. A certain Mrs. Goadby had visited the French *sérails,* esp. those of Justine, Paris and Montigny: in all such establishments high standards were maintained; many beautiful girls were employed with various talents. Mrs. Goadby even went so far as to employ a physician to look after the health of the girls; and she imported fine silks from France. The result of such enterprise was that she became extremly wealthy and later retired to the country.

434. Brothel—most recent to offer children
In 1810 a well-known London brothel specialized in girls under fourteen years of age; and a number of other English brothels employed adolescents. In the nineteenth century a reporter for the French newspaper *Figaro* noted that in one stretch of London streets, about 300 yards long, could be seen nightly some 500 girls, most of them between 12 and 15 years of age, engaged in soliciting. The same was true of Paris and other European cities. As recently as the 1930s Paris had a very well-known child brothel (274).

435. Brothel (homosexual)—most famous in nineteenth-century England
This brothel was opened by a certain Charles Hammond around 1884 in a house of the Tottenham Court Road. It was soon doing well and included a number of aristocratic and well-to-do homosexuals. It was suspected that one of the clients was the 25-year-old Prince Eddy, later Duke of

Clarence, eldest son of the Prince of Wales. One speciality in this establishment was the "telegraph boy", willing both to sleep with customers and to deliver telegrams; they earned a few shillings a week by all their efforts! Eventually the police raided the place. Hammond escaped but Veck (a 40-year-old clergyman) and Newlove (an 18-year-old clerk) were given four months and nine months in jail respectively (275).

436. Brothel—first established as part of the English court

Court brothels existed during the time of Charlemagne; and later a well-equipped brothel was established by contemporaries of George III. This latter establishment comprised a group of houses near St. James's Palace, in a lane called "King's Place:" the employed girls were only allowed to walk in the royal parks, and only the *innermost circle of the court* was allowed to frequent the court brothel (276).

437. "Love club"—most exclusive

The English Aphrodites comprised an eighteenth-century Love Club—which arranged wife-swapping and a variety of other sexual diversions. Membership was £10,000 for a gentleman and £5,000 for a lady, plus a gift compatible with economic status. Fortunately the journal of a female member has been preserved. She provides a list of 4,959 amorous rendezvous for a period of twenty years. Among her lovers were—

272	princes and prelates	929	officers
93	rabbis	342	financiers
439	monks	420	society men
288	commoners	117	valets
2	uncles	12	cousins
119	musicians	47	negroes

and 1,614 foreigners (277).

438. Prostitute—most famous in Greece

Aspasia, the daughter of Axiochus, arrived in Athens from Miletus in Asia Minor. Soon she became one of the high-ranking *hetairai*. In addition to her sexual abilities she had immense political ambition and in due course became a lover of the law-giver Pericles; eventually he had a divorce on her account. Aristophanes blamed her for starting the wars against Sparta and Samos. Socrates spent time in her company and Plato wrote well of her (278).

439. Prostitute—most popular in English history

Nell Gwynne has been represented as "the only darling strumpet of the warm-hearted British public (279)" Swinburne wrote of her—

> *"Nell Gwynne*
> *Sweet heart, that no taint of the throne or the stage*
> *Could touch with unclean transformation, or alter*
> *To the likeness of courtiers whose consciences falter*
> *At the smile or the frown, at the mirth or the rage,*
> *Of a master whom chance could inflame or assuage,*
> *Our Lady of Laughter, invoked in no psalter,*
> *Praise be with thee yet from a hag-ridden age.*
> *Our Lady of Pity thou wast: and to thee*
> *All England, whose sons are the sons of the sea,*
> *Give thanks, and will not hear if history snarls.*
> *When the name of the friend of her sailors is spoken;*
> *and thy lover she cannot but love—by the token*
> *That thy name was the last on the lips of King Charles."*

She was born in 1650. In 1665 she appeared on the stage as Cydaria in Dryden's *Indian Emperor*.

440. Prostitute—most successful in eighteenth-century London

Kitty—"one of the most beautiful and talented *demi-mondaines* of the eighteenth century"—moved in such wealthy circles that she could command the extraordinary sum of 100 guineas a night. The Duke of York, after spending a night with Kitty, gave her a mere fifty-pound note, since it was all he had with him. She promptly dismissed him and refused to receive him again. To further show her contempt, she sent the banknote to a pastry chef with instructions that it be baked into a tart and served up for breakfast (280).

441. Prostitute—most successful in nineteenth-century London

Laura Bell, ex-Belfast shop-girl, whose apogee as what Sir William Hardman called "The Queen of London Whoredom" occurred in the mid-nineteenth century, was an immensely successful prostitute. When she visited the Opera in 1852 the whole house rose to watch her departure. In 1856 she married Captain Augustus Thistlethwaytes, a nephew of the-then Bishop of Norwich. They lived for a time in Grosvenor Square in what may be considered a somewhat eccentric fashion. The Captain, for instance, summoned servants by firing a pistol through the bedroom ceiling. Laura had brought to the marriage a dowry of £250,000, earned from a Nepalese prince. Later she "got religion" and "she was, by all accounts, as successful a preacher as she had been a whore—no mean achievement (281)." Cora Pearl, another nineteenth-century prostitute managed to accumulate a few hundred thousand pounds.

442. Prostitutes' client—most famous in the Bible

The powerful and wealthy Judah, praised and worshipped by his brethren (*Genesis* XLIX, 8), slept with a harlot (*Genesis* XXXVIII, 18), and made no secret of the fact. The Bible is truly a compound of immense sexual license and sternest sexual prohibition—possibly the one generated the other.

443. Prostitutes—highest status

Many societies, ancient and modern, have made provision for high-ranking prostitutes (we have already met Kitty and Laura Bell). The Greek *hetairai* were a class of high-status prostitutes, as were the English and French courtesans. The temple-harlots of ancient Babylon (mentioned in Herodotus) had their own high status in society, as did the Japanese geishas. In ancient China high-class prostitutes were classified as *ch'ing-kuan-jen* and *hung-kuang-jen* (pure official attendants and popular official attendants respectively), since in the Manchu Dynasty their important customers were mainly high officials. It is a sobering thought that the derogatory connotation of the word *pros-*

titute springs mainly from the influence of the Judeo-Christian tradition. Many societies in history have viewed things differently.

444. Prostitutes—lowest status

Native girls are available in various parts of the world "for baubles" (282). The lowest-priced prostitutes in the industrial cities are invariably the skid-row "fleabags"—often 60-, 70-, or 80-years of age and venereally diseased. Such women will go with a customer for fifty cents or less in the U.S. Fees are generally determined on the basis of "what the traffic will bear." Seldom does such a prostitute earn more than two dollars from a customer. The fleabag leaves skid-row only when she dies or is placed in an institution. Contrast this situation with that of a former Miss Denmark who is known to have earned fifteen hundred dollars from a single client for one night's work!

445. Prostitutes (animal)—most bizarre

In a number of the ancient temples a variety of animals were trained to copulate with women and to have intercourse *per anum* with men. Monkeys and baboons were encouraged to play with the genitals of both sexes. Attending priests accepted the customer's payment for this service. Use was also made of such creatures as dogs and goats in various establishments. In more recent times geese and turkeys have been placed at the disposal of frequenters of brothels in various parts of the world. A more frequent use of animals is in erotic displays: dogs, small horses, etc. have been made to copulate with women in front of a paying audience. Such practices still take place today.

446. Prostitutes (human)—most bizarre

Every imaginable type of human being has been required for purposes of prostitution. In Italy a ring of grandmother-prostitutes was uncovered by the police. Amputees have also been immensely popular. Not so long ago a woman with one leg was operating in the San Francisco area: "she claimed to have more business than she could handle." Hunchbacks and women with one or both breasts amputated have also been immensely popular. Similarly some men apparently desire a woman with a club foot or females with hideous scars. And hermaphrodite or trans-sexual prostitutes have also been much in demand (283).

447. Prostitutes—youngest

Child prostitution has always existed in history. Temple harlots were as young as six and seven; and in China boys as young as four years were trained "in the fine art of passive pederasty;" girl and boy brothels were common in the ancient world and in more modern times also. The Chinese boy prostitutes were sanctified by *Tcheou-Wang*, God of Sodomy. Without doubt the youngest prostitutes of all were the babies in the brothels of ancient Rome (284). It has been noted that "sucking babes" were introduced into the brothels. The Emperor Domitian was praised when he attempted to stamp out all forms of infant prostitution. In the Japanese *Yoshiwara* or Whores' Quarter, little girls were kept for fellatio. The high-status geishas, contrary to some imaginings, were only avaliable for vaginal coitus.

448. Prostitution—most famous use of army funds

Soldiers and sailors have always been keen to frequent prostitutes. This is as true of the modern conscript in foreign lands as it is of the enlisted man in the armies of antiquity. One startling use of campaign funds was brought to the attention of Richard I at the beginning of a European enterprise. When Richard arrived at Marseilles he found that the English knights who had preceded him had squandered all the campaign funds on prostitutes."

449. Prostitution—most prevalent in London

Those pessimistic souls who declare with paradoxical relish that the nation's morals have never been worse should take time off to glance at the extent of Victorian English prostitution. Archenholtz talked of the 50,000 prostitutes in London, Marylebone alone having no less than 13,000 (such figures are generally thought to be exaggerated). The Kronhausens reckoned that the number of prostitutes in the London of Walter's day was around 80,000 (in a total London population of only about two million). If we add to this figure the estimated number of "semi"—or *occasional* prostitutes we find a figure of something like 100,000—150,000 women engaged in full-time or part-time prostitution at the height of the Victorian era in the London district alone!

450. Prostitution—oldest form

The oldest type of prostitution must have been the ancient form of "street-walking," where a woman clearly desported herself in the hope of financial or other reward. It is likely that there are professions as old as prostitution, but unlikely that there are any older. It has even been suggested that a form of prostitution can be detected in pre-human animal communities: for example, if a baboon offers herself sexually to a male she may at the same time contrive to steal his food—he may detect this but tolerate the transaction!

451. Prostitution (temple)—earliest instances

Sacred temple prostitution existed throughout the bulk of the ancient world. It has been described for Egypt, Babylon, Greece, etc. and was generally seen as having deep religious significance. The first recorded instances of such types of prostitution are for the Mesopotamia of 2300 B.C. From this region it spread throughout the Near East.

452. Prostitution (temple)—most recent instances

In some countries temple prostitution survived into modern times. One writer notes (285) that "In no country in the world did religious prostitution flourish more than in India, and in no country has it longer survived the advance of civilization." There is ample evidence that temple prostitution survived into the twentieth century. Thurston, quoted by Scott (p.80), has cited a number of cases culled from court records concerning the activities of the *Devadasis* (handmaidens of the gods), the name given to the dancing-girls attached to the Tamil temples. In connection with one court case, "the accused, a Madiga of the Bellary district, dedicated his minor daughter as a Basavi by a form of marriage with an idol." It emerged that a Basavi "practices promiscuous intercourse with me."

453. Prostitution—earliest in China

Prostitution in China is certainly as old as human life in that part of the world. But as a thorough-going institutionalized form it can first be dated to the Feudal Period of 841-221 B.C. At that time the aristocracy keep huge numbers of courtesans, paid companions, actors and musicians, not merely for use but as status symbols. The courtesans were chosen to abilities which could be sexual, musical, poetic, etc.

454. Brothel—first publicly administered

Solon, the law-giver, introduced the first publicly administered brothel in the Athens of 550 B.C. The brothel, soon copied in nearby cities, was run by slaves; and the inmates were also slaves, the lowest class of Greek prostitute. From the taxes collected from the licensed brothels (*Dicteria*), Solon built a temple to the Goddess Aphrodite. There is a passage in Athenaeus to show the gratitude of the citizens for Solon's wisdom in establishing a brothel which would give an outlet to lustful impulse without endangering the social order—

> Solon, you were a true benefactor of humanity, for our city is full of young men with exuberant passions that might spur them on to criminal excesses. However, you bought women, provided them with everything they might need, and put them in places where they would be available to all who wanted them. There they are as nature made them; no surprises, everything on view! Isn't that something? To open the door, all you need is an obolus. Have a go—no false modesty or coyness, no fear that they'll run away. You can have it now if you want it, and whatever way you like it . . .
> These fillies of Cypris, built for sport, stand in a row one behind the other, their dresses sufficiently undone to

let all the charms of nature be seen, like the nymphs nurtured by the Eridanus in its pure waters. For a few pence, you can purchase a moment of bliss with no risks attached . . .

There are thin ones, thick ones, round ones, tall ones, curved ones; young, old, middle-aged, mature as you wish—yours for the taking, and you don't need to bring along a ladder or sneak in through a hole in the roof . . . If you are old they'll call you "Daddy;" if you are young it will be "Little brother." At any rate there they are where anyone can have them without fear, day or night . . .

455. Prostitution provisions—by least expected organizations

It may seem odd that royal courts should have established their own brothels, but most of us know that such was done. Similarly, in our prudish times the idea of *municipal* brothels may appear somewhat startling; but again we know that such an arrangement was commonplace in times past. What is also interesting is that the Armed Forces made special provision for prostitution. Thus, in the Army and Navy Estimates of 1870-1871, no less than $110,000 was set aside for 2700 registered prostitutes in eighteen naval and military stations. And the London Stock Exchange maintained its own brothel in the eighteenth century.

456. Virgins "repaired"—most frequent

In the nineteenth century, bands of young English gallants would seek out virgins. The demand generated a shameful trade in young girls. One problem was that there were just not enough available virgins to go around. An answer was to "manufacture" virgins, i.e. to sew up girls who had had previous sexual relations. Some poor young girls were treated in this fashion repeatedly, their maidenheads being restored after each coitus with a new client. In some areas of London disreputable surgeons specialized in "revirginising"—and some girls were reported to have gone in for repairs as often as 500 times.

457. White slave traffic—most bizarre instance

There are many bizarre (and well-authenticated) tales from the world of *white-slaving*. One case was publicized at the trial of 1964 of three sisters of Mexico who, with immense brutality, ran a wholesale business of sex slavery (286). Girls were abducted—and then branded on the thigh or the breast with a red-hot iron; then they were locked up for months in tiny cells to break their spirits. When the girls were thought ready—through starvation, beating, and gross sexual exploitation—to satisfy any brothel frequenter they were sold to establishments in Mexico or elsewhere. Some girls were beaten to death; one was burned alive; some were buried or tied to a bed by means of barbed wire. At the range-house of the three sisters there was a makeshift crematorium in an oil-drum, in which the police discovered charred bones.

Chapter Five

PRUDERY, SUPERSTITION, AND LAW

458. Bowdlerizing of Bible—first attempt
All societies, primitive and advanced, have worried about
the magical power of words. From the savage community,
where the name of the chief may not be spoken aloud, to
the great industrial nation, where "four-letter words" ter-
rorize decent folk, there are endless efforts to castigate
those who have wrong sounds on their lips. The printed
word, the prerogative of civilization, has also come in for
attention: no work has been sacred. In 1833, Noah
Webster, the famous lexicographer, began the task of
bowdlerizing the Bible. "He replaced *teat* with *beast, in
the belly* with *in embryo, stink* with *smell, to give such*
with *to nurse* and *to nourish, fornication* with *lewdness,*
whore with *lewd woman* and *prostitute, to go a-whoring*
with *to go astray,* and *whoredom* with *impurities, idola-
tries,* and *carnal connection.*" He even obliterated whole
verses, "as beyond the reach of effective bowdlerization
(287)."

459. Coitus during pregnancy—first opposed
In certain circumstances there can be medical reasons for
discouraging coitus during pregnancy. Often, however,
there is nothing more than an odd moral scruple to the effect that sex is wrong at such a time. We are not sure
which category Hippocrates comes in to, but he was one
of the first medical men to oppose sexual intercourse with
a pregnant woman; he also thought that hill-walking,

washing and sitting on soft cushions were inadvisable (288).

460. Prude—most vigorous

The modern professional prudes are lazy ineffectual people compared with their great forerunner, Anthony Comstock. Peter Fryer has pointed out (289) that from its inception in 1873 to the end of 1882, Comstock's New York Society for the Suppression of Vice was responsible for 700 arrests, 333 sentences of imprisonment totalling 155 years and 13 days, fines totalling $65,256, and the seizure of 27,856 lb. of "obscene" books and 64,836 "articles for immoral use, of rubber, etc." Much of Comstock's battle was against the use of artificial contraceptive precautions. The prudes have lost that fight: today they struggle to campaign on other fronts.

461. Prude—most famous

Comstock may be the most vigorous prude but a number of modern exponents of the art of practical prudery are better known. In England there are three candidates for the title of number one prude—Mary Whitehouse, Malcolm Muggeridge and Lord Longford. All have a powerful religious sense, complete conviction that their own subjective judgments should bear on all mankind, and the undaunted eagerness to campaign vigorously in a permissive age. Mary Whitehouse expanded her interests from an early preoccupation with television; Malcolm Muggeridge, after a spell in journalism, discovered religion; and Lord Longford, determined to "hate the sin and love the sinner," managed to combine an eagerness to help prison inmates with a fervent desire to put more people, of a certain kind, inside. For my money Lord Longford just about beats Mary, who leads Malcolm by a short head. For it is only the conscientious Lord, with his immensely publicized anti-pornography crusade, who managed to make headlines in the national press. Lord Longford, a man who possesses great social conscience, two English baronies and one Irish earldom, was, under a sympathetic Tory Home Secretary, a force in the land. Optimistically, he will go the way of Comstock.

462. Prudery—most absurd instances

We could write a book on this one (people have). There
are endless instances of prudish silliness in Fryer, Find-
later, and others. One instance will suffice here—after
which you can read superlative 463. Many women have
been positively repelled by the sight of the male body. A
woman of seventy, the mother of seven children, said that
she had never seen a naked man in her life; and her sister
admitted she had never looked at her own nakedness, because it *frightened* her (290).

463. Prudish society—most ridiculous

Until quite recently America boasted a Society for Indecency to Naked Animals. As Peter Fryer nicely observes it
should have been "against" rather than "for"—"but the
founder was stricken in years when he drew up his will."
What worried the Society was the sight of naked sex organs on animals. In consequence efforts were quickly
made to design bikinis for stallions, petticoats for cows,
knickers for bulldogs, and boxer shorts for small animals
(291).

464. Prudery—most extreme modern behavior

Prudish attitudes do not always result in absurdity. Sometimes they generate a brutal and callous response. The
case of Dr. Magnus Hirschfeld, German sexologist, is particularly illuminating. In 1921 he had been attacked by
Anti-Semites in Munich and left in the street for dead. In
1933 his famous Sex Institute in Berlin was destroyed by
the Nazis. I quote from *The Brown Book of the Hitler
Terror* (Gollancz)—

"On the morning of May 6th, the *Berliner Lokalan-
zeiger* reported that the cleansing of Berlin libraries of
books of un-German spirit would be begun that morning, and that the students of the Gymnastic Academy
would make a start with the Sexual Science Institute . . .
"... an attempt was made to remove for safe-keeping
some of the most valuable private books and

manuscripts; but this proved to be impossible, as the person removing the books was arrested ... The students demanded admittance to every room, and broke in the doors of those which were closed ... they emptied the ink bottles over manuscripts and carpets and then made for the book-cases ..."

Books, manuscripts, charts, and other material was destroyed. When the students were told that Hirschfeld himself was abroad, suffering from an attack of malaria, they replied, "Then let's hope he'll die without our aid: then we shan't have to hang him or beat him to death." They later carried Dr. Hirschfeld's bust in a torch-light procession and threw it into a fire. The Nazi report devoted to this "deed of culture" carried the headlines—*Energetic Action Against a Poison Shop, German Students Fumigate the Sexual Science Institute*. The report spoke of the institute as an "unparallelled breeding-ground of dirt and filth" (*Angriff*, 6 May 1933).

465. Sex book—most abused

Perhaps the most abused "sex book" in history was *Married Love* (1918) by Marie Stopes. Based on the unyielding premise that sexual happiness was the right of every person, it offended the Church, conservative medical opinion, reviewers and professional moralists. Inevitably there were publishing problems: two major publishers rejected the book—and Walter Blackie, who had published her *Journal from Japan* (1910), asked: "Don't you think you should wait publication until after the war at least? There will be few enough girls for the men to marry; and a book would frighten off the few." She is said to have replied: "*What* an idea of marriage you must have if you think the truth about it will frighten people off."

466. Sex research (Kinsey)—most extreme reactions

When the Kinsey reports—*Male* (1948) and *Female* (1953)— were published, the reactions were, inevitably, mixed. Many specialists in various disciplines rejoiced. But the moralists, the pious, and those simply terrified of all things sexual, were hostile. One hysterical reaction will suffice here. One woman wrote, after the publication of the volume on the male, that the whole study was a waste of time as it merely confirmed her opinion "that the male population is a herd of prancing, leering goats."

467. Sex organs (female)—most number of synonyms
The invention of synonyms can serve a variety of purposes. It can, for instance, add poetic color. It can also—as a euphemistic or circumlocutory device—shield people from unwelcome aspects of life or thought. Many synonyms for matters sexual have been invented to reduce the "carnal component" in speech and thought. Fryer notes many synonyms for the sex organs and coitus. And he cites the publication, *The Slang of Venery,* as listing over one thousand popular and literary synonyms for the female pudenda as a whole (292).

468. Four-letter word—the most obscene
We all (?) know the four-letter words—*fuck, cunt, cock, arse, shit, piss,* and *fart.* Doubtless imaginative readers can think of others. It is convenient that *dick* has four letters, but such words as *tit* and *prick* do not oblige. Edward Sagarin has suggested in his *Anatomy of Dirty Words* that there is only one four-letter word in the English language—*fuck.* We know what he means. It could be argued that to many people this word has a unique status, a peculiar aura of foulness, and that where other four-letter words may be tolerated, *fuck* would still be beyond the pale. Until recently the word was banned from all dictionaries ever since the eighteenth-century. The earliest dictionary to record the word is John Florio's Italian—English dictionary, *A Worlde of Wordes* (1598).

469. Coitus (human)—most extreme hostile comments
Considering how delightful sexual intercourse can be it is quite extraordinary how many people have been eager to condemn it. The Christian Church has been particularly keen to represent sex as something repulsive; and this attitude has influenced law, education, and the status of women in society and the home. Examples will be given of the clerical attitude. For now we will content ourselves

with one secular condemnation. The German philosopher, Schopenhauer, reckoned that sex was "an act which on sober reflection one recalls with repugnance, and in a more elevated mood even with disgust." (This parallels the view of W. T. Stead who saw the act as "monstrously indecent" and who wondered how two self-respecting people could face each other after performing it (293)."

470. Coitus (human)—most significant inhibiting factors

Kinsey investigated, inevitably, the restraints on sexual intercourse for various educational levels. The factors considered were such things as moral objection, fear of public opinion, fear of pregnancy, fear of venereal disease and lack of opportunity. Of all the inhibiting factors, moral objections were the most powerful deterrent—at least for what Kinsey termed the 13+ educational level, i.e. the upper educational levels.

471. Coitus (human)—most thorough cleansing to follow

The religious suspicion of sex is not confined to Christians. The leaders of other world religions have also expressed doubts about the propriety of carnal relations. One example—from the Moslem faith—will suffice. After sexual intercourse or any discharge of semen (though nocturnal emission, masturbation, etc.) a Moslem is obliged to wash himself all over as thoroughly as he can. Until this is done he is in a state of ritual impurity and is not allowed to pray. It is extraordinary the lengths that the pious will go to in order to sanctify gross anti-sexuality.

472. Masturbation—earliest historic disapproval

We are accustomed to associating the most hysterical opposition to masturbation with the pious souls of the nineteenth century. It is sobering to realize that men and women thought masturbation quite disgusting long before that. In fact the opposition to any form of masturbation goes back at least as far as the *Book of the Dead* (1550-950 B.C.) (294). Later, e.g. in Greece and Rome, the act of masturbation was mildly condemned. In Jewish history it was sometimes punished by execution! In America it has been illegal.

473. Masturbation—first condemned in France

Of course we don't know when masturbation was first condemned in France. It happened, probably, long before the nineteenth century. Perhaps the earliest *authoritative* condemnation is that to be found in Esquirol who declared (in 1816) that masturbation "is recognized in all countries as a common cause of insanity;" by 1838 he had decided that masturbation also caused melancholia, epilepsy and suicide.

474. Masturbation—most famous hostile book in eighteenth-century

There are several candidates for this title. For instance in 1724 there appeared a book called *The Crime of Onan* or *the Heinous Vice of Self-Defilement with all its Dismal Consequences*. There were ten detailed chapters. The first gave reasons for publishing the treatise—"As this Branch of Uncleanliness, viz., Sinning with a Person's own Self, is the most general of any Sin of Impurity whatsoever, by consequence some instructions concerning it are the most of any wanted in the World, in order to awake the Guilty, and deter the Innocent and Unwary from falling into it, through Inadvertence or Ignorance." After this explanation the author dwells on the repulsiveness of the sin and describes the fate of those in Hell who succumb to it. In the same year another work, *Eronania*, on this theme appeared. More than a decade earlier, in 1710, *Onania, or the Heinous Sin of Self-Pollution* was published. All these works were influential and laid the basis for the absurd hysteria that was to follow.

475. Masturbation—first hostile book in eighteenth-century

All the books already mentioned (superlative 474) were anticipated in a work by Boerhaave (1708). He declared, with the certainty of the bigot, that "the rash expenditure of semen brings on a lassitude, a feebleness, a weakening of motion, fits, wasting, dryness, fevers, aching of the

cerebral membranes, obscuring of the sense and above all
the eyes, a decay of the spinal cord, a fatuity and other
like evils."

476. Masturbation—most famous hostile book in the nineteenth-century

Again there are several possible works that would qualify
for this title. Perhaps the most influential was J. L. Milton's *Spermatorrhea*—which had run through twelve editions by 1887. He describes special cages with spikes,
which were worn by boys at night, and even a device
whereby an filial erection was made to ring an electric bell
in the parents' room (295). In the interest of Christian piety anything was possible!

477. Masturbation—first scientifically condemned

The impact of *Onania* was greatly increased because its
cause was taken up by a respected authority, the physician
and hygienist Tissot. His aim was the promotion of the basic tenets of Roman Catholicism: he was the Pope's advi-
sor on the control of epidemics and also an author of an
important work on public health. In consequence, his
word was influential. He used the earlier title and his
*Onania; a treatise on the disorders produced by mastur-
bation* appeared in Lausanne in 1758 and spread far and
wide in translation. All sexual activity is, according to Tissot, harmful as it causes a rush of blood to the brain with
the consequent danger of insanity. But solitary orgasm is
the worst of all. Because it can be done by young people,
and in private, excess is inevitable. The masturbator is
seen as liable to melancholy, fits, blindness, catalepsy, impotence, indigestion, idiocy and paralysis.

478. Masturbation (male)—most severe cure

Many measures were tried to stop boys (and men) as
masturbators. Where pious exhortation failed sterner tactics had to be adopted. The most trivial of these were to
ensure that boys slept with their hands tied; even adults
were counselled by William Acton to adopt the "common
practice" of sleeping with the hands tied. Milton suggested
a chastity belt. S. G. Vogel had advocated infibulation, i.e.

inserting a silver wire through the foreskin, in his *Unterricht fur Eltern* (1786): such a practice was in fact adopted. Comfort has quoted a paper by Yellowlees—"I was struck by the conscience-stricken way in which they submitted to the operation on their penises. I mean to try it on a large scale, and go on wiring all masturbators ..." If a recalcitrant mental patient tore out the wire, he should simply be tied up. Milton also suggested blistering the penis with red mercury ointment; and cauterization of the spine and genitals were recommended as late as 1905. The most severe cure for masturbation of a man was surely the penile amputation inflicted on a Texan towards the end of the nineteenth century (297).

479. Masturbation (female)—most severe cure

Like men, women were also forced to undergo spinal and genital cauterization and to wear chastity belts in a vain attempt to prevent masturbation. Krafft-Ebing refers to a girl who "at the age of ten was giving up to the most revolting vices," e.g. masturbation. He adds that "Even a white-hot iron applied to the clitoris had no effect in overcoming this practice (298)." After this sort of treatment the Moodie girdle of chastity, designed for a similar purpose, seems almost mild. In 1894, a surgeon was asked at St. John's Hospital, Ohio, to bury a girl's clitoris with silver wire sutures (clitoral masturbation not having been effectively stopped by means of severe cauterization). The girl tore the sutures and resumed the habit. The entire organ was then excised! Six weeks after the operation the "patient" was reported as saying, "You know there is nothing there now, so I could do nothing (299)." Holt's *Diseases of Infancy and Childhood* (New York) continued, as late as 1936, was "not averse to circumcision in girls or cauterization of the clitoris."

480. Menstrual blood—most famous ancient description of baleful effects

There is a much quoted passage in Pliny—"It will not be easy to find anything with more miraculous effect than the menstrual blood of women. If they are in this condition and come into contact with new wine it turns sour, at their touch the fruits of the field become unfruitful, grafts and cuttings wither away, seeds in the garden are parched, and fruit falls from the tree under which a woman with her periods has sat. Should they look in a mirror its brilliance is blurred, the blade of an iron knife is blunted. Ivory loses its lustre, even bronze and iron rust and give forth an evil odor. Dogs which lap up menstrual blood go mad and their bite works as a poison for which there is no cure." Such things have been said of menstruating women throughout all recorded history. In the sixteenth-century, for instance, Agrippa Nettesheim said similar things; and in the Lebanon it was said that when a menstruating woman casts her shadow on flowers they fade, that trees rot away, and snakes creep off to die (300).

481. Menstrual contact by men—direst consequences

We have seen that menstruating women are fraught with hazard. Some consequences were alleged to be even more catastrophic. Anthropologists have laboriously catalogued the supposed consequences of menstrual contact: a first reading of Fraser or Crawley is a revelation. The following brief examples are culled from Crawley (301). An Australian, discovering that his wife had lain on his blanket during her menstrual period, killed her and died of terror within a fortnight. Among the Veddas of Travancore, the husband of a menstruating woman dared not eat anything but roots, for fear of being killed by "the devil." And according to *The Laws of Manu* if a man approach a woman covered in menstrual blood he will at once lose his wisdom, strength, vitality, etc. There is a nice rhyme that may be quoted—

Oh! menstruating woman, thou'rt a fiend
From whom all nature should be closely screened.

482. Menstruating girls—most harshly treated

Many societies have decided on cruel ritual to afford protection from menstruating women. Often the *first* menstruation was thought to be particularly hazardous; and so a number of precautions evolved as part of puberty initiation rites. The main worry was about the supposed magical power of menstrual blood. The Canadian Beaver Indians, for example, thought that to walk on the same path as a menstruating woman would cause sores to develop on the legs. Girls menstruating had therefore to be "disinfected." One measure was that adopted by the Guarani Indians of South America. The girl was sewn up in a hammock as if she were a corpse, a tiny opening allowing her to breathe. The hammock was then suspended over a smoking fire for several days; in such a fashion the girl was purified (302).

483. Vaginal infibulation—most recent case in U.K.

Vaginal infibulation—the sewing up of the vagina to ensure chastity—has been historically common but most unusual in modern industrial society. A Sudanese woman was examined in a Sheffield hospital in 1962 (303). She was then half way through pregnancy, though her vagina was extremely small, preventing normal sexual relations. An infibulation had been performed when she was eleven, in 1951, and she had become pregnant after her marriage. Sheffield surgeons restored her vagina to normal and the subsequent delivery of a boy was entirely satisfactory. The girl later declared that, although the procedure was illegal, female mutilation of this sort was still the rule in certain Moslem families.

484. Chastity belts—finest surviving examples

The best-known "girdles of chastity" still in existence are generally said to be those in the Cluny Museum in Paris. (304). One has a stout steel band, covered with velvet, and is adjustable. Beneath the front lock is a piece of convex ivory which, with an oval dentated opening, presses firmly against the vulva. This device is dated to either the sixteenth or early seventeenth century. The second specimen is a finer device, thought to be made in Germany in the early seventeenth century. It has two iron plates jointed together at their narrowest point, to one of which is attached two jointed iron bands for passing round the hips. Both the plates are engraved, damascened, and picked out in gold. One carries a design showing Adam and Eve in the Garden of Eden. Drilled holes were provided to allow velvet or silk coverings to be attached. Both belts give abundant evidence of high-quality workmanship.

485. Chastity belts—only one in the Tower of London

Chastity belts are rare; many collectors are eager to possess a genuine one. Sir James Mann, Master of the Armouries at the Tower of London, managed to purchase one shortly before his death in 1962. It cost him around £350 and appeared to date from the early seventeenth century (305). However, experts at the Tower have decided that it is a fake and sent it for sale at Christie's in March 1974. A spokesman declared that "It does not seem strong enough for its purpose."

486. Chastity belts—first described in detail

Few chastity belts date to a time anterior to the sixteenth century; and a fair number of those on exhibition are thought by experts not to be genuine. A number of well-authenticated specimens however do exist and there are representations in early MSS. One of these can be found in Konrad Kyeser von Eichstadt's military encyclopedia, the *Bellifortis* (306). The MS, dealing largely with Kyeser's military experiences and dated 1405, is now in the library of the University of Gottingen: a girdle of chastity is shown and described. It appears to have been made of iron and could be locked; in appearance the girdle in question is heavy and had little in common with the more elegant later models. Laborde declared that chastity belts were heard of as early as 1350, but he gives no evidence.

487. Chastity belt fibula—first invented

A fibula closes the female genitals by actually having a piece of metal, ivory or wood pass through the labia. A chastity belt which was really a fibula of this sort was invented by a certain Francesco de Carerra, an imperial judge in Padua in the fifteenth century. His invention was a padlock which "locked up the seat of voluptuousness." Carerra was eventually ordered—on account of various crimes—to be judicially strangled. One charge was that he locked up all his mistresses by means of his fibula. The device was also known as the Bernasco padlock, and it was sold briefly in France during the reign of Henry II. According to one tale, an itinerant Italian peddler opened a stall at the fair of San Germain and sold the locks so quickly that French gallants became alarmed. The enterprising tradesman was soon obliged to flee the town.

488. Chastity belts—earliest pictorial representation

According to Dingwall(307), one of the earliest pictorial representations is the woodcut published first in the 1572 Bale edition of Sebastian Brant's *Das Narrenschiff* (The Ship of Fools). A woodcut illustrating a poem shows to the left in the foreground a fool pouring water into a well, while to his left is a nude woman seated upon a block and partly hidden behind a curtain. Around her waist is a belt and in her left hand she holds a chain from which is suspended a stout padlock. In other editions of the work the chastity belt is not shown.

489. Chastity belts—finest early representation

Perhaps the finest early representation of a girdle of chastity is that found in one of Heinrich Aldegrever's delicate engravings; a copy is contained in the British Museum. A naked young man has his right hand on the shoulder of a young girl, also naked but for a girdle of chastity. In her right hand she holds a key which, we may deduce, the fellow is imploring her to use. The girl appears to be uncertain.

490. Chastity belts—first appearance in Europe

There has been much controversy as to when the first chastity belt appeared in Europe. There is little doubt that the idea of such a device was current at least as early as the second half of the twelfth-century. Thus in the Guigemar Epic, which exhibits strong traces of Oriental influences, Marie de France narrates an event which suggests knowledge of such devices. It has also been suggested that a passage in the *Livre du Voir-Dit* of the fourteenth century poet Guillaume de Machaut can be interpreted in this way (308).

491. Chastity belts—most recent book to advise their use

The last book published in Great Britain to advise the use of chastity belts was the one published in Edinburgh in 1848 entitled *A medical treatise: with principles and observations to preserve chastity and morality*. The book has three main parts: one section is concerned with the asserted widespread use of the dildo among Scottish ladies of the period; the second section gives a detailed account of the need for, and means of manufacturing, girdles of chastity for Scottish maidens; the third section is devoted to an ingenious piece of equipment for preventing masturbation among boys.

492 Chastity belts—most thorough listing of types

Dingwall has given a listing of seven types of chastity belts. The various belts vary according to bulk, number of component parts, material of construction, facility of adjustment, etc. Chastity belts are still being manufactured in the modern world.

493. Chastity belts—most recent application for a patent

As late as 16 March 1903, Frau Emilie Schäfer, of 26 Rigaerstrasse, Berlin, applied for a patent (Sch. 16096: Gebrauchmuster 30. d. 204538) for a "Verschliessbares Schutznetz für Frauen gegen echeliche Untreue" (Girdle with lock and key as a protection against conjugal infidelity) (309). Writing in about 1930 Dingwall noted that enquiries about the availability of chastity belts were still being made of surgical instrument makers in London— "and doubtless such sometimes supplied."

494. Brassiere advertisement—most controversial in U.S.

Today we tend to take the brassiere in our stride. Some unhappy folk are still nervous about it and their unease gives scope for simple-minded comedy in West-End theater and elsewhere. The most controversial bra ad in America was that of the early fifties—those unpermissive times— when the jaunty slogan "I Dreamed I Stopped Traffic in My Maidenform Bra" was coined. The situations varied but the girl was always dressed the same: she wore only a brassiere above the waist and wandered around with a vacant look among normally dressed people. The idea was that the undressed state was permissible as the girl was only dreaming. Psychologists debated the implications of the ad and what its impact on women would be. Moralists, as ever, fulminated.

495. Married Roman Catholic priest—first in Australia

Of the many issues attacking the authority of the Roman Catholic Church that of celibacy in priests is one of the most significant. The dissatisfaction among priests with the traditional teaching on celibacy has been shown by the greatly increased number seeking dispensation. For instance in one five-year period in the sixties the number rocketed from 167 (in 1963) to 2,263 (in 1968). A poll of Italian priests on the celibacy issue was published in the Rome weekly magazine *L'Espresso*: of 465 priests questioned, 301 believed that the Roman Catholic clergy should have a free choice on the celibacy issue. Over the last six years no less than 7000 priests throughout the world have asked to be allowed to marry. In Sydney (7/10/69) a former Anglican minister, Peter Rushton, watched by his wife and two of his three children, was ordained as Australia's first married Roman Catholic priest. The papal dispensation permits him to live with his family but requires that they live "a simple and unworldly manner."

496. Sex in confessional—first "exposé"

The Roman Catholic confessional has often intrigued those who have little or no experience of it and some of those who have an intimate acquaintance with the device. From time to time exposés have appeared of what actually takes place in the confessional; after all, in more dissolute times the confessional was used by randy priests as a means of recruiting likely women! In the nineteenth century a number of publications, mostly of poor quality, appeared claiming to reveal what went on in nunneries, monasteries and the confessional. One such was the *Awful Disclosures of Maria Monk:* the author claimed to have been a nun in the *Hotel Dieu* in Montreal. Her disclosures, first printed in New York in 1836, were reprinted again and again in the U.S. and Europe, and by 1851 more than a quarter of a million copies of the book were in circulation. A leading Catholic called the book "blasphemous fiction" and it was mentioned during debates in Parliament. In 1874 a certain Father Chiniquy published a book called *The Priest, The Woman, and the Confessional:* harrowing accounts were given of sex in the confessional. A more sensational book had appeared in London ten years earlier—*"The Confessional Unmasked: showing the Depravity of the Romish Priesthood, the Iniquity of the Confessional and the Questions Put to Females in Confession."*

497. Tranvestism—first Christian condemnation

There is no form of sexual activity that has not been roundly condemned, at one time or another, in the name of Christian piety. The damage that the Church has done to human sexual relations is inestimable. Coitus itself has been frequently denounced as inherently sinful, and only achieving a modicum of legitimacy through the need to procreate. The traditional Church has always been brutally hostile to all forms of sexual experimentation, and this intractable opposition has inspired both fervent moralizing and repressive law. As one example—and others will be given—transvestism was first condemned in the fourth century. St. Asterius, Bishop of Amasia in Cappadocia, censured the males in his diocese for dressing up as women on New Year's Day and roaming the streets "in long robes, girdles, slippers, and enormous wigs" (310). And Bishop Isidor of Seville (560-636) remarked of New Year dancers in Spain—"These miserable creatures transform themselves into monsters, womanizing their masculine faces and making female gestures, romping, stamping, clapping, both sexes together in the ring dance, a shameful thing, a host with dulled senses intoxicated by wine!"

498. Sexual temptation—most famous saintly instances

The early Christian saints, struggling to remain sexually "pure," were often *tempted* in odd ways. Thus, St. Anthony of Egypt (A.D. 251-356) was worried at night by a devil "throwing filthy thoughts in his way" and "imitating all the gestures of a woman." On one occasion "the devil, unhappy wight, one night even took upon him the shape of a woman and imitated her acts simply to beguile Anthony." His disciple, St. Hilary, was, on lying down to sleep, "encircled by naked women (311)."

499. Chastity—first urged in Buddhist law

It is of interest that Christianity is not the only world religion to urge chastity on disciples. The oldest existing scripture of Buddhism is the Pratimoksha, or collection of rules for observance by the bhikshus, which tradition ascribes to Sakyamuni. Here any infraction of chastity falls under the first of the four Parajika rules: it is classed with murder, among the most serious offenses, bring excommunication and expulsion without any hope of forgiveness. The solicitation of a woman comes within the scope of the thirteen Sanghadisesa rules, entailing penances and probation, after which the offender may be absolved by an assembly of not less than twenty bhikshus. Various punishments were stipulated for even a suspicious act and detailed regulations were laid down for social intercourse between the sexes (312).

500. Sexual activity—most thorough clerical efforts to restrict it

As well as condemning sexual "variations," the Christian Church was also keen, at various times in its history, to cut down on the amount of *licit* intercourse between man and wife. First, coitus was made illegal on Sundays, Wednesdays and Fridays—which effectively removed the equivalent of five months in the year. Then it was banned for forty days before Easter and forty days before Christmas and for three days before attending communion (and rules stipulated frequent attendance at communion). It was also made illegal from the time of conception to forty days after parturition. And it was forbidden during any penance.

501. Sexual behavior—most thorough early Church condemnation

Part of the Church's early hostility to sex was occasioned by the prevalence of phallic cults which celebrated sex in all its aspects. The early Christian Fathers must have had a close acquaintance with a variety of sex practices and beliefs. Arnobius, an African rhetorician writing at the beginning of the fourth century, gave his fellow-theologians the requisite data in no less than seven separate books "Against the Heathen," describing the *libidinous perversions* of the sex impulse. He laid particular emphasis on those activities which "through the wicked sophistry of their advocates, might appeal to Christians" (313). By 595, Gregory the Great was stating that sexual intercourse, even when conception resulted, was at least a venial sin.

502. Celibacy—first Church efforts to impose it on priests

There were a number of restrictions on priestly sex in the pre-Christian pagan world. Thus the hierophants of Demeter in Athens were obliged to remain continent; and the priestesses of the Delphic Apollo, the Achaian Hera, the Scythian Artemis, and the Thespian Herakles were all virgins. The earliest recorded attempt by the Church to invoke such restrictions was made in 305 by the Spanish Council of Elvira, which declared that all concerned in the ministry of the alter should maintain entire abstinence from their wives under pain of forfeiting their positions (314).

503. Celibacy—most famous modern encyclical

The most celebrated encyclical in modern times on celibacy is *Sacra Virginitas* (Holy Virginity) produced by Pope Pius XII in 1954. It includes a long theological argument to show the nature of virginity and its superiority over the married state. On page 6, CTS publication (315), we learn that "Holy Virginity and absolute chastity pledged to the service of God unquestionably take rank among the priceless values which the Church's Founder bequeathed to the society which He established." One whole section of *Sacra Virginitas* is headed "Superiority of

Virginity"—"holy virginity is more excellent than matrimony"—"The superiority of virginity to marriage ... is ... due to the superior purpose which it envisages"—"The superiority of virginity stands out in still bolder relief if it is considered in terms of its manifold results." A subsequent section is headed "Virginity the Angelic Virtue." And a Bishop of Milan, St. Ambrose is quoted approvingly—"You have heard, O parents—a virgin is a gift from God, her parents' oblation, chastity's priesthood. A virgin is her mother's victim, by the daily sacrifice of which God's anger is appeased."

504. Celibacy—keenest ecclesiastical advocate

This is a tricky one. There are many competitors for the title. Saints rushed off into the desert least they even *see* a woman in more densely populated parts; other divines, later canonised, ran from their wives on the wedding-night. In the view of Lea, "no doctor of the Church did more than St. Jerome to impose the rule of celibacy on its members." It is interesting that even he was obliged to admit that at the beginning there was "no absolute injunction" to that effect.

505. Love in marriage—most famous theological condemnation

St. Jerome was such an interesting—not to say extreme—character that we will give him another superlative! Theological condemnation of sexual love is so abundant in history that it is difficult to know which instance to select as *most* famous. One that I, at least, keep coming across in the literature is Jerome's pleasant little dictum that "he who loves his wife too ardently is an adulterer"—"A wise man ought to love his wife with judgment, not with passion. Let a man govern his voluptuous impulses, and not rush headlong into intercourse (316)."

506. Sex penitentials—first promulgated

The famous penitentials were first promulgated in England: these were collections of rules for the guidance of confessors in estimating penances to be imposed for an extraordinary large number of sins, mainly of a sexual nature. The bulky Anglo-Saxon penitentials were quickly copied out and used in other lands. The first comprehensive penitentials were those of the Northumbrian historian and theologian Bede (672-735). Ecgbert followed with his own detailed book of canonical writings in 729. The penances ranged widely, according to the supposed heinousness of a sin (317). (See superlatives 315 and 316).

507. Sex penitentials—most severe

As medieval punishments went the penitentials (superlative 314) were not all that harsh. In general they prescribed such things as fasts, prayers, etc. The "fasts," often meaning a bread-and-water diet, ranged from a few months to many years—though it is hard to see how any such provision could be enforced. In one set of penitentials bestiality could bring a ten years' fast, as could habitual fornication by a beneficed priest. A fornicating nun could get a seven-year fast. One of the longest fasts is the twelve years given to an adulterous bishop; and this penance was accompanied by almsgiving in bulk, tears, and prayers. Incest with a mother gets a fifteen years fast!

508. Sex penitentials—least severe

Little boys who had "unnatural coition" forced upon them (*si parvus puer a majori opprimatur in coitu*) were punished nonetheless—this time with a five days' fast. If the child did not resist then the penalty was increased to a twenty-day fast. If someone "weakens" (*imbecillitatem intulerit*) *another genitals,* or wounds them, must pay for the appropriate medical treatment and fast, as a minimum, for two or three days.

509. Sexual euphemism—most obvious biblical examples

Many of us have known for some time that the Bible is a sexy book. In fact it is even sexier than a superficial reading would indicate! Part of its inherent sexiness has been emasculated by careful translation. It is interesting to reflect on some of this. In ancient Israel, the zārāh (tight women or adventuress) was distinguished from the zōnāh (loose woman or whore) in that she engaged only in extracoital activities with strange men. Zārāh stems from the root zūr to press or squeeze, to take hold in the hand). The zārāh, being married, pursued her illicit pleasures for the simple thrill of it; and she is frequently mentioned in the Book of Proverbs; e.g. 5:3, "The lips of a strange woman drop with honey, and her mouth is smoother than oil [an allusion to *fellatio*]; 7:12 "Now in the street, now in the market, and at every corner she lies in wait [to masturbate men]; 22:14, "The mouth of a strange woman is a deep pit [she will 'swallow up' the largest penis];" and 23:27, "A whore is a deep pit [she offers her cunnus], and an adventuress is a narrow well [she offers her anus]." And Edwardes and Masters have also pointed out the words in Numbers 24:7—"water shall flow from his buckets" (*yizzel mem mi-dolyav*, semen shall pour out of his testicles).

510. Contraception—first theological condemnation

Here is another Christian example. The Christian opposition to birth control—not so long ago universal in Christendom—can boast the most prestigious historical authorities. The first clear statement of the sinfulness of artificial birth control, even among married people, is to be found in the works of St. Augustine. In a famous work, *Marriage and Concupiscence,* he categorically condemns the use of "poisons of sterility" (contraceptives), even when used by man and wife. In fact those who use an "evil deed" or an "evil prayer" to prevent conception are married in name only (318).

511. Contraception—most extreme Papal encyclical

Part of the Roman Catholic problem on contraception stems from the fact that the Church is so committed to a position. In the light of modern developments in medical science and within the Church itself one may have expected some modification in the traditional teaching on birth control. But the Church has been so dogmatic, historically and today, that useful reform is not possible. A number of encyclical have underlined the basic Roman Catholic opposition to contraception. One of the most vigorous of these is *Casti Connubii* (1930) produced by Pius XI. Brief quotes form this encyclical shows both its tone and the extreme philosophy with which the Church has saddled itself—". . . . the conjugal act is destined of its very nature for the begetting of children . . . ," so "those who in exercising it deliberately deprive it of its natural force and power act against nature and commit a deed which is shameful and intrinsically vicious . . . the Catholic Church, to whom God has entrusted the defense of the integrity and purity of morals, standing erect in the midst of the moral ruin which surrounds her, in order that she may preserve the chastity of the nuptial union from being defiled by this foul stain, . . . proclaims anew: any use whatever of matrimony in which the act . . . is deliberately deprived of its natural power to procreate life is an offense against the law of God and of nature, and those who commit such are branded with the guilt of a grave sin."

512. Phallic oath—most widespread ancient type
It was an ancient and widespread custom for anyone making a vow to place his hand on his own genitals or on those of the other person. The Biblical translators deliberately used the word "thigh" for what should have been "penis." Thus, when Abraham asked his servant to swear to him, he said (Genesis 24, 2): "Put, I pray thee, thy hand under my thigh: and I will make thee swear by the Lord, the God of Heaven, and the God of the earth." There is another instance of the phallic oath in Genesis 47, 29; and yet another in Ezekiel 17, 18. Nor is the phallic oath confined to the Judeo-Christian tradition. The ancient Egyptians had a similar practice and there is a well-known print of Osiris holding his penis to take such an oath (319).

513. Phallic worship—earliest signs in Scandinavia
There is unmistakable evidence of phallic worship, dating back to the early Stone Age, in Norwegian rock carvings. A Stone Age petroglyph from Bardal, Norway, has often been depicted. There is also prolific evidence in the Bronze Age (1600-400 B.C.) and in the later Iron Age. In all of Europe and most other parts of the world there is evidence that the mysteries and wonders of sex have been

celebrated with religious devotion from the earliest times (320).

514. Phallic worship—most celebrated evidence in Britain
This is unquestionably the Cerne giant, the two hundred feet figure carved in the Dorset hills. It is thought that the figure is around two thousand years old. The lines defining its body, head, and limbs are no less than two feet wide; each finger is seven feet long; and the club that the man wields is no less than 120 feet in length. The figure has an erect penis—a circumstance that caused a woman living in a nearby house to complain to the County Council (321). There is an ever larger—but less publicized—naked man carved in a hillside in the village of Wilmington in Sussex. This "Long Man," outlined in white bricks in 1874 and preciously cut in the turf, is 226 feet long!

515. Phallic worship—most frequent biblical type
There are various signs that phallic worship occurred at the time of the writing of the Old Testament. Most commonly there is evidence of pillar-worship. Thus Joshua worshipped a pillar Shechem; and Solomon paid homage to a stone at Gibeon (1 Kings, 3,4). Scott has suggested that there was stone or pillar worship "everywhere throughout Palestine" until Hezekiah began his campaign of destruction. In the twenty-eighth chapter of Genesis the story is given of worship of a pillar by Jacob. This is significant in connection with the phallic worship of the age (322).

516. Phallic worship—most ingenious device
Phallic worship, common in all lands at one time or another, sometimes presented practical problems. For example the statue of Saint Guingnole or Guingalais near the town of Brest received so much attention from pious women that there was a serious danger that its penis would in due course be worn away altogether; the women, in accordance with the custom of the time, scraped the phallic member in the hope that this would make them fertile. The priests hit upon the idea of fitting the Saint with a

penis in the form of a rod through the statue. A blow with a mallet at the rear propelled the rod forward, with the result that, despite continual scraping, the sacred organ never seemed to diminish. The end of the rod was described as "strikingly characteristic."

517. Phallic worship—most thorough eighteenth-century work

Richard Payne Knight wrote *A Discourse on the Worship of Priapus* in 1786, a work which has influenced all other writers in this field. Knight caused the book to be published despite the fact he knew he would be comdemned personally for what it contained. Unfortunately the uproar was greater than even he envisaged, so, to quote from the preface of a later edition, "Rather than endure the storm of criticism aroused by the publication, he suppressed during his life-time all copies of the book he could recall, consequently it became very scarce and has continued so." The book, now rare and expensive, is in general only to be found in the special collections of libraries and museums. It finally became generally available in 1957 when Julian Press published an edition in conjunction with a later work, *The Worship of the Generative Powers During the Middle Ages in Western Europe by* Thomas Wright.

518. Sex cults—most famous in India

The most famous Indian sex cult is Tantra. This is not to say it is the most influential in Indian culture but more that it has recently been well publicized in the West. For instance Philip Rawson wrote an article, The Art of Tantra, in the ill-fated magazine *Scorpio;* and a large paperback book followed. Tantra is more than a sex cult, embodying as it does a complex philosophy of man and his place in creation. In particular, Tantra teaches the use of ecstasy—sexual as well as the rapture derived from other sources—to enrich human existence and generate insights into the nature of reality.

519. Sex deity (female)—most important in Rome

In the Roman pantheon there were many gods, often belonging to competing cults and having overlapping functions. The pre-eminent goddess of love was of course Venus, the deity who acquired great fame after Vergil had in the *Aeneid* shaped many old legends into a national epic. In some contexts Venus is the patron of gardens and flowers; only later did she become the goddess of race and beauty. Eventually she merged with the Greek importation Aphrodite, becoming in effect the Aphrodite of Rome. Venus had many functions. She was, for instance, both the guardian of honorable marriage and the patroness of prostitutes (*meretrices*). Sulla honored her as his patroness as did Pompey; Caesar consecrated a sanctuary to her and claimed that "The Julian clan, to which my house belongs, is sprung from Venus (323)."

520. Sex deities (male)—most important in Rome

No male deity dominates the sex scene in ancient Rome as does Venus (superlative 324). Mutunus Tutunus is perhaps the best known "sexual" deity; there have been efforts, for instance, to connect him with the later arrival, Priapus. Janus was sometimes thought to attend in matters sexual "in order to open the way for the conception of the seed, when the fruit of the body is conceived." And Saturn was given the role of protecting the seed of the husband. Liber, identified with the Greek god Dionysus, was also assigned a variety of sexual responsibilities (324).

521. Religion—most sexually inhibiting

There is dispute, inevitably, about the effect of religious belief on sexual behavior and sexual responsiveness. Kinsey found "little evidence" that the frequency of marital coitus among the females in the sample had depended upon their religious background. Similar the evidence indicated that the proportion of the copulations that led to orgasm in marriage did not seem to have differed significantly between most of the religiously devout, moderate, and inactive groups of women. One finding may be viewed as significant—"Only the more devout Catholic groups seem to have been more restrained in their first year of marriage, with a distinctly higher percentage completely failing to reach orgasm, and a distinctly lower percentage reaching orgasm in most of their coitus." Fisher found

that "the greater a woman's religiosity the less the satisfaction she derives from masturbation."

522. Sexual genetics—most ancient superstition
The story of Jacob in the Old Testament has been high-
lighted as containing an ancient superstition about genetics. According to Genesis 30, Jacob had bargained with
his father-in-law that he should have all the speckled and
spotted sheep and goats for his hire; since Laban tried to
cheat him of his wages he resorted to a genetic trick—

> Jacob took him rods of green poplar; and of the hazel
> and chestnut; and pilled white strakes in them, and
> made the white appear which was in the rods. And he
> set the rods which he had pilled before the flocks in the
> gutters in the watering troughs when the flocks came to
> drink, that they should conceive when they came to
> drink. And the flocks conceived before the rods, and
> brought forth cattle ringstraked, speckled and spotted.

In the words of Wendt—"The present-day geneticist, acquainted with Mendel's laws and Morgan's researches on
mutation, can only shake his head at this."

523. Sex as aid to immortality—first proposed in China
As early as the Eastern Han Dynasty (A.D. 25-220), a
school of Taoists created the Yin Taoism which proposed
a theoretical basis for immortality through sex. The theory
and practice were seized upon by the emperors as the key
to longevity, if not immortality. One of the Taoist manuals
asserted that the Yellow Emperor became immortal after
having had sexual relations with 1200 women and that
Peng Tsu, through the "correct way of making love to ten
to twenty girls every single night," was able to live to a
good old age. Peng Tsu thought it a fine idea to have intercourse with virgins—"He ought to make love to virgins
and this will restore his youthful looks. What a pity there
are not many virgins available ... My late master observed
these principles strictly. He lived to 3000 years of age ...
one cannot achieve one's aim by using one female. One

will have to make love to three, nine, or eleven women each night, the more the better (325)."

524. Castration—most famous Greek myth

In Greek mythology the sovereign Uranus, the god of heaven, imprisoned his sons as soon as they were born so that they could not seize his power. The strongest and youngest son, Cronos, under the influence of Gaea, his mother, castrated his father and threw his genitals into the sea. Aphrodite sprang from the sea foam that gathered around the severed member of Uranus. Cronos later married his sister Rhea—and, fearing his own sons, swallowed them as soon as they were born. After Zeus was born Cronos was tricked into swallowing a stone instead. Zeus caused his father to disgorge a series of gods; then he castrated him, and shared his power with his now-disgorged brothers and sisters.

525. Castration—most famous Buddhist myth

In the Pali culture there are many tales about Buddha's early life. One of these relates how Brahmadetta, fearing dethronement, castrated his sons by biting off their testicles. One son, Buddisata, was hidden by his mother and went on to defeat his father with skill and cunning. This tale has obvious parallels with the Greek myth (superlative 327). (326).

526. Contraceptive superstitions—earliest

Pliny the Elder (A.D. 23-79) reckoned that if you took two small worms out of the body of a certain species of spider and attached them in a piece of deer's skin to a woman's body before sunrise, she would not conceive. Other ancient and dark-age writers believed that if a woman spat three times into a frog's mouth she would not conceive for a year; and that a jaspar pebble clasped in the hand during coitus would also stop conception. St. Albert the Great (1193-1280), who taught Aquinas, advised women to eat bees as an effective contraception procedure. Aëtios of Amida (fl. 527-565) suggested that a man should wash his penis in vinegar or brine; and that a woman should wear a cat's testicle in a tube across her naval. The oldest contraceptive beliefs hinged acceptance of the efficacy of magical practices (327).

527. Sexual superstitions—most prevalent in Rome
The superstitions of ancient Rome were broadly representative of antiquity as a whole. The Roman sages were influenced—as were the thinkers of Greece, China, India, etc.—by the accumulated tradition that sprang from the most primitive communities. Inevitably factors such as sympathetic magic, witchcraft, and the like were spread, in the absence of a sceptical scientific world-view, from one ancient land to another. It suffices to mention one prevalent Roman superstition: that the sex of a child was determined by the testicle which supplied the sperm in question. (See also superlative 331.)

528. Sexual superstitions—most prevalent in Greece
The Romans derived much of their art and much of their superstition from Greece. In Pliny the Elder there is abundant cataloguing of superstitions common in Greece, many of which were absorbed by the Romans. In Pliny it is suggested that the sap of the flea-wort is effective in securing the birth of boys; and Glaucias ascribed the same effect to the thistle. A pregnant woman could guarantee to have a boy-child if she ate the testicles, womb, or rennet of a hare; and to eat the foetus of a hare removed barrenness permanently. One prevalent superstition was that the hyaena changed its sex every year, though Aristotle had his doubts about that one (328).

529. Sexual superstitions—most prevalent in Arabic thought
A variety of Arabic superstitions are recorded in *The Perfumed Garden* (329). For example, you are not supposed to leave your member in the vulva after ejaculation, as this may cause gravel, or softening of the vertebral column, or the rupture of blood vessels, or inflammation of the lungs. Coitus with old women acts like a fatal poison—"Do not rummage old women, were they as rich as Karoun"—"The coitus of old women is a venomous

meal"—"Do not serve an old woman, even if she offered to feed you with semolina and almond bread." Too much coitus was supposed to injure the health.

530. Sexual superstitions—most prevalent among Trobrianders

The work of Malinowski immortalized the Trobrianders. One view was that the male and female discharges (vaginal fluid and semen) to an action of the bowels. There was total ignorance of the physiological function of the testes. Women were seen to have no testes, yet they produced *momona,* the sexual secretion. The only function of the testes was to make the penis look proper (330). In the most important Trobriander myth a woman, called Mitigis or Bolutukwa, mother of the legendary hero Tudava, lives alone in a grotto on the seashore. One day she is asleep under a dripping stalactyte. The drops of water pierce her vagina and deprive her of her virginity. In other origin myths the means of piercing the hymen are not mentioned, but it is often stated that the ancestress had no male consort and so could not have had sexual intercourse (Malinowski, pp. 155-6).

531. Sexual superstitions—most prevalent among Marquesans

It is widely believed among the Marquesans that the best part of the menstrual cycle for achieving conception was the period immediately following the menstrual flow, while the period for avoiding conception was thought to be the days midway between two menstruations. Thus the Marquesans had a clear concept of a "safe period": they just got it all the wrong way round (331). It was thought that the male would become impotent if he copulated with a menstruating woman.

532. Sexual superstitions—most prevalent in science

Science is not supposed to be superstitious but it often is. I have already collected a number of scientific superstitions together (332). Hippocrates suggested that the right testicle should be tied if boys were wanted. Aristotle said that a dominating woman will necessarily produce girls. Dawson, a fellow of the Royal Society of Medicine, reckoned that the right ovary produced boys and the left ovary produced girls (333). The scientific superstitions, so contrary to the spirit of true science, have been frequent throughout history!

533. Uterine superstition—longest lived

One superstition deserves particular mention on account of its remarkable persistence from the earliest times. It was thought in antiquity that the womb could wander around the body. The Greeks even regarded it as a separate animal. Thus Plato, in the *Timaeus*, remarked that—"That part of the woman which is called the womb, being an animal desirous of generation, if it become unfruitful for a long time turns indignant, and wandering all over the body stops the passages of the spirits and the respiration and occasions the most extreme anxiety and all sorts of diseases." If the womb wandered it could sometimes be coaxed back into position by fumigating the vagina with sweet and pleasant substances. The notion of the wandering uterus was accepted for many centuries—"Even 300 years ago some textbooks of medicine recommended types of treatment which were based directly on the idea (334)."

534. Sexual superstitions—most prevalent in Britain today

Superstition persists. In Britain there are still many odd beliefs that had currency hundreds of year ago. Some of the popular newspaper and magazine advice columns are deluged with questions and worries revealing a superstitious orientation on sexual matters. According to Marjorie Proops, for instance (335), the commonest myths cropping up in correspondence from readers are—

A man with a small penis is always sexually inadequate.
Masturbation will cause hair to grow on palms of hands, make men impotent, women frigid or sterile, cause madness, etc.
Women who never reach a climax are always frustrated.
Women with small breasts are poor risks in bed.
Women with large breasts are always sexy.
Men, according to many wives, are perverted if they take girlie magazines, talk about erotic things during love-making, like oral sex, etc.

535. Sperm mobility—most famous eighteenth-century superstition

During the eighteenth century a clergyman produced one of the best-sellers of the age, which postulated an aerial origin for spermatozoa; and a contemporary remarked that "the whole extent of the air . . . is full of the seeds of everything that can live on earth." A tale was also told by Averroes of a woman who "conceived in a bath, by attracting the sperm or seminal affluxion of a man admitted to bath in some vicinity unto her." Many men thought that a woman could conceive if a man ejaculated some distance away from her: sperm were tricky little fellows who needed watching! It was said that one woman was made pregnant when caressed by a female friend who had just had sexual relations with her husband.

536. Penis—coldest

Viewed in a scientific spirit this question may be treated in terms of cold-blooded animals who also possess a penis. Viewed in a different spirit, and with a clear interest in human experience, we find that demons and devils are the coldest creatures to copulate with human females. Rossell Hope Robbins has commented that testimony on this subject "is almost unanimous as to the coldness of the devil" (336). Boquet has quoted Jacquema Paget, a witch of Franche—Comté who "had several times taken in her hand the member of the devil which slept with her, and that it was as cold as ice . . ." Similarly, Sylvine de la Plaine, condemned to be burned by the Parliament of Paris in 1616 admitted that "the devil had known her once before, and his member was like that of a horse, and on insertion it was as cold as ice and ejected ice-cold semen." Mother Bush of Barton in 1649 said that the devil who visited her was "colder than man." And in 1662 Isobel Gowdie found the "nature" of the devil "as cold within [her] as spring well water." Such examples could be extended.

537. Coitus with devil—first woman to be burned for it

At Toulouse in 1275 it was alleged that a certain Angela de Labarthe gave birth to a monster with a wolf's head and a snake's tail. This woman was the first to be burned for intercourse with the devil. Many tales have been told of monsters born to human females, following sexual intercourse with Satan or his devils. Apart from anything else such accounts were a convenient explanation, to ignorant and superstitious folk, of the congenitally deformed child (337).

538. Celibacy—saddest consequences

It is always sad when a human being cannot find a mate. There is such a need for love in people that its denial—deliberately or without intention—may be expected often to generate a distortion in the personality. People forced, possibly through no design of their own, into celibacy have been known to create phantom lovers. In two reported cases (338), two paranoid single women actually believed that their lovers gave them coded messages and would send for them one day! Such a situation may well have been the case with the frequent reports of incubi and succubi in medieval times (338).

539. Semen—most popular ways acquired by demons

Medieval demons, and the supernatural creatures of other times, were not supposed to have bodily substance. This presented a problem when such demons felt the urge to copulate with women (or men), which is why the lustful denizens of the supernatural realms often assumed human form to facilitate their sexual exploits. Another problem was how to get hold of some handy semen with which to inseminate the lucky human females. Various tactics could be adopted. Martin of Arles suggested that the incubi squeezed out semen from corpses; whereas Guazzo asserted that they stole nocturnal emissions of men and "by speed and experience of physical laws perserved that semen in its fertilizing warmth." Sometimes, it was also alleged, a demon (in the form of a woman) would copulate with a man to acquire his semen: then the demon (who

really wanted only to copulate with women) would assume
a male form and make use of the newly acquired seminal
fluid (339)!

540 Brothel—least likely

There have been some pretty unlikely brothels in history—ones offering babies, young boys, geese and donkeys
have all been known at one time or another. Perhaps the
most unlikely, however, is the bordello allegedly staffed by
succubi (or female demons). For running such a brothel a
man was condemned to death at Bologna in 1468.

541. Phallic relic—most famous in France

At one time there were at least a dozen foreskins of Jesus
Christ circulating in Europe, and all claiming to be the
real thing! The most famous was in the Abbey Church of
Coulombs, a little town between Maintenon and Dreux, in
the diocese of Chartres. The "Holy Prepuce" of Coulombs
was believed to make sterile women fertile and to mitigate
the pains of the resulting childbirth—a real package deal!
Today there is no trace of this much vaunted relic, and the
Abbey itself is in ruins. It is remarkable how, even today,
the Roman Catholic Church is still ambivalent on the
question of the magical power of human or saintly relics.

542. Sexual purity (animal)—most celebrated species

Animals have been assigned, rightly or wrongly, a variety
of sexual and other predispositions. Snakes were thought
to be singularly lecherous, as were baboons and other
apes. Various creatures have been granted a singular
moral rectitude—for no obvious reason. The elephant
ranked high among the "good" animals. Thus Pliny credited the pachyderm with every possible virtue: sense of
honor, righteousness, conscientiousness, and above all a distinct sense of shame: "Out of shame elephants copulate
only in hidden places . . . Afterwards they bathe in a river.
Nor is there any adultery among them, nor cruel battles
for the females." Medieval writers embellished the legend
with further details. Albertus Magnus declared that the elephant had no sexual instinct, but conceived and bore in

all innocence. In the fourteenth-century one of the first popular zoologists, Konrad von Megenberg, compared the frivolous morals of those animals which "live for their lust without divine worship" with the sobriety of the elephants who copulate only to generate offspring and who after achieving this purpose "do not touch the female for a space of three years."

543. Sexist conventions—most vicious

We are accustomed to a degree of patriarchalism in modern society. Some men, to their shame, laugh at the attempts of women to gain equality in law, opportunity, employment, marriage, etc.—and gloat over tales, e.g. of bra-burning, which probably have no relation to truth but which save the "male chauvinists" the trouble of uncomfortable thinking. Though the developed nations manage to exploit women quite effectively in many ways (and men also in a few ways) their injustices hardly rank with those known in various other communities in history and today. The Koreh of Arabia buried alive all girls at the age of seven, only keeping a few for reproductive purposes(340). In Arab lands also the adultress, but not the adulterer, had a broad metal spike driven through the forearm. In India widows, no longer of value, were immolated on their dead husband's funeral pyre. In Egypt women, but not men, were—like animals—sacrificed to the gods. In Formosa it was a convention to trample a certain number of women to death when they became pregnant. And a Greek playwright asked Zeus why he did not create a better means of reproducing the race without the agency of females.

544. Sexist publication (anti-female)—most extreme historical example

Pamphlets, articles, and books attacking women have been a commonplace of history. Some of the polemical tracts are almost incredible. The Roman Catholic inquisitors discussed why it was that women were particularly addicted to evil superstition. And Knox, that Christian gentleman, wrote his fulmination, *First Blast of the Trumpet Against the Monstrous Regiment of Women*. For my money the most extreme anti-feminist publication is surely *Women*

Are Not Human Beings, produced in Leipzig in 1595. The very question as to whether women were human beings was learnedly discussed by (male) theologians at a celebrated Synod of Macon in the sixth century. St. Thomas declared, as we all know, that woman was only an "occasional" and incomplete being—"Man is above woman, as Christ is above man." And that, it would seem, is that (341)!

545. Sexiest publication (anti-male)—most extreme modern example

This is without doubt the S.C.U.M. (Society for Cutting Up Men) Manifesto. Written by Valerie Solanas this is a "violent, excessive, obnoxious and totally fascinating little book"—to quote from the words on the back of the Olympia publication (342). One quote is sufficient to illustrate the tone of this unusual tract— ". . . the male is an incomplete female, a walking abortion, aborted at the gene stage. To be male is to be deficient, emotionally limited; maleness is a deficiency disease and males are emotional cripples (pp. 3-4)."

546. Sexist publication (pro-female)—most extreme historical example

It is arguable (see superlative 346) that women have a variety of innate superiorities to men, that they are biologically prior to the male of the species, that they are more independent physically and emotionally, and that all culture is derived from women. Such views, in various combinations, have been espoused at regular times through history. In 1613 a book entitled *The Excellence of Women* appeared, indicating—perhaps above all—how the pendulum had swung from the earlier medieval patriarchalism (343).

547. Sexist publication (pro-female)—most extreme modern example

Many readers may nominate Greer or Millett, Figes or Mitchell, for this one. I do not. In all the books of the above writers—*The Female Eunuch, Sexual Politics, Patriarchal Attitudes,* and *Woman's Estate*—there are "limited ambitions," efforts to *set the record straight* by simply denouncing male injustice and pointing to female capacities and potentialities. In one book, however—*The First Sex* by Elizabeth Gould Davis (344) there is no stopping, no limit beyond which the feminist should not venture. In Miss Gould (should it be Ms. Gould?) women are *first* is virtually everything. We owe culture and civilization to them, they were biologically prior to the male, etc., etc. It is an extreme thesis and I have my own objections to it. But it is well argued and there is nice documentation (the notes, some of the spurious, run on for around thirty pages in the Dent edition).

548. Sexual harmony—first acknowledged in China

What does this one mean? It means that sexual harmony has often been seen as necessary to the ordered running of a society. Where there are sexual tensions, for whatever reason, there will be social conflict; where sexual needs are met this will have beneficial ramifications in other areas of communal living. All this seems obvious but it was not always so. It was around 3000 B.C. that the Emperor Fu-hsi began to realize the importance of sexual harmony for his subjects. Though a confirmed bachelor, he is said to have introduced the marriage system into ancient China.

549. Marriage age—youngest permissible in twentieth-century England

When moralists rail against sexual intercourse in young people they often pay no account to cross-cultural studies of young spouses, nor to recent history in Britain. The idea that it is wrong for young teenagers to have sexual relations is comparatively new. It is often forgotten, for example, that before the coming into force of the 1929 Marriage Act in England, a girl could marry at twelve and a boy at fourteen—"even below those ages a marriage was not absolutely void but only voidable on such attainment . . . ; even the Catholic Church recognized the legality of a marriage down to the age of seven provided it could be consummated."

550. Marriage ceremony—oldest in Rome

The oldest and most ceremonious form of marriage, the equivalent of the modern Church wedding, is called *confarreatio* (345). The name is derived from a sort of meal-cake, *farreum libum,* used in the ceremony. Dionysius has spoken of *confarreatio*—"The Romans of ancient times used to call a wedding which was confirmed by ceremonies sacred and profane a *confarreatio,* summing its nature up in one word, derived from the common use of *far* or spelt, which we call *zea* . . . Just as we in Greece consider barley to be the oldest grain, and use it to begin sacrifices under the name *oulai,* so that Romans believe that spelt is the most valuable and ancient of all grain, and use it at the beginning of all burnt offerings . . ."

551. Marriage—oddest forms

Marriages between young children and old men were not unknown at various times in history, not—more recently— are marriages between people of the same sex. More strange than any of these is surely marriage between a human being and an animal (which history has recorded) or between a human being and a tree! Tree marriages were prevalent in various parts of India. Among the Brahmans of southern India it was the custom that a younger brother should not marry before an older one. To satisfy the requirement, when there is no bride in sight for a senior brother, he is ceremoniously married to a tree (or to the spirit inside the tree) to allow the younger brother to take a wife. In some instances tree marriages occur at the same time as the marriage of the couple, the idea being that evil influence which may attach to the married pair be diverted to the tree (346).

552. Polygamist—first in China

Throughout history there must have been plenty of polygamists who did not make a fuss about it. For this reason we often do not know of them. We do at least know of Huang Ti in China. He violated Fu-hsi's idea of the Yin-Yang harmony by taking many wives and concubines and so became the forerunner of the Chinese polygamists (347). Huang Ti, the Yellow Emperor (2968 B.C.), had a reputation for many sexual exploits. His polygamy was the first on record in China, but we can hardly doubt that there were practicing polygamists before him.

553. Bride—youngest

Child brides have been commonplace throughout history. Megasthenes pointed out that in his time (306-298 B.C.) early marriages prevailed in India in the case of girls, who were sometimes married when they were seven years of age (348). A census in the early nineteen-sixties showed that there were sixty million girls in India under the age of fifteen and of these eight and a half million were married. Among infants five years of age and under, fifteen in a thousand were married or widowed. There were nearly four hundred thousand girl widows under fifteen years of age, who under the existing codes of the day were not allowed to remarry. The most famous child bride of Mohammed is said to have experienced sexual intercourse with the Prophet when she was only six years old. And there is a saying attributed to a certain Rabbi Joseph—"Come and hear! A maiden aged three years and a day may be acquired in marriage by coition." And it has been pointed out that in many parts of North Africa, Arabia, and India, girls are still wedded between the ages of five and nine; and no self-respecting female remains unmarried beyond the time of puberty. The record for young brides has been achieved by men and women seeking to guard against an estate reverting to the crown under feudal law: in such cases it was not unknown for the Church to perform the marriage ceremony over a babe in arms (349)!

554. Puberty rites (male)—most severe

Many primitive peoples have felt it necessary to initiate both males and females into adult life. Sometimes simple seclusion in a hut apart from the village has been sufficient; on other occasions various forms of mutilation have taken place. Degrees of circumcision, even to the point of splitting the urethra, have been known; and in one society at least (Ponapeans) hemi-castration (the removal of one testis) has been part of the initation ceremony for boys

(350). In a few societies a ritual of sodomy has been part of the initiation ceremony for boys.

555. Puberty rites (female)—most severe

In some societies girls are deflowered at puberty with a special tool made of horn, after which they are forced to live apart from the village for a period. Attempts to enlarge the labia, ear piercing, tattooing, and sacrification have all been associated, in one part of the world or another, with puberty initiation. In some societies it was the custom, when a girl reached puberty, to put black ants into her vagina—to make the labia and clitoris swell (351).

556. Brideprice (Africa)—as most expensive outlay

It is still the case, in various parts of the world that brides have to be purchased. Among the Sebei, for instance, the task of acquiring a bride "costs a man a substantial fee in cattle, cash, clothing, pots, tobacco, milk, beer, and other commodities (352)." In fact it has been pointed out that of all expenditure "brideprice is the largest single outlay of goods that an ordinary Sebei makes in his lifetime." Some indication is given of the cost by stressing that the expenditure on acquiring a bride is equivalent, in terms of proportion of income, to what the average American spends on buying a house, ordinarly his greatest single capital outlay. Brideprice has not been limited to Africa.

557. Brideprice (England)—most recent cases

Marriage by purchase continued in England up to the time of the nineteenth-century. In a much-quoted article in *All the Year Round* (20/12/1884), more than twenty cases are cited: the names of the women and many other details are cited. In some instances women were actually led to market with a rope around their necks! And prices for women ranged from 5 and 20 guineas plus half a pint of beer (!), to a penny and a dinner (353). Archenholtz commented, writing of eighteenth-century England, "Never was the sale of women so frequent as now."

558. Sex laws—earliest

There are a number of ancient codes of law, of which the most frequently instanced is the Babylonian Code of Hammurabi. It has been stressed that the ruler Hammurabi was bringing up to date a corpus of common law which had long before his time been codified by Libit-Ishtar of Isin, by Ibi-Sin and by Ur-Nammu of Ur; and by earlier rulers of Sumer, as well as by Hammurabi's own ancestor, Samu-la-ilum of Babylon. As one example, Ur-Nammu, a king of the third dynasty of Ur, dates to something in excess of two thousand years before Christ. There are provisions in the Libit-Ishtar law code for the penalization of extra-marital coitus. Middle Assyrian laws include the following—"If he has kissed her—the wife of another—they shall draw his lower lip along the edge of a blade and cut it off (354)." In the Code of Hammurabi a man might divorce his wife at will but must restore her dowry and provide maintenance. Both parties to adultery were liable to drowning; incest was punished by death or exile; seduction was punished by fines; sodomy is not mentioned. The later Hittite Code, centuries after Hammurabi but deriving from his code, is generally said to show a marked ethical advance. For instance private revenge, not uncommon in old Babylonian law, is only allowed in one case—where a husband catches his wife in adultery: if the wronged husband thereupon kills both his wife and her lover he is guiltless in the eyes of the law; but if he does not act at once the moment of just vengeance is passed and he must then have recourse to lawful procedures (355).

559. Sex laws—earliest in Christendom

The early Christian emperors were not remarkable for their lenience in the face of sexual "crime". For instance; pimps, panders, and procurers had molten lead poured down their throats (356). In the case of forcible seduction both the man and the woman, if she consented, were put to death (357). In the reign of Valentinian I (fourth century), sodomites were burnt alive. And in 390 Theodosius I proclaimed—"All persons who have the shameful custom of condemning a man's body, acting the part of a woman's, to the sufferance of an alien sex, for they appear not to be different from women, shall expiate a crime of this kind in avenging flames in the sight of the people (358)." The doctrine of Christian forgiveness was quite alien to the early Christian legislators.

560. Sex laws—most vicious

This was a tricky one—not because it is hard to find vicious sex laws in history and today, but because there are so many! One could fill a book with the most horrible and cruel practices visited upon ordinary men and women in the name of Christian piety and sexual purity. Vicious penalties are of several kinds: a person may be imprisoned for life, mutilated, or executed. Of all sexual "crimes", there is hardly a one which, at one time or another, has not been a capital offense. One or two examples will suffice. Among the Babylonians and the Zulus (to name only a couple), incest brought the death sentence, as did homosexual behavior in medieval Europe, and rape in modern America. In old Judaic law, masturbation was punished by death (359). In Rome the seducer of a Vestal Virgin was scourged to death (360). According to a law of Jovian in 364, any effort to marry a nun was a capital crime (361). The list could easily be extended. Sometimes the punishments, as least in theory, did not lead to death. For example, rapists have been legally castrated; adulterers have had their noses, lips, and ears cut off; and concubines in the arms of a court eunuch in ancient China risked, upon detection, being sentenced to having their arms and legs torn from their sockets, their eyes being gouged out, and liquid lead being poured into the open wounds as well as into the vagina and anus (362). Throughout history people followed their sexual inclinations at their peril!!

561. Sex offender—youngest

An Inquiry initiated in 1950 and carried out in 14 districts of England and Wales covered 2000 cases of conviction for sexual offenses, about a quarter of these crimes known to the police. It was found that the youngest sex offender was nine years of age; the oldest was ninety. Most of the sex offenders were between the ages of 21 and 50 (363).

562. Sex criminal—most classic example of sexual psychopath

The case of Neville George Clevely Heath—tried at the Central Criminal Court, London, on 24 September 1946, on the charge of murder—has been represented as "the classic example of the sexual psychopath, almost a human blueprint of the type (364)." One of Heath's victims was found with her ankles tied together, her wrists having at some time also been tied. Seventeen lash blows from a riding switch were counted on the body. And the breasts had been bitten until the nipples were almost severed. A second woman was found with similar breast injuries; and in this case the genitals had been wounded with a sharp instrument (in the earlier case, while the woman was still alive, an instrument had been rotated in her vagina, badly tearing the tissue). One of the ribs of the second woman had been broken. Heath was hanged at Pentonville Prison, London.

563. Sex criminal—most famous in modern Britain

The most famous sexual offender in modern Britain is almost certainly Ian Brady and/or Myra Hindley. When they met, in the early nineteen-fifties, Brady told Myra Hindley of his interest in the Marquis de Sade and sexual perversion. Hindley became more and more emotionally involved. A short time after she became a willing partner in the murder of a twelve-year-old boy and a ten-year-old girl, both of whose bodies were discovered on the moors above Saddleworth. Photographs were discovered of the girl and Brady in obscene poses; the girl had been tortured and a tape-recording had been made of her screams. There is some suspicion that other children missing in the area may have been killed by Brady and Hindley. A third known victim was a youth of seventeen, killed with an axe. Some people have pointed to Brady's liking for pornography as a reason why such material should be banned; others, perhaps more persuasively, have noted that Brady had a reputation for sadism as a child, long before he gained access to erotic literature. Myra Hindley has stayed in the news, partly because she was later befriended by Lord Longford, partly through an abortive prison escape attempt in March 1974.

564. Sex criminal—most famous in nineteenth-century Britain
Jack the Ripper committed the famous Whitechapel murders in London in 1888, before he disappeared without trace. The Ripper claimed six* victims, all of them female prostitutes (365). What is particularly remarkable about the Whitechapel murders was how skillfully the victims were dismembered after being killed. Thus a number of the women had precise cuts in their bodies, organs removed, etc. This circumstance led to speculation that the Ripper had at least superficial medical knowledge; and one of the crimes suggested that dental forceps had been employed. Hardly surprisingly, London prostitutes organized themselves into a "Defense committee against Jack the Ripper" and some of them, friends of murdered colleagues, attended identification parades. Jack the Ripper wrote letters to Scotland Yard. One of the letters is at Madame Tussand's—"I like my work and I mean to go on with it. You will hear of me and my little games again. I have kept a little of that lovely red liquid in a glass of beer and I wanted to use it to write with but it's become thick like glue and I can't use it. But even red ink can serve the purpose. Ha! Ha! Ha! Next time I'll cut the ears off the lady and send them to the police. Keep my letter until my next success and then publish it maybe. With luck, I'll begin again soon. Good luck!"

565. Sex crime—most vulnerable social group in the U.S.
For sex offenses against minors in the U.S. it is estimated that between 20 to 25 per cent of middle-class children will become victims as compared to one-third to two-thirds in the lower classes. This means that every year in America about a half a million children are sexually victimized (367). It has also been suggested that many instances of sex offenses against children are never reported. In one survey, for example, it was suggested that there were two

*There is dispute about the number, some writers suggesting there were as many as nine victims (366).

million families in the U.S. who concealed the fact that one of their daughters was a victim of incest (368).

566. Sex criminal—most religious

Religious commitment is no guarantee against sexual criminality; indeed in some cases deep religious devotion seems to promote sexual excess! In 1949 John George Haigh admitted that he had murdered nine people, three of them total strangers. In each case he drank a glassful of the victim's blood. He was brought up in a fanatically religious atmosphere—and the belief in salvation through drinking the blood of the sacrificial lamb of God was deeply etched on his mind. He was haunted by a recurrent dream of a bleeding Christ on the cross; and in his mind, crucifixes turned into trees which dripped with blood. It has been suggested that Haigh's upbringing—within the terms of a frightening religious doctrine—was largely responsible for his later perverse behavior. "Again and again we find that the sadist suffered from a warped upbringing (369)."

567. Sex criminal—most vicious

We have already seen a few candidates for this title (see superlatives 359, 360, 361). There is, perhaps, one man in history who outdid them all! Gilles de Rais was a notorious French sadist of the fifteenth century. In one estimate he murdered "at least two hundred children (370)." In another, the figure was set at "eight hundred little boys (371)." Before he killed them he would first use them sexually in various ways and, before they died, he would mutilate them with a sharp knife. He read of the lives of the Roman emperors and then dedicated himself to "pederasty, voluptuous infanticide, necrophilia, devil-worship, sacrilege, and mysticism." Gilles de Rais was a Marshal of France and a famous scholar. In 1440 he was tried before a tribunal of the Bishop of Nantes and sentenced to be hanged.

568. Sex criminals—tallest

It was found (372), in the Kinsey Institute survey of sex criminals, that the range of median height was from 5 ft.

8 in. to 5 ft. 10 in. "Curiously enough the one group in which tallness would be an advantage in the *modus operandi* of the offense is the tallest of our groups: the average peeper stood 5 ft. 10 in."

569. Sex crime—most under-reported

A significant proportion of sex crimes are not reported. This is true of crime as a whole but particularly so in the field of sex—one obvious reason being the shame that people feel if they have been sexually violated. It is difficult to know which sex crimes are *least* reported, as a proportion of the total. There appears to be a feeling that rape is the most under-reported sex crime. Thus the U.S. Uniform Crime Report estimated that in 1960 only 30 per cent of rapes committed were reported, which suggests that in that year only 7000 of 20,000 cases of rape were brought to the attention of the authorities. It has been suggested (373) that as few as 5 per cent of rapes are reported. And Geis has stated elsewhere (374) that rape is the most under-reported major criminal offense in the U.S.

570. Sex crime—most under-studied

It has also been suggested that rape is one of the most under-studied crimes in the modern world. One authority, M. Amir, has pointed out that as late as 1965 there was not even a single book available in English dealing exclusively with rape. And Geis has categorized group rape as the most under-studied major criminal offense in the U.S. (374). In view of the startling high incidence of rape in many parts of America this neglect is difficult to comprehend.

571. Sex crime—most serious to Chinese

Different societies and cultures vary on the gravity they attach to the different sorts of sexual offense. Some societies cannot stand pornography, others even have a down on adultery, many are virtually hysterical about youthful sexual indulgence. Common to many societies is a dislike of a cross-cultural phenomenon. Incest has ben represented incest, but the incest "taboo" has been seen to be strong as a cross-cultural phenomenon. Incest has been represented as the most serious sexual offense in Chinese eyes. And it has been noted that owing to the large family system, the Chinese connotation of incest has often been much broader than it appears to Western moralists and law-makers. Thus, in ancient China, if a man had an affair with the wife of his father's cousin three times removed, it would still have constituted a case of incest. In the countryside, detected offenders were tied up and buried alive by their relatives with the full support of the rest of the villagers.

572. Sexual offence penalties—greatest dispairities in U.S.

One of the troubles of a Federal system of law is that odd disparities often exist in legislation from one state to the next. This has the consequences that wrong-doers tend to move towards "lax" states, and that the concept of law is brought into disrepute. Here are some disparities in law in the U.S.—fornication in Virginia brings a twenty-dollar fine, whereas in Arizona you may get landed with a three-year prison sentence. By contrast, North Dakota and Rhode Island give fornicators 30 days in jail and ten-dollar fines. In New York, homosexual behavior can result in minor fines; in Nevada, the same behavior can result in life imprisonment! In some states the age of consent is 12 years; in other states the age of consent is 21 years (375)!!

573. Penile manipulation by woman—most severe penalty

Most men enjoy having their penis caressed by a woman; happily, many women enjoy doing it. Occasionally, however, there have been laws against such dissolute goings-on. Perhaps the most severe of all such prohibitions is to be found in old Judaic law. We have already met the phallic oath in the ancient world (see superlative 319), so we know how the penis has been worshipped. Among the Jews, for a woman to touch with her hand the sacred genitals of her husband was a severe crime. If a woman committed such a crime, then the offending hand would be amputated (376).

574. Legal plea—oddest

There are many candidates for this one. For at least one authority the oddest plea found in the law books is that of keeping a concubine at home. Many societies have covered this type of activity under a general concept of adultery, or the keeping of concubines in general, as was the case in Panama. Belgium has been cited as the only country which regarded the installation of one's mistress in the matrimonial home as sufficiently heinous to be particularized in her divorce laws.

575. Coitus (human)—youngest legal allowed in nineteenth-century

The youngest legal age for permissible coitus has varied throughout the world and through history in individual countries. Three examples may be quoted for nineteenth-century England. The permissible age was only ten in the 1861 Offenses Against the Person Act; 12 in the 1875 Act; and 13 in the Criminal Law Amendment Act of 1885. In such legislation, coitus required that penetration occur, but emission was not necessary.

576. Court ruling—most bizarre

The judicial world is capable of absurd and bizarre behavior from time to time: many rulings have bordered on fantasy. For example, it used to be the case that animals appeared in court, allocated defense counsel, their grunts and whines being interpreted as denials or guilt or confessions. Court rulings followed in accordance with such interpretations. In the realm of human sexual behavior the rulings have often been harsh in the extreme (see superlative 357). Sometimes the judgments seem so ridiculous as to be almost incredible. Here's just one example —in Dittrick v. Brown County 1943: 9 N.W. (2d) 510 the Supreme Court of Minnesota unheld the commitment as a sexual psychopath of a 42-year-old father of six who "was mentally bright, capable, and a good worker," because of the extreme craving for sexual intercourse with his wife, amounting in the year before his commitment to approximately 3 or 4 times a week (377)."

577. Sex crime—most frequent

It all depends what country you live in. It is hard to be a sex criminal in Denmark by publishing pornography, but easy to be so rated in South Africa for the same activity. Oral sex, common in Britain and America, is not illegal in the former but can result in prosecution in some states of the Union. Similarly adultery, legally O.K. in some states, can bring a prison sentence in others. The most frequent sexual offenses in America are oral sex, adultery and rape (in the respective states where such activities are against the law): this does not mean that prosecutions are frequent, only that there is a nominal infringement of statute. In Britain the commonest sexual offense is exhibitionism.

578. Sex crime—least frequent

The considerations here are the same, *mutatis mutandis,* as those indicated in superlative 577. Rare sexual behavior may be illegal in some parts of the world but legally permissible elsewhere. In Britain and most other countries such activities as necrophilia and bestiality tend to be frowned upon by the authorities: such indulgences are extremely rare. (See superlative 579).

579. Bestiality—only conviction of woman in U.S.

As far as can be judged there is only one recorded case of a woman convicted of coitus with a non-human animal in the United States. It is the case of State v. Tarrant (1949: 80 N.E. 2d Ohio 509), mentioned by Kinsey, Masters (378) and others.

580. Homosexual law—most absurd

Laws against homosexual behavior have varied from the severe (e.g. mutilation and execution) to the ridiculous and ineffectual. Homosexuals (i.e. *male* homosexuals rather than females) have often been prosecuted on charges of indecency for simply holding hands or trying to dance together. Perhaps the most absurd law was the one instanced by Robitscher (379)—the sale of alcoholic drink to homosexuals, or permitting their congregation at licensed premises, was represented as a ground for suspension or revocation of a liquor license, 27 ALR. 3d (1954).

581. Homosexual law—first introduced in Britain

Action has been taken against homosexuals throughout all recorded history. Sometimes the action had the sanction of official statute, sometimes not. In England homosexual offenses did not become a matter for the secular courts until 1533 when a statute was introduced (25 Henry VIII c. 6) making sodomy a capital crime (380). So it remained until the nineteenth century when, under the reforming influence of Sir Robert Peel, the maximum penalty became life imprisonment. (See also superlative 374).

582. Homosexual behavior—first made non-capital crime in Britain

From the time of Henry VIII to that of Queen Victoria, those convicted of the "abominable crime" of buggery or sodomy were liable to be executed. In 1861 in England and 1889 in Scotland the maximum penalty for homosexual acts was changed to life imprisonment. In the 1885 Criminal Law Amendment Act, acts of "gross indecency" not amounting to buggery, hitherto not regarded as a crime, were made subject to two years hard labor: it was under this act that Oscar Wilde was prosecuted (381).

583. Lesbian behavior—most recent attempt in UK to impose legal sanctions

In 1921 a new Criminal Law Amendment Act was introduced into the House of Commons as a Private Member's measure. During the report stage, after the Bill had been considered by a standing committee, a Scottish conservative lawyer and son of the *manse*, Frederick Macquisten, representing one of the Glasgow divisions, moved the following new clause under the heading of "Acts of Indecency by females"—

Any act of gross indecency between female persons shall be a misdemeanour and punishable in the same manner as any such act committed by male persons under section eleven of the Criminal Law Amendment Act, 1885.

According to Macquisten the new clause was "long overdue in the criminal code of this country" and he referred with some relish to "an undercurrent of dreadful degradation, unchecked and uninterfered with." Sir Ernest Wild, supporting the clause, declared it "an attempt to grapple with a very real evil." The clause was passed in the Commons on 4 August 1921 by a vote of 148 to 53, but defeated in the Lords (382).

584. Vasectomy—first approved in English law

Vasectomy, nervously seen by some males as akin to forcible castration and the consequent surrender of virility, has often been opposed in law. For a number of years vasectomy has been legal when performed under conditions of appropriate medical control. It was in 1972 that Parliament added vasectomy to the methods of contraception which may be provided by local authorities. This was largely due to the sustained advocacy of the Simon Population Trust.

585. Castration (human)—most recent legislation for therapy

Castration, variously defined and interpreted, has featured in the laws of many lands—sometimes in relation to punitive measures against sexual offenders, sometimes in reference to the entitlement of those seeking remedial action in cases of sexual pathology. In Czechoslovakia and Germany in recent years the question of castration has received considerable attention. Therapeutic castration has been employed in both countries and as late as 1969 a new law was introduced in Germany legalizing therapeutic castration when appropriately defined.

586. Castration (of self)—first outlawed by Christian Church

In A.D. 211, as we all know, Origen castrated himself in a fit of religious enthusiasm. This of course follows Jesus's remark that "there be eunuchs, which have made themselves eunuchs for the kingdom of heaven's sake . . ." We may suspect that various devout men tried to emulate the example of Origen, who was, after all, the first great scholar among the Greek Fathers. In A.D. 325 the Council of Nicaea ruled that church servants who had gelded themselves should leave their holy offices immediately (Canon 1).

587. Sterilization—first eugenic legislation in Europe

In the early part of the nineteenth century various European countries were considering means of preserving the imagined racial purity of their own respective stock (383). It is sobering to realize that much of the disreputable eugenic legislation in Nazi Germany was foreshadowed in serious discussion in nations that were to fight against Hitler. (There is an intriguing piece of courtroom drama in the film *Judgment at Nuremberg* where a counsel points out that much of the Nazi race philosophy can be found in the earlier pronouncements of American jurists!) In 1928, the first Eugenic Act was passed in Europe, and this in Switzerland, not noted for racial intolerance. Denmark followed in 1929; Germany, Sweden, and Norway in 1934; Finland and Danzig in 1935; and Estonia in 1936. England, in 1934, "came periously close to taking the plunge (384)" The first castration associated with a Danish court was carried out in 1925 (385). (See superlatives 378 to 381).

588. Sterilization—first eugenic legislation attempted in Europe

The success of sterilization legislation in Europe (see superlative 377) followed many years of agitation for such statutory provision. For instance, bills making provision for sterilization on eugenic grounds were introduced in Germany in 1903, 1907, 1923, and 1925 (384).

589. Sterilization—first eugenic legislation

As we may suspect, having read superlative 377, the first eugenic legislation was achieved, not in Europe, but in America. The first statute was in Michigan as early as 1897, but the bill was later vetoed. The world's first operational law for eugenic sterilization came into force in Indiana in 1904: this legislative provision was declared unconstitutional in 1921.

590. Sterilization—first compulsory legislation achieved

From 1907, until overtaken by Germany in the nineteen-thirties, the United States of America was to lead the world "in drafting and implementing laws for compulsory sterilization (386)." The Wolfers add, parenthetically that "there is something to be said for the leisurely tradition-bound processes of the older democracies if they can protect from surrender to the malice and hysteria of the day." (Maybe, but take a look at the accomplishment of one of the older democracies, as shown in superlative 381.) As early as 1855, the Territory of Kansas introduced judicial castration. The law stipulated castration of a Negro or mulatto male who had raped, attempted to rape, or tried to force marriage upon a white woman. This law is mentioned by G. von Hoffman in 1914, but Langelüddeke points out that von Hoffman could not obtain information on whether or not the law had ever been applied (387).

591. Sterilization law—most effective

Nazi Germany wins this one without a serious rival on the horizon. One German law passed on 24 November 1933 provided castration for a man over 21 years of age who—

1. was convicted of forcing someone to indecency, of raping children, or of having committed a sex crime, and who, therefore, was imprisoned for at least six months, and who, in addition, had been thus sentenced for a sex offense once before and was evaluated as a dangerous sex criminal; or

2. was convicted and sentenced to imprisonment for a

period of not less than one year and, in addition, was evaluated as a dangerous sex criminal; or
3. had committed murder in order to satisfy his sexual drive.

The German "Law for the Prevention of Hereditary Disease to Posterity" was promulgated in July 1933, operative from 1 January 1934. More sterilizations were performed under this law than under all the rest of the world's sterilization laws put together. Persons suffering from a long list of diseases* were considered "hereditarily diseased in this sense of the law." Severe alcoholism was also considered a ground for sterilization. Estimates of the number sterilized between 1934 and 1945 vary from 200,000 to 2,000,000 (388).

592. Artificial insemination by donor—first court case (US)
In California in 1967 a man divorced three years earlier was charged by the District Attorney in Sonoma County with violating a law which makes willful non-support of a child a misdemeanour. The child in question was born by AID six years earlier with the husband's consent. In this particular case the wife had refused offers of financial help from the husband. The judge convicted the man on the ground that "all children born in wedlock are presumed the legitimate issue of the marital partners." (A much earlier case, in Bordeaux in 1883, concerned a Dr. de Lajatre who advised patients to overcome their infertility by an infallible treatment known as a "la fécondation artificielle." The worth doctor was ordered to pay costs and damages following an unjustified advertisement which *enticed* a couple to pay for treatment.)

593. Exhibitionism—first court case in U.K.
Exhibitionism, as we have seen, is a common sexual offense in Britain. It must always have occurred. Men and women not infrequently have an urge to divest themselves of their clothes and we should hardly be surprised if this is done for conscious or unconscious sexual reasons. In sev-

---

* Innate mental deficiency, schizophrenia, manic-depressive insanity, hereditary epilepsy, Huntington's Chorea, hereditary blindness, hereditary deafness, severe hereditary physical abnormality.

enteenth-century Ireland, as Fynes Moryson has testified, aristocratic ladies would throw off their clothes indoors, even in the presence of strangers. And Havelock Ellis tells us (389) that "as early as 1476 a London priest appeared before the Ecclesiastical Court charged with showing his privates to several women in the parish"—"No doubt his sacred profession led to scandal. We are not told that anything was done about it."

594. Obscene publications—first English legislation against public exposure

The crime of creating or distributing "obscene" material is of relatively recent origin in Anglo-American law. In England it was held as late as 1705 that such materials were not indictable at common law, although "obscene libel" was found punishable in England through judicial decision in 1727. The first legislation in England stipulating the prosecution of obscene materials was enacted in 1824, and covered public exposure of what were considered obscene books or prints. General legislation affecting the distribution of "obscenity" was not enacted until Lord Campbell's Act of 1857, and a broad legal definition awaited the celebrated decision of Queen v. Hicklin in 1868.

595. Obscene publications—first international conference

The first International Conference on Obscene Publications was held in Geneva in 1923; the representatives of half the governments of the world declared that —"After careful examination of the question as to whether it is possible to insert in the Convention a definition of the word "obscene" which would be acceptable to all the States, the Conference came to a negative conclusion and recognized, like the conference of 1910, that each State must be allowed to attach to this word the signification which it might consider suitable." Or in other words, having decided resolutely that they did not know what they were talking about, the nations of the world sat down to condemn this, that and the other!

596. Obscenity—first made an obscene libel

The eighteenth-century in England saw little strenuous attention to concepts of pornography and obscenity: that was to come later. There was a ruling in 1729 that an obscene libel constituted a common-law misdemeanour.

597. Obscenity case—most famous in nineteenth-century England

The much quoted Hicklin case of 1868, arising out of the seizure of a pamphlet entitled *The Confessional Unmasked* which had been published by the Protestant Electoral Union as part of its program to advance Protestantism and oppose Catholicism, was taken as a model for many later judgments. In affirming the obscenity of the pamphlets the Chief Justic Cockburn created a new legal test for obscenity—a test quickly adopted in both English and American courts. The Lord Chief Justice remarked that he thought the test of obscenity "is this, whether the tendency of the matter charged as obscenity is to deprave and corrupt those whose minds are open to such immoral influences, and into whose hands a publication of this sort may fall." There has been endless debate on the *deprave and corrupt* issue.

598. Obscenity—first prosecution under 1959 Obscene Publications Act

The 1959 Obscene Publications Act, still in operation, has been represented as embodying a number of progressive or liberal principles. For instance, expert testimony is allowed in defense of the artistic or social merit of a work being prosecuted; and the onus is on the prosecution to prove a tendency to deprave and corrupt. *Lady Chatterley's Lover* by D. H. Lawrence was the first work to be tried under the 1959 Act. A procession of expert witnesses came forward to argue the merit of the work. The result was an acquittal, a verdict generally taken as a triumph for liberal opinion in the U.K. (390).

599. Obscenity legislation—first enacted in American colony
In the United States the distribution of "obscenity" was
never established as a common-law offense, although there
were a number of common-law prosecutions in the 1800s.
Only one colony enacted an obscenity statute; this was
Massachusetts. The other colonies left the subject unregu-
lated. The first state statute was enacted in Vermont in
1821; the first federal statute, prohibiting the importation
of pictorial obscenity was enacted in 1842; and obscenity
was first prohibited in the mails in 1865.

**600. Obscenity legislation—first in New York only to restrict
children**
The most repressive obscenity legislation is sweeping in its
spirit and application; there are no exceptions in terms of
favored persons according to age, sex, professional qualifi-
cation, etc. Slightly less repressive, but equally indefensi-
ble, is the legislation that allows certain élitist groups to
have access to material not allowed to the general public.
More liberal still is the provision of total freedom for
adults while maintaining restrictions on children. The most
liberal situation is evidently total absence of restriction in
any shape or form: no country, in terms of obscenity legislation, is liberal in this last sense. Some legislation attempts to give freedom to adults while "protecting" children. There is a paradox here in that adults seem more
adversely affected by pornography than do children: we
cannot debate this here. In 1968 the US Supreme Court
for the first time approved a New York obscenity law that
applies only to children, a statute that prohibts the sale to
persons under seventeen "girlie" magazines and other literature depicting nudity, "sexual excitement, sexual conduct,
and sadomasochistic abuse." Justice Brennan, in handing
down the 6-3 decision, "noted that most experts doubt
that nude pictures and girlie magazines are harmful to
children. But he said it was 'not irrational' for the Legisla-
ture to find otherwise.

601. Obscenity legislation—first to include defense provisions

We have already mentioned this one. The 1959 Obscene Publications Act in Britain allowed the calling of defense experts to show that a prosecuted work had artistic, scientific, or other merit. In English courts the extraordinary picture emerged of great numbers of highly qualified men and women being prepared to come forward to defend material that to simpler minds would seem to be indecent or obscene. The 1959 Act must have facilitated a degree of public education not previously possible in English courts. A clause in the Act, sponsored by Roy Jenkins, runs as follows—

A person shall not be convicted of an offense against section two of this act and an order for forfeiture shall not be made under the foregoing section if it is proved that publication of the article in question is justified as being for the public good on the ground that it is in the interests of science, literature, art, or learning, or of other objects of general concern.

602. Obscenity legislation—most absurd sentences

There are those among us who think that all legislation against obscenity is absurd (391). But even such hardy souls will concede that some legislative deliverances are more ridiculous than others. The selection of a particularly absurd ruling is an arbitrary business. One choice example will suffice here—In 1923, Sir Archibald Bodkin told the International Conference for the Suppression of Obscene Publications, "I have got two people in prison now for having exchanged and lent and dealt with each other in indecencies, photographs, pictures, books, etc." This is akin to the sentence in 1932 of six months imprisonment on a man who submitted translations of poems by Rabelais and Verlaine to a printer (392).

603. Obscenity report—most thorough

This is the British Arts Council report (550). The report is not all that thorough but it is the best we have. What it lacks in depth it makes up for in nice presentation and readability. Happily, it reaches liberal conclusions.

604. Obscenity trial—longest in England

The longest obscenity trial in English legal history was that of the Oz magazine under the 1959 Obscene Publications Act (393). The proceedings lasted for nearly six weeks in the hot summer of 1971. It was also the first major obscenity trial which produced a guilty verdict since the pre-*Lady Chatterley* days (1960). The trial was a remarkable affair with Judge Argyle able to make remarks such as "so-called defense experts"—in fact the *experts* including such people as Michael Schofield, Lecturer in Psychology and Caroline Coon, director of "Release."

605. Obscenity trials—earliest in England

In 1663, Sir Charles Sedley, an intimate of Charles II, and two friends got themselves drunk and climbed to a balcony of the tavern, whereupon they removed their clothes and (the reports differ) either urinated on the crowd below or emptied bottles of urine on to them. In any event the crowds did not enjoy the proceedings and Sedley found himself in court. The case is often referred to as the first reported obscenity case, since it showed that common-law courts would, even in the absence of a statute, penalize conduct which was grossly offensive to the public. But in 1708, in the case of *Reg. v. Read,* where the defendant had published *The Fifteen Plagues of a Maidenhead* (said in court to be "bawdy stuff") for gain, Mr. Justice Powell dismissed the case saying there was no law under which it could be tried. In 1727, however, when a man named Curle published a pornographic book, the Attorney-General submitted that the publication was an offense at common law because "it tends to corrupt the morals of the King's subjects and is thus against the peace of the King." The submission was accepted with reluctance: the conviction of Curle's *Venus in the Cloister or the Nun in her Smock* became a precedent for further prosecutions (394).

606. Obscene publications legislation—most famous in nineteenth-century England

In 1857, an Obscene Publications Act was passed which had much importance. Sometimes known as Lord Campbell's Act, it provided a summary procedure whereby obscene publications might be searched for by the police and brought before justices who had power to order the destruction of offending publications if the case was made out.

607. Pornography—only country totally to repeal adult legislation

Denmark is at present unique in that there are currently no statutory restrictions on the consumption of pornography by adults. In the past, Danish governments signed international conventions for the control of pornography. Increasingly however there was unhappiness that material that could be deemed *obscene* under existing provisions had clear artistic merit. A turning point came with the publication in Denmark in 1964 of *Fanny Hill*: the publisher was prosecuted but acquitted. The case was then taken to the Supreme Court where the acquittal was upheld. This and other cases led to a great increase in the amount of pornographic material being circulated. In 1964 the Ministry of Justice requested the Permanent Criminal Law committee to consider existing legislation on pornography and to recommend changes. The report was completed in June 1966; the majority conclusions favored repeal of obscenity legislation in so far as it affected adults. In the spirit of the report the Danish Parliament repealed existing legislation (395).

608. Prostitutes—first property legislation

Brothels and prostitution in general have often served as a taxable source of revenue for municipalities, church, etc. One Pope, Clement II, even found a way of taxing prostitutes after they had died. He issued a bull requiring anyone who had ever engaged in prostitution must leave half of her property to the Church (if she had not made the contribution earlier). Prostitution was taxed in Spain, Portugal, Germany, Switzerland, France, and elsewhere. In

Nuremberg in the Fifteenth-Century, money spent visiting prostitutes was tax-deductible (396). No, I don't advise you to try it on your next income-tax return!

609. Topless fashions—first ordered for prostitutes

Prostitutes were often ordered by the municipal authorities to wear dress by which they could be distinguished. The fifteenth-century authorities of Venice decreed that the town prostitutes must sit with completely bare breasts at the windows. The idea, so the story goes, was that it was required so that the young men would be diverted from the "unnatural aberration" of homosexuality (397).

610. Prostitution—first abolished in China

Prostitution has flourished in China over the centuries. Only in 1949, with the revolutionary success of the communists, was a systematic effort made to destroy it once and for all. The ordinary Chinese people have been urged to lead a sexually pure life in the "new China." Prostitutes were "abolished" in 1949: those who had musical talents were trained to be actresses at the Peking Opera, while the rest were sent to work in factories or on farms. In 1953, dance halls were ordered to close and the dancing-girls were urged to follow the example of the erstwhile prostitutes.

611. White slave traffic—first UN convention

In December 1949 the United Nations General Assembly adopted the "Convention for the Suppression of the Traffic in Persons and of the Exploitation of the Prostitution of Others" which brought international attitudes up-to-date. The Parties to the Convention are bound to punish any person, who, to gratify the passions of another:

1. Procures, entices or leads away, for purposes of prostitution, another person, even with the consent of that person.
2. Exploits the prostitution of another person, even with the consent of that person."

The implications of Article 1 of the Convention have been discussed in a UN *Study of Traffic in Persons and Prostitution* (1959) (398).

612. White slave traffic—most recent legislation (France)

Various systems have operated in France and elsewhere to acquire girls for induction into a life of prostitution in France and other countries. Many apparently innocent organizations have functioned as recruiting grounds for the unsuspecting. A most successful line was the "dancing studio" where ambitious girls tended to congregate and were only too glad if the "ballet master" himself (or herself) gave them advice and helped them kindly to a promising contract abroad. The studios were mushrooming so fast and their activities were so blatant that on 1 December 1965, a new French law (No. 65-1004) was promulgated that forbade any previously convicted procurer to give dancing lessons or to run a dance studio (399)."

Chapter Six

SEXOLOGY AND SEX EDUCATION

613. Sexology—first practiced

We're in semantics again. If sexology is nothing more than the observation and cataloguing of sexual features in the animal world then Aristotle and his brother Greeks were sexologists a few hundred years before Christ. Some people want to date the origins of the science to sexology to Leonardo da Vinci in the fifteenth-century; or to Leeuwenhoek (see superlative 426) in the seventeenth. But perhaps the systematic study of sex *per se* really began in the nineteenth-century with such specialists therapists and writers as Krafft-Ebing and Havelock Ellis. One modern writer suggests (400) that "the science of sexology begins with the more theoretical generalizations about sexual behavior which Freud articulated in his *Three Essays on the Theory of Sexuality,* written in 1905 and revised in subsequent years."

614. Sexologist—first liberal in modern times

Most writers on sex are liberals these days. There can be little doubt that progressive views are fashionable; they are also, some of us may believe, desirable. At the moment it is relatively easy to be liberal and progressive, a situation which we largely owe to the early progressive writers in the field of sex. Among these Havelock Ellis was perhaps the most significant. In Brecher's nice phrase Havelock Ellis (1859-1939) was "the first of the Yea-Sayers." He contributed vastly to an enlargement of man's view of human sexuality; and he brought to all his work a humanistic sympathy and tolerance which have informed psychosexual therapy and research ever since (401). Healer and educator, writer and scholar, Havelock Ellis recorded the results of his studies in a multi-volume work, *Studies in the Psychology of Sex,* which he published and periodically revised in the years between 1896 and 1928. This monumental work was first published in America, English prudery being too vigorous to allow the book to be published here! (See superlative 395.)

615. Sexological study—most comprehensive in nineteenth-century

Havelock Ellis deserves another superlative! His main work, the *Studies,* constituted the most weighty contribution to sexological research in the late nineteenth and early twentieth centuries. One of the volumes was almost entirely devoted to the topic of sexual inversion, or homosexuality. And he felt, for instance, that there were both congenital and psychological factors influencing the predisposition to homosexuality. It has been suggested that Havelock Ellis paved the way for the significant sexological developments that were to begin with Freud.

616. Sexologist—most famous

Alfred Charles Kinsey bestrides the sexological world like a giant. His two reports on the sexual behavior of the human male and female respectively (1948 and 1953) have no equals before or since in their scope, thoroughness or the richness of their data. Kinsey has been criticized in his methods (so have Marx, Darwin, and Freud); but where is the sexologist in the modern world who does not owe a debt to Kinsey? All serious sexological social surveys, all compilers of statistical and other information in this field, all specialist writers on one aspect of sex or another soon or later have to acknowledge the pioneering work of Kinsey at the institute he founded (superlative 402). There can be no doubt that the headline-making work of Masters and Johnson is well grounded in the firm empirical approach established by Kinsey.

617. Sexological survey—most comprehensive

The first Kinsey report (403) was based on detailed interviews held with more than five thousand white males; the second report (404) was based on data gathered in the same way for more than five thousand females. In the *Male* volume it is pointed out (p.6) that "about 12,000 persons have contributed history to this study" Furthermore, this represents *forty times as much material as was included in the best of the previous studies.* Kinsey estimated that no less than 100,000 histories would have been required to complete the project—hence the dedication in the *Male* volume. There are no signs that any such figure will ever be reached.

618. Sex institute—most celebrated

It is hardly surprising that, in view of Kinsey's sexological contributions, the institute he founded at Indiana University should be the most famous in the world. Sometimes still referred to as the Kinsey Institute, its correct title is the Institute for Sex Research: it is a mark of the reputation of Kinsey himself that many people seem to be under the impression that the Institute died with its founder. The Institute's primary purpose is represented as the conducting of research into human sexual behavior by gathering data analyzing them and making the resultant information available to those who need it. The Institute is a nonprofit organization governed by a board of trustees. The library subjects being college and club women; a high percentage there is a vast archive of other sexological and erotic materials photographs, films, drawings, paintings, *objets d'art*, trinkets, diaries, love letters, records, etc. In recent years various police departments have contributed confiscated sexual material. Institute staff have produced books, book chapters, and journal articles in a wide range of publications.

619. Sexologist—first woman

A number of the early female writers on sexual matters were mainly concerned with a specific measure, e.g. Margaret Sanger wrote on birth control. It can be argued that such a preoccupation, though praiseworthy, is not strictly sexological in nature. The first woman sexologist in the true sense was Katherine Davis who performed a detailed questionnaire study of 2200 women in the New York area and who published in 1929 (405). The questionnaire was originally mailed to 20,000 women, only a tenth choosing to reply. The survey was said to be confined to "normal" women of good standing in the community, most of the currently holds more than 20,000 bound volumes and terial, such as pamphlets, magazines, newspaper clippings, were graduates. The ages of the women, many of them teachers, ranged between 25 and 55. The treatment of the data has been represented as "simple but statistical (406)." (A much smaller study, perhaps justifying the adjective *sexological*, was carried out by Anita Newcomb McGee from 1888 to 1891; interviews were taken and data compiled with respect to the famous Oneida Community in New York.)

620. Sex research—most active modern country

In view of superlatives 396 to 399 the reader will hardly be surprised to learn that the most active country in the world in the field of sex research is the United States. Paul H. Gebhard, who became director of the Institute for Sex Research on Kinsey's death in 1956, has commented (407) of the United States that "the proliferation of universities and the vast number of behavioral scientists and in sex research" that it is possible to name "only a minority of them (408)." Various important organizations have been identified; in addition to the Institute for Sex Research, there are the group focused on Benjamin and Masters, the Society for the Scientific Study of Sex (Albert Ellis), etc.

621. Sex research—least active modern developed countries

Of many countries we do not expect sex research—simply because such nations are too poor to fund such investigations (or because they are too pious). Other countries, neither poor nor pious, have a surprising dirt! of research effort into human sexuality. Of the Soviet Union, for example, Gebhard has remarked—"I know—and only by surname—of only two qualified persons interested in sex research: Milman, a Lenigrad urologist, and Vasilcenko, a Moscow psychiatrist." There have been rumors from time to time that Moscow was to create a new sex institute. East Germany apparently only boasts one or two serious sexologists: for instance the survey, organized by H. Rennert, via questionnaires distributed to male and female students in 1963, has been quoted (409).

622. Sex institute—first
The first sex institute was the Magnus Hirschfeld Institut für Sexualwissenschaft, Berlin, and doomed only to survive a few years (see superlative 464).

623. Sexual activity (maximum by age)—earliest survey
The earliest serious attempt to ascertain the age of maximum sexual activity, and the effect of age on sexual performance in the human male, was made by R. Pearl in 1925. This has been termed a nicely analyzed study by a biostatistician using hospital data on 257 older, married, white males, most of them over 55 years of age. They had all undergone prostatic operation. In particular, data from 213 men (average age 65.53 years)—who felt they could recall the frequencies of marital intercourse in their earlier histories—were analyzed. The age of maximum sexual activity for this group was located in the 30-39 year period, a circumstance thought to have sociological (e.g. lack of opportunity) significance rather than physiological. On a limited empirical basis Pearla concluded that the peak of activity "is in the 20-29 decade and that thereafter there is a steady decline." The survey has been criticized on account of its neglect of education as an influential parameter in making rural and urban comparisons.

624. Coitus (human)—first scientifically observed
The observation, for scientific purposes, of human beings in coitus is generally associated with Masters and Johnson. They were not the first to study sexual behavior in this way. Kinsey had already moved to such a means of investigation and even he had his predecessors. The earliest

efforts to study human sexual activity through direct observation were those of Félix Roubaud who, in 1855, published his 804-page volume entitled *Traité de l'Impuissance et de la Sterilité chez l'Homme et chez la Femme*. Kinsey declared that Roubaud's descriptions of sexual activity had not been surpassed by later writers. Part of the Roubaud findings were later confirmed by Masters and Johnson. Brecher lists (410) more than a dozen pre-Masters sexologists who observed human coitus directly. The first American observations of orgasm were made by Dr. Joseph R. Beck of Fort Wayne, Indiana, on 7 and 8 August 1872.

625. Coitus (human)—first efforts to measure heart rate
In modern observations of human coitus efforts are made to measure heart rate during sexual excitement, climax, the resolution phase, etc. The first attempts to measure heart rate during sexual intercourse date back to 1896, when G. Kolb carried out a range of experiments in this area. In the 1930s E. P. Boas and E. F. Goldschmidt made similar observations, and in 1950 G. Klumbies and H. Kleinsorge included heart rate, blood pressure and respiratory changes in their experiments.

626. Coital observance taboo—first effectively eliminated in research
For reasons that have yet to be explored in detail the vast bulk of people are reticent about having their sexual activity observed by others. That such an attitude is not innate is shown by various cross-cultural studies. Any effective scientific project, involving direct observation of human coitus, has to begin by overcoming the reticence in people about having sexual intercourse in public. In a number of small scale projects (see superlative 624) this was accomplished but it was not until the work of William Masters and Virginia Johnson that the taboo was effectively combatted for hundreds of men and women. Brecher describes how this was achieved.

627. Orgasms—most observed in research

Over a period of twelve years Masters and Johnson observed and recorded more than 10,000 male and female orgasms. Dr. Masters began his program of sex research in 1954 after specializing for many years in gynaecology and hormone replacement therapy for postmenopausal women. He found his assistant, Mrs. Virginia Johnson—now Mrs. Masters—through an advertisement. Their first subjects were prostitutes—eight female and three male—but gradually they collected non-professional volunteers: their final sample was 694 individuals.

628. Orgasm observations—first in America

The rich tradition of American sexological research began early in the nineteenth-century. As we have seen, by the 1870s it became possible, on a limited scale, to observe human coitus directly. Dr. Beck observed human orgasm in August 1972. In fitting a woman with a pessary to correct retroversion of the uterus she was quick to request that Beck take care lest she experience orgasm, a likelihood in view of her nervous temperament and passionate nature. However, out of scientific curiosity, Beck decided to provoke an orgasm in the woman and observe what happened. "I now swept my right forefinger quickly three or four times across the space between the cervix and the pubic arch, when almost immediately the orgasm occurred ..." Dr. Beck reported his observations in the *St. Louis Medical and Surgical Journal* for September 1872. An enlarged paper was delivered before the American Medical Association on 2 June 1874 and published in the *American Journal of Obstetrics and Diseases of Women and Children* for November of the same year (411).

629. Orgasm physiology and arousal—first detailed account

There were many account of orgasmic response before the work of Masters and Johnson. Theirs however was without doubt the most detailed research study ever undertaken in this field. Their findings were published in 1966 in *Human Sexual Response*. In particular it was concluded that the long-standing debate about the "clitoral" vs "vaginal" orgasm was largely misplaced, there being only one type of female orgasm no matter how it is caused.

630. Orgasm (women)—most thorough study

The main studies of human sexuality—Kinsey (1948 and 1953) and Masters and Johnson (1966)—drew conclusions largely from statistical and physiological research. A recent publication—*The Female Orgasm* (412) by Seymour Fisher—aims at adding the psychological component to the earlier studies. In addition to giving the most comprehensive review of earlier sexological work in this area, *The Female Orgasm* includes a detailed presentation of Fisher's own research findings. A major positive finding is that the greater a woman's feeling that love objects are easily lost or may disappear the less likely she is to attain orgasm and that this anxiety may frequently be traced to the dominant socialization practices for women in our society.

631. Sexological surveys—earliest

A few small surveys into sexual behavior were carried out in the nineteenth-century; but perhaps the first of any account was that carried out by P. S. Achilles in 1923 (413). As a psychologist he organized a group-administered questionnaire study of 1449 males and 483 females, all of the subjects from the New York City area. The study was mainly concerned with the effectiveness of certain social hygiene literature in disseminating information about venereal disease, but a number of the questions related to the sexual activities of the subjects. The size of the group is larger than most for that period, but was not broken up into homogeneous groups for analyses.

632. Sexologically studied groups—largest pre-Kinsey

The only three studies, pre-Kinsey, which approached nationwide coverage in the U.S. were limited to college students. The largest pre-Kinsey study—which just preceded the first Kinsey report—was *The Sex Life of Unmarried Men* (1947) by L. B. Hohman and Bertram Schaffner, based on interviews with 4,600 selective service selectees at military induction centres in New York State and Balti-more. The study was remarkable for its finding that only three or four inductees per thousand reported homosexual experience. However, the Kinsey group later pointed out that "three-to-five-minute interviews ... held in army in-duction centers were not conducive to winning admissions of socially taboo behavior."

633. Sexological study—smallest pre-Kinsey

Some research studies have been too small to appear as regular references in the literature. Kinsey himself iden-tified on 19 studies of sex behavior which are in any sense taxonomic. Of these the smallest were based on data gathered by a probation officer who interviewed a hundred boys who were passing through a juvenile court in Seattle, on interview returns from a hundred handicapped females, and on data derived from a study "of 40 superior single men." This latter investigation, the smallest of the nineteen cited by Kinsey, was based on single males between 21 and 30 years of age and for the most part superior college graduates from Universities in Eastern Massachusetts. "Because of the uniformity of the population, the results are better than such a small sample might be expected to give."

634. Sexological study—first to be statistically based

Broadly based statistical studies into sexual behavior are largely confined to the twentieth century. If we stretch the term *sexological,* however, we can find statistical studies as early as the sixteenth-century. François Rabelais (c. 1490-1553) checked the monthly distribution of christenings in his part of France and discovered a peak incidence in October and November—leading him to the conclusion that the first thaws of January and February resulted in increased sexual activity. A later French researcher, Villermé, had reported in 1831 on the basis of 17,000,000 births, that the maximum of French conceptions occur in April, May, and June (414).

635. Woman—oldest discussion of types

One of the oldest discussions of types of women, with relation to their sexual characteristics, is set in the form of a dialogue between the Chinese Yellow Emperor and the goddess-instructress, *The Forthright Female* (Su Nu). The dialogue forms part of the I-hsing Fang, a collection of such writings compiled by the Chinese authority Yeh Te-hui (1864-1927). *Women to be avoided*—"If the pubic hair is coarse and stiff, like bristles, or if it sprouts wildly and in different directions, this woman is unsuited. If the lips of the vagina do not cover the Jade Gate, and it hangs below, if the secretions are pungent, then such women are harmful. To have intercourse once with such creatures can bring a withering to the Jade Stem equal to that of one hundred battles with a good woman." *Women to be sought*—"A young woman is the best choice for such a partner, and she should be a virgin with the Flowery Field as yet unseeded. Her breasts will then be high and not yet milked, and her Yin-essence unspilled. Her flesh should be firm, her skin well-oiled and silky to the touch, and her "hundred joints" should be well-hinged and smooth in their movements."

636. Sexological survey (Women)—largest in England

This is the survey published as *The Sexual, Marital, and Family Relationships of the English Women* (Hutchinson, 1956) by Eustace Chesser, hence sometimes known as the Chesser Report. Around 6000 general practitioners were approached: they were invited to distribute a self-administered questionnaire to their patients. 1688 doctors agreed to co-operate, but 190 subsequently refused on seeing the questionnaire. In the event some 1498 doctors received between them about 18,000 questionnaires. The eventual report was based on material derived from 6251 informants of whom 1474 were in the London area. Only 23 per cent of the questionnaires distributed were returned and it has been suggested that "the sample was over-represented in the higher educational and income groups (415)."

637. Sexological study—first to involve questioning of women

The Achilles survey (superlative 407) also deserves mention a second time as the first American study (1923) to include women in the sample surveyed. The study was carried out for the American Social Hygiene Association—an organization engaged in fighting venereal disease, with primary emphasis on suppressing prostitution.

638. Sexological anthropology—most thorough surveys

Some anthropological studies relate only indirectly to sexual matters. In Frazer (*The Golden Bough*) and Crawley (*The Mystic Rose*), there is a vast amount of both sexual and non-sexual information. The two most famous anthropological studies that bear *directly* on sexual matters are Malinowski's *The Sexual Life of Savages* (416) and *Patterns of Sexual Behavior* (417) by Ford and Beach. If any hardy reader is ploughing through the superlatives in this book he will already have met Ford and Beach several times. Their book, as one of the few cross-cultural studies to include reference to animal behavior also, is perhaps the most quoted of anthropological studies of human sexual behavior.

639. Sexological anthropology—most detailed "one-culture" study

If Ford and Beach are the most quoted for their cross-cultural contribution (superlative 411) then Malinowski produced the most detailed sexological study of a single society. *The Sexual Life of Savages* deals in depth with many aspects of sexual relations among the Trobriand Islanders. Topics analyzed include—relations between the sexes, the status of women, prenuptial intercourse, avenues to marriage, divorce, procreation, lovemaking and the psychology of erotic life, erotic dreams, incest, etc.

640. Marriage prerequisite

Many propagandists have suggested that people contemplating the step of marriage should first acquaint themselves with the facts of life. What is generally recommended is that the intending person read some appropriate biology or sex technique book, the more to understand the peculiarities of the opposite sex. Sometimes the suggestions are altogether more thorough-going. For instance, Balzac (in his *Catéchisme conjugal*) suggests that "No man should marry before he has studied anatomy and dissected the body of a woman." Van de Velde speculates that careful study may obviate the need for actual dissection.

641. Prostitution—first effort to study it in social and scientific terms

The first attempt to approach the subject of prostitution from a social, philosophical and scientific viewpoint "bereft of all hypocracy and cant" was made early in the eighteenth century, when Bernard de Mandeville wrote his *The Fable of the Bees*. In this connection another Bernard (Shaw) has been quoted as suggesting that any vice that cannot be suppressed "should be made into a virtue."

642. Psychosexual disorders—first study written

De Sade's *Les 120 Journées de Sodome* is the first detailed study of psychopathia sexualis ever written and it remains the most complete in its descriptions. This extensive study describes in minute detail as many as 600 types of deviant sexual activity. The value of the work has been acclaimed by medical, scientific and scholastic authorities. And Bloch suggested that this book placed de Sade in the front rank of the important writers of the eighteenth-century.

643. Psychosexual disorders—first detailed nineteenth-century study

The *Psychopathia Sexualis* by Dr. R. v. Krafft-Ebing is the first systematic study of sexual disorders in which the author utilized both medical literature and a relatively large number of case histories. The first German edition of the book was published in 1886. Baron Richard von Krafft-Ebing was born at Mannheim on 14th August 1840, becoming Professor of Psychiatry and Nervous Diseases in the Royal University of Vienna. He died in 1902.

644. Masturbation—most thorough pre-Masters study
A number of sexologists studied the effects of masturbation before the extensive program launched by Masters and Johnson. One of the most thorough investigations of female response during masturbation was conducted by the American gynaecologist Dr. Robert Latou Dickinson whose findings were summarized in his Atlas of *Human Sex Anatomy* (first published in 1933). Dickinsons explored theories about vulval and clitoral masturbation and was responsible for introducing, with Robie and LeMon Clark, the electrical vibrator or massager into American gynaecological practice. Dickinson asked subjects to demonstrate their masturbatory techniques in order to correlate their methods with such factors as the degree of clitoral excursion(418).

645. Homosexuality—most important modern report in U.K.
This is the *Wolfenden Report*, which dealt also with prostitution. The committee, chaired by Sir John Wolfenden, was appointed on 24 August 1954 to consider the law and practice relating to homosexual offenses, the treatment of offenders by the courts, and the law and practice of prostitution. Recommendations were asked for. It was largely because of the liberal recommendations of the Wolfenden Committee that the 1967 Sexual Offenses Act gave a measure of freedom to consenting homosexual adults in their private behavior. That the 1967 Act was inadequate in many respects has repeatedly been pointed out by such bodies as the Campaign for Homosexual Equality (CHE).

646. Hermaphrodite gender roles—first study
Drs. Money, Hampson, and Hampson studied 76 hermaphrodites and other mixed-sex cases of various kinds and reported in a pioneering 1955 paper that adult psychological gender role and identity agreed with sex of assignment and rearing in all except four cases. If babies were assigned as male at birth and brought up as boys by their parents, they thereafter thought of themselves as male, played with male toys, enjoyed male sports, preferred male cloth-

ing, developed male sexual fantasies, and in due course fell in love with girls. Similarly, babies reared as girls accepted female roles, in due course falling in love with boys (419).

647. Castration (human)—most thorough pre-Kinsey study

The most thorough pre-Kinsey study of this sort is generally attributed to J. Lange. It was based on 310 cases which included 242 complete castrates and 68 partial castrates. The data are drawn from a long-time study of 247 injuries incurred through war, and 63 cases in which there had been a surgical removal of testes following tuberculosis. A summary of the conclusions is given in Kinsey. The sexual desire of many of the subjects had exceeded their potency. Lange discussed the fallacy of castration as a cure for sex criminals, since criminal violence is often the result of the conflict of weakened potency and strong sexual impulse.

648. Castration (human)—first scientifically discussed

The first scientific discussion of the effects of human castration took place long before the birth of Christ. The scholars of antiquity knew that the effects of castration varied according to the age at which castration took place. In the *Historia Animalium* (Bk. IX: 631b-632b), Aristotle (384-322 B.C.) has a lengthy discussion of the effects of castration in man and other male animals. He differentiates between pre-adolescent and adult castration, and refers to the removal of the ovaries of sows to reduce their sexual responsiveness. Data for a study of the effects of castration would always have been available throughout human history through the consequences of war injuries.

649. Castration studies—earliest

The earliest modern study of the effects of castration is that attributed to M.W. Barr, predating the Lange investigation but less comprehensive (420). Barr studied six male castrates, most of them with records of low intelligence and aged from eleven to twenty. The reported results are in general terms and are not useful for evaluation.

650. Sex-change clinic—first in the world
In 1966 the Erickson Educational Foundation provided funds for the world's first clinic for gender-reversal problems. The Gender Identity Clinic was formed at Johns Hopkins Hospital despite objections by a number of resident psychiatrists. Initially the clinic's committee comprised nine men headed by a plastic surgeon. Two applicants were selected each month for transformation and follow-up. Soon afterwards a gender committee for study and treatment was created at the University of Minnesota Medical School, and in 1970 two Chicago hospitals began to practice sex-change surgery (421).

651. Menstruation—first related to ovarian behavior
In 1896 Dr. E. Knaner found that excising the ovaries abolished menstruation; and transplanting ovaries into some suitable site reestablished menstruation—"Even the most reactionary vestiges of medieval opinion could not rationalize this."

652. Breast tumescence—first described as symptom of sexual excitement
R. L. Dickenson (see also superlative 644) first described breast tumescence as a sign of erotic arousal. This sort of knowledge is so commonplace today that it is amazing it was not remarked upon in the literature long ago.

653. Blushing—first studied as sexual phenomenon
In the April 1897 edition of *Paedagogical Seminary*, G.E. Partridge described the blush. He had collected 254 cases of blushing, 213 of them in girls and young women, and had discovered "an astonishing fact"—that the blush does not just affect the face but is a general physiological response in which many other parts of the body may participate. The face-reddening may be preceded by many other symptoms—"tremors near the waist, weakness in the limbs, pressure, trembling, warmth, weight, or beating in the chest, warm wave from feet upward, quivering of heart, stoppage and then rapid beating of heart, coldness all over

followed by heat, dizziness, tingling of toes and fingers, numbness, sometimes rising in throat, smarting of eyes, singing in ears, prickling sensations of face, and pressure inside head (422)." Darwin had studied blushing earlier but on several points was mistaken.

654. Sexual cycle in men—first evidence adduced

He often hear mention of the possibility of a sexual cycle in men to correspond with the female menstrual cycle, but little research has been done. As far back as 1888 Julius Nelson brought forward evidence to suggest a monthly cycle in men of a twenty-eight day length. Perry-Coste, in a more detailed investigation, also produced what he took to be evidence of a monthly sexual rhythm in men. Von Römer brought the evidence from involuntary emissions into line with that from voluntary emissions in coitus, by showing that the acts of coitus of an unmarried man fall into a monthly cycle, with two maxima approximating to Perry-Coste's; he also noted that the chief maximum occurs at the time of the full moon, and the secondary maximum at the time of the new moon (423). Havelock Ellis has also referred to an annual cycle of involuntary sexual activity—"which I first showed in 1898 and which I have since been able to confirm by additional evidence."

655. Pornography study—most detailed

There have been a number of studies of pornography, notably in Scandinavia, but also in West Germany, Israel, Britain, and America. The most thorough study of pornography is without doubt the one carried out by the Presidential Commission in the U.S. In 1967 the Congress created a Commission to investigate the effects of obscenity and pornography on the people of the United States, each member of the Commission being appointed by President Johnson. The final report was remarkable in that it recommended repeal of obscenity legislation as it related to adults. The findings—that pornography could not be shown to do harm to individuals or to society—would not surprise liberals, who already know as much. The publication of the report (424) occasioned a brief but heated controversy in the U.S. and elsewhere. Predictably the President—by now it was Nixon—ignored the report. Presumably another expensive effort will be made in the future; presumable also, the conclusions will be substantially the same.

656. Pornography effects—best recent survey

The most recent effort to study pornography in Britain came in *The Longford Report*. In the main this report is abysmal—poorly argued, uninformed by a mature grasp of human sexuality, bereft of supporting evidence, etc. We need spend no more time on it here. What *is* surprising is that this publication should contain a nice little appendix (Appendix V) by Maurice Yaffé as a Research Survey and Bibliography. This appendix, tucked away on pages 460 to 498, is quite out of tone with the rest of the report. In fact the conclusion undermines all Longford's efforts— "In the present state of knowledge it is not possible to draw any useful conclusions which might be applied to this problem and related issues . . ."

657. Gonorrhoea—earliest recorded knowledge

Moses, Hippocrates, Galen, the Roman doctor Cornelius Celsus, a contemporary of Christ, and the later Arab physicians were all familiar with gonorrhoea, which in general they regarded as an ordinary skin infection. Moses austerely recommended slaughter of the victims. A mural in a Pompeii brothel complains of a girl who, though extremely good-looking, was discovered to be "a dunghill within." At least one writer has taken this to mean that she had gonorrhoea (425).

658. Syphillis—first noted

There is much debate as to when syphillis first happened upon the scene. One theory is that it was brought back to Europe from Haiti by Columbus's sailors in 1494, whereupon it spread rapidly reaching France, Germany, and Switzerland in 1495, Scotland in 1497, and Hungary and Russia in 1499. Vasco da Gama took it to India in 1498 and it reached China in 1505. The Archbishop of Crete is said to have died of it in 1506 (426). Diaz is said to have

encountered syphillis in 1493 (427). Some writers have
suggested that syphillis was present in medieval
Europe (428) and "merely flared up in 1494." And some
evidence for the existence of syphillis in England is given
in C. Creighton's *A History of epidemics in Britain* (Cambridge, 1894); according to this account syphillis existed
in England in the first part of the fourteenth-century.

659. Syphillis—first country to abolish it

There is good evidence that China is the first country in
the world to have abolished syphillis. J. S. Horn describes
how this was done (429). Felix Greene has made similar
impressive claims for the record of modern China in the
area of venereal disease. Thus—"Perhaps one of the most
spectacular victories achieved by the new regime has been
the virtual wiping out of venereal disease. I visited, in all,
ten hospitals in China in city and country, old and new. In
each one I asked about the incidence of syphillis. In each
it drew a similar response: 'None for two years,' 'None
for a long time,' etc. Wassermann tests are required from
both partners before a marriage certificate is
granted" (430).

660. Veneral disease—most famous sufferers

A great number of famous and talented men have had one
sort of venereal illness or another. Here are one or two of
them—Abraham, David and Job, Caesar, Herod, Tiberius,
Charlemagne, Charles V and VIII of France, John of
Gaunt, Popes Alexander VI, Julius II and Leo X, Henry
VIII, Erasmus, Albrecht Durer, Thomas Wolsey, Ivan the
Terrible, Benvenuto Cellini, Richelieu, John Aubrey,
Casanova, Boswell, Goethe, Schopenhauer, Keats,
Schubert, Nietzsche, Mussolini, Hitler, Gauguin, Strind-
berg, Oscar Wilde, etc., etc. (431). This list could easily be
extended.

661. Sperm—first discovered

Human sperm were first discovered by a student of An-
tonij van Leeuwenhoek in 1677 in the city of Delft. The
name of the student is not known for certain: he is vari-

ously written up as Ludwig Hamm, van Hamm or von Hammen. According to some writers he is a Dutchman, to others a German. One day he brought to the acknowledged master of microscopy, Leeuwenhoek, a bottle containing semen and pointed out that small animals could be seen moving about in the ejaculate. Van Leeuwenhoek went on to study the seminal emissions from a wide range of sick and healthy men; in the semen of them all the odd creatures could be detected. He described his findings to the Royal Society in London—

I have seen so excessively great a quantity of living animalcules that I am much astonished by it. I can say without exaggeration that in a bit of matter no longer than a grain of sand more than fifty thousand animalcules were present, whose shape I can compare with nought better than with our river eel. These animalcules move about with uncommon vigor and in some places clustered so thickly together that they formed a single dark mass. After a short time they separated. In fine, these animals astonished my eye more than aught I had seen before (432).

But perhaps Leeuwenhoek and his student were not the first men to gaze upon sperm. There is a suggestion that Roger Bacon may have been so lucky in the fourteenth-century (433). Of course at the end of the seventeenth-century there was still a mystery as to what sperm actually were. Some thought them to be parasites in the seminal fluid—and saliva and urine and other bodily secretions were quickly examined in the search for more sperm. Others thought them coagulating agents.

662. Sperm—first realized to be a fertilizing agent
It was not realized that sperm were concerned in the process of fertilization until the nineteenth century. Various names are associated with the discovery—Prevost and Dumas (1824), Peltier (1835), and Dujardin (1837).

663. Sperm/egg nuclei—first known to contribute chromosomes to body cells
The realization that the male and female sex cells each

contribute half the chromosomes to the other body cells did not dawn until 1883 when Van Beneden grasped the fact that fertilization results in the zygote receiving an equal number of chromosomes from each parent. This new insight laid the basis for the Chromosome theory of inheritance.

664. Sperm (human)—first to survive experimental freezing

Sperm, both animal and human, have been frozen to aid storage for purposes of artificial insemination. Human sperm was first successfully frozen and unfrozen (from a temperature of around −17 degrees centigrade) by Mantegazza in 1866. He himself was quick to see the consequences for artificial insemination. The next serious work in this area was not attempted until 1938 (Jahnel).

665. "Ovary"—word first coined

Ovaries were at first called "female testicles," which was bulky as well as being rather male chauvinist! Ovaries were so called in 1662, when van Horne decided that female testicles deserved a name of their own.

666. Ovum (mammalian)—first discovered

Von Baer first discovered the ova in dogs in 1827 by working backwards from 24-day-old embryos. He opened an ovarian follicle and found a yellowish white speck floating in the follicular fluid. Under the microscope he discerned an "ovule," similar to the ones already found in the Fallopian tubes.

667. Ova (human)—first cultured in test-tube

Research is being conducted into "test-tube" fertilization. If successful there could be significant ramifications for family planning and in enabling seemingly infertile women to have children. In 1966 Dr. Robert Edwards of Cambridge University (England) showed for the first time how eggs extracted from human ovaries (removed for therapeutic reasons) could be cultured in a test tube so that large numbers developed into ripe eggs (434).

668. Fertilization (external) of human eggs—first accomplished
Another area receiving attention is the introduction of sperm to ripe human eggs in artificial circumstances to achieve actual *in vitro* fertilization. A *New Scientist* article (435) discussed two papers in *Nature*. The first was a report by Y. Toyoda of efforts by "possibly the most patient of all workers in the field, Dr. M. C. Chang" of the Worcester Foundation of Experimental Biology, Massachusetts. After 844 attempts to fertilize rat eggs outside the body of the female (all unsuccessful) the researchers tried dissolving the tough outer membrane of the egg with an enzyme, after which sperm taken direct from the male tract were able to penetrate the egg and begin the process of activation following successful fertilization. The success was qualified, however, since without the external membrane the eggs soon died. In the second *Nature* paper, a description is given of the successful fertilization on a watch-glass in a "simple chemically defined medium" of mice eggs. Some workers in the same laboratory, at the Department of Veterinary Physiology at the University of Sydney, succeeded in developing eggs *in vitro* up to the stage at which they were ready for implantation—previously no one had succeeded in passing a mysterious barrier at the four-cell stage. In *Nature* (14/2/68), Cambridge scientists reported the successful fertilization of human eggs in artificial laboratory conditions. The vatican termed the experiments "immoral acts and absolutely illicit."

669. Fertilization (external) of human eggs—most controversial experimenter
One of the most active and controversial figures in the field of "test tube" fertilization is Dr. Landrum B. Shettles, a fellow of the American College of Obstetricians and Gynecologists. In one series of experiments he managed to keep a fertilized human egg alive for a period of six days, longer than any similar time previously achieved. The religious press immediately claimed that the scientist was creating a "monster." When Shettles attended the International Fertility Conference in Italy in 1954 the Pope took

the opportunity to condemn those who "take the Lord's work into their own hands."

670. Pregnancy tests—first animals to be used

The urine of pregnant women will cause certain species of animals to ovulate. This circumstance has enabled doctors to give an early diagnosis of human pregnancy. The first creature to be used in the test for human pregnancy is the *Dactylethra*, the African clawed frogs. (The small male clawed frog is at some disadvantage when trying to copulate with his massive spouse—so he spins her around several times until she loses consciousness, whereupon he rapes her!)

671. Uterus (prolapse)—first medical account

There is a recommended treatment in Hippocrates for prolapse. First he describes the condition—"When the uterus bears down on the ischium if it does not withdraw itself promptly and return to its proper place it starts to become dry; its entrance ... closes. With this change of position and subsequent closure it becomes hard, contracted and misshapen. The normal route for the menstrual flows is obstructed and they are rerouted to the breasts upon which they lie heavily." Hippocrates (in Book 2) then goes on to describe how the condition can lead to great obesity, to cancer of the breast, to mental derangement and ultimately death. The Greeks adopted fumigation of the uterus to cure the condition, employing garlic, seal oil, fennel root, etc. And efforts were made to open the cervix using pine dilators—"as smooth and round as possible, and without splinters." There is no way of estimating the success of the physicians of antiquity.

672. Vagina (artificial)—first follow-up study

There are at least two broad classes of artificial vaginas—those used in the sex-aid sense as a masturbatory device; and those artificially constructed in women without a vaginal tract for congenital, disease, or other reasons. Artificial vaginas have been built into women using a variety of surgical techniques; and the methods have been improved and developed over the decades. The first detailed follow-up study after the artificial creation of a vagina was carried out by William Masters and Virginia Johnson. According to one estimate there are around 20,000 women in the United States alone who were born without a vagina. Masters and Johnson made use of the perineal dilator method of gradually "stretching" a vagina into the pubic area where previously there was no orifice. The Brechers give details of such treatment and the follow-up work (436).

673. Sexual physiology—most thorough book in early twentieth-century

This is undoubtedly F. H. A. Marshall's *Physiology of Reproduction*, a multi-volume classic edited by A. S. Parkes. When the book first appeared in 1910 it was an event in the history of biological literature: the book contained virtually everything known at that time about the physiological processes of reproduction. By the time the book had gone into several new editions Marshall realized that the project was beyond the scope of a single author; and so a number of British experts were asked to contribute. With each new edition the book grew in size. As some indication of the scope of the work it can be pointed out that a single part (Part 1) of Volume One runs to nearly seven hundred large pages with immensely detailed sections on the breeding season, the morphology of the reproductive tract, the oesrous cycle, etc. In this one part alone the bibliography runs to fourteen close pages.

674. Sex organs (female)—most famous seventeenth-century study

It has often been immensely difficult to publish serious sexological works. Even if a publisher could be found there has often been a problem with legal forms of censorship, pressure groups and the like. Sometimes authors, conscious of the fuss that would follow publication, have refused to give permission for research to be printed; on other occasions they have apologized for the nature of their sexological studies. This latter course was adopted by R. de Graef in the Preface to his famous treatise on the sex organs of women, *De Mulierum Organis Generatione*

Inservientibus, dedicated to Cosmo III de Medici in 1672. A century later, Linnaeus in his great *The System of Nature* dismissed as "abominable" the exact study of the female genitals.

675. Sex organs (human)—first scientific depiction

The human sex organs have been drawn throughout all human history, but mostly for magical, religious or artistic purposes. The effort to depict the sex organs—and the coital act—in a strictly *scientific* spirit is relatively recent in origin. Probably the first effort to show the human sex organs actually engaged in coitus was made by Leonardo da Vinci. He included in his drawing the anatomical peculiarity of a tubal connection between breast and womb, as was believed to exist at the time. The real connection between the two has only recently been understood and relates to the hormone oxytocin released by the brain in response to stimulation of the breast or the vagina.

676. Sex organs—most famous nineteenth-century work

In 1857 William Acton published *The Functions and Disorders of the Reproductive Organs, in Childhood, Youth, Adult Age, and Advanced Life, Considered in their Physiological, Social, and Moral Relations.* Within a year a second edition was called for; and as late as 1894 an eighth edition appeared in Philadelphia. The book was popular, influential, and—in the words of Steven Marcus (437)—"misleading and inaccurate". The most remarkable thing about the book, particularly in view of its startlingly comprehensive title, is that it says nothing (!) about the *female* genital organs: there are two extremely short passages and nothing more. In short we may remark that the book, detailed and thorough though it purports to be, is little more than a vehicle for hysterical prudery, a true representative of the worst of Victorian hypocrisy and cant.

677. Sex organs (external)—first account of embryological development

The Greeks and many later observers were certainly interested in embryological matters but we have no accounts before the nineteenth-century of the embryological growth of the external genitalia. Perhaps the first truly scientific account is that of Tiedemann.

678. Penis and clitoris (embryological)—first described

The development of the external genitalia in the embryo was first described in 1813 (see superlative 677). The penis and the clitoris as featuring in the male and female embryos were first described by Meckel a few years later.

679. Sex (plants)—first scientifically denied

Natural philosophers throughout history have often been unhappy about sex. Infected by puritan theology and perverted loathing of carnal relations they have often struggled to deny that sex is as compulsive in the natural world outside human intercourse as it is for men and women. Thus animals were sometimes said to copulate "innocently", without passion or lust; Original Sin was a human prerogative. On occasions the scientists deny that certain animals were bisexual, when in fact the male and female were well defined if the scientists cared to look. On many occasions, and more understandably, it was denied that plants had sex. Thus one of the great natural philosophers of the Middle Ages, Albertus Magnus, wrote seven books on plants and twenty-six on animals; yet he denied that there were sexes in plants. (He also proposed that weasels are fertilized through the ear and give birth through the mouth!) (438).

680. Sex (plants)—first established

In 1695 Rudolf Jacob Camerarius advanced the shocking notion that the stamens of flowers corresponded to the male genital organs of animals, and that the pistil was the female organ. Forty years later, Linnaeus produced a thesis on the *Nuptials of Flowers* in which he noted that "in the springtime when the bright sun rises to the zenith, the plants also are gripped by love:" Linnaeus had not the slightest idea how sex in plants worked. In 1787 Christian Konrad Sprengel, the assistant headmaster in a school in Spandau, published an essay called *The Newly Revealed*

Mystery of Nature in the Structure and Fertilization of Flowers. For the first time the illusion that flowers were free of sex was destroyed. Sprengel dared to compare the blossoms of plants with the sex organs of animals. He also described how plant sexual intercourse took place, by means of insect and wind intermediaries. Uproar followed: he was dismissed from his teaching post and his book was banned! Some broad-minded citizens of Spandau allowed Sprengel to earn a living by giving tutorial instruction to their children.

681. Inheritance of sex—first demonstrated

The differentiation of organisms according to sex is primarily a characteristic of animals, but the inheritance of sex was first demonstrated in a plant. In 1907 Correns provided evidence that in the white bryony, *Bryonia dioica*, the sex of the plant is determined by the pollen grains. These, he discovered, were of two classes, male-producing and female-producing, while in this particular respect the eggs were all the same. It was also shown that sex in mosses and liverworts is genetically determined.

682. Cotyledon—first discovered

In 1759 Kaspar Friedrich Wolff, son of a Berlin tailor, presented a dissertation entitled *Theoria generationis* in which he declared that all previous embryologists had been proceeding from false premises, in particular from the premise of a minute preformed organism. He stated that the unfertilized chicken egg, for instance, contained no preformed organism, nor was there any such thing in the freshly fertilized egg. All he had found was a small round disk, a *cotyledon*, from which the organs and various other parts of the body gradually developed. The concept of the cotyledon, or "seed leaf," later became an established part of the vocabulary of biology.

683. Sex in animal kingdom—first treatise

Much in science can be traced to the ancient Greeks. With Euclid and speculative philosophy the Greeks have often been depicted as theoretical, and unsuited to the observational needs of empirical science. This is partly a matter of interpretation. In Aristotle there was observational commitment as well as metaphysics, cataloguing of facts as well as imaginative cogitation. The impact of Aristotle in biology, as in logic and metaphysics, led in later times to a freezing of new enquiry. Aristotle was seen as the fount of all wisdom: to argue against the followers of Aristotle was to commit heresy. Aristotle wrote about sex in animals—and was probably the first natural philosopher in history to do so—and he also preserved scientific myths. In, for instance, his *History of Animals* there is both observational biology and rank superstition. In particular he believed in the theory of spontaneous generation, a notion that survived for centuries before being overthrown.

684. Sex in animal kingdom—most famous nineteenth-century book

Towards the end of the nineteenth-century a writer on popular science, Wilhelm Bölsche published a three-volume chronicle of *Love Life in Nature*. This "Kaleidoscope of Love" covered all that was known of reproduction and sexuality in nature. It ran from one-celled animals to man, discussing everything from the origins of life to the absurdity of the human sex act, from the bewitchment of love to the venereal diseases (these latter called "love's dance of death").

685. Sexual forms—first established for various species

We now know that polyps, worms, and many other animals can exist in two entirely different sexual forms: an asexual generation which propagates by budding, and a sexual generation which begets offspring only after fertilization. In the early nineteenth-century it was not known, for instance, that jellyfish were the sexual forms of polyps, that miracidia and redia were the asexual generation of the liver fluke. Consequently Chamisso was ridiculed when, in 1819, he published a treatise on alternation of generations. His efforts were ignored until 1842, when the Danish zoologist Johann Japetus Steenstrup took up the thesis and proved that Chamisso had been right: unfortu-

nately by that time the 1819 pioneer had been dead for
four years!

686. Courtship (mammals)—first scientific description

The naturalist Steller wrote in 1753 of the sea-cow—"In
the spring they mate like human beings, particularly
towards evening when the sea is calm. Before they come
together many amorous preludes take place. The female,
constantly followed by the male, swims leisurely to and fro
eluding him with many gyrations and meanderings, until
impatient of further delay, she turns on her back as if exhausted and coerced, whereupon the male, rushing vio-
lently upon her, pays the tribute of passion, and both give
themselves over in mutual embrace."

687. Sex chromosomes (insects)—first discovered

When examining the spermatozoa of an obscure species of
insect, *Pyrrhocoris apterus*—one of the "true bugs"—in
1891, the German naturalist named Henking noted a com-
plicating detail. About half of these insect sperm cells contained eleven chromosomes; the others contained a
twelfth, "accessory" chromosome. After Henking's discovery chromosome counts were quickly made of the sperm
cells of other species, including some mammals. And in
1902, in a paper entitled "The Accessory Chromosome—
Sex Determinant?" an American investigator announced a
solution to the central mystery. The extra chromosome
carried the qualities "which belong to the male
organism" (438).

688. Sex chromatin—first discovered

The term "sex chromatin" generally denotes a body in the
nuclei of cells which shows a special relationship to the sex
of the organism from which the cell originated. The behavior of sex chromatin has been studied for both man
and other animals, and such work is seen as one of the
growing points in cytogenetics. One reason is practical, for
the sex-chromatin test helps in diagnosis of patients with
sex chromosome abnormalities. The discovery of sex chromatin is usually dated in 1949, when Barr and Bertram in

London, Ontario, described a morphological distinction between neurons of male and female cats.

689. Sex of offspring (animal)—first controlled

Sex is determined at conception by the sperm. Around 50 per cent of all spermatozoa contain a "female-determining" X sex chromosome while the rest have a slightly smaller "male" Y sex chromosome. When they meet the X sex chromosome of the female egg the result is either XX (a girl) or XY (a boy). One way to determine the sex of offspring would therefore be to separate out the two types of sperm. This has not yet been achieved with predictable success. To date, the only reliable sex choice method that has been accomplished in mammals relates to embryos, not to sperm. In April 1968 Gardner and Edwards announced (440) that for the first time ever they had successfully controlled the sex of a mammal, in their case of rabbit offspring. They flushed out embryos from female rabbits, used a sex-chromatin test to ascertain the sex of the embryos, and then replanted them—this time with known sex—into female rabbits. Of those embryos that developed the sex predictions were correct.

690. Spontaneous generation—first disproved

Naturalists and zoologists, from Aristotle to Buffon, believed in the theory of spontaneous generation, the idea that life-forms could simply emerge from appropriate material—the earth, slime, excrement, etc. One of the first scientists to oppose this notion was René Antoine Ferchault de Réaumur. He repeated an earlier experiment by Needham who had tried to demonstrate that infusoria would spring forth in substances boiled to destroy all life within. Réaumur in effect showed that the life-forms developing within the boiled meat, plants and other organic substances came in fact from the air, growing and multiplying when they found congenial conditions. Abbé Lazzaro Spallanzani repeated the Réaumur experiment in sterile conditions and finally disproved the idea of spontaneous creation.

691. Reproductive method as classification—first established
The means whereby animal species reproduce are so
varied that the possibility of classifying species in terms of
such methods has occurred to many naturalists. (The sex
organs of insects are so various in their morphologies that
they could be used for a similar purpose.) In the
eighteenth century Linnaeus introduced the idea of classifying animals by their means of reproduction—and the
notion was taken up by the first great zoologists and pale-
ontologists of France (such men as Cuvier, Lamarck,
Geoffroy de Saint-Hilaire and Ducrotay de Blainville). In
particular, mammals were divided up according to the
structure of the internal and external organs of embryonic
development and the connection between mother and infant. Thus the three great mammalian groups were seen to
be the monotremes, marsupials, and placental animals, a
division retained by the evolutionists of Darwin's time and
by modern biologists. The monotremes still reproduce in
the manner of reptiles, the marsupials bear undeveloped
larvae, and the placental mammals are equipped to bear
children that are replicas of their parents in form, mobility
and sense functioning.

692. Reproduction (tapeworm)—first discovered
The reproductive methods of most of the lower animals
have only been understood following extensive observation
and experiment. For example, until half way through the
nineteenth century the reproductive cycle of tapeworms
was not understood. In 1851 the German doctor named
Friedrich Küchenmeister addressed naturalists in Gotha on
the subject of tapeworms. He claimed to have discovered
the route by which fertilized eggs, which entered sewage
systems along with the excrement of infected human
beings, became tapeworms in human intestines. Küchenmeister asserted that formations in the muscle tissue of
certain domestic animals, usually called cysticerci, were in
fact the encapsulated larvae of tapeworms. Tapeworm
eggs reached meadows and gardens when these were fertilized with "night soil", whereupon the eggs would be
taken in, first by plant-eating animals (mice, rabbits, pigs
and cattle) and then by meat-eating animals (cat, dog,

man). Finding itself in the appropriate environment the tapeworm head crawls out of the cyst, enters the small intestines, and develops into a tapeworm (441).

693. Reproduction (squid)—first discovered

Aristotle observed reproduction in squids with some accuracy. In particular he took note of the male's copulatory tentacle which, he remarked, was inserted in the breathing funnel of the female. But there was long-lasting confusion about what happened in a deviant type of squid, *Argonauta argo*. This creature's mantle cavity was often found to be alive with highly active worm-shaped animals—Aristotle thought them to be parasitic worms and for two thousand years all subsequent naturalists (from Pliny to Cuvier) accepted this view. Cuvier is even credited with assigning a scientific name to this supposed parasite: *Hectocotylus*. Around the middle of the nineteenth-century the truth was discovered: during an expedition in 1853 the naturalist Johannes Müller concluded that hectocotylus must be the copulating tentacle of the argonaut male.

694. Reproduction (lamprey)—first discovered

The lamprey, a primitive form of fish, enjoys a sophisticated form of sexual reproduction, discovered in 1646 by an Alsatian fisherman named Leonhard Baldner, an "untrained" student of fish life in the waters of the Upper Rhine. He set forth many of his observations in a book entitled, *Right Natural Description and Depiction of the Water Birds, Fishes, Four-footed Beasts, Insects, and Vermin which Are to Be Found in the Waters near Strasbourg.* Of the smallest European lamprey he wrote— "These lampreys or lamprons have their spawn in March and April. They hang close together to the stones; where the water runs fast they make deep pits in which the pair put their bellies together to perform their lust, which else I have seen of no other fish but the lampreys, since they spawn in water which is not deep, so that it can be easily seen" (442).

695. Reproduction (hydra)—first discovered

In the eighteenth-century Abraham Trembley enjoyed himself messing about with fresh-water polyps. He beheaded them, cut them up, etc., etc. Surprisingly each piece not only survived but grew into a whole animal. He even induced two polyps to grow together to form a sort of monster. One idea was to turn a polyp inside-out over a hog bristle. Trembley remarked, "It is nothing to a polyp to be impaled on a spit." About fifteen years after Trembley's original discovery of the reproductive powers of the polyp (or hydra) the German naturalist August Roesel von Rosenhof pulped up a number of polyps of a larger type, the more to understand their reproductive capacities. In 1753 he began publishing a monthly magazine of biology, *Allmonatliche Insecten-Belustigungen* (Monthly Insect Diversions), in which many of his findings were recorded (443).

696. Reproduction (clam worm)—first discovered

Clam worms usually crawl through the ooze on the ocean bed and don't do much else. But when they start feeling sexy they change into swimming worms so different in appearance that for a long time they were thought to be an entirely different species. In 1860 a Göttingen naturalist recognized that these *heteronereids* were sexual forms of the ooze-dwelling nereids. The males even dance about— often at new moon and high tide—during which they emit sperm; and hormones released from the clouds of sperm stimulate the females to lay eggs.

697. Reproduction by "cloning"—first accomplished

In June 1966 a team of Oxford biologists announced that they had grown seven frogs from the intestine cells of tadpoles, i.e., they had achieved what is commonplace in the garden, produced a new organism from a cutting of a single parent. With animals the process is generally called "cloning". The biologists took a frog's egg, removed its gene-bearing nucleus, and replaced it with the nucleus from a body cell of a tadpole. They then planted the new nucleus plus egg in a female frog and induced the whole system to start the egg developing. The result was a frog, an identical twin of its single parent. It has been confidently asserted that the "cloning" of human beings will soon be technically feasible.

698. Virgin birth (vertebrate)—first scientifically documented

Parthenogenesis or virgin birth—reproduction via unfertilized eggs—in commonplace among plants and invertebrates; for example, it is a major feature of reproduction in aphids, bees, ants, and termites. It also occurs among vertebrates. The first scientifically documented report on vertebrate parthenogenesis dates to 1932, when a small fish, *Poeciliops formosa* (a molly from Texas), was observed to reproduce without the presence of any males (444). It was shown that P. formosa was in fact initially the hybrid progeny of P. latipinna and P. schenops.

699. Virgin birth—first achieved in sea-urchins

In 1899 the French (later American) Jacques Loeb declared—"when I announced the successful chemical fertilization of sea-urchins the almost unanimous opinion was that I had been the victim of an illusion, and at first I myself was afraid that I had been mistaken." The *Annales des Sciences Naturelles* was skeptical, and talked of "chemical citizens, the sons of Madame Sea-Urchin and Monsieur Chloride of Magnesium." Then Eugène Bataillon managed to do the same thing with a frog: he produced tadpoles by treating frog's eggs with chemicals. The fact that the egg has only half the number of chromosomes inhibits such a method of reproduction in the higher life-forms. But clearly the method would be relevant to reproduction by cloning (445).

700. Virgin birth (vertebrate)—key experimental animal

The Caucasian lizard is a key experimental animal in the field of naturally occurring parthenogenetic vertebrates (see superlative 442). Reference has been made to the work, during the 1950s, of Russian herpetologists working with Soviet zoologist J. Darevsky (446). They collected more than five thousand specimens of *Lacerta saxicola* from certain areas of the Caucasus—and failed to find any males! It was also evident that more than one species was involved. Difficulties in classifying parthenogenetic species are far from having been overcome.

701. Sex experiments (animal)—creature most used

The fruit fly *Drosophilia* (also called the vinegar fly or pomace fly) had been used more than any other animal in sex experiments and research into various aspects of genetics. It was first established as a laboratory animal in America during the first decade of the twentieth century. It proved an ideal subject for breeding experiments since it reproduces prolifically in milk bottles and 25 generations can be obtained within a year. The chromosomes have been observed directly and a wealth of genetic information has been obtained by a variety of experimental procedures. *Drosophilia* has made a fundamental contribution to the science of cytogenetics in general and to the genetics of sex determination in particular.

702. Oestrus in sheep—most detailed study to correlate with time of day

A flock of forty Cheviot (North Country) ewes were studied over a seven-week Autumn period. Once an animal had mated she was removed from the flock. It was observed how the ram searched the paddock for animals coming into oestrus, which was observed to begin in 56 cases that were not uniform through the day. A "bimodal" situation was noted, i.e. equal numbers of ewes came into oestrus during the period 04.00 to 11.00 h and during the period 13.00 to 22.00 h. Later in the breeding season the onset of oestrus was found to be uniform through the 24-hour period.

703. Menstrual cycle (orang)—first reliably recorded

The first record of the menstrual cycle and pregnancy in the orang was given by Aulmann in 1932 (447). The animal was about 9½ years old when studied but had previously menstruated for an unspecified period of time. Four complete cycles were observed, lasting 32, 32, 32, and 31 days. No details are given about the amount or duration of the bleeding, or about any aspects of the appearance of the genital region.

704. Nymphomania—first induced in cattle

This frightening condition was first induced in cattle by the careful administering of chemicals. Pellet implantation resulted in continuous oestrogen administration with resulting changes in the sexual enthusiasm and receptivity of cattle.

705. Sex ration in eels—first related to temperature

Grassi in 1919 studied the migrating eel and discovered that a low sex ration existed in the higher reaches of the river, and a high sex ration existed in the estuarine parts. Temperature and salinity were given as the causes of this interesting phenomenon. (In 1929 E. Witschi found a similar relationship between temperature and sex: he exposed frog larva to high temperature and converted females into males).

706. Sex change in embryo—first accomplished in cow

The masculinizing of a genetic female embryo in the cow when twinned with a male was first noted in 1917, though the phenomenon of the modified female known as the freemartin was known long before that in the non-scientific literature. The freemartin is a sterile intersex exhibiting vas deferens, seminal vesicles, and ovaries. Rudimentary oviducts and uteri are also present. The situation arises when the testes of the male twin secrete androgens into the common blood supply (448).

707. Oviducts—first accurately described

Fallopius was the first observer accurately to describe the human oviducts—which is why they became known as the Fallopian tube. He also gave the first precise description of the clitoris and the skeletal system of the foetus. It has also been suggested that he was the first to use the word "placenta". He was also interested in the digestive tract, the ear and the nervous system. In addition he described the invention of a simple linen condom as a guard against venereal infection.

708. Egg grafting (animals)—first attempt
The first to "graft eggs" was made by the French physiologist Paul Bert, a pioneer in various forms of animal grafting. He wrote in 1863—"To my learned master, M. Gratiolet I owe the idea of an experiment which in execution presents the greatest difficulties. The problem is to take from the Fallopian tubes or the uterine cornua of mammals fertilized ova, but nothing else and to transfer them into the peritoneum of another animal in order to see if the eggs will develop ..." He then speculates on whether eggs would develop in the bodies of animals of a different but close-related species. He concludes unhappily—"Unfortunately I have not succeeded in grafting eggs.

709. Egg laying (platypus)—first established
For the bulk of the nineteenth-century scientists had struggled to understand the reproductive methods of the monotremes. Milk glands were found in female platypuses but no nipples. Hence the newborn young could not suckle in the usual mammalian fashion. Australian observers maintained that platypuses and *echnidas* laid eggs, but many zoologists were convinced that montreme offspring must be born alive, possibly in a primitive embryonic state. The speculations were ended in August 1884 when two scientists, the Australian W. H. Caldwell and the German Wilhelm Haacke, each established independently that both platypuses and echnidas laid eggs. Monotreme eggs are peculiar in that they contain little food, so that the growing embryo has to be nourished through the shell by secretions from the mother's womb (449).

710. Eggs (fertilized)—first transferred from one rabbit to another
Walter Heape of Cambridge University wrote—"On the 27th April, 1890, two ova were obtained from an Angora doe rabbit which had been fertilized by an Angora buck

32 hours previously . . . These ova were immediately transferred into the upper end of the Fallopian tube of a Belgian hare doe rabbit which had been fertilized three hours before by a buck of the same breed as herself . . . In due course this Belgian hare doe gave birth to six young—four of these resembled herself and her mate, while two of them were undoubted Angoras." The remarkable experiment was not repeated successfully until well into the twentieth century. Egg transfer has now been carried out successfully in sheep, goats, pigs, cows, mice, rats, rabbits, hamsters, and at least one species of marsupial.

711. Sterilization (camels)—first scientifically recorded
There is a text in Aristotle that has been taken to refer to the insertion of an intrauterine device in a camel. At least one modern author has argued, however, that the text refers to an actual removal of the ovaries of the female beast in question.

712. Erection—first experimentally induced
In 1863 Eckhard first demonstrated that stimulation of the sacral nerves produced penile erection; he called the nerves the *nervi erigentes*. Semans and Langsworthy (1938) demonstrated in the cat that stimulation of the sacral and hypogastric nerves would result in a sexual response in the male organ. Dilation of the penile arteries and erection of the penis was produced by stimulation of the first, second, and third sacral nerves. Stimulation of other appropriate regions ultimately resulted in ejaculation of semen. Finally, stimulation of the sympathetic nerves produced constriction of the penile arteries with subsidence of the erection. In 1957 Hotchkiss summarized the peripheral mechanisms in the male.

713. Sperm capacitation—first demonstrated for rabbit, etc.
One of the intriguing discoveries about spermatozoa was their need to undergo a number of physiological changes (termed "capacitation") before they can fertilize the egg, i.e. penetrate the *zona pellucida*. It was only as late as the

nineteen-fifties that this phenomenon was demonstrated for rabbits and other creatures (450). Various researchers established the phenomenon of capacitation for various species—Noyes showed it in the rat (1953), Braden and Austin in the mouse (1954), Chang and Scheaffer in the hamster (1957), Mattner in the sheep (1963), Chang and Yanagimachi in the ferret (1963), etc. (451).

714. Fertilization process—first observed in detail

As early as 1843 Barry claimed to have observed spermatozoa inside the egg (452). The first detailed work on fertilization, however, was done years after this. In 1875 Oskar Hertwig, a pupil of Ernst Haeckel, decided to study the sex cells of sea-urchins to trace the actual events of fertilization. He placed a sea-urchin egg under the microscope, added seminal fluid, and watched the sperm swarming around the egg. He saw one of the sperm actually penetrate the egg. Then the egg formed a firm shell, a *fertilization membrane,* which prevented the entrance of additional spermatozoa. A whole range of subsequent processes were observed (453).

715. Fertilization (external)—first discovered

Spallanzani took one hundred and sixty-five female frogs in the act of copulation, cut them open, removed the eggs which had remained in their bodies, and put the eggs in water. All of them quickly rotted; showing they could hardly have been fertilized inside the frog. But those eggs which had already left the female's body during the act of copulation developed normally into tadpoles. Spallanzani experimented carefully to determine whether the eggs were fertilized at the moment of emission or some time afterwards. In such a way he demonstrated the phenomenon of "external" fertilization, a process widespread in the animal kingdom from one species to another. (In an ingenious and much-quoted experiment Spallanzani dressed some male frogs in *little breeches of oilskin,* left others undressed, and placed all the males with females ready for copulation. Hardly surprisingly the eggs emitted in copulation with a trousered male remained sterile: "The eggs are never fruitful, for want of having been bedewed with semen, which sometimes may be seen in the breeches in the form of drops.")

716. Ovum transportation—first in oviduct of a different species
In 1962 two South African Dorper ewes gave birth to two healthy Border Leicester lambs. The eggs were flown to South Africa in the oviduct of a living rabbit. In such an environment the eggs would survive for up to eight days (454).

717. Female mounting behavior (monkeys)—first recorded
A wide variety of animal species are capable of homosexual behavior, and this is often instanced by such activity as females mounting other females. In 1914 such behavior was described for adult female monkeys. They also displayed the lip-smacking and pelvic movements that normally characterize heterosexual coitus. The animals studied were in an outdoor compound but were not confined. Carpenter found in 1942 that such behavior took place in natural conditions, the activity "resembled in many respects a male-female consort relationship." It was pointed out that the mounted creature was likely to be in oestrus. Similar findings have been recorded by such workers as Yerkes and Bingham.

718. Graafian follicles—first discovered
In 1672 Regnier de Graaf, a Delft physician, cut open a number of female rabbits and discovered organs similar to the ovaries of birds. When he looked at them under the microscope he saw they contained numerous small bladders—the rabbit's "eggs". One hundred and fifty years later it turned out that de Graaf had been mistaken. He had not found *eggs*, but the *Graafian follicles*, small sacs of fluid in the wall of the ovary in whose protection the eggs themselves grow. In spite of the error, de Graaf's main conclusion was correct—the female mammal has ovaries and produces eggs.

719. "Pheromone"—word first coined

For a long time it was a mystery how insects attracted mates for reproductive purposes. Eventually it was discovered that a principle means was through the exuding of powerful chemical attractants. In 1959 the word *pheromone* was coined to describe these chemical "messengers".

720. Pheromone (beetle)—first proposed

It was demonstrated in 1931 that a beetle (*Tenebrio molitor*) (455) released a sex attractant chemical from the tip of the abdomen to stimulate the male. The attractants were not at that time called "pheromones".

721. Pheromone (gypsy moth)—first isolated

A number of efforts have been made to isolate and synthesize the powerful sex attractants used by insects. Jacobson and his colleagues managed to do this for a principle chemical attractant exuded from the gypsy moth (456). They isolated, identified, and synthesized pheromone extract from the last two abdominal segments of one half million virgin female moths. This vast number of creatures yielded 20 mg of a colorless blue-fluorescing liquid soluble in petroleum ether, liable to solidify in the cold and to melt at room temperature. For the enthusiasts the isolated pheromone is identified as—

$$(+)\text{-}10\text{-acetoxy-1-hydroxy-}cis\text{-}7\text{-hexadecene}$$

722. Pheromone (Bombyx mori)—work first begun

In 1939 work was started on the pheromone of various species of moths. By 1959 the pheromone of Bombyx mori, a potent volatile material, was characterized by Butenandt et al (*Z. Naturforsch*, 14b, pp 283–284) as "Bombykol". It was found that a mere 10,000 molecules of the substance at the end of a glass rod were able to arouse around fifty per cent of a population of one hundred male moths.

723. Hormone—first discovered

Of all the hormones—sometimes depicted as "chemical messengers"—only a proportion are connected with evident sexual behavior. The first hormone was discovered by Ernest Starling at University College, London, on 16 January 1902 (457). He was investigating the origin of the pancreatic juices produced in the intestines to aid digestion. He introduced into the mucus membrane of the small intestine a few drops of hydrochloric acid, whereupon pancreatic juice started to come from the intestine. But how was the intestine stimulated to act under the influence of the acid? Without nerves, it was responding as if nerve impulses were being fed to it. Starling decided that there must be some sort of *chemical reflex*. With this insight he was on the road to establishing the concept of the chemical communicators, or *hormones* (from the Greek "hormnein", to set in motion or spur on).

724. Hormones—earliest medical usage

The Chinese of the Middle Ages (and possibly before) were well aware of the relevance of sex hormones to behavior. In 1378 Yeh Tzu-Chhi recorded information that was known to other medieval peoples—that sex hormones are responsible for the growth of facial hair in the male. In his book, *Tshoa Mu Tzu*, he says that "the outer glory of the seminal essence is manifested by the beard". Similarly, Wang Shih-Chên says in his Lei Yuan (1575) that "the beard pertains to the kidneys and testes". In the Pên Tshao Kang Mu (1596) by Li Shih-Chên there are accounts of numerous preparations of testicular tissue, taken from the pig, the dog or the sheep, and administered for male sexual debility, spermatorrhoea, hypogonadism, impotence, and "other conditions for which androgens would be prescribed today". In the West similar treatments began in the nineteenth-century. The use of placental tissue, a rich source of oestrogens, was mentioned by Chhen Tshang-Chhi in his Pên Tshao Shih I pharmacopoeia as far back as A.D. 725; and in the fourteenth-century Chu Chen-Hêng was encouraging its use in the treatment of various forms of debility, including sexual weakness (458).

725. Hormones (androgens)—first injected into developing reptiles

In experiments carried out in 1939 the eggs of *Chrysemys marginata bellii* were injected at the gestrulation stage with 250ug testos. propionate in 0.05 ml sesame oil. The eggs were incubated for sixty days, then the embryos were removed. The treated female gonads showed varying degrees of intersexuality, but the actual oviducts, penis, clitoris, etc., showed no effects.

726. Hormones—first related to testicular atrophy

In 1937 it was shown that testicular atrophy was related to inhibition of pituitary gland activity or to a decrease in the production of gonadotrophic hormones. Part of the significance of such discoveries lay in the possibility of developing various forms of hormonal therapy for a variety of illnesses.

727. Hormones—first shown as necessary to masculinization of cockerels

In 1849, Dr. A. A. Berthold of Göttingen described experiments in which he castrated six young cockerels in which the comb, wattles, and spurs had not yet developed. Two birds were allowed to become typical capons, unable to crow; in two other of the birds Berthold returned one of the removed testicles to a new site among the intestines, and the birds in question became typical cockerels—they grew combs, crowed, and showed typical interest in the hens. It was not until about 35 years ago that the first of the androgens was synthesized.

728. Hormones—first detailed study of influence on sexual development

Four researchers at the University of Kansas (Phoenix, Goy, Gerall, and Young) performed in 1959 a breakthrough series of experiments on guinea pigs. Earlier work had shown that when male hormones are administered to pregnant female guinea pigs, the female offspring are anatomically masculinized—born with penises and scrotums. And some experiments had shown that when female guinea pigs are spayed and latter given male hormones they display only a limited amount of malelike sexual behavior. Phoenix *et al* combined the two types of experiments. Pregnant female guinea pigs were given androgens. The ovaries of the masculinized female pups were removed after birth and at maturity androgens were administered. The females behaved much like males. Brecher has termed this the Phoenix-Goy-Young effect.

729. Testicular functions—first demonstrated
It was first shown by John Hunter in 1792 that the functional activity of such structures as the seminal vesicles and the prostate gland was dependent upon the behavior of the testis. Such findings laid the basis for modern endocrine system theory.

730. Sexual behavior (rats)—first identification of antiandrogen drugs
Neumann and his colleagues, working with rats in West Berlin in the early sixties, first discovered the antiandrogenic properties of cyproterone and cyproterone acetate (459). Not long afterwards, there began the clinical application of the new drugs on an experimental basis in selected clinics in West Germany and Switzerland. Sex offenders were chosen as patients. In the U.S. the new drugs were not released by the Food and Drug Administration (FDA) for behavioral research.

731. Masculinization (rats)—first achieved through testicular transplant
In 1936 it was shown that if a baby rat was treated with gonadal steriods, the female sexual rhythm is abolished and the adult rat fails to ovulate. The experiment involved grafting gonadal tissue in the anterior chamber of the eye.

732. Sex educator—first

Aristotle was the main sex educator in antiquity and remained as the provider of basic source material for many centuries afterwards. His philosophical and scientific literary output was so enormous that it has been speculated that many of the works attributed to Aristotle were in fact written by his pupils. Aristotelian treatises on animals, childbirth, etc. continued to circulate well into the nineteenth century, even when it could be shown that a fair portion of what was said in the name of Aristotle was little short of absurdity. At the same time a number of Greek insights were preserved over the centuries. Aristotle describes the persistence of sexual prowess to high ages and points out that acquired characteristics are not normally transmitted. Sometimes—as with the little edition of *The Masterpiece of Aristotle* from the early nineteenth-century—authors without any particular merit tried to borrow authority from The Master.

733. Sex educator—most controversial in modern Britain

Dr. Martin Cole, a lecturer in genetics at Aston University, Birmingham, first hit the headlines with his production of a sex education film, *Growing Up*, in 1971. The film, a candid outline of the sex act, male and female sexuality, etc., included a sequence showing a young woman masturbating. This innocent and commonplace activity, various prudes and bigots decided, should never be shown on film. *Growing Up* was discussed throughout the country, in various local authority meetings, and in the House of Commons. A Birmingham counselor made the recommendation that you should "Leave your sex organs with your bedroom slippers . . ." and another counselor remarked that soon human beings would be copulating on the streets—with dogs having to throw cold water on them! Dr. Cole—inevitably dubbed Sex King Cole in the popular press—possibly not the most tactful of men, added fuel to the controversy by urging that young girls be provided with the pill, by introducing the use of sexual surrogates into England (first used for therapy by Masters and Johnson), and by making a second film. Dr. Cole's efforts, a

breath of fresh air, are inevitably opposed with fury by
those nervous souls more concerned with the preservation
of taboo than the enlargement of the areas of human happiness.

734. Sex education pamphlet (modern)—least enlightened

There are so many reactionary, obscurantist, and repressive sex "education" pamphlets and handbooks about that
it is hard to select one for particular mention. I have decided on "Sex-Instruction in the Home" by the Rev. Aidan
Pickering, a Catholic Truth Society publication intended
"for private circulation ONLY . . . not to be displayed for
general sale." It really is an extraordinary little pamphlet.
Published in 1965 it preserves intact the traditional Roman Catholic teaching on matters of sexual immorality,
"purity," and the like. The facts of life are to be given
"only as a means to purity." The approach is contrasted
with modern educational methods—"You would be ap-
palled to see the anatomy charts of the sexual organs and
the growth of the unborn child published for use in schools
with boys and girls of twelve and thirteen." Pius XII is
quoted approvingly as urging that questions not be answered with evasions or untrue statements; yet on the following page, it is suggested that when children ask how a
baby begins, "they are quite satisfied if you tell them that
you can feel it begin."

735. Sex education pamphlet (modern)—most enlightened

The choice here was a simple one. It fell naturally upon
Sex Education, the Erroneous Zone by Maurice Hill and
Michael Lloyd-Jones, a National Truth Society Publication
(1970) with a foreword by Brigid Brophy. In part the
booklet is a survey of 42 other publications purporting to
provide sex education. It is shown conclusively that the
profiled books and pamphlets rest not only on bogus moralizing but on quite inexcusable factual error. *Sex Education* really is a pamphlet to read: one brief quote conveys
a little of the flavor—"Making love is normal, healthy and
pleasurable, and a means of communicating delight between human beings. Provided you are sincere with each

other, and safe, then if you feel like fucking, do it with a clear conscience; and we hope you enjoy it."

736. Sex education—first voluntary organization in Sweden
Scandinavia has long been associated with progressive ideas in sexual matters. Sometimes this is an inflated reputation; but there are some grounds for it. In 1933, for instance, the Norwegian-born Mrs. Elise Ottesen-Jensen founded a voluntary organization to spread sex education and called it *Riksförbundet för Sexuell Upplysning* (RFSU) (National League for Sex Education). The organization fought many battles against repressive legislation and against conservative public opinion. In particular it presented radical ideas in the field of sex education, birth control, and abortion. Mrs. Ottesen-Jensen had been a member of the World League for Sexual Reform.

737. Sex book collections—largest
There are sex books and sex books! There is all the difference between a piece of cheap nineteenth-century pornography and a detailed research publication in sexology. Prudes have often failed to make a distinction, and when a distinction has been attempted it has often been bogus. The biggest sex book collections in the world contain *all* types of sexual literature—from the simply titillating to the driest scholarly tome. The leading sex institutes—associated with the names of Bloch, Hirschfeld, etc.—all had associated libraries. The Kinsey Institute (more properly The Institute for Sex Research) has around 20,000 books of all sorts, as does the British Museum. According to one writer (460), the Vatican Library tops them all with something like 25,000 volumes.

738. Sex books—longest titled
We have already met a number of book titles that seem needlessly lengthy. The longest I have come across is the one by Schurig (it is apparently typical of his book titles in general) (461)—

MULIEBRIA Historico-Medica, hoc est Partium Genitalium Muliebrium Consideratio Physico-Medico-Foren-

sis, qua Pudendi Muliebris Partes tam externae, quam internae, scilicet Uterus cum Ipsi Annexis Ovariis et Tubis Fallopianis, nec non Varia de Clitoride et Tribadismo de Hymen et Nymphotomania seu Feminarum Circumsisione et Castratione selectis et curiosis observationibus traduntur. A. D. Martino Schurigio, Physico Dresdensi . . . MDCCXXIX.

After which you may feel there is little point in reading the book!

739. Sex book (historical)—most unreliable

All historical sex books are unreliable for one reason or another. The vast bulk of them are full of superstition, special pleading, sterile moralizing, or simple ignorance. Despite all this, perhaps Giovanni Sinibaldi wins with his *Geneanthropeia.* In the words of Alex Comfort (462)— "This extraordinary treatise (it is one of the most beautiful of medical books, typographically) is the fount and origin of very nearly all the major nonsense about reproduction, inheritance and sexual matters generally which was to haunt counseling literature to the present day." The book first appeared in 1642 in Rome; by 1658 it had reached England in a popular version entitled *Rare Verities, the Cabinet of Venus Unlock'd . . . Printed for P. Briggs at the Dolphin in St. Pauls Church-yard.* It would be impossible to list the absurdities written up by Mr. Sinibaldi (or Mr. Briggs). One or two examples will have to suffice. He reckons that excessive venery is accompanied by various symptoms (such as red nose, baldness, constipation, and gout), that ravished virgins are "never with child," that coital positions other than "missionary" (woman underneath and on her back) are harmful, that a little forehead denotes "an unbridled appetite in lust," etc., etc. There is also some dangerous advice on "How to shorten the Yard, being too long" and "How to enlarge the pudenda."

740. Sex book (modern)—most unreliable

Here too there are a number of candidates, often written by prudes or pious souls with several axes to grind. Perhaps David Reuben's *Everything You Always Wanted to Know About Sex* (Pan, 1971), not least (and not only) because of its appalling section about homosexuals. He suggests, for example, that male homosexuals wear women's clothes, adopt female mannerisms, have impersonal relationships, are primarily interested in the penis and not the person, and that when homosexuals are sado-masochistic they are "the cruellest people who walk the earth." All this, and a number of related remarks by Rueben, are untrue. There have been protests about the Reuben book in various countries. In Holland, for example, in January 1971, the Central Committee for the Dutch Society of Homosexuals (COC) lodged a complaint with the public prosecutor at Utrecht against the company publishing the book in Holland. In July 1972 the prosecutor agreed that the book was very shallow, insignificant, and bigoted, but thought nevertheless that it should not be banned. The publisher, however, in discussion with COC, came to agree that the book should not be distributed. In England the Campaign for Homosexual Equality managed to get a "correction sheet" inserted in the book in sympathetic retailers (I have quoted from the insert in my *Sex and Superstition*, Abelard-Schuman, 1973, pp. 179–80). Nor is the homosexual section the only weak part of the book. In a personal letter to me a leading sex aid and sex technique expert has commented how poor the sex technique section is; and Reuben's suggestion as to how women come to have two breasts—that some higher power decided it that way—is perhaps not the most persuasive from an evolutionary point of view!

Chapter Seven

CON(TRA)CEPTION . AND CASTRATION

741. Contraceptives—earliest

Fragments of Egyptian papyri, found at Kahun in El
Faiyūm in 1889, are the oldest medical literature that has
come down to us from antiquity. They reveal that upper
class Egyptian women of the Twelfth Dynasty, about 1850
B.C., used crocodile dung as a pessary, irrigated the vagina
with honey and natron (native sesquicarbonate of soda),
and inserted a gum-like substance in the vagina. Though
elephant's dung was later substituted for that of the crocodile, a similar prescription was used in various places
for some three thousand years. It is likely that the contraceptive measures had some effect. Honey and gum
would clog the motile sperm; and crocodile's dung, slightly
alkaline, would not be much different from a spermicide
carried in a sponge. The Ebers papyrus (about 1550 B.C.)
contained a prescription for the use of lint tampons mois-
tened with juice from fermented tips of acacia shrubs, i.e.
lactic acid (463).

742. Contraceptive methods—most ridiculous

Soranus (A.D. 98–138) was a Greek physician who studied
in Alexandria and later practiced in Rome under Hadrian.
He found enough time to write forty books or so. In his
Gynaecology he suggests—". . . that a woman ought, in
the moment during coitus when the man ejaculates his
sperm, to hold her breath, draw her body back a little
so that the semen cannot penetrate into the *os uteri*, then

289

immediately get up and sit down with bent knees, and in this position, provoke sneezes" (464). Thus, it is hoped, she will avoid conception.

743. Contraceptive methods—most bizarre

Many of the most bizarre contraceptive measures date from antiquity and involve magical practices and gross superstition. Many odd recommendations can also be found in modern times. William Godwin, for instance, in the early nineteenth-century, was not averse to a bit of infanticide (hardly contraceptive but at any rate a form of family planning). He remarked—"if the alternative were complete, I had rather such a child should perish in the first hour of its existence, than that a man should spend seventy years of life in a state of misery and vice" (465). In 1838 the idea of systematic infanticide was put forward in all seriousness by an author calling himself "Marcus." In this man's view all babies after the third born into a poor family should be killed during their first sleep by mixing a deadly gas with the air they were breathing. Less drastically, in 1806, Thomas Ewell suggested that couples only copulate in "vessels filled with carbonic acid or azotic gas." This on the grounds that "coition will always be unfruitful unless it be done in pure air." Weinhold recommended the infibulation of poor men, invalids, servants, apprentices, etc.—until they found themselves capable of supporting a wife and children. Noyes and others suggested *coitus reservatus* as an effective contraceptive measure (466).

744. Contraceptives—first mentioned in ancient Greece

The first Greek writer to mention contraceptive methods was, again, Aristotle. He and his wife collected eggs from many different animals, birds, insects, and spiders. As a method of birth control Aristotle recommended the use of oil to cover the cervix and coat the inside of the vagina. As with the Egyptian honey and gum we would expect the oil to reduce sperm motility and thus have a degree of success. If it blocked the entrance to the uterus there would be an effective barrier to the influx of sperm (467).

745. Contraceptive experts—foremost in ancient Greece
Three Greek experts—Dioscorides, Soranos, and Aetios—
come down to us as having been outstanding in the field of
contraception. The *Herbal* of Dioscorides, written in the
first or second century A.D., was a standard work until the
sixteenth-century; though it was not available in English
until 1655 when the first translation was made. Dios-
coroides thought that various substances could be taken orally to cause sterility. In common with various earlier
writers he also urges the use of various viscous substances.
The books of Soranos (see also superlative 468) were lost
for many years. Aetios of Amida described Soranos as a
great master. Soranos discussed contraceptives and aborti-
facients in detail and appears to have been the only author
of antiquity to have made a distinction between the two;
apart, that is, from Aetios who probably borrowed from
the earlier writer (468).

746. Contraception—briefest literary reference in ancient Greece
There is a brief but ambiguous line in Horace's *Odes*
which has been taken as a reference to contraception, but
which may equally refer to the heavy casualties of the
civil war—*vitio parentum rara inventus* (the evil of the
parents makes children scarce).

747. Intrauterine devices—first medically employed
We find details in Hippocrates, a few hundred years before Christ, of pessaries that were employed in a totally
intrauterine fashion. It is not known, however, that the usage was for contraceptive purposes.

748. Intrauterine devices—first employed in modern times
Astwell, half way through the nineteenth-century, remarks
(469) on the great number of pessaries in use. Thomas, in
1891, declared (470)—"The first to devise an intrauterine
support was Möller who in 1803 constructed a stem composed of an elastic catheter with a flexible wire stylet.
Amussat followed in 1826 with a smooth ivory stem, and
Velpeau, Simpson, Valleix, and Kiwisch about 1850 al-

most simultaneously revived the idea . . . the intrauterine or stem pessary unquestionably counteracts directly and immediately all flexions of the uterus" (471).

749. Intrauterine device—first described in modern times

The first intrauterine device, as it is known in current contraceptive usage, was described in 1909 and it was employed early in the twentieth-century, following the efforts of Grafenberg and others. The earliest devices were in the form of rings made of silver ("Grafenberg ring") or silkworm gut, placed in the uterus after dilation of the cervix. Adverse reports cause this method of contraception to fall into disrepute for a time.

750. Intrauterine device—least expected

In 1924 an American woman was involved in a car crash in France. X-rays were taken in the expectation of abdominal injuries. No damage was discovered but the X-ray gave "a very singular picture." In the middle of the pelvis was "a cylindrical metal object . . . bearing three linear appendages which ended in knobs." The observers first thought it must be a swallowed denture. But the woman informed them it was an IUD—"un pessaire anti-conceptionnel." She described its advantages and they concluded that—"Social attitudes are decidedly curious on the other side of the Atlantic: prohibition is a state institution but people drink their fill behind closed shutters; everyone prides himself on his virtue but the women wear pessaries against conception."

751. Intrauterine device—first usage to result in jail sentence

In April 1902 a physician in Magdeburg was given six months in jail for alleged negligence in fitting an "Obturator" (invented by Hollweg). The device was a vaginal disc on a hinge to allow menstrual flow to escape. It was estimated that the physician in question had fitted about 700 of the devices. By 1914 German physicians were demanding government control over the fitting of such devices. As early as 1891 Thomas had listed 26 "prominent writers" against intrauterine devices (472).

**752. Intrauterine device—highest incidence of uterine perfora-
tion on insertion**
We all know that *every* contraceptive means is supposed
to have a number of drawbacks. One disadvantage of the
intrauterine device is that uterine tissue may be damaged
upon insertion. In general this very rarely happens but the
incidence does vary from one part of the world to another. In one series of insertions, in Singapore in the
1960s, there were 125 perforations in 18,000 insertions.
Even this seems a relatively low figure, yet it is much
higher than figures quoted elsewhere (see superlative
753).

**753. Intrauterine device—lowest incidence of uterine perforation
on insertion**
Questionnaires were sent to physicians in Taiwan concerning insertion of the Lippes loop, a form of intrauterine
device. An incidence of uterine perforation of about one
in 8000 was revealed, but it has been suggested that this is
perhaps a low figure.

754. Intravaginal pessary—most popular in nineteenth-century
An obloy with rounded ends and bent at each end, so S-
shaped in cross section, was described by Hodge in 1860.
The device was immensely popular, surviving well into the
twentieth century—but estimates as to its value varied.
Thomas commented wryly that "on more than one occasion we have heard the most unmeasured denunciation
against pessaries upon the part of men who we found had
been persistently using them upside down."

755. Contraceptive pessaries—first marketed
The chemist W. J. Rendell began making up quinine and
cacao-butter pessaries in about 1880, which he distributed
among the poor who lived around the Clerkenwell area of
London, where his shop was situated. The demand soon
became so great that producing the suppositories soon became a full time job (473). Rendell, in common with
many of the conception pioneers in the nineteenth-

century, was a convinced freethinker: when he advertised himself in Bradlaugh's National Reformer in 1885 he styled himself "M.N.S.S." (member of the National Secular Society) (474).

756. Occlusive contraceptive—first nineteenth-century mention

A German doctor, C. W. Hufeland, is generally credited with the first mention of an occulsive method of preventing pregnancy in the nineteenth-century. A relevant text dates to 1823.

757. Condom—first used

Hercules Saxonia recalled, in 1597, that Fallopius had invented the linen condom, and further suggested that it could be improved by soaking it in a chemical solution several times and allowing it to dry in the shade (475). While it is conceded that Fallopius was one of the first to mention the sheath or condom it is also stressed that such a device was probably invented in many different parts of the world at different times. It is possible that sheaths of various types were used in ancient Rome (there is a legend, related by Antoninus Liberalis, of a goat's bladder being employed as a female sheath). Sheaths could also have been used in ancient times for decoration as well as for contraception. There is an illustration of an Egyptian wearing a sheath that hangs in clumsy fashion before him. And it has been suggested that use of the condom in ancient Egypt could well date to the XIX Dynasty (1350 B.C. to 1200 B.C.) (476).

758. Condom—first invented in modern times

In 1564 the *De morbo gallico* of Gabriello Fallopio (1523–1563) was published posthumously. Here the Italian anatomist described the linen sheath he claimed to have invented. Made to fit the glans of the penis it was devised essentially as a protective against venereal disease. The foreskin had to be pulled over the device to keep it in place. An alternative usage suggested by Fallopius must have been even more difficult—to insert the sheath in the urethra. He did claim however to have tested the sheath on 1,100 men, with not one of them becoming infected.

759. Condom—first reference in Rome

The legend told by Antonius Liberalis (already mentioned, superlative 476) may have related to either a male or female sheath. According to the tale, Minos, the King of Crete, had a problem—his semen contained serpents and scorpions which injured the women with whom he made love. Happily his wife Pasiphae was immune to the creatures, yet the union was sterile. A remedy was discovered when a goat's bladder was placed in the vagina of a second woman. Minos ejaculated his serpents into this obliging lady and then could cohabit with Pasiphae who thereupon conceived.

760. "Condom"—word first used

There has been immense debate about the origin of the word *condom*. One suggestion was that there was a Dr. (or Colonel) Condom (or Condum, Condon, or Conton)—a physician at the court of Charles II—who invented the device. The word first appeared in print in a poem written in 1706—"*A Scots Answer to a British Vision,*" which refers to contemporary instruments for combating venereal disease (*Sirenge and Condum/Come both in Request*). A 1708 poem has "a Word or two in Praise of Condons" (477).

761. Condom—only instance in preliterate peoples

Many early peoples may have used the condom, in some form or another, without a record of such usage having survived to modern times. We do know of the employment of the contraceptive sheath among the Djuka Bush Negroes of Dutch Guiana forty or so years ago. The women inserted into the vagina a seed pod, about five inches long, from which one end had been snipped. The man inserted his penis into the open end. Despite such a formidable obstacle, the tribe "was described as highly promiscuous."

762. Condom—first used in France
It is certain that the glans sheath was used in Paris as early as 1655. French sources also refer to a number of contraceptive alternatives of that time, including withdrawal. Not everyone was enthusiastic about the new invention. Madame de Sévigné described the condom as "armour against enjoyment and a spider web against danger."

763. Condom—first used in England
The condom was probably first used in England, as in much of the rest of Europe, in the seventeenth-century. A witness before the first English Birthrate Commission testified that condoms were in use in London at the time of the Great Fire (1666).

764. Condom—first full discription in modern times
One of the fullest early descriptions of the condom is to be found in the amusing *Histoire Amoureuse & Badine du Congres & de la Ville d'Utrecht*, published anonymously in Liege in 1714 (authorship was attributed to the historian Casimir Freschot). Freschot wrote of a very fine covering or bladder, more effective than if made of iron; this device was put over the "gallant" at the moment he was ready for insertion. It covered the penis like an impregnable armor, and was tied with a ribbon.

765. Condom (modern)—first manufactured
The historical condoms must have been unreliable to a marked degree, simply because of difficulties in manufacture. Developements in rubber technology in the nineteenth-century allowed, for the first time, the standardized production of improved contraceptive sheaths. Of particular relevance was the vulcanization process, first carried out in 1843.

766. Contraceptive propagandist—first to be jailed

Charles Knowlton, born in 1800 in Massachusetts, became the first man in history to go to jail for advocating birth control. He was a self-taught freethinker who never left New England, except for two brief visits to New York State. In 1832 he published a birth control classic, *Fruits of Philosophy, or the Private Companion of Young Married People;* and the work helped to establish him as the founder of American contraceptive medicine. At the time the value of *Fruits of Philosophy* were not noticed. The *Boston Medical and Surgical Journal* primly talked of the "unnatural measures" proposed, adding that "the less that is known about it by the public at large, the better it will be for the morals of the community." Three sets of prosecutions were launched against Knowlton, one resulting in a fifty dollar fine and costs, another in three months hard labor in a house of correction.

767. Contraceptive propagandist—first in Britain

Francis Place, born in Drury Lane in 1771, began the birth control movement in Britain in 1823. After immense early struggles he managed to become a prosperous tradesman, expressing the ambition that he would retire at forty-five and devote himself to politics. His commitment to birth control was only one facet of his deep social and political involvement in reformist philosophy on several fronts.

768. Contraceptive propagandist—first woman in U.S.

If Knowlton (superlative 481) was the first male propagandist for birth control in America, then Margaret Sanger was the first woman to be active in the same field. Her role in America has been compared to that of Marie Stopes in Britain. Mrs. Sanger was a declared socialist and took part in the various activities of the Labor movement. She marched with the "Wobblies" (The Industrial Workers of the World), and in 1914 began to publish a magazine called *The Woman Rebel,* determined to make it as "red and flaming as possible." Apart from the *Rebel,* Mrs. Sanger produced a small pamphlet called *Family Limitation.*

It was soon announced that Mrs. Sanger had violated nine federal statutes; and under the Comstock regime (superlative 283) she was prosecuted. She fled to England the day before the trial was due to be held. She met Marie Stopes and is said to have fallen in love with Havelock Ellis (478). Later she returned to America and lived through many tumultuous events.

769. Malthusians—first international conference

Thomas Robert Malthus (1766–1835), an English clergyman, argued in 1798 that population increases faster than the means of subsistence, and so population increase should be checked, mainly by "moral restraint." The nineteenth century Malthusian League, the equivalent of today's Family Planning Association, held its first international conference in London in 1881 when about forty doctors assembled in the hope that the importance of Malthusianism would thus be drawn to the attention of the medical profession. "As it happened, the medical men were among the last people to show much interest, at least in Europe and the English-speaking world" (479).

770. Family planning clinic—first

The first birth control clinic in the world was opened in Holland in 1882 under the auspices of the *Nienw Malthusiaanschen Bond* (the Dutch Malthusian League). The League was founded in 1881—and was immediately opposed by the medical profession! Two doctors, however, joined the organization in the early days—Dr. de Rooy (1881) and Dr. Aletta Jacobs (1882), the first woman to become medically qualified in Holland. From 1883 Dr. Jacobs held a clinic twice a week to give advice on infant welfare to working-class women. Soon she became aware of the Mensinga Diaphragm and started giving birth control advice.

771. Family planning clinic—first in U.K.

The first birth control clinic in Britain was opened by Marie Stopes and her husband in Holloway on 17 March

1921. A framed inscription on the wall of the clinic ran as follows—

> This, the first Birth Control Clinic in the British Empire, was opened on the 17 March, 1921, by Humphrey Verdon Roe and his wife Marie Carmichael Stopes, in order to show by actual example what might be done for mothers and their children with no great difficulty, and what should be done all over the world when once the idea takes root in the public mind that motherhood should be voluntary and guided by the best scientific knowledge available.
>
> The clinic is free to all, and is supported entirely by the two founders. Those who have benefited by its help are asked to hand on a knowledge of its existence to others and help to create a public opinion which will force the Ministry of Health to include a similar service in Ante-Natal and Welfare Centers already supported by the Government in every district.

772. Family Planning Association—first in United Kingdom
The British Family Planning Association was founded in 1930 on a voluntary basis. A number of other countries had already set up similar organizations.

773. Family Planning Association—first in US
The first Family Planning Association on the American continent was created in 1917, despite the lingering influence of Comstock, hostile contraceptive legislation in many states, etc.

774. Family Planning Association—first in South Africa
South Africa, perhaps not the most liberal of countries managed to get a Family Planning Association started in 1932. Today the government provides a variety of family planning services.

775. Family Planning Association—first in Australia
The Australian Family Planning Association was started in 1926, four years before the creation of a similar body in

the UK. As with other FPAs, the Australian organization was on a voluntary basis.

776. Family Planning Association—first in Bermuda
It would be possible to chart the commencements of voluntary birth control organizations for every country in the world (where such organizations are not forbidden in law). One more will suffice for our purposes. The Bermuda Family Planning Association was begun in 1937.

777. Family planning clinic—first in India
India has an impressive record in family planning. There is some uncertainty as to when the first clinic was opened on the subcontinent. A Neo-Malthusian League was founded in Madras in 1916; and Bombay State was probably the first in the region to embark upon practical family planning work. A clinic was opened in Poona in 1923 by R. D. Karve, a professor of mathematics in Bombay—he lost his job due to his advocacy of birth control.

778. Family planning—first government program
It is to India's credit that it began the first government-sponsored program of birth control in 1951. At that time no other Asian country or country elsewhere, could boast a family planning scheme supported out of government funds.

779. Family planning—first all-India conference
In December 1951 the First All-India Conference on Family Planning was staged in Bombay. About one hundred people attended, many traveling from other parts of the country. The conference was generally held to have been a success. While it was being held, the organizers, Lady Rama Rau and her team, received a cable from Margaret Sanger, asking if they would be prepared to hold the next International Conference in India. The team agreed but warned Mrs. Sanger about the possible smallness of the audience and the likelihood that the publicity would be limited.

780. International Planned Parenthood Federation—first proposed
The International Planned Parenthood Federation (IPPF) was first suggested at Bombay in 1952, and ratified at Stockholm a year later. The IPPF came into existence on 29 November 1952 under the joint Presidency of Mrs. Margaret Sanger and Lady Rama Rau.

781. Population control—first U.N. declaration
The Secretary-General of the United Nations, on Human Rights Day (10 December 1966), issued a Declaration on Population, developed on the initiative of the Chairman of the Board of the Population Council in New York, and signed by the heads of state of twelve countries. A year later, a further eighteen signatures were added to the same declaration which described briefly the problems of unplanned population growth and asserted, among other things, that governments should become actively involved in family planning (480).

782. Family planning—first enabling legislation in England
Under the Family Planning Act of 1967 birth control was placed on an official footing for the first time in this country. Local authorities can now make provisions for family planning advice and appliances, and contraceptives can be given free of charge at their discretion. The FPA noted that eighteen months after the Act only thirty-four out of 204 local authorities were providing a family planning service for everyone who wanted it, married or single; 129 were giving a restricted service, e.g. advice but not supplies, or not advising the unmarried; and thirty-nine authorities had done nothing about the act or were still talking about what they intended to do.

783. Contraceptive sales—first made legal in modern Japan
Partly due to the continuing efforts of Mrs. Shidzue Kato, elected to the Diet in 1946 in the first postwar General Election, the Japanese laws on contraception were modified in 1948. The Pharmaceutical Affairs Law removed

the prohibition on the sale of contraceptives, with a resulting surge in the production of both mechanical devices and chemical contraceptives. The competing manufacturers swamped the market with many products and the voluntary organizations did their best to advise confused users. 1948 also saw in Japan the legalization of abortion and sterilization for medical, social and economic reasons.

784. Contraceptive information—dissemination first made illegal in U.S.

In 1873 in the United States the dissemination of any information about birth control suddenly became illegal. The Comstock Bill came to Congress in February of that year, was passed by both houses, and was signed by the President before the Session closed on 4th March. There were no speeches, virtually no discussion, and no public hearings. The Bill was represented as "a measure for the suppression of trade in and circulation of articles for immoral use."

785. Contraceptives—most recently condemned in U.S. federal law

As recently as 1971 Federal law grouped contraceptives with "obscene or pornographic materials," and until only a few years ago the laws of many states restricted not only their sale but the provision of information about them. *Comstockery* (a Bernard Shaw word) lingers on.

786. Family planning—first made legal in modern U.S.

In the early nineteen-thirties, ten bills were introduced into Congress. They differed in detail but their main aim was the same, to liberate the country from the restrictive Comstock laws which regarded contraceptive materials as obscene and pornographic. Seven of the Bills died in committee; one was tabled without discussion; and one was given an adverse report by the Ways and Means Committee. One was passed by the Senate Judiciary Committee and passed to the floor of the Senate, where it was opposed and recalled. Birth control was more or less freed by a decision of the United States Circuit Court of Appeals on 30 November 1936. The issue was settled by a test case (481). In 1961 the Planned Parenthood League opened a clinic and treated forty-two patients in ten days. Then a Roman Catholic father of five complained: the Executive Director of the League and the Medical Adviser (who happened to be the Chief of the Department of Obstetrics and Surgery at Yale University) were arrested, found guilty of violating the law, and were fined one hundred dollars each.

787. Family planning—first reforming legislation in modern Canada

In 1936 a Miss Dorothea Palmer, a social worker doing birth control work, was arrested at Eastview, Ontario. The trial took place under section 207 of the Federal Criminal Code, which forbade birth control activities, "unless for the public good." The trial, with twenty-three days of hearings, was spread over six months. Some of the evidence given by women interviewed for the prosecution rebounded since it emerged they were in need of birth control advice. On 17 March 1937 the Magistrate, Lester H. Clayton, acquitted Miss Palmer. The decision was upheld, the same year, by a higher court. Some time after this important case significant reforming legislation came on to the Canadian statute.

788. Contraception—most recent papal encyclical

In the summer of 1968 the Pope issued the encyclical *De Humanae Vitae* (On Human Life), reaffirming the Vatican opposition to all means of artificial birth control. A public opinion poll after the publication of the encyclical showed that only a minority of Catholics in Britain supported the ruling. Many observers felt that the Pope had given a reactionary ruling and had seriously damaged the spirit of the Ecumenical Movement (482).

789. Contraception—most repressive country

Not all the world is permissive. In Spain the manufacture of contraceptives is forbidden. The advertising of contraceptives is forbidden. The distribution of contraceptives is forbidden. And giving advice on contraceptives is forbidden. And even though it is allowed to bring contraceptives into the country for personal use, the practice of contraception is prohibited under Article 416 of the Criminal Code (483).

790. Contraception—first hostile book in twentieth-century

In a book by Dr. Stall (484) (1900) a certain Dr. Pomeroy is quoted, a name-dropping device to lend authority—"As before noticed, it is surprising to what extent the laity believe that the course of Nature can be safely interfered with, even by those who understand her laws the least. Those who fear to turn back the hands of a watch lest they injure the complicated and delicate machinery do not hesitate to use violent means to interfere with the natural workings of the human mechanism, which is a thousand-fold more complicated and delicate. Nature is tenacious of her rights; she resists grandly, but if forced to yield, she visits the offender with punishment which is no less sure because it is sometimes long delayed."

791. Contraception—earliest academic censorship

The earliest example of academic censorship designed to restrict the spread of birth control knowledge dates to the nineteenth-century. In 1875, Professor Burt Green Wilder (1841–1925), professor of physiology, comparative anatomy and zoology at Cornell University, published *What Young People Should Know*. One aim was to make birth control knowledge available to young people. But the chapter on this subject was omitted from his book at the request of Cornell's governing body.

792. Contraceptive methods—first named in US national magazine

It was not until 1955 that an American national magazine hazarded to name specific methods of contraception; and not until 1959 did a television network have a program that mentioned the subject. Serious constraints were also apparent in the administrative policies operating in Government hospitals and health agencies. Even for people who did not rely on publicly funded health agencies for medical care, public policy stigmatized contraceptive practice and made it difficult to obtain medical contraception.

793. Contraception—most famous medical hoax

A Canadian doctor, a certain J. S. Greenstein, published a paper on a wholly fictitious contraceptive which he called "Armpitin," for which he sketched the chemical formula, including several molecular groups represented by the initials NO. "Armpitin," he explained, was found to affect males by way of the olfactory nerve, and rendered them sterile for a number of days equivalent to the number of NO groups in the formula. The paper was seriously reviewed in an annual review of pharmacology, and Dr. Greenstein received requests from pharmaceutical companies to sell them the patent (485).

794. Contraception—most progressive countries

The degree of tolerance a country shows to the idea of contraception is revealed by looking at what is permissible in certain areas. (See superlative 483.) Not many countries allow contraceptives to be manufactured, imported in bulk and in private, to be distributed, to be advertised, and for practical advice to be given. In one IPPF survey (mostly devoted to Europe) the following countries are found to be tolerant (or "permissive") in all these respects—Belgium, Britain, Denmark, Finland, West Germany, Luxembourg, Netherlands, Norway, Sweden, and Switzerland. The following countries are restrictive in one or more of the areas indicated—Austria, Bulgaria, Czechoslovakia, France, East Germany, Greece, Hungary, Iceland, Ireland, Italy, Malta, Poland, Portugal, Romania, Spain, Turkey, and Yugoslavia (486).

795. Contraception—most recent practical invention

The C-film has been described as the first "his-or-hers" contraceptive. It consists of a thin, transparent, flexible film about 1½ in square impregnated with a spermicide chemical of which the formula has not yet been published. In use the C-film can either be placed on the tip of the penis just prior to coitus; or it can be pushed into the

vagina up to three hours before sexual intercourse takes
place. Once in the vagina the film dissolves at once and
makes the cervical mucus impenetrable to sperms. C-films
have been on sale in Hungary since December 1968. The
editor of *World Medicine* reported that as many as 100,-
000 Hungarian couples were using C-films by November
1969 and that the results of a three-year trial with 720
highly fertile couples gave a pregnancy rate of 3.4 per
hundred woman-years. C-films are now being tried in
more than ten countries under the auspices of the International Planned Parenthood Federation.

796. Contraceptive failure rates—highest estimates
Various figures have been given for failure rates for contraceptive measures of various sorts. Highest estimates
have been quoted as follows (figures for pregnancies/100
woman-years of exposure) (487):

pill	2.0
condom	11.1
diaphragm and jelly	17.5
withdrawal	20.0
safe period	35.0
foaming tablets, douching	42.8

797. Contraceptive failure rates—lowest estimates
Lowest estimates for contraceptive measures of various
types are as follows (figures for pregnancies/100 woman-
years of exposure) (487). (See also superlative 497.)—

pill	0.1
condom	7.5
diaphragm and jelly	7.2
withdrawal	12.0
safe period	14.4
foaming tablets, douching	11.9

798. Contraceptive methods—least popular in UK
According to one estimate, the least popular methods of
contraception in Britain are the coil/IUD (used by five

per cent of married couples), spermicides (five per cent), rhythm method/safe period (six per cent), and the cap/diaphragm with spermicidal cream or jelly (six per cent).

799. Contraceptive methods—most popular in UK
The same estimate gives the most popular contraceptive methods in Britain as the condom/sheath (used by thirty-nine per cent of married couples), the oral contraceptive (used by twenty-seven per cent), and withdrawal or coitus interruptus (twenty-five per cent).

800. Contraceptive technique—most popular internationally
The bulk of the world is poor and underdeveloped, without access to the benefits of modern technology. A large number of primitive societies are still reported as using various plants and herbs to reduce fertility in males and females, but their efficacy is not known. A post-coital douche has also been reported for a number of countries. By far the most commonly reported contraceptive technique is withdrawal or *coitus interruptus*. Only in the United States has it ceased to be one of the major techniques employed. In general *coitus interruptus* is a male-initiated technique but there is some evidence in the anthropological literature of where women, e.g. the Kgatla of Botswana, move their hips or turn over as they feel the man nearing ejaculation (488). It is also reported that such female behavior not infrequently leads to quarrels.

801. Contraceptive technique—most reliable
The most reliable contraceptive method of all is undoubtedly total abstinence. Only in such a fashion is it certain that the energetic and resourceful sperm will be defeated in its aims. Few writers are eccentric enough these days to recommend such a means of family limitation. Of methods that *are* recommended, sterilization (male or female) and the pill (oral contraceptive) are generally conceded to be the most reliable—though neither is foolproof! With sterilization, some men have a third *vas deferens* and women sometimes have a third ovary, making a doctor think that

a successful operation has been performed when in fact the man or woman is still not protected at all! With the pill, it may be vomited out before digestion, it may be taken at the wrong time, etc., etc. (See also superlative 498).

802. Contraceptive technique—least reliable
Here we have all the old wives' tales—sneezing, coughing, holding one's breath, drawing up one's knees, lying in an East—West direction, etc., etc. The safe period (see superlative 796) is not much better: for good cause has it been termed "Vatican roulette." In general such contraceptive methods as prayer, wishful thinking, unsullied optimism, etc. are to be avoided: sperm and eggs have a way of behaving quite indifferent to our hopes and dreams. Try something *safe*: sex can still be magic.

803. Progesterone—effect on rabbits first shown as prelude to pill
A paper published in 1937 by Makepeace, Weinstein and Friedman of Pennsylvania showed for the first time that progesterone, if injected into rabbits would stop them ovulating even though they had been mated. This finding had great significance for the development of the oral contraceptive. Much was already known about the effects of oestrogen, but for progesterone to have such effects was an altogether different matter (see superlative 804).

804. Progesterone—effect on rabbits most fully shown as prelude to pill
Dr. Min-Chueh Chang repeated the Pennsylvania experiment and established new facts about the dose of natural progesterone needed to inhibit ovulation and about the timing of the dose. Given by mouth, between two- and five-thousandths of a gramme were needed per rabbit. (The hormone is more active by mouth in rabbits than in humans.) But if injected or deposited in the rabbits' vaginas, it had to be given at least five hours before they copulated and in a dose of between one- and two-thousandths of a gramme. This dose could be given up to twenty-four hours before mating and still work. The bigger the dose the longer the period of effectiveness. It was also possible

to show that a pellet of progesterone lodged under a rabbit's skin would inhibit ovulation for a matter of months. The Chang paper ("constructed" by Pincus) was published in 1953, after which Chang moved on to rats. Female rats, unlike rabbits, do not have to copulate to produce an egg: they are "spontaneous ovulators," and so biologically a step nearer to human beings.

805. Progesterone—first synthesized as prelude to pill

Carl Djerassi, a professor of chemistry at Stanford University and a man with more than 650 scientific publications to his credit, began in 1950 to tackle the problem of creating synthetic progesterone that could be taken by mouth, the step that was to lead directly to the formulation of the contraceptive pill. By late 1951 Djerassi ran through seven separate chemical processes, at the end of which an entirely new molecule emerged—

19-nor-17-alpha-ethinyltestosterone (or norethisterone, for short).

The new chemical had a high order of potency and achieved the required effect when swallowed. The way to the contraceptive pill was becoming clearer.

806. Oral contraceptive—first

Following the work of Chang and Djerassi and others, Gregory Pincus, the Director of the Worcester Foundation for Experimental Biology had developed an effective contraceptive pill by 1957. The Pincus team, including Chang, began a systematic study, in the nineteen-fifties, of more than two hundred substances with varying effects on such things as ovulation, menstruation, and conception. One substance, gestagen type, called "norethynodrel," formed the basis of the first large-scale trial of the contraceptive pill, a trial carried out in Puerto Rico in 1956. The gestagens, however, gave poor control over menstruation, a problem overcome by combining the gestagen with a synthetic oestrogen. It was a combined pill of this type (marketed commercially as Enovid) that proved so successful in the Puerto Rican trial. Now there are literally dozens of contraceptive pills available (489).

807. Oral contraception—first approved by FDA

Enovid (see superlative 502) was placed before the U.S. Food and Drug Administration with application for a license as a contraceptive product. Backing up the application was evidence on experimental work and the Puerto Rican trials. Approval was granted by the FDA in 1960 for use of the drug as a contraceptive. The FDA ruled that its use was to be limited to two years for any one person, a ruling that was relaxed some years later.

808. Contraceptive testing—first in human vagina

Chemicals ultimately intended for human use are first tested, appropriately enough, in animals and the test tube; and various contraceptives—hormonal preparations, spermicides, etc.—have been tested in this way. One of the unique contributions of Masters and Johnson was to embark upon an extensive program of testing contraceptives in the human vagina. The results were published in papers which appeared through the fifties and sixties. A singular feature of the program was the use of artificial coital technique in testing various contraceptive products. For example, a woman would introduce a spermicide, then use a plastic penis until she reached orgasm. At the time of orgasm a specimen of semen from a fertile man was injected into the vagina with the cervix capped. Samples of the vaginal contents were then withdrawn at various intervals and examined for moving sperm. The whole procedure was then repeated. No spermicidal products was found to be perfect but some results were more than twice as good as others for different products.

809. Oral contraception—first British trial

The first British trial of any size took place in Birmingham, under Family Planning Association—CIFC auspices, in the early nineteen-sixties. When the project began, forty-eight women were involved, and they were expected to have sexual intercourse at least once a week.

Enovid tablets were given to the women: the intention was that the tablets would contain 2.5 milligrammes of progesterone and 0.05 milligrammes of oestrogen. Unfortunately something went wrong with the manufacturing process, and it was later found that by this time the tablets contained only 0.036 milligrammes of the oestrogen. Within only a few weeks, fourteen of the women were expecting babies! The women were switched to other pills and none of the ones not already pregnant became so. The results of the trial, including the subsequent births of the unplanned babies, were written up in the British Medical Journal.

810. Oral contraception—country of widest use
The United States of America is the country of maximum oral contraception consumption. Today there are in excess of ten million women taking the pill. The figure has fluctuated widely with each new "scare" about possible links between the pill and cancer, thrombosis, later sterility, etc.

811. Oral contraception—first connected with blood-clotting
The first published report of a woman developing a blood-clotting disorder while taking the pill came comparatively early, in 1961, only four years after the pill had first been made commercially available. She was a forty-year-old nurse who had been given Enovid, not for contraceptive purposes but because she had a disorder of the uterus which was expected to respond to hormone treatment. After several weeks the treatment was stopped because she was vomiting severely. She was soon found to have blood clots in both lungs. She later recovered (490).

812. Oral contraception—first connected with menstrual disorder
In 1966 Dr. Rodney P. Shearman of Sydney University in Australia published a paper in which he reported having studied eighty-six women whose menstrual periods had ceased for no apparent reason. Nine of these women had been using oral contraceptives. It might, he admitted, have been a coincidence. Some considerations, however, suggested that the relationship between the pill and menstrual

peculiarities was in fact real. Shearman was cautious—
"We cannot yet be certain whether the association is
causal or casual, and we present our findings to stimulate
future clarification."

813. Oral contraception—most bizarre correlates

Many strange occurrences have been laid at the door of
the pill. Sometimes there are good grounds for thinking
that oral contraception can have very strange effects on
some women. One patient complained that whenever she
turned over in bed, or sneezed, she could feel and hear
something crackling in her chest. It transpired that her
breastbone was loose—the doctor advised her to go off the
pill! A Manchester dentist found that a patient with loose
teeth was on the pill. One particularly bizarre finding was
that women who were taking the pill were supplying green
(!) blood plasma to the Leeds Regional Blood Transfusion
Center in 1968. A case described in the *British Medical
Journal* indicated that the pill might be able to cause the
equivalent of St. Vitus's Dance (491).

814. Oral contraception—most persistent British critic

The most persistent critic of the pill in Britain has been
the Australian-born specialist in human metabolism, Professor Victor Wynn, head of the Alexander Simpson Laboratory for Metabolic Research at St. Mary's Hospital,
London. His concern over the subject grew out of his
study of the pill's effects on how the body handles carbo-
hydrates, and on the pattern of blood fats in women. His
studies in this area have been extensive.

815. Oral contraception—first seen as relevant to court damages

A rich market for the pill manufacturers is Australasia,
where around one million women "contracept orally"—a
figure that represents more than one third of the women
of childbearing age. The pill is coming to be regarded as
one of a woman's natural entitlements. In November 1969
a news sheet was circulated amongst British drug firms
stating that a Melbourne bride-to-be, who had hurt her leg
in a car crash, had been awarded £230 by a court, be-

cause the risk of thrombosis probably meant she would never be able to take the pill!

816. Contraception—first blamed for difficulties in the menopause

In 1902 a certain Dr. Emma Angell Drake of Boston argued (492) that contraception would be likely to affect the menopause adversely. One quote will suffice—"Of the cases which ... have denominated 'serious' and 'severe,'" many of the women through ignorance of their physical natures and of the penalty which must be paid for neglecting or tampering with them, were they arraigned before a tribunal where all the testimony must be given, would be found to have incurred the consequences themselves ... the prevention of conception or the production of abortion when conception has taken place, is another large factor which contributes to the discomfort and disease of the women who lend their hand and heart to this soul-destroying business."

817. Contraception—first "morning-after" drug in widespread usage

The drug di-ethyl stilboestrol (DES) has been in widespread use in the U.S. for several years as a "morning after" contraceptive—and this despite the drug's proved carcinogenicity in animals. The drug is a synthetic ostrogen approved by the Food and Drug Administration for the treatment of various gynaecological problems. There is no mechanism to ensure that the drug is for an approved purpose. The widespread use of DES as a morning after pill was first publicized in an article in the *Journal of the American Medical Association* (25th October 1971), where Dr. Lucille Kuchera of the University of Michigan described her use of the drug as a post-coital contraceptive in 1000 women.

818. Contraception (animal)—first success in applying chemical to brain

At an American Endocrine Society meeting in Chicago it was announced that a biologically-active chemical had been made which, in rats, will shut down the activity of one of the brain hormones that regulate fertility. A year was spent synthesizing antagonists to the luteinising releasing factor (LRF) produced by the hypothalamus in the brain. When this drug reaches the pituitary gland it causes the gland to release luteinising hormone and follicle stimulating hormone—the two hormones that control reproduction in the female. The synthetic material reported by David Coy, a worker at the laboratories of Andrew Schally of the Veterans Administration Hospital in New Orleans, reduces the release of luteinising hormone in rats.

819. Fertility survey—largest
A World Fertility Survey is currently taking place, involving between forty and sixty underdeveloped countries, the U.S. and various European countries. This is represented as the largest social survey ever attempted on a global scale. It is being financed by the United Nations Fund for Population Activities and AID (the Agency for International Development), the entire project costing in the region of twenty-five million dollars. The task of handling the vast amount of data has been facilitated by the use of computers, and this aspect has been discussed in the technical press (493).

820. Infertility—oddest causative factors
Some of the oddest reasons for infertility lie in peculiar congenital abnormalities of egg and sperm. A picture showing deformed sperm is really quite remarkable. Whereas sperm are generally nicely symmetrical, having a head (carrying the genetic material) and a tail (to give mobility), a wide range of abnormalities can occur. Heads may appear in semen without any adjoining tails, and tails themselves may appear in similar isolation. Individual heads may be oddly curved or distorted, not unlike the sperm heads of some nonhuman animals; or the heads and tails may be "paired." One peculiarity, resulting in effective sterility, is where the sperm clump together in a mysterious fashion, quite incapable of fertilizing anything. It has been suggested that this clumping factor could be identified and injected into men who wish to be made infertile. When the condition occurs naturally it cannot be

cured—so presumably the contraceptive provision, if accomplished artifically, would be irreversible.

821. Sterilization—first proposed as eugenic measure
A certain Dr. Rentoul first proposed sterilization in England as early as 1903 in his *Proposed Sterilization of Certain Mental and Physical Degenerates.*

822. Sterilization—first committee recommendation for eugenics
In 1934 a Departmental Committee on Sterilization, known as the Brock Committee, recommended unanimously that sterilization be made legal for mental defectives, those suffering from, or believed likely to transmit, mental disease, and persons suffering from or believed to be carriers of grave physical disabilities which had been shown to be transmissible (710). The recommendations referred only to the *right* of such people to be sterilized and required the consent of the person to the operation. But if the person was a minor, or "incapable," then the guardian could give permission for the operation to be performed. The question has been asked—who is the guardian of a mental defective or lunatic in a public institution? An official of the state! The Brock Committee's report was never adopted.

823. Sterilization—first proposed as eugenic measure
The earliest published recommendation of sterilization on eugenic grounds is that of a Swiss, Dr. August Forel, in 1892. It was such early agitation that let up to the European enthusiasm for sterilization in the nineteen-thirties.

824. Sterilization (family planning)—most progressive countries
The legal position on sterilization for family planning and other purposes is, from an international point of view, confused. There are in several countries precise laws either permitting or refusing the right to sterilization (male or female), yet in other parts of the world the law has to be interpreted. Sometimes "consent" is written into legislation; sometimes it is declared to be irrelevant. Some liberal states in America specifically allow vasectomy—and

this specific operation appears by name in the statutes. As one specific example, Virginia authorizes "a vasectomy or salpingectomy, or other surgical sexual sterilization procedure." Other countries allow sterilization without specifically referring to any particular surgical operation, e.g. Britain and Czechoslovakia (494).

825. Sterilization (family planning)—most repressive countries
Some national laws specifically forbid operations designed to make a person sterile; others laws condemn sterilization as part of more general legislation relating to "mayhem" or "bodily harm." Some American states, for example, are hostile to sterilization for family planning purposes, and in South Vietnam, Law No. 12 of 22 May 1962 forbids propaganda to encourage "the unnatural prevention of pregnancy," except in cases where the life of the woman would be threatened by a childbirth (494).

826. Sterilization (women)—first recorded
Male castration was common in ancient Egypt, as in other countries of antiquity. There is also an account of a king who created female eunuchs by removing their ovaries. According to the Greek historian Strabo, the Egyptians were well acquainted with this practice, as were their neighbors in other areas. One motive for this hazardous operation appears to have been the desire to keep women young and beautiful, rather than to prevent conception (495).

827. Vasectomy (animal)—first
The first recorded animal vasectomy, in this case the tying of the *vas deferens* in a dog, occurred in 1823. Sir Astley Cooper, Bart, F.R.S. (1768–1848), who had experimental surgery as a hobby, wrote—

In 1823 I made the following experiment on a dog. I divided the *vas deferens* on one side and the spermatic artery and vein on the other.

The testis upon that side on which the artery and vein were divided gangrened and sloughed away . . .

The testis on the side on which the duct was divided became somewhat larger than natural. I kept the dog for six years; during that time he was twice seen *in coitu,* but the female did not produce. This was in 1827.

In 1829 I killed him, and found the *vas deferens* below the division excessively enlarged and full of semen (sic), and entirely stopped, with some separation of its extremities; but it was open from the place of division to the urethra (496).

828. Vasectomy (human)—first

Maurice Meltzer, writing in 1928 (497), has decalred that four men—Guyon, Burket, Hilton, and Harrison—performed vasectomies between 1885 and 1896; but doubt has been expressed about this claim. Guyon wrote of his experiences with "resection of the vasa deferentia" in 1895 and it is clear that Isnardi performed vasectomies in 1896 (498), but the first human vasectomies were performed either by Harrison in London (possibly as early as 1893) or by Lennander in Uppsala, Sweden (in 1894).

829. Vasectomy—first conceived as treatment for criminals

The origin of the idea of using vasectomy as a treatment for sex criminals is usually attributed to Dr. A. J. Ochsner of Chicago. He performed two vasectomies for prostatomegally in 1897.

830. Vasectomy—first used as treatment for criminal

In 1899, Dr. Harry C. Sharp, as medical officer of the Jefferson Reformatory in Indiana, performed the first vasectomy as treatment for a "criminal," i.e. a compulsive masturbator. A young man of nineteen called Clawson, greatly worried by his masturbatory habits, approached Dr. Sharp to request castration. Even in 1899 no sane doctor would have granted such a request. Dr. Sharp, remarked, forty years later, "I did not feel justified in performing that mutilation," However, he did think that a vasectomy would help; and on the 12th October 1899 Clawson was sterilized by vasectomy. The operation apparently did the trick. Clawson reported later that he had stopped masturbating.

But why this should be so is rather a mystery. Dr. Sharp's "success" with "this fellow Clawson" encouraged the doctor to carry out further vasectomies. In 1902 he published a report of forty-two voluntary vasectomies on men aged between seventeen and twenty-five, all offenders imprisoned in Jeffersonville.

831. Vasectomy—first used as treatment for impotence

Meltzer has the "dubious distinction"(499) of being the first to use vasectomy as a treatment for impotence. There is of course little reason to suppose that any such operation should help a man's potency. The Meltzer effort dates to 1928.

832. Vasectomy—first attempted for rejuvenation

Throughout history various methods have been employed to make old men young again, to restore lost potency, etc. With Voronoff, monkey glands came into vogue, and even vasectomy was drafted as a means of restoring youthful vigor. Steinach advocated such a method, and was also connected with the monkey gland business. Under Steinach's direction, Lichtenstern had performed an apparently successful testicular graft. On 1 November 1918, Lichtenstern performed the first Steinach rejuvenation on a "prematurely senile" coachman of forty-three. Thousands of operations followed. One approach was to tie one vas and later, when the effects of that had "worn off," to tie the other! In such a way repeated rejuvenations could be accomplished.

833. Vasectomy inducements—first introduced

It is one thing to devise a means of contraception, quite another to get people to employ it. In some circumstances they can be bribed. The payment of inducements for vasectomy was first introduced in Madras State (Tamil Nadu) in 1956, where thirty rupees was paid to each man agreeing to submit himself for the operation. Later, payments were even made to anyone who successfully induced a man to undergo vasectomy.

834. Vasectomy—country most practiced

India has been represented as the home of vasectomy, the Indian government claiming to have performed upwards of 8,000,000 sterilization operations of which more than eighty per cent are vasectomies. The need for extensive birth control in India is evidenced by the fact that in a population of nearly six hundred million the population is growing at the rate of up to 14,000,000 every year. In the India of today there are around 120,000,000 married women of reproductive age and the Indian government is pledged to provide contraceptive services of some kind to all of them.

835. Vasectomy—spontaneous recanalization first reported

Vasectomy, normally achieved by tying or cutting the *vas deferens* to prevent sperm being ejaculated in the seminal fluid, is by no means a foolproof method of birth control. The sperm ducts have the astonishing facility, in some rare circumstances, of joining themselves up again, so hard will Nature struggle to thwart efforts to tamper with its processes! Spontaneous recanalization of the divided *vas* has been known since it was first reported by Rolnick (500) in 1954.

836. Vasectomy—least expected recanalization

The recanalization of the sperm ducts (see superlative 518) can occur following the most thorough vasectomy operation. Marshall and Lyon have reported a case (501) in which recanalization took place even though a section of *vas* had been removed, the *lumina* had been diathermized, and the ends doubled back and ligated with no-nabsorbable sutures. Despite such remarkable occurrences perhaps it should be stressed that in the vast majority of cases vasectomy is both trouble-free and effective as a contraceptive means.

837. Vasectomy—longest period to subsequent detection of non-motile sperm

It is conventional medical practice to test a man's ejaculate, after vasectomy, to ensure the absence of viable sperm. Ideally this is done on more than one occasion, some weeks or months after the operation. In one study (502) a man was still producing (non-motile) sperm in his fourteenth specimen, no less than 17 months after the operation. If even non-motile sperm appear in the ejaculate after a vasectomy, is a man to be told that he is still fertile? Of 208 men who sent in a semen specimen in the study about 3 per cent showed a reappearance of non-motile sperm. Can a pregnancy be caused by non-motile sperm? Unfortunately there are still no records of any long term follow-up of men whose semen contains non-motile spermatozoa (503).

838. Vasectomy—first attempt at reversal

In 1886 Bardenheurer was experimenting with methods of restoring continuity between the *vas deferens* and the epididymus in cases of blockage through disease or injury. The first description of a feasible operation is credited to Martin in an article in the *University of Pennsylvania Medical Bulletin* in 1902. Two Italians, Penzo and Gutti, wrote on the subject in 1903 and 1905, while Swinbourne, an American claimed success in 1910 in one of five cases, using Martin's technique. The first British report is a note by Wheeler, of Dublin, in 1914. The first repair carried out for the reversal of vasectomy, rather than in a case of accidental blockage, was performed in 1919 by W. C. Quinby, the patient having undergone a voluntary vasectomy in 1911 (504).

839. Vasectomy (animal)—most serious consequences

If we forget about fatalities caused through careless operations then a number of alarming consequences can still be detected in animals as a result of vasectomy (505). In a series of experiments on male rats in New York vasectomies were performed: at week 28 the rats were killed and their testes and other organs were examined. In less than one-third of the vasectomized group did the testes appear normal. In 17 of the 31 rats examined the testes were "small, less turgid or soft and had an abnormal purplish coloration." More alarming still were "numerous small-to-large yellowish cysts" observed either around the *vas*, closer to the testes, or elsewhere in the body. The authors suggested that "pending extensive study of the endocrine and somatic effects of vasectomy in man, greater caution be observed in the use of vasectomies as a routine contraceptive measure."

840. Vasectomy (human)—most serious consequences

Vasectomy, like any other surgical operation, involves a number of risks. What follows must be regarded as quite exceptional and in no sense likely to occur in the vast bulk of vasectomies carried out in a modern medical environment. In the Gorakhpur vasectomy camp in India in 1972 there were at least fourteen cases of tetanus infection. This circumstance led to the first reported deaths due to vasectomy—eight of them were described in the *Times of India*. There can also be a number of allergic reactions. Also, the handling of the structures of the spermatic cord can lead to shock and even to cardiac arrest. In one such reported case prompt resuscitation led to a restarting of the heart and to full recovery. Mention has also been made of such things as auto-immune conditions and anaesthetic mishaps (506).

841. Castration (animal)—first practiced

The significance of castration among domestic animals has been known for a very long time. In Kinsey there is the suggestion that "the understanding and practice of castration may have begun as early as 7000 B.C. in the early Neolithic age when animals were first domesticated(507). It has also been pointed out that many primitive peoples were at a Neolithic cultural level when first visited by Europeans; in such societies castration was generally practiced.

842. Castration (human)—first practiced on massive scale

It is likely that the first tribes engaging in warfare on a systematic basis indulged in castration of defeated foes on a grand scale. It is common knowledge that ancient nations regarded a collection of male testicles as a sign of a warrior's bravery and skill in combat; and foreskins were given in tribute in biblical times to signal the defeat of an enemy. According to Schurig's *Gynocologia*, the legendary Syrian queen Semiramis was the first practitioner of mass castration. According to one theory she had men so mutilated in order to prevent opposition to her female rule—a latter-day Valerie Solanas! Another idea was that she was simply motivated by jealousy. It was said that after having spent the night in the arms of a lover the queen would have him castrated to prevent him giving the same pleasure to any other woman!

843. Castration (human)—first therapeutic instance

The human body has always been mutilated in various ways in the cause of medical treatment. We have already noted vasectomy practiced for such a purpose (see superlative 832). A therapeutic castration, based on psychiatric considerations, was carried out in 1892 on a suggestion from August Florel in Zurich. The case concerned an imbecilic man who was on the verge of auto-castration because of neuralgic pains in the testes.

844. Castration (human)—most extreme form

The severest form of male castration involves the removal of all the scrotum with the testes, and the penis! The most prized eunuchs in the harems of Arabia were the *Sandali*, who possessed neither testes nor penis. The provision of eunuchs for the ancient Chinese harems could also involve total loss of the genitals. There is a graphic description of the operation, written by Carter Stent, an authority on Chinese court life, in the *Journal of the Royal Asiatic Society (North China Branch 1877)*.

845. Castration (human)—least extreme form

Now it depends what you mean by castration. In a mild form it may involve the remove of a single testicle or the crushing of same (one cannot begin to imagine the suffering that such a "mild" form of castration must have caused). In the Chinese harems, three kinds of castration were practiced—removal of all the male genitals, the removal of the penis only, and the severing of the testicles. Perhaps we may regard the last of these as the mildest form of ancient Chinese castration.

846. Castration (human)—most famous case in eighteenth-century England

There is a much quoted case of castration that occurred in April 1790, near London. A half-wit named James Trotter had sired three illegitimate children who had to be supported by the parish. The Parish Council, apparently resenting this situation, decided to have the man castrated. He was taken by force and castrated, naturally enough without anaesthetic, by the local pig-butcher. No details are given of how Mr. Trotter behaved thereafter.

847. Eunuch system—first established in China

The first mention of eunuchs in during the time of the Chou Dynasty, around 1100 B.C. Cjou-kung, the younger brother of Wu-wang, the first monarch of the Chou Dynasty, framed a Code of Laws for China; and one of five modes of punishment was castration. Castration punishments carried such names as *kung-hsing* (palace punishment) and *lao-kung-yen* (royal palace castration). The systematic creation and employment of eunuchs appear to have occurred some time during the Chou Dynasty (1122–221 B.C.).

848. Eunuchs—most famous biblical reference

The most famous reference in the New Testament (Matthew 19, 12) to eunuchs has sanctified hostility to sex, the persecution of sexual deviates, and such excesses as self-castration—

> For there are some eunuchs that were so born from their mother's womb; and there are some eunuchs that were made eunuchs of men; and there be eunuchs, which have made themselves eunuchs for the kingdom of heaven's sake. He that is able to receive it, let him receive it.

849. Castration—most recent of Vatican choir boys

We all know that the popes of old used to have young boys castrated so that they would continue to sing sweetly in the Vatican chapel. How many young males so emasculated there is no way of knowing. What we do know is that as late as 1890, Vatican choir boys were still being castrated to conserve their soprano voices.

850. Castrati—most famous

During the sixteenth, seventeenth, and eighteenth-centuries in Europe the theatrical stage was dominated by the castrati, often immensely wealthy and influential performers. Describing Farinelli (subject of an Abelard book, 1974), D. Charles Burney, eminent eighteenth-century musical historian remarked—"He was able to project the tone to such a length as to incite incredulity even in those who heard him, who imagined him to have the help of some wind instrument." A French commentator, writing of Cresentini, another famous male soprano, observed that this "great balloon" could expand his breath for ten minutes without inhaling! Farinelli became a hero of his time, evoking rapture and adulation. On hearing Farinelli, a woman is reported as swooning in her box, exclaiming— "One God and one Farinelli."

851. Castration (of self)—most famous cases

The single most famous case of self-emasculation is that of Origen who severed his own genitals in a fit of religious devotion. He was but one of many who took the Matthew injunction (superlative 525) at its face value. Whole sects grew up to practice self-castration and the emasculation of all men and boys who fell into their clutches. In one of the *Dialogues* of Lucian there is a famous tale of self-castration. A young Syrian nobleman named Cambobus, ordered to accompany the queen on an extended journey, decided to castrate himself so that he would not betray the king en route. He had his testicles placed in an ornate casket, which he secured with a royal seal, and then presented to the king. The queen tried to seduce Cambobus on the journey. Various rumors got back to the king, and the young nobleman was arrested and charged with adultery. But then—of course—Cambobus played his trump card and the king, opening the casket, saw that he was innocent. Whether everyone, including Cambobus, lived happily ever after, we do not know.

852. Eunuchs—most influential in modern times

The court eunuchs in Arabia, China and elsewhere were often close to the monarch: at least they could be trusted not to ravish the harem girls or seduce the queen! In modern times the two most powerful eunuchs were An Tehai and Li Lien-ying, both of whom were favorites of the Empress Dowager Tzu Hsi (1835–1908). On the death of her husband she was installed as Regent until the Crown Prince came of age, but this formidable woman never really relinquished power throughout her life. A principal aim of Chief Eunuch An was to ensure that the young Crown Prince left the means of effective rule in the hands of the Dowager Empress. In part this was achieved by involving the prince in harem facilities at an early age. The prince eventually became chronically weak and, to a degree, insane. Both An Te-hai and Chief Eunuch Li, his successor were skilled at operating the financial affairs of state: both became extremely wealthy men. An eventually overstepped himself and was beheaded, his eunuch companions being strangled and thrown into the river. Chief Eunuch Li stayed at the side of the Dowager Empress for forty years.

853. Castration (chemical)—most recently discovered drug

It is claimed that a new drug, *Cyproterone acetate*, chemically castrates both hetero- and homosexuals more effectively than hitherto possible. The drug is a steriod, which counters the effects of androgen, without feminizing side effects; it blocks testosterone both peripherally and at the hypothalamus in the brain. In particular, it reduces the sexual impulse, the capacity to have an erection, to experience orgasm, etc. It has also been claimed that the drug creates a "sexual calm as a starting point for psychotherapy. The drug was developed first by Schering Chemicals in Germany, where the law permits sexual offenders to be surgically castrated. In the *New Scientist* article, David Cohen properly expressed disquiet at the apparent circumstance that experiments are being conducted in Britain and elsewhere using this drug "without systematic, detailed and available knowledge and a code of ethics to govern" its use.

854. Artificial insemination (animal)—first attempted

There appears to be evidence that the Arabs were practicing artificial insemination with horses at the beginning of the fourteenth-century. An old Arabian document (much quoted), dated around 1322, tells of an inhabitant of Darfur who introduced a wad of wool into a mare's genitals. Then he took the wool, let a stallion smell it to stimulate the sexual urge, caught the ejaculate, and then introduced it into the mare's vagina. The mare conceived (508). Artificial (in)semination of fishes was tried with fishes by Jacobi in 1765 (*Kumstliche Fischzucht,* Hannover Magazine).

855. Artificial insemination (animal)—first experiments

If we allow that the Arabs (superlátive 854) were not carrying out scientific experiments but merely adopting a practical and logical technique for the economic viability of the community then the first technical experimentation in animal artificial insemination probably began with Spallanzani towards the end of the eighteenth-century. In particular his name is associated with the first artificial insemination of a bitch in 1785.

856. Artificial insemination (animal)—first techniques

The first modern techniques of artificial insemination were not that much different to those attributed to the Arabs in the fourteenth-century. Some methods relied on sucking semen from a served vagina and using the extract to inseminate other females (generally domestic cattle). Semen could be collected from inserted sponges or gelatin capsules. Such methods were used with mammals (1912) and birds (1913) (Iwanow). Later methods included the use of a pulsating device (vibrator!) to stimulate male emission; chemical means were used for the same purpose. A number of particular devices were invented; for instance, the special rubber device for collecting boar semen is usually associated with the name of McKenzie (1931).

857. Artificial insemination (animal)—first efforts to cross-breed

Various efforts have been made, in the nineteenth and twentieth-centuries, to cross-breed between species. The following instances have been selected for the last century—

In 1876 Plonnis bred a lap-dog with a male setter; the pup resembled the father. In 1895 Albrecht carried out a similar experiment.

In 1897 Millais bred a bloodhound with a Basset hound.

In 1938 Walton and Hammond bred a large shire horse with a Shetland pony.

In 1912 Iwanow bred a white mouse and a rat.

Many similar experiments have been attempted with varying degrees of success, for both wild and domestic animals(509).

858. Artificial insemination (human)—first recommended method

In 1550 Bartholomeus Eustachius advised the wife of a physician who consulted him on her infertility to persuade her husband, after coitus, to insert his finger into her vagina and push the semen upwards towards the mouth of the uterus. The method is said to have been successful on more than one occasion. Rohleder remarked, with good cause, that this must have been a pretty rough and ready method (510).

859. Artificial insemination (human)—earliest medical methods

These were more sophisticated variants of the methods that would appeal to common sense, the main task being to ensure that the semen be deposited as near to the cervix as possible. One early method aimed at the *accumulation* of semen in the hope that this would produce a higher sperm count in the case of men suspected of low fertility. An inevitable difficulty is maintaining sperm in a viable state where they are not directly injected into the vagina.

860. Artificial insemination (human)—first instance

Around 1887 the Catholic gynaecologist Mantegazza demonstrated that artificial inseminated with the semen of an impotent or otherwise sexually handicapped husband could lead to conception. He was treading on dangerous ground, theologically speaking! In March 1897 the question of the legitimacy of artificial insemination was put to the Holy See, and the answer was a straight *"non licere."* But Mantegazza was by no means the first to have successfully achieved the artificial insemination of a human being. Artificial insemination was first used a century before Mantegazza, in 1781, to enable a man suffering from a malformed penis—a case of hypospadias—to procreate. The earliest successes in this area are generally attributed to John Hunter, who had a wide interest in sexual matters and, in addition to various other enterprises, wrote an influential treatise on venereal diseases. The first artificial insemination *by donor*, as opposed to *by husband*, is reckoned to have been performed by Professor Pancoast about 1884 in the Samson Street Hospital of Jefferson Medical College. A rich merchant (aged 41) and his wife (31) were childless; the husband had had gonorrhoea as a young man. Professor Pancoast eventually collected semen from "the best looking member of the class," after which it was injected into the wife, who was chloroformed. The husband was told of what was happening, but the wife was not. As can be imagined, immense controversy followed this experiment.

861. Artificial insemination (human)—first theologically condemned

There is a clear sense in which artificial insemination is condemned in terms of the overall sexual philosophy of the Roman Catholic Church. With its stress on "natural"' as opposed to "artificial" sexual behavior the Church may be expected to object to any measures that involve a clinical interference with the circumstances of the sex act. And if one adds to this the general theological horror of masturbation—the means whereby semen has traditionally been obtained for inseminatory and other clinical purposes—then Church opposition to medical insemination by husband is easy to understand. With insemination *by donor* the question of adultery is raised and Church opposition is even more predictable. The first formal opposition to artificial insemination (in 1897) merely made explicit what was inherent in traditional teaching.

862. Artificial insemination (human)—first adopted as practical technique

The first systematic use of artificial insemination was probably in the 1890s by the American doctor, Robert Dickinson. He worked, with varying degrees of success, with a number of patients—and in immense secrecy, knowing full well the consequences of exposure. Today there are up to 10,000 successful AID births in the United States every year, with Europe achieving around a thousand (a few hundred of these being British) (511).

Chapter Eight

THE ARTS

863. Coitus (human)—earliest depiction

Human beings, we may reliably assert, first made love a very long time ago. Estimates as to the age of the human race seem to vary between one and two million years, give or take a few hundred thousand years. In any event we have been around a long time (though not yet as long as the dinosaurs, who managed one hundred and twenty million years). Some time after man first made love he got around to the idea of describing it and depicting it in drawings and other artistic forms. In fact he soon became an enthusiast at this type of art, a circumstance that is not immediately apparent in most of our nicely respectable art galleries. Many of the ancient depictions of human coitus will have been lost due to the ravages of time and the ravages of self-styled (and officially appointed) censors. Some ancient drawings and paintings do, however, survive. According to one authority (512) the oldest known depiction of human coitus, in the Ur excavations in Mesopotamia, dates to between 3200 and 3000 b.c. But much older than this are the representations of coital activity on the walls of the Grotte des Combarelles in the Dordogne in France. One particular drawing is thought to date from the Aurignacian period of the late Old Stone Age, about 40,000 (513). If there are more ancient depictions than this we do not know of them.

864. Coital positions (human)—earliest depicted
These ancient drawings are of some interest and so we'll
give them another superlative. What do we know of the
first positions shown for coital activity? In the most ancient drawing, the one in the Dordogne, the woman is
shown crouching forward while the man approaches her
from behind. According to Havelock Ellis (514) the
oldest picture of human coitus that we have—of the
Palaeolithic Solutrian age—shows the man as supine while
the woman squats (in fact the Solutrian, or Solutrean age,
ante-dates the Aurignacian). One prehistoric rock
drawing, this time from Bohusian in Sweden, shows two
couples standing up and copulating (515). And the seals
from Ur of the Chaldees (around 3000 B.C.) have the copulating pair with the woman on top of the man. Kinsey
et al have pointed out that the position with the woman
above is common in ancient art, e.g. that of Peru, India,
China, Japan and other civilizations (516). (See also superlative 184).

865. Coitus (animal)—earliest depiction
In Ariége in France there is the famous grotto known as
Tuc d'Audoubert. At the end of the last gallery three ex-
ploring boys found, in 1912, an "art work which has become one of the most significant items in any history of
sex"(517). The creation is a sculpture in clay showing
clearly a male bison about to mount a female bison; and it
has been dated to the prehistoric life of palaeolithic man.

866. Sexual symbols—earliest
Man's early preoccupation with sexual matters led to the
literal depiction of human and animal coitus, and to the use
of sexual symbols for magical and religious purposes. Crude
representations of the male and female genitals were employed in ritual to aid fertility of man and beast. Sometimes the symbols were shown in conjunction to signal the
union of the sexes and the fruitful outcome of intercourse.
The use of symbolic imagery, through painting and sculpture, can be dated to the time of palaeolithic man, around

20,000 B.C. One modern writer (518) has pointed out that the ancient symbols of paleolithic Europe "can be accurately matched with symbols still used by Tantrikas."

867. Sexual symbols—oldest in China

According to some authorities the most ancient Chinese representations of sexual subject matter date from the Han dynasty (ca. 206 B.C.–A.D. 24)—"Excavations from that period have unearthed bricks from tombs and gifts buried with the dead which show definite sexual motifs." In view of the great antiquity of other aspects of Chinese erotic life these sexual motifs do not seem particularly ancient. The sexual manuals in China (see superlative 298) suggest that various forms of sexual imagery would have been employed two or three thousand years before the birth of Christ.

868. Sexual figures—most famous Palaeolithic drawings

We have already cited instances of ancient palaeolithic art. The early interest of man in sexual art is well established. Perhaps the most famous of all the palaeolithic sexual depictions are those to be found in the Les Trois Frères cavern: a human figure, wearing an animal skin and antlers, is crouching, his genitals clearly shown (this drawing has often been cited as evidence of early witchcraft. Elsewhere in Trois Frères is an ithyphallic bison with human legs. And half-human, half-animal depictions are shown to suggest sexual mounting. A bone engraving from the Abri Murat (Lot) is based on the same theme. And in Pech Merle there is a finger drawing in clay of a woman "crouched in a sexually receptive posture beneath animal-like lines"(519).

869. Nude (female)—earliest sculpture

The prehistoric sculptures such as the Venus of Willendorf are among the oldest to show the nude female figure. Such works are generally dated to palaeolithic times. The relief carvings such as the Venus of Laussel may also be mentioned (520). What is particularly interesting about these early representations is that they are not naturalistic, in the way that the early paintings of animals are naturalistic. Instead certain sexual features are exaggerated, such as the thighs and breasts. The apparent desirability of fatness, common also to primitive societies in the modern world, has been attributed to the survival value of stored body food. In the late Stone Age an Aurignacian sculptor created what has come to be known as the Venus of Lespugue, a palaeolithic female figure carved in the ivory of a mammoth's tusk found in the Haute-Garonne in 1922 (521). The period runs from about 30,000 B.C. to 10,000 B.C.

870. Nude—first invented as art-form

After the superlatives already presented in this chapter the following quote may seem a bit odd—"What is the nude?" It is an art form invented by the Greeks in the 5th century B.C., just as opera is an art form invented in 17th century Italy. The conclusion is certainly too abrupt, but it has the merit of emphasizing that the nude is not the subject of art, but a form of art. This is at least partly a semantic point, but perhaps we can appreciate the underlying point.

871. Nude (female)—most famous ancient sculpture

The Cnidian Aphrodite (or Venus) of Praxiteles is generally said to be the most famous statue in the ancient world. It has been dated to the fourth century B.C., and the work was seemingly known throughout many of the lands of antiquity. In the tenth century the work, having been taken to Constantinople by Theodosius, was praised by the Emperor Constantine Porphyrogenitus; and the statue, in original or copy, is mentioned by Robert de Clari in his account of the taking of Constantinople by the Crusaders.

872. Erotic sculpture—most famous

The most famous erotic sculpture in the world is certainly that of the Hindu temples of India(522). Most of the best examples were created in the North between the ninth and thirteen centuries A.D., and in the South between the sixth and seventeenth-centuries A.D. The sculptures show every imaginable form of sexual activity—different coital positions, oral sex, masturbation, rape, bestiality, etc. Many temples still used for worship make use of immense wooden-wheeled chariots or "cars," constructed after the pattern of the temples, with high canopies and spires. The chariots are used to carry the sacred images during the festivals, and they are adorned with the same sorts of erotic scenes as are the temples themselves. The carvings, elaborate and meticuolusly excuted, show all forms of sexual behavior.

873. Nude (female)—most famous rock relief

The Venus of Laussel (already mentioned, superlative 869) is the most famous rock relief of a nude woman. Originally deriving from a rock shelter, it is now in a museum at Bordeaux. The figure (about 46 cm tall) was originally carved on a block overhanging a sanctuary, and is probably Solutrian in date. She had been colored red to signify power and life; and her breasts, belly, hips and thighs bulge with fat. Her hand rests on his stomach, and the pubic triangle is emphasized. Her attributes are clearly sexual. There has been speculation about the relationship of the figure with animal fertility cults.

874. Penis (human)—largest (fiction)

In fiction and legend the human penis can be any size. Malinowski wrote of the Legend of Inuvayla'u, who was the head of his clan and possessed of a remarkably long organ. When the women of the tribe were cleaning the ground or weeding he would stand behind a fence and push his penis through a convenient aperture. It would wriggle along the ground like a snake, and when the women went bathing the penis would chase them through the water like an eel. Eventually he left the village, before he went cutting off his penis and testicles: they turned to stone as they fell. The testicles can still be seen, as large round boulders; and the glans penis is a pointed helmet-shaped piece of coral (523). In the *Arabian Nights* many vast organs are paraded. In one of the stories there is a description of a *zabb*, "as great as an ass's or an elephant's, a powerful sight to see." In another of the stories a man is able to wish for a large penis, whereupon the zabb grew enormously until it resembled a calabash lying between two pumpkins. The weight was so great that the poor fellow could no longer stand. And at a more mundane level we have the straightforward exaggerations common in pornographic fiction of all ages. In de Sade's *The 120 Days of Sodom* Hercule boasts a 13-in. long penis. In Chinese fiction there are similarly impressive items of equipment, with organs invariably described as of "incredible length," "bigger than a sea cucumber" or "too thick to be encircled by a lady's fingers." The hardness of such monsters was comparable to that of an iron post, and such organs could support, when erect, a bushel of wheat hung from the end (524)!

875. Sex organs (human)—largest in erotic art

Some erotic art, notably that of Japan, is characterized by immense exaggeration of the sexual organs. The penis and vulva are often drawn three or four times their proper size: the penis, for example, can resemble a forearm, and the female organ often "assumes the length and width of the folded sleeve opening of a kimono" (525). One extraordinary feature of Japanese erotic art is the depiction of the penis as a duelling weapon. Drawings show two men, both equipped with mighty organs, fencing with the erect members. There are also other forms of penis competitions: men are depicted going along to have vast organs measured to see who possesses the largest. In one drawing a man equipped with a penis about the size of all the rest of him is obliged to support the mighty organ on a pair of wagonwheels trundling before him! A sexual hero of China was said to be able to smash a copper pot with one blow of his penis!

876. Penis transplant—earliest in fiction

In a seventeenth-century Chinese tale, *Jou-pu-t'uan*, there is an account of a penis transplant, or, perhaps more accurately, a penis graft (526). A Scholar inquires of the Master of Medicine how a gigantic organ can be acquired. One technique, as carefully explained, is to make use of the erect organ of a dog. It is arranged for the dog and bitch to copulate; in the midst of the act the Master of Medicine cuts off the penis of the dog and, slicing it up, inserts the parts into the incised organ of the man requiring a larger member—"With luck, there will be a perfect grafting of man and dog."

877. Penis (supernatural)—largest

Devils and demons have often worried pious folk on account of their absorbing interest in sexual matters. Neither men nor women, in medieval times and after, could sleep soundly in their beds for fear of being visited by randy beings from the supernatural realm. In such circumstances it was hardly surprising that such lecherous creatures should be assigned vast sexual organs, the more accurately to depict their true natures. Thus the devil, simultaneously invented and castigated by religious people, was said to possess a vast penis; a circumstance thought to bring pain to his witch-followers when they copulated with him at esbat and sabat. A witness cited by De Lancre testified that when the devil appeared as man or goat "he always had a member like a mule's . . . that it was as long and as thick as an arm . . . and that he always exposed his instrument, of such beautiful shape and measurements" (527). But this is as nothing compared with the organ of an Arab demon called an Ifrit. Thus Kashkash ibn Fakrash ibn Atrash, of the line of Abu Hanfash, had a zabb forty times larger than that of an elephant; the organ ran between his legs and rose in the air behind him (528).

878. Penile thrusts (human)—most number in erotic fiction

Chinese and Japanese erotic fiction features men and women of gigantic sexual prowess. In one instance, a couple "sported for a long time," not all that remarkable until we find that "he thrust his sword, continuously in and out of her scabbard over three thousand times" (529). This makes another Chinese claim—never less than a thousand thrusts without pause (530)—look positively feeble. One Japanese best seller carries the title, "How to Make a Nymphomaniac Faint in One Foray."

879. Testes (human)—largest (fiction)

We have already met the weighty testicles of Inuvayla'u (superlative 541). There are others, e.g. in the *Arabian Nights.* For instance, a certain King Samandal was said to have testicles that normally hung to his knees (531). This remarkable pair of organs did, however, rush up to his navel when he was cross! (Vast organs, as we have seen (superlative 87), can be caused by diseases such as elephantiasis. Atkins quotes a note in Douglas—"Whoever wishes to see what this organ can do in the way of size should go to Pernambuco, where it is nothing out of the way to see a man wheeling his testicles in front of him in a barrow. I suspect the disease (elephantiasis) was imported by African Negroes" (532).

880. Semen—best quality (fiction)

The medieval demons were particular fellows. If they wanted to copulate with human women then they used only the best quality semen. Of course it first had to be acquired from human males, a requirement satisfied by gathering up nocturnal emissions or squeezing seminal fluid out of the nearest handy corpse. That the demons worked to get the best semen they could is attested by two late sixteenth-century experts, the Dominican Thomas Malvenda and Dr. Franciscus Valesius. "What incubi introduce into the womb is not any ordinary human semen in normal quantity, but abundant, very thick, very warm, rich in spirits and free from serosity. This, moreover, is an easy thing for them, since they merely have to choose ardent, robust men, whose semen is naturally very copious, and with whom the succubus has relations; and then the incubus copulates with women of a like constitution, taking care that both shall enjoy a more than normal orgasm, for the greater the venereal excitement the more abundant is the semen."

881. Ejaculate (human)—largest (fiction)

Some heroic characters in erotic fiction manage to ejaculate over and over again without apparent effort or fatigue. Try de Sade again! In *The 120 Days of Sodom* the Duc de Blangis, though fifty years of age, maintained a constant erection (priapism?) and could ejaculate any number of times a day! Perhaps, though, Hercule was the most accomplished—he could fill a pint measure to the brim with only eight discharges!!

882. Orgasms (men)—most frequent (fiction)

Some literary accounts of sexual experience may or may not be true. It is not a field where men are apt to be modest. Boswell gives us a nice account in his *London Journal*. In one encounter, which took place with Louisa on 12 January 1763, he was "fairly lost in supreme rapture" no less than five times, and the worthy Louisa declared him a prodigy. Atkins suggests that "Boswell was probably truthful." Debate about frequency or orgasm often centers on six or seven times as remarkable. In literature there are many examples around such figures—in *Teleny*, "As true votaries of the Grecian god, we poured out seven copious libations to Priapus." In *Catullus*, a bigger figure is mentioned—

> . . . . *and bid some servant bar the door;*
> *and don't rush out to call or shop,*
> *but nicely wait for what I'll bring,*
> *and then—nine hugs without a stop!*

And Ovid, though growing old, managed it nine times with Corinna—but he is not at all satisfied. In de Sade's *Juliette*, Minsky never goes to bed without first discharging ten times ("It is a fact that the inordinate amount of human flesh I eat contributes greatly to the augmentation and thickening of my seminal fluid") (533). Such men are weaklings compared with the performers in Arab and Japanese legend. In the *Arabian Nights* one man manages to make love forty times in one night; Japanese sexual athletes are similarly insatiable. And there is a pleasant little joke I cannot resist including—An English sailor got into an argument with a Chinese sailor in Shanghai, each boasting how many times he could do it. They decided to put the matter to the test. Each took a girl to bed. The Englishman performed once, then again, and finally—with difficulty for he had drunk too much—a third time. He marked each one on the wall with an upright stroke. In the morning the exhausted Chinese crawled into his room. He looked at the Englishman's tally and exclaimed—"One hundred and eleven! Beaten by one, by God!"

883. Aphrodisiac—most effective (fiction)

Every imaginable concoction has been tried in efforts, mostly futile, to increase sexual capacity and performance. Sometimes the recommendations are not what we would immediately expect. Thus Omar Haleby played the part of sexual adviser to the Prophet Mohammed and was keen on sexual stimulants. In his view no aphrodisiac was superior to prayer, which he advocated before coitus along with the shouting of "Allah" at the moment of ejaculation. One complicated recommendation involved the preparation of a paste (with many ingredients)—"You must eat this paste two hours before the sexual approach but for three days before that you must eat nothing but roast pigeons excessively seasoned with spice, male fish . . . and lightly fried ram's eggs. If after all that you do not pierce the very walls of the room and get THE FOUNDATION OF THE HOUSE WITH CHILD, YOU CAN CUT OFF MY BEARD and spit in my face . . ." (534) A Chinese concoction enables a man to make love to more than ten women every night (535). But most impressive of all is the plant mentioned by Theophrastus which, held in the hand, enabled a man to achieve sexual relations seventy times in one night! ". . . but he forgot to name the plant, and thus deprived all succeeding generations of vital knowledge" (536).

884. Promiscuity (male)—most extreme (fiction)

Samson is said to have made love to around 3000 Philistinian women during his time at the prison in Gaza. The Rabbi Hiyya speculated, interestingly enough, that the Philistines seized Samson, who was playing with Delilah, "while he was in the state of erection." And the Hercules of Western mythology was reputed to have prodigious sexual capacities. For instance, on one occasion he is said to have deflowered around fifty daughters of Thespios in a single night. The mighty club carried by Hercules in sculptures and other depictions has been said to represent his penis. It is hardly surprising that such performers should be valued as studs, and that women should want children sired by them. It has been said that the main reason the Philistines captured Samson was to breed a race of supermen.

885. Clitorises (human)—most (fiction)

One clitoris per (female) person is the usual quota—but fiction, and legend, are not so limited. Malinowski gives examples from Melanesia of a woman who had five boys and five clitorises! The giant stingaree used to terrify her: it would copulate with her and then cut off a clitoris. She complained (who wouldn't?) to each of her sons in turn, but it was only the fifth and youngest, when she only had one clitoris left, who faced the creature and killed it (537).

886. Clitoris (human)—longest fiction

In de Sade's *Juliette* there is a woman named Volmar who carries a clitoris three inches long, and, "destined to insult Nature whichever be the sex she adopts, the whore's got either to play the nymphomaniac or the sodomite: with her, there's no median alternative." Yes, this one is an impressive length, but try superlative 114 (truth longer than fiction?).

887. Vagina (human)—most capacious (fiction)

In the main a vagina is only required to accommodate a penis, though eventually it will have to accommodate a baby's head! There are big vaginas in fact, though, as Germaine Greer remarks, "no woman wants to find out that she has a twat like a horse collar" (538). In fiction, however, there are bigger ones. There is the tale of Digawina (the name means Store-cunt) who had such a capacious vagina that she used to pack it with coconuts, yams, taro, areca nuts, betel pods, large chunks of sugar cane and whole bunches of bananas. She met her match, however, when some unpleasant fellow concealed a large black mangrove crab among the food!

888. Vagina (human)—most voracious (fiction)

There is an Eskimo legend about the unhappy fate of Nukarpiartekak. He visits a girl in an igloo but then finds he has bitten off more than he can chew. He starts to make love to the beautiful creature but then finds to his presumed horror that *all of him* is being sucked into her vagina. Gradually he disappears, bit by bit. In the morning Nukarpiartekak no longer exists; his kayak lies untended on the river. The beautiful girl goes out of the igloo to urinate and out falls the skeleton of her erstwhile lover (539). What is singularly interesting about this sort of myth is how it crops up from one society to another: the toothed vagina is a frequent apparition in the dreams of mentally disturbed people.

889. Nipples—largest (fiction)

Lots of fictional and legendary giants may be presumed to have gargantuan nipples. Usually there is no mention of this part of a giant's anatomy. Occasionally we see reference to the sexual features of such creatures. There is a nice section in the unexpurgated version of Swift's *Gulliver's Travels*. At one time in his adventures, Gulliver finds himself sitting astride a nipple of one of the female giants of Brobdingnag—"The handsomest among these maids of honor, a pleasant frolicksome girl of sixteen, would sometimes set me astride upon one of her nipples; with many other tricks, wherein the reader will excuse me for not being over particular (540)." A nipple that a man could sit astride must have been a pretty weighty appendage!

890. Reproduction—oddest method (fiction)

A fair number of odd methods of propagation of the human race have been described in fictional literature. Perhaps none is odder than the one found in Lucian. For a start, in Lucian's *The True History* it is the men who get pregnant—and the child grows not in a uterus but in the calf of the leg, "which grows extremely fat on these occasions." At the right time a Caesarian operation is carried

out, and the baby is taken out dead; but then it is brought
to life by being placed in a high winds with its mouth open.
Another Lucian mode of reproduction is that adopted by
the Tree-men. A man's right testicle is cut off and placed
in the ground, where it soon grows into a large fleshy tree
rather like a phallus. Vast acorns are produced which,
when ripe, allow the babies inside to be hatched.

891. Sex aids—most famous mention in Greece (fiction)

We like Lucian so we'll give him another superlative.
We said Greece in the title of this one but it may just
as well have been Syria, Rome or France. Lucian was a
well-traveled (and well-read) fellow. I think of him in
connection with Greece because some of his funniest dialogues involve poking fun at the Greek philosophers. Anyway, he also talked about sex aids, briefly but amusingly.
In *The True History*, talking of some of his fanciful people, he remarks that "It is not uncommon up there to have
artificial private parts, which apparently work quite well.
If you are rich, you have them made of ivory, but the
poorer classes have to rub along with wooden ones."

892. Sexual deformations (deliberate)—most bizarre

There are many ways in which the human body has been
mutilated in order to enhance sexual attractiveness. We
need only mention a few. The binding of the feet of
Chinese women immediately springs to mind, as does piercing of the ear lobes in many cultures. Teeth have been
filed to sharp points, as among the Bogobo women of
Mindanao Island. Similarly the shape of the skull has been
modified by tight binding from infancy onwards. Some societies have pierced noses and nipples (or even amputated
the latter). And Musgu women were known to insert
larger and larger plates into their lips to cause a greater
and greater distortion of the flesh. In our own society, ear-
piercing is commonplace and there is quite a vogue for
nipple-piercing in some areas—but multilatory steps rarely
proceed beyond such things (541).

893. Brassieres—first

It all depends what you mean ... In various parts of ancient Greece the brassiere, in one form or other, was employed; paradoxically, in view of the free attitudes towards mixed nudity, naked athletics and the like, brassieres have been associated which the ancient inhabitants of Sparta. There were also used in China and elsewhere. The now almost extinct ancient Chinese brassiere has been likened to a small apron, introduced by Yang Kwei-fei, a concubine of Emperor Hsuan Tsung of T'amg in the eighth-century. In fact the charming creature only decided on the creation of a "brassiere" to cover bites made by an "illegitimate" lover.

894. Topless dresses—first

The topless dress fashion of a few years ago may have seemed like a new thing. It wasn't. In fact an early purpose of the corset was to show as much of the breast as possible. As early as 1388, Johann de Mussi, a Lombard author, wrote—"Women show their breasts and it looks as if their breasts would wish to jump from their bosom". And he adds, reflectively, "Which gown would be beautiful if it did not show the breasts?" The beautiful Agnes Sorel (1409–1450) was said to display her shoulders and breasts, including the nipples (783). The early Christian Church termed the laced openings to women's bodices "the gates of hell". By the fifteenth century much of the breast was again being shown; and in James I's time young unmarried women (784) displayed the whole of their breasts. John Hall, a sixteenth-century poet comments "That women theyr breastes dyd shew & lay out." But the early Anglo-Saxons were predated by centuries in the use of topless fashions. In various mediterranean lands of antiquity the exposed breasts was a commonplace.

895. Breast piercing—first modrn mass incidence

Breast piercing, as a modern fashion has already been mentioned (superlative 892); but again it is really nothing new. An earlier craze swept England in the 1890s.

896. Erotic jade and ivory—first in China

Erotic carvings gradually appeared in Chinese jade and ivory. An eye-witness in the Ming Dynasty described such things from the Ming Palace—"The two Happy Buddhas were carved out of two huge pieces of flawless jade. With their sex organs in close contact they gave the viewers the basic concept of the man-woman relationship. The eunuch in charge told me that these jade figures were actually left behind in the palace by the Mongols after their downfall. He also said that they had been used by the Mongol imperial family to enlighten their descendants about the facts of life. It is believed that after our empire had been established, these figures continued to be used for the same purpose during the reign of our first few emperors. However, I cannot help congratulating myself secretly for having the good luck to see these finished products of artistic perfection (542)."

897. Erotic coins—first

China also boasted erotic coins ("spring coins"), as early as the Han Dynasty. On one side of a coin would be words of good omen; on the other, a god and a goddess would be copulating. It was claimed that such coins could dispel evil spirits, as a consequence of which, parents frequently gave them to their children as a form of protection against supernatural forces. By the time of the Sung Dynasty the coins were showing a variety of coital positions: they were no longer called "spring coins" but "bed curtain-spreading coins." They formed an integral part of a dowry when a daughter married; on the wedding-night the coins would be scattered on the bridal bed. In other cultures with a strong erotic tradition and a coinage system coins were also used to depict sexual activity. For example, in pre-Christian Greece some coins show an eager satyr carrying off a complaisant nymph (mid-sixth-century B.C.). And there is a Green scaraboid of the fifth-century B.C., showing a cock treading a hen; an identical scene appears on an Etruscan gem of the same period.

898. Erotic porcelain ware—first in China
Sexual designs were used for porcelain ware by the Manchu emperors such as Ch'ien Lung and Hsien Feng, as a form of sexual elaboration. Erotic motifs and designs were used on vases, bowls, plates, etc.; it has been established that such designs were painted on earthenware in the first and third-centuries. One early Chinese habit was to bury earthen bowls and plates where "future rebel leaders or rulers might be born." It was thought that earthenware carrying erotic designs would bring ill luck to future rulers and thus forestall possible uprisings. This is in interesting contrast to the supposed beneficial effect of erotic coins.

899. Erotic paintings—first promoted in China
According to Han Shu (*Historical Records of the Han Dynasty*) Prince Kuan Ch'uan, during the reign of Emperor Hsuan Ti (71–48 B.C.) was the first promoter of erotic (or "pornographic") paintings ... It is said that the prince commissioned a couple of famous painters to paint the palace ceiling with vivid pictures of men and women making love in various positions. When drinking and carousing with guests he would ask them to look up at the ceiling. The prince is also said to have committed adultery with his own sisters. When his favorite concubine invited one of the painters to have sexual intercourse with her, Prince Kuan Ch'uan drew out his sword and "cut her body into eight pieces (543)."

900. Erotic painter—greatest in China
Chou Fang is regarded as the greatest Chinese erotic painter. Mi Fei, a famous painter in the Sung Dynasty, held Chou in the same class as Ku Kai-chih (one of whose pictures is in the British Museum), Lu T'ang-wei, and Wu Tao-tzu. The women in Chou's paintings are all rather plump—which relates to the T'ang Dynasty concept of beauty. Chou Fang, in common with many oriental artists, also tended to exaggerate the size of the genital organs: it is said that he influenced Japanese erotic art (see superlative 542).

901. Erotic model—first Chinese emperor
Emperor Hsuan Tsung, called Ming Huang (the Enlightened Emperor) by his subjects, used his favorite concubine as a model for erotic paintings. Chiu Fang (superlative 900) was one of the court painters. In one painting Chou portrayed Hsuan Tsung with five women, one of them making love to him. The pictures are described by numerous scholars as successive dynasties, but no trace of these particular works have been found in China. Portraits by Chou Fang are held in the Palace Museum of Taiwan. Two hundred years later, in the Sung Dynasty, an unnamed court painter painted Emperor T'ai Tsung making love to the captured Little Queen Chou of Li Yu, the poet-king of Southern T'ang.

902. Erotic pictures—first recommended as aid to love-making
It is a commonplace in the modern world to expect illustrations to aid love-making. The biggest and best sex manuals (e.g. *The Joy of Sex*, Comfort) come equipped with fine pictures—drawings or photographs. In China the first reference to erotic pictures used for the guidance of bride and groom occurs in a poem from about A.D. 100. This is the *T'ung-sheng-ko*, a verse-treatise written by the famous poet Chang Heng (A.D. 78–139)—

Let us now lock the double door with its golden lock,
And light the lamp to fill the room with its brilliance,
I shed my robes and remove my paint and powder,
And roll out the picture scroll by the side of the pillow,
The plain girl I shall take as my instructress,
So that we can practice all the variegated postures,
Those that an ordinary husband has but rarely seen,
Such as taught by T'ien-lao to the Yellow Emperor.
No joy shall equal the delights of this first night,
These shall never be forgotten, however old we may
    grow.

903. Erotic art (Japan)—period of highest development
Japanese erotic art is generally regarded as reaching a peak during the Edo period, 1600–1868; Edo refers to

the small fishing town which was to succeed the old city of Kyoto as capital of Japan and which was to become the Tokyo of today. The Edo period saw a quite unparalleled development of erotic art and literature, one consequence of which was that the Japanese government started to take an interest in censorship!

904. Love painting—most famous in Spain

The most famous of the few Spanish love-paintings is the fairy-tale *Saint George and the Dragon* (c. 1438, Art Institute of Chicago) by Bernat Martorel. The style is linked in its conventions to the illumination of manuscripts. The original Saint George is thought to have died about A.D. 300 at Lydda in Palestine. He seemingly assumed his role of a slayer of dragons from Perseus who slew a sea monster that had threatened the virgin Andromeda. The ideals of courtly love "were exalted to the sanctification of the perfect, gentle knight."

905. Nude (reclining figure)—first used in European art

It is thought that Giorgione and Titian were the first painters to use a reclining nude woman as the subject of a painting. Where, before their time, such a position occurs, as on some Roman sarcophagi, the figure is only a detail, filling in the corners to complete the design. The use of the nude woman in such a way was secondary to the main design. Giorgione and Titian in both sculpture and painting elevated the reclining nude to a significant status, and this is the teeth of opposition from the Christian Church to all things carnal.

906. Nude sculpture—first in Renaissance

There are nudes and nudes. Some are desiccated and sexless, others jaunty and provocative. According to one authority(544), the first nude of the Renaissance—a nude that is "not unaesthetic and submissive, the usual appearance of the Byzantine and medieval Eves"—is Lorenzo Ghiberti's *Eve* on the eastern door of the Baptistry in Florence, sculptured in relief in 1425. She is given the Hebrew name of Eve and she is being called into existence by Jehovah, but she has the beautiful expression reminiscent of the Greek Venus on the Ludovisi throne and the body is "unashamedly beautiful . . ." (Ghiberti also wrote the earliest known autobiography of an artist.)

907. Erotic art—first Italian Renaissance painter

Antonio Pisanello (c. 1395–c. 1455) has been taken as one of the first Italian artists to see in the nude form the wide scope for erotic art. He produced copies of the Bacchic Sarcophagi in the Campo Santo collection of antique art in Pisa, and then added to some of these an erotic component; for instance he drew the legs of a young girl to suggest "uninhibited delight in sexuality."

908. Pornographic artist—earliest in England

The earliest pornographic artist in England, with name unknown, functioned halfway through the eighteenth-century. In about 1755 he produced seventeen drawings to illustrate *"The Pleasures of Love: Containing a Variety of Entertaining Particulars and Curiosities in the Cabinet of Venus."* The frontispiece shows a fat woman, with a basin of cordial in her left hand, the right drawing aside the curtains of a bed on which can be seen four naked legs. On the curtain is inscribed "The Pleasures of Love 1755." The book was reprinted in 1881 as "The Adventures of a Rake," and in reprint the book carried inferior illustrations (545).

909. Prostitutes—most poetic in China

Ancient (and, sometimes, modern) prostitutes exhibited considerable artistic and literary ability in many cases. One task of the early prostitute was to make the wedding ceremony go with a swing, and this she would sometimes accomplish by reciting her own poetic compositions. In China there were great numbers of poetic prostitutes in the T'ang period; and among them, Hsueh Tao has enjoyed lasting fame. She became a prostitute after the death of her parents and later became the Official Compiler of Classics. In her old age she became a nun (Taoist) and lived in a small hut by a well. A commercial fellow did well by making a special notepaper out of the

water of the well and calling it "Hsueh Tao's notepaper."
Another poetic prostitute was Su Hsiao-hsiao of the
Southern Sung Dynasty (13th century). She was so famous that one of her contemporary poets considered himself honored to have been born in the same city,
Chient'ang. In many anthologies of Chinese classical poetry there are poems that were written by ancient prostitutes. A famous example is the poem from *Tzu Tsung*
(An Imperial Manchu Anthology of Classical Poems),
written by an anonymous prostitute from Szachuan in the
Yuan (Mongol) Dynasty: the poem is a sad one about a
man going away and leaving his lover.

910. Love-poet—most important in Rome
This is Catullus, the first Roman love-poet. He has been
considered "more sympathetic to modern minds than all
his famous successors; for he is a man, not a rhetorician,
and he tells us frankly and beautifully of his passion
(546)." Catullus has been seen as bisexual, with the
heterosexual side of his nature predominating. Inevitably
he has been portrayed as a coarse and pornographic
writer.

911. Kissing—most famous poet
Robert Herrick has been dubbed the "Kissing Poet." For
instance, his *Hesperides*, 1648, is replete with kisses and
kissing. In Catullus (superlative 564) there is a kissing
poem. Herrick has his own version—

Ah my Anthea! Must my heart still break?
(Love makes me write, what shame forbids to speak.)
Give me a kisse, adde to that kisse a score;
Then to that twenty, adde an hundred more;
A thousand to that thousand; so kisse on,
To make that thousand up a million.
Treble that million, and when that is done,
Let's kisse afresh, as when we first begun.
But yet, though Love likes well such Scenes as these,
There is an act that will more fully please:
Kissing and glancing, soothing, all make way
But to the acting of this private play:

Name it I would; but being blushing red,
The rest Ile speak, when we meet both in bed.

912. Sexual love—greatest European poet

This superlative, like many of the others, is a matter of opinion. But for this one a fair number of people seem to opt for Racine. Racine has been represented as seeing love as a passion—"that is, something suffered by mankind, a thing imposed upon mankind from outside—and ultimately, therefore, an ill."

913. Homosexuality—most famous sonnets

Homosexual poets, like heterosexual poets, write sonnets. The most famous sonnets that may legitimately be dubbed "homosexual" are undoubtedly those by Shakespeare, in particular Sonnets 20, 26, 36, 53, 54, and 126. The extent to which Shakespeare was a homosexual can of course be debated—if you want to. For my part it seems a waste of time. To discern homosexual content in sensitive verse is merely to extend the range of human love. Many of the Italian Renaissance poets wrote homosexual sonnets.

914. Female body—most famous poem

If the Song of Solomon is a poem then it qualifies for this one. Some people say it is a poem, some disagree. It all depends upon where you stand, semantically. Another name for the Song of Solomon is the *Song of Songs,* a title which—like the equivalent *King of Kings*—suggests something quite outstanding. In the nineteenth century the Reverend E. P. Eddrupp, Prebendary of Salisbury Cathedral, wrote in a commentary on the Old Testament— "Such a book as the Song of Solomon may not be fitted for public reading in a mixed congregation, or even for private reading by the impure in heart." The first century Pharisees wondered whether the Song should have a place in the Canon: the problem was that the Song so clearly celebrates physical (or carnal) love and makes no reference to God. Inevitably there were endless attempts to interpret the Song metaphorically or allegorically. It is supposed to have been written about 400 B.C., during the reign of Artaxerxes II (547).

915. Virgin birth (human)—first lampoon

A lampoon published in 1750, and quoted by Rostand (in his *La Biologie et l'Avenir humain*), comments upon the idea of fertilization without copulation—

> May couples riven by conflict return to harmony, trust, and mutual respect! May slandered women bid gossiping tongues be silent! A woman living apart from her husband can nevertheless present him with the joys of fatherhood, fruit of a boating trip or a country walk. The woman only wanted to get a breath of fresh air, and the organic molecules needed only a draft, a slight breeze to establish themselves in her. A widowed lady has children, and gossip names their fathers. But there is no need for any such assumption: she merely breathed the air and the molecules crept into her along with it. A girl becomes a mother before marriage: again only the air she inhaled is to blame. Why should humanity be in a worse plight than ordinary insects? . . .

Today, parthenogenesis in higher animals is no longer seen as quite so ridiculous!

916. Anti-papal philippic—most extreme

It is likely that the most vicious philippic ever published was a twenty-six page pamphlet that appeared in 1700. It was entitled, *Reasons Humbly Offer'd For a Law to Enact the Castration of Popish Ecclesiastics. As the Best Way to Prevent the Growth of Popery in England.* The author asserted that the Roman clergy had kept 100,000 whores before the Reformation. A variety of other arguments are introduced to establish beyond reasonable doubt that depraved nature of "popish ecclesiastics." This pamphlet, a poisonous diatribe, was distributed in the 1860s by the Protestant Evangelical Mission and Electoral Union.

917. Graffiti—most frequent sexual (by females)

Graffiti, as we all know, is not always sexual in nature. It is more often sexual when produced by men than when produced by women. Kinsey and his colleagues investigated sexual and non-sexual graffiti (as they appear to have investigated everything else)and documented and tabulated their results (548). A high proportion (86 per cent) of the inscriptions on the walls of the male toilets were found to be sexual; but not more than 25 per cent of the toilet wall inscriptions made by women dealt with sexual topics (genitals, oral and anal sexual behavior, "obscene" words, etc.). Most of the female inscriptions referred to love, or names were associated ("John and Mary," "Helen and Don"); the drawing of hearts was common in the female toilets. In 331 female inscriptions, there were 69 per cent depicting lips, 35 per cent making non-erotic references to love with the opposite sex, and 12 per cent making non-erotic references to love with own sex. The scores in the other Kinsey categories were considerably less.

918. Graffiti—least frequent sexual (by females)
Surprisingly, amongst the 331 female inscriptions (superlative 917) there were no references to heterosexual dating (homosexual dating scored one per cent). There were no homosexual references to anal contacts, and only one per cent heterosexual reference to anal activity. Oral contacts scores two per cent (heterosexual) and one per cent (homosexual); "other erotic items" also scored two per cent (both heterosexual and homosexual).

919. Graffiti—most frequent sexual (by males)
The investigators (see superlative 917) found 1048 sexual and nonsexual inscriptions in male toilets, of which the largest category (30 per cent) were homosexual oral contacts, with heterosexual oral contacts scoring only eleven per cent. Twenty-one per cent of the inscriptions were to homosexual dating and eighteen per cent to homosexual anal contacts.

920. Graffiti—least frequent sexual (by males)
The least frequent references by men were to "non-erotic" items such as lips and hearts (none recorded). Three per

cent of inscriptions related to the genitalia of the opposite sex; and non-erotic references to love (both with the same and the opposite sex) also scored three per cent. Five per cent of the inscriptions referred to heterosexual dating.

921. Love-songs—foremost fourteenth-century composer

Guillaume de Machaut, born in Champagne around the year 1300, was the dominant figure both in lyric poetry and music in fourteenth-century France. Many of his own poems were specifically arranged for musical setting. In a famous work combining both poetry and music, Le Livre du Voir Dit, probably written between 1361 and 1365, Machaut recounts the progress of his love affair with a young girl called Péronne. At this time the poet was more than sixty years old and blind in one eye. It is likely that the girl was more impressed by the man's reputation as a poet and composer than by the amorous possibilities of the situation. Machaut is considered one of the central figures in the art of courtly love (569).

922. Sex translator—most prolific

Sir Richard Francis Burton (1821–87) was one of the most accomplished and many-sided men of the nineteenth-century. As well as being a man of action (explorer, swordsman, etc.) he possessed immense intellectual ability—as ethnologist, linguist, poet, amateur botanist, zoologist, and geologist. He published forty-three volumes describing his travels, two volumes of poetry, and more than one hundred articles. In particular he translated sixteen volumes of the *Arabian Nights,* six volumes of Portugese literature, two volumes of Latin poetry, four volumes of folklore (Neapolitan, African and Hindu), etc. In the words of his (perhaps) most skillful biographer (550)— ". . . Burton was no ordinary translator; the inflexible integrity, brilliance, and vigor of his translations are an index to the man himself. One stands in awe of the ease with which he moved from Hindustani for his Pilpay's Fables and *Vikram and Vampire*—to Portugese for his *Camoens* and *Lacerda*—to Arabic for the *Arabian Nights* and the *Perfumed Garden*—to Neapolitan Italian for his *Il Penta-*

merone—to Sanscrit for his *Kama Sutra* and *Ananga Ranga*, and to Latin for his *Priapeia* and *Catullus.*"

923. Erotic novels—most prolific period (China)
Chin Ping Mei, an erotic novel of the early sixteenth-century, "seemed to set a trend for pornography in fiction." A great number of erotic works appeared in China in the seventeenth and eighteenth-centuries. Chou has mentioned *Jou Pu Tuan* (The Prayer Mat of Flesh), The Apricot Blossoms Sky, The Monk of Lamp Wick, The Biography of a Silly Woman and Yeh Sou Pu Yen (The Frank Words of a Rural Old Man).

924. Erotic novels—first emerging (China)
It is likely that many fictional forms that could be termed sexual or erotic appeared in China in the fourteenth and fifteenth centuries. The first novels *per se*, in the sixteenth century, would not have sprung up in a literary vacuum. Literature that may be termed "pornographic" (without the moral overtones) first appeared in China during the reign of the Emperor Shih Tsung of Ming in the early sixteenth century. A few books have survived from this period. One of them, *Hsiu Ta Yeh Shih* (A Tale of the Embroidered Bed), describes in detail the sexual exploits of Hsia Chi, a great beauty of the time. Similarly, *Ju Yi Chun Chuang* (The Biography of Mr As-you-wish) describes the ways in which Hsueh made love to Empress Wu.

925. Erotic writer—first in English
This is a debatable one. Atkins plumps for Spenser as "the first writer in English to be consciously erotic (551)." The *Faerie Queen* is represented as a "mine of sensuality." A *Spectator* article (552) is cited to indicate the sexual significance of the Spenser imagery—"You do not need any psychoanalytic training to see here a rather grisly amalgam of the male and female sexual organs," after quoting the description of the lustful monster in Book IV, Canto VII. Now it's Atkins again—Spenser reckoned to be preaching chastity and religion, but he "allowed his imagi-

nation to luxuriate in obscenities which would have impressed both Shakespeare and Donne."

926. Erotic writer—foremost in sixteenth-century

Pietro Aretino has been termed the "greatest erotic writer in Christendom." (809) Perhaps his most famous work is the *Ragionamenti*, partly biographical. Aretino was active as a writer for more than forty years, during which time he produced poetry and pornography, plays and theological works, lives of the saints and lampoons on the living. He was a friend of Michelangelo and Titian. He talked with popes. He has been depicted as "the Renaissance counterpart of Petronius in the ancient world, or of the Marquis de Sade in the period of European revolution."

927. Erotic writer—foremost seventeenth-century woman

The most famous female Restoration writer of erotica was Aphra Behn (1644–89), the daughter of a barber named John Johnson. She had a childhood in Surinam and then returned to England to become the wife of a London merchant (553). She is best known for her novel *Oronoko*, a tale of South American sex and violence. The aim of *Oronoko* has been compared to that of Harriet Beecher Stowe's *Uncle Tom's Cabin* two centuries later (554). In her play, *Lover's Watch* (1686), she gives advice that rivals much in modern marriage guidance manuals ("Those snow-white breasts, which before you durst scarce touch with your little finger you may now, without asking leave, grasp by whole handfuls ... O unspeakable pleasure! Now you may practice an hundred delicious things to please your appetites and do as many Hocus Pocus tricks more."). One writer compared Aphra Behn to Susanne Centlivre, her "sister spirit in the Lord Priapus:(555)."

928. Erotic novel—most famous French (apart from de Sade)

The most famous erotic novel in the French language, apart from those of the Marquis, is *Gamiani*, attributed to Alfred de Musset. This book, hardly heard of in modern England, went through forty-one editions before 1930. In one preface it is claimed that the author wrote it to prove that an erotic novel could be written without resort to "coarse" words. The theme in *Gamiani*—the title is from the surname of the heroine—is largely lesbian. A young man inadvertently witnesses a lesbian scene, whereupon he comes out of the cupboard and joins in! Most of the book is occupied with the ensuing love-triangle. One scene has Gamiani climbing onto the erection of a just hanged man. The plots ends with the two lesbians taking poison and experiencing orgasm and death simultaneously. A happy tale!

929. Erotic novel—most famous
Fanny Hill wins this one hands down. Henry Cleland's *Fanny Hill or Memoirs of a Woman of Pleasure* was first published in London in 1749. The author sold it for twenty guineas to a bookseller, who is said to have made £10,000 from it (556). The book was quickly translated into several European languages. The style of the book is simple and artless, and "obscene" words are avoided by means of circumlocution and euphemism. The theme is straightforward to the point of cliché: a young innocent girl journeys to the big city and finds herself in a brothel, whereupon she quickly falls in love with one of the clients. The book ends with a happy marriage. *Fanny Hill* has been represented as the first truly erotic novel, and as providing useful insights into brothel-life in eighteenth-century London. Like all similar famous books of the genre, it has been prosecuted and praised.

930. Erotic novel—most detailed in nineteenth-century England
The Romance of Lust by William S. Potter was published privately in four volumes between 1873 and 1876. It has been termed a "veritable Thousand and One Nights of Perversion." The author traveled the world extensively and acquired a vast collection of erotic books, paintings and other *objets d'art*. The hero of the book starts a life of depravity at fifteen years of age; he is soon a keen fornicator, favoring incest, sodomy, and flaggelation. Perhaps the most remarkable aspect of *The Romance of Lust* was the inclusion of twelve letters allegedly written by a young

French diplomat to his mistress, a married Englishwomen some years his senior. The letters are full of "sexual excesses."

931. Erotic novel—first "to acknowledge its own purpose"

Well, what is the purpose of an erotic novel? Put candidly it is to make the reader, if male, have an erection. This is not often admitted by erotic writers, and their works are usually defended in terms of sexual realism, literary integrity and such like. But if a sexy tale does not turn the reader on then surely it has failed in its central purpose. Erotic novels eventually came to admit their main aim. Mirabeau wrote pornographic novels, of which *Ma Conversion* is a good example, based on the life of a gigolo. It contains an explicit notice to the reader—*"Eh bien, lis, dévore, et branie-toi."* (Or, "And now, read, devour, masturbate")

932. Erotic book—first in Christian Europe

According to one authority, the first book of purely or mainly erotic content to be published in Christian Europe was the *Hermaphrodite* of Antonio Beccadelli, written in about 1426. The Latin text was re-issued in 1892 with a French translation by Isidore Liseux, the scholarly French publisher or erotica and the literature of love. Beccadelli, who wrote under the name of Panormita, was one of the group of men later called humanist; he modelled much of his work on the writings of the poets of antiquity. Wayland Young suggests that Beccadelli, like Martial, was half fascinated and half disgusted "by women and fucking."

933. Sexual autobiography—first in Christendom

The *Confessions* of St. Augustine, who was born in 354 in Tagaste, South of the Algerian coastal city of Bône, may be regarded as the first "Christian" sexual autobiography: there has been talk of this as the *locus classicus* of Christian sexual morality. In the work Augustine bewails the sinfulness of his youth. It also emerges that he tried Manicheanism and then turned away from it. He was keen to forbid marriage and procreation; and he reckoned that to become pure one should practice celibacy—and vegetarianism! Finally he studied St. Paul and became a Christian. His Christian phase lasted somewhat longer than the Manichean phase of nine years.

934. Sexual autobiography—most uninhibited
My Secret Life by "Walter" is the most candid sexual autobiography in existence. For a start there are no diversions: the work is all sex. In Casanova's *Memoirs* there are many asides, about gambling or magic or some such; and Frank Harris has given us a travelogue as well as an account of personal sexual experience. The 4000-odd pages of *My Secret Life* deal with nothing other than the sexual activities, enjoyments, frustrations, and insights of the author: in this sense the work is unique (557). (See also superlative 191)

935. Sexual autobiography—most expensive
Walter deserves another superlative! The full eleven volumes of *My Secret Life* are extremly rare, a real collector's item. What the work would cost today, if it were available is anybody's guess, but a copy is supposed to have been sold in 1926 for no less than seven thousand dollars.

936. Erotica bibliography—first
Henry Spencer Ashbee, writing under the name of Pisanus Fraxi, declared in his introduction to the *Index Librorum Prohibitorum* that the only bibliography of erotic literature that existed at the time (1877) was the *Bibliographie des Ouvrages relatifs a l'Amour aux Femmes, au Mariage et des Livres Facétieux, Pantagruéliques, Scatologiques, Satyriques, etc., per M. Le C. D'I . . .*

937. Erotica collection—greatest in nineteenth-century
The collection of erotica of Henry Spencer Ashbee was the greatest private collection in the nineteenth century (some people thought Ashbee to be Walter—superlative 934). His *Index Librorum Prohibitorum*—the title mod-

eled on the Roman Catholic *Index of Forbidden Books*—represented a guide to his unique collection of erotic works. Each entry in Ashbee's *Index* comprises three sections—the publishing history of the book, a summary of its contents, and a critical commentary on its literary value. All the most important books are quoted extensively.

938. Erotic periodical—first in England

This emerged in 1773, under the title *The Covent Garden Magazine,* "Amorous Repository, Calculated Solely for the Entertainment of the Polite World." In the words of Hurwood (558) "This, inauspicious as it may have seemed at the time, the great granddaddy of a multi-million dollar business was born." Ten years later London acquired a new publication—THE RAMBLER'S MAGAZINE: Or, *The Annals of Gallantry, Glee, Pleasure, and the Bon Ton; Calculated for the entertainment of the Polite World; and to furnish the Man of Pleasure with a most delicious banquet of Amorous, Bacchanalian, Whimsical, Humorous Theatrical, and Polite Entertainment.* As a principal item readers were offered the histories of ladies "whom the attracting charms of gold can conquer." And typical story titles were *The History and Adventures of a Bedstead, The Adventures of a Eunuch, Memoirs of Lydia Lovemore,* and the *Adventures of Kitty Pry.*

939. Pornographic magazine—most famous in nineteenth-century England

It is difficult to say what the difference is between erotica and pornography. Those who praise sexual manifestations in art will tend to use the former word, those who are perpetually disgusted by all things carnal will incline to savor the latter. To say of a magazine that it was "pornographic" is not necessarily to condemn it, nor, *mutatis mutandis,* is it to praise it. However, one publication popularly dubbed *pornographic* in the nineteenth century was *The Pearl*—which carried the happy subtitle, *Journal of Facetiae and Voluptuous Reading.* The journal appeared monthly between July 1879 and December 1886, and declared as its imprint, Oxford: Printed at the University

Press. The entire run, in three volumes, contained 36 obscene colored lithographs—said by Ashbee to be of "vile execution." Six serialized novels were also included, as well as short stories, numerous ballads, poems, "gossip" notes and anecdotes, amounting to a total of five hundred pages. Some items, in translation, were simply stolen from elsewhere. *The Pearl* was neither the first nor the last of its kind; it was the most famous (559).

940. "Girlie mags"—first

The first "girlie magazines" were intended to be *respectable*, emphatically not "pornographic" (see superlative 578). The first magazine to merit the adjective "girlie" was *Esquire*, which, in the 1930s, was the only one of its kind. The decision to carry pin-ups was bold and innovative; *Esquire* began, incidentally, as a men's fashion magazine, hence the status title. The first issue of the magazine had a printing of 105,000 copies, 5000 of which were to be distributed to newsstands and 100,000 to clothing stores throughout the U.S. The first issue was, however, so popular that 95,000 copies were recalled from clothiers and redistributed to newsstands. The first issue was also significant in that it carried George Petty's famous pin-up girl, appearing at first more as a cartoon than a pin-up. She soon represented a singular female type that was destined to become almost as much a legend as the Gibson girl had been thirty years earlier. In early 1941, the Petty girls began to appear regularly in *Esquire*'s first foldout pages (560).

941. "Girlie mags"—highest selling

Penthouse was the first of Britain's *Playboy* counterparts, beginning life in the U.K. in 1965; *Mayfair* followed in 1966, and *Men Only*, in its new format and now under Paul Raymond (see superlative 585) in 1971. All three magazines are high-quality "glossies," with concentrated emphasis on beautiful (and seductive) women, expensive cars, fashion, and status. In 1974 the highest selling of these magazines was *Men Only* with something approaching half a million copies being sold in the U.K. The figures for *Penthouse* were slightly lower—still remarkable for a monthly periodical! *Men Only* also pioneered a number of new production techniques and undoubtedly has the appearance and feel of a high-quality product. It has also been involved in a court case: copies of one month's issue, printed abroad, were seized by British customs. *Men Only* lost the following court case—in a trial that could only have been held in a prurient, sexually maladjusted society.

942. Pubic hair—first magazine exposure

The first exposure of pubic hair—"albeit modest to the point of invisibility" (561) was accomplished by *Penthouse* (April 1970). The appearance of pubic hair in the girlies is now so commonplace that it is remarkable that there was such a fuss about it in 1970. But at the time the *Penthouse* initiative was seen as little short of revolutionary! Almost all the other "pin-up" magazines followed suit within a matter of months.

943. Erotic magazines—first for women

It is a commonplace of sexological research that women are supposed to be less easily aroused by visual erotica than are men: this is found in the bulk of relevant research from Kinsey onwards, but some of the findings are ambiguous. Recently various women, possessed of immense feminist ardor, have been involved in the creation of "pin-up" magazines for women. The two most famous of such magazines are *Viva* and *Playgirl*. One idea is that nude male figure should adorn the pages: "full frontals" are permissible in these enlightened times. The magazines can now be purchased on bookstalls in the U.K. Judging by the immense difficulty in obtaining a copy of the first issue of *Playgirl* it has a good future on this side of the Atlantic. But does it work? Are women, suddenly confronted with a graphic centerspread penis fastened onto a handsome male, stimulated to lustful urges? I don't know. The only girl I asked declared that it didn't do much for her—but she kept looking!

944. Erotica publisher—most famous woman in nineteenth-century

Perhaps the most famous woman publisher of erotica in the nineteenth-century was Mary Wilson. Whether she published primarily for men or for women is not known, but she produced a wide variety of literature. She was called by the famous "governess," Theresa Berkeley "The reviver of erotic literature in the present century." Mary Wilson had a number of peculiarities, one of which was an intense dislike of sodomy in any form; she would allow no mention of it to appear in any of her books. She also wrote an essay in a collection called *The Voluptuarian Cabinet;* the piece was called *Adultery on the Part of Married Women, and Fornication on the Part of Old Maids and Widows defended by Mary Wilson, Spinster, With Plans for Promoting the same, Addressed to the Ladies of the Metropolis and its Environs.* The plan was for the establishment of a palatial brothel for women only. It was to be a sanctuary "to which any lady of rank and fortune may subscribe, and to which she may repair incog; the married to commit what the world calls adultery, and the single to commit what at the tabernacle is termed fornication, or in a gentler phrase, to obey the dictates of all powerful Nature, by offering up a cheerful sacrifice to the God Priapus, the most ancient of deities." The premises purchased by Miss Wilson for this purpose are then described in detail. The plan, alas, never materialized (562).

945. Erotica publisher (books)—most famous in twentieth-century

The most famous modern dynasty in the publishing of erotica is centered in Paris. Before the war an Anglo-Irishman named Jack Kahane founded the Obelisk Press and published Joyce's *Haveth Childers* (a foretaste of *Finnegan's Wake*), Durrell's *The Black Book,* Connolly's *The Rock Pool,* and Harris's *Life and Loves*). His son, Maurice Girodias, continued the family business and has published Nabokov's *Lolita,* Donleavy's *The Ginger Bread Man* and Burrough's *The Naked Lunch.* The firm now publishes as Olympia Press. In 1972 *Scorpio* ran an article, "Is Maurice Girodias Being Forced Out of Pornogra-

phy?", indicating the immense difficulties under which he
was operating. At the same time there appears to be an
increasing willingness to admit that Girodias has made a
significant and enduring contribution to modern literature.
After all he was even asked to contribute a piece to "To
Deprave and Corrupt . . . ," a compilation including items
from such respectable people as Lord Birkett and Norman
St. John-Stevas (563).

946. Erotica promotor (magazines and theatre)—most successful in England

Paul Raymond, born Geoffrey Anthony Quinn, the son of
a Liverpool haulage contractor, is without doubt the most
successful individual promoter of magazine and theatrical
erotica in Britain today. His *Men Only* (superlative 580)
is the best-selling girlie magazine in Britain, with *Club International*, from the same Fleet Street stable, also chalking
up impressive sales. In addition he now has five London theaters, including the Revuebar, the Windmill, and
the Whitehall (this latter is said to have cost him £340,-
000). His most expensive show—costing around £300,000
to stage—is the *Royalty Follies*; the £25,000 production
costs of *Pyjama Tops* at the Whitehall were recouped in
just two months. Paul Raymond—one-time drummer,
salesman, barman, and miner—claims he could have sold
the Revuebar for £1.25 million. One Raymond quote—
"Tits, bums and a few laughs. That's what people like.
That's what I like. I'm not a pornographer, I'm an entertainer. And I have a knack of judging what people want
at any given moment (564)."

947. Erotic work—first effort at clandestine production in England

In 1674 an effort was made at All Souls College, Oxford,
using the university press, to prepare an edition of Aretino's *Sonnets*, illustrated by Romano's celebrated drawings
of coital positions. Alas, it so happened that the Dean appeared unexpectedly—with no less than sixty reproductions already produced. Consideration was given to the
possibility of expulsion—"And I think they would deserve
it, were they of any other college than All Souls, but there

I will allow them to be virtuous that are bawdy only in pictures."

948. Erotic publisher—most famous in nineteenth-century
William Dugdale has been dubbed the "most notorious of publisher-booksellers of pornography of his time (565)." In fact he produced both poor-quality "pornography" and good-quality "erotica." He was responsible for publishing *The Romance of Lust*, a book termed by Ashbee, "the most lascivious book ever written." The police raided Dugdale on information supplied by the Vice Society, and on a single occasion took away two cartloads of books and prints, "all of a most obscene nature (566)." William Dugdale was active in the pornography (or erotica) trade for a total of forty years, during which times he had nine convictions. He died in prison.

949. Pornography debate—most famous in the House of Lords
In the early 1970s the peers of this realm were much concerned at the spread of pornography in Britain. Their concern was manifested at a vigorous, and frequently rather absurd debate, in the House of Lords on 21st April 1971. It was at this debate that Lord Longford first revealed his plans for a private enquiry into pornography (try superlative 588 also)(567).

950. Pornography—most publicized modern work
The most publicized work on pornography in Britain is *Pornography, The Longford Report* (568), which appeared in 1972. Prudes welcomed the report; others were not so sure. At least one writer (569) was prepared to use language that many would consider rather extreme—"In short, this effort is a confused mishmash of prejudice, clear anti-sexuality, and downright self-contradiction. The document, a poorly organized tome resulting from the reflections of many disparate personalities, is one of the clearest signs of sexual superstition in the modern world ..." (See also superlative 284.)

951. Sexual words—richest language

German, as a language, is said to be good for "rabble-rousing." English and Russian are reckoned to be rich in poetic possibilities. What is the best language for sexual expression? Paldamus, in his book *Roman Sexual Life* (1833), draws attention (p. 19) to the fact that "no literary language is so rich in words for the crudest of physical sexual relationships as early Latin. This can be proved by a glance at the old glossaries, namely Nonius and Festus ..." At the same time "All the words are entirely lacking in a gay and frivolous charm; they are dull sensual utterances."

952. "Fuck"—first used in poetry

Fuck—as currently spelled or in near approximation—appears a number of times in sixteenth-century Scottish poems. Its first known use was in the poem "Ane Brash of Wowing" ("A Bout of Wooing") (*c.* 1503) by the Franciscan friar, or pretended friar, William Dunbar—

> *His bony beird was kemmit and croppit*
> *Bot all with cale it was bedroppit,*
> *And he wes townysche, peirt, and gukit,*
> *As with the glaikis he were ouirgane;*
> *Yit be his feirris he wald have fukkit;*
> *Ye brek my hart, my bony ane!* (570)

(*cale*, broth; *townysche*, lively; *gukit*, foolish; *glaikis*, feeling; *ouirgane*, overcome; *feirris*, manner)

953. "Fuck"—most unexpected appearance

In some circumstances the word *fuck* is used where we more or less expect it—in pornography, modern novels, and "progressive" talk. Historically it has sometimes appeared when least expected: for instance the dread word slipped into the columns of *The Times* (London) on 13 January 1882. The report of a speech delivered by the Attorney General, Sir William Harcourt, included one man's sentiment that "he felt like a bit of fucking." The shock at this in Printing House Square was so great that a full four days elapsed before "the management of this journal" could steel itself to issue an apology—it spoke of "gross outrage," of a "malicious fabrication" that was "surreptitiously introduced" and noted that the matter was under legal investigation—"it is to be hoped that the perpetrator of the outrage will be brought to punishment." *The Times* suffered another terrible blow when an advertisement for a book about the public schools was discovered, after the paper had been printed, to include the line—"With a Glossary of Some Words used by Henry Irving in his disquisitions upon fucking, which is in common use in these schools." And this only a few months after the first incident! Not a good year for *The Times*. It is also noted that in a daily paper reporting the birth of a royal child—"the substitution of an F for a B in the name of the palace where the queen was confined gave the heading of the notice a suspiciously suggestive appearance." All in all, Kenneth Tynan's delivery of the work *fuck* on BBC television had one or two "establishment" precedents.

954. Obscene language lexicon—best known in eighteenth-century

The best known lexicon of improper language in the eighteenth-century was *The Classical Dictionary of the Vulgar Tongue*, published in 1785 by Captain Francis Grose. This glossary of underworld jargon, unlike many similar works, is more than a mere dictionary, giving as it does a vivid portrayal of the seamy side of life in eighteenth-century London—"a sexy, brawling, rum-soaked playground, where petticoats flew up at the clink of a tuppence, and swordsmen were kings of the streets."

955. Theatre (English)—most hostile seventeenth-century diatribe

Theater has always been criticized by those of puritan disposition. In 1698, for instance, Jeremy Collier, a veritable fanatic, published a diatribe against the theater entitled *A Short View of the Immorality and Profaneness of the English Stage.* Everyone connected with the theater was condemned as "whoring, cursing, filthy, atheists," and the sheer bombast of the attack seemed to astonish many contemporary observers. Even the playwrights of antiquity were attacked—Aristophanes was accused of atheism, and Shakespeare was called "too guilty" because "when there is too much smut, there is least sense." Collier said of one play, *The Relapse*—"I almost wonder, the smoke of it has not darkened the sun, and turned the air to plague and poison." *A Short View* sold well.

956. Female actresses—first appearing in Shakespeare

The appearance of women on the stage got under way in earnest when Tom Killigrew, one of the King's best friends, produced *Othello* on 8 December 1660. Women had already appeared in plays on the Continent. In England no self-respectiong young woman would have thought of a career in acting—and so all the casting was done in brothels! The subject-matter of plays being performed was such that whores fitted naturally into the female roles. Theater thrived on love intrigues, rape, seduction, and the like. It has been said that Restoration theater "not only fostered lewdness by depicting it in glowing and attractive colors, but its actors spread abroad the corruption it was their business to delineate"—"Their personal character corresponded, in too many instances, with the parts which they performed, and they re-enacted in private the debaucheries which they presented on the stage (571)."

957. Erotic play—"most outrageous gang of sexual miscreants..."

John Wilmot, the second Earl of Rochester, the "greatest of sinners," led an eventful life which included the kidnapping of his bride, the composing of satirical verses and lampoons, and the writing of controversial plays. His most controversial work was a play written for "the Royal Company of Whoremasters," entitled *Sodom; or The Quintessence of Debauchery*. The play was said to be a vicious satire on the court of Charles II. The *dramatis personae* are a remarkable bunch, at least as far as their names go. The leading characters are *Bolloxinon*, King of Sodom; his offspring, *Prince Prickett* and *Princess Swivia; Buggeranthos*, General of the Army; *Borastus*, Buggermaster General; *Pine* and *Twelv*, Pimps of Honor; *Flux,* the king's physician; and *Virtuoso,* "merkin and dildoe maker of the royal family."

958. Erotic plays—most famous nun author

The tenth-century German nun Hrotswitha wrote, in Latin, a remarkable series of plays strongly influenced by the pagan Roman dramatist Terence (c. 190–159 B.C.). But she manages to be sexier! In fact some of her scenes are set in brothels. One represents a cemetary where a lover interrogates a sexton. The intruder wants to dig up his mistress's corpse. Go ahead, says the sexton, She's not putrid yet. You'll find her still in fair condition for fornication. Ha, cries the lover, as he seizes a spade, Now I can offer that bitch all the insults I please! (*Abutere, ut licet—Nunc in mea situm est potestate quantislibet iniuriis te velim lacessere.*)

959. Lesbianism—first time on the American stage

The first major effort to present lesbianism on the American stage was suppressed by the police. This was in 1927, and the play was the French importation, *The Captive,* by Edouard Bourdet. The play was devoid of any message. It concerned a love triangle, two women and a man. One of the women, inevitably enough, did not know to which of the others to turn. This, evidently, was too strong for the authorities of the day!

960. Nude—first in Folies-Bergère

The first time that a woman appeared on the stage completely nude was at the Folies-Bergère in 1912. She was only visible for a moment (573). It was feared that a scandal would follow, but France survived, and after the war every Paris revue featured at least one naked woman.

961. Censorship (theatre)—most absurd examples

There are endless absurdities in the history of censorship (see, for instance, John Trevelyan's *What the Censor Saw*), and we have given examples of censorship absurdity elsewhere ... The following instances of theatrical censorship in Britain are taken from *Banned,* by Richard Find-later (576)—

It is understood that, wherever the word "shit" appears, it will be altered to it." *Spare,* by Charles Wood.

The killing must be semi-hidden from the audience. There must be no severence of the head. *Afore Night come,* by David Rudkin.

There must be no scratching of private parts. *Meals on Wheels,* by Charles Wood.

The Doctor's trousers must *not* be hauled down. *The Happy Haven,* by John Arden.

The huge Spanish Crucifixion must not be visible in the brothel room. *The Balcony,* by Jean Genet.

The statue of President Johnson must not be naked. *Mrs. Wilson's Diary,* by Richard Ingrams and John Wells.

All these, "by order of the Lord Chamberlain." It is not difficult to see why playwrights and theatrical producers welcomed the demise of the Office of the Lord Chamberlain.

962. Sex in advertising—first instances

In one view, Eve tempting Adam is the first case of sex in advertising, though perhaps this is not normally what we think of by the phrase. Another candidate for the title is a woodcut produced in 1491 by a Belgian publisher to promote a new translation of *Histoire de la Belle Melusine* by Jean d'Arras. The woodcut may be regarded as the first known illustrated advertising poster. Melusine's breasts are exposed (she is bathing), and there is some suggestion of auto-eroticism in the position of her right hand. The text beneath the illustration reads—"A beautiful, pleasing, and most marvelous story of a lady named Melusine, of her ancestors and descendants, and the wonderful and devout works and deeds they wrought and performed. Lately

translated from the French into Flemish and adorned with
fine personages and scenes as the text demands. This story,
as well as a great number of other new books, can be purchased at the price written hereunder (575)."

963. Sex in advertising—most famous early "double entendre"

Elliott White Springs, in 1947, shocked the business community in the U.S. with his double entendre concerning
the Springmaid name. Making use of sex appeal to sell
sheets, Springs—a pioneer of quarter of a century ago—
used a cartoon of an Indian couple on a sheet hammock.
The caption read—"A buck well spent on a Springmaid
sheet."

964. Sex in advertising—first introduced as a new subject category

The "respectable" acknowledgment of sex in advertising
was in 1968 when the *Business Periodical Index* com-
menced using "sex in advertising" as a new subject category. The majority of references—few in number—are
primarily concerned with ethics in advertising and not
with the effects on consumer purchasing.

965. Sex in architecture—most candid (ecclesiastical)

Architectural erotica is frequent in history. The Hindu
temples have already been remarked upon (superlative
540). But it must not be thought that architectural adorn-
ment was the prerogative of the pagan world. Within
Christendom erotic embellishment to architecture was
commonplace, and was indulged in, doubtless, to help gain
the allegiance of pagan folk already wedded to creeds with
a strong phallic element. One famous example of ecclesiastical erotica will suffice. Over the main entrance to a village church in the French department of Deux-Sèvres
there can be seen a carving of the male and female genitals in coitus. The design is flanked on either side by a
man and a woman. Their contorted features are clearly
intended to depict orgasmic rapture (576). Other church
architecture, in England and elsewhere, has been decor-
ated by models of the penis, by statues masturbating, and
by various sculpted figures engaged in various sexual pre-

occupations. There is more to Christian history than some of us may think!

966. Nude athletes—first allowed in Greece

We think of the ancient Greeks as a pretty liberal lot. We are led to believe that their sculpture was uninhibited in matters of sex and that such activities as homosexual behavior were not condemned. The Greeks had their liberal moments but doubtless there were hangups as well; even the Solon-instigated brothel appears to have been a singularly low-grade institution, an unfortunate necessity. As we all know from the surviving bits of pottery, the Greeks (at least the adult men) were allowed to enjoy athletic pursuits in the nude. As far as can be judged this sort of naked indulgence first occurred in 720 B.C. Greek "streaking" was regarded, in healthy fashion, as perfectly normal and desirable. The sex organs, it can well be argued, only need covering up if they are shamefull (577).

967. Nudes (male)—first in Greek art

Male nudes are generally thought to be more daring than female nudes. It's all to do with the genitals. A woman's genitals, you will have noticed, retire gracefully in pubic hair and between the thighs; a man's genitals are not so obliging. With a man a full frontal is quite unambiguous; with a woman a full frontal is often no more revealing than a full anything else! The earliest male nudes in Greek art, "not beautiful" (according to Clark), are generally known as Apollos. They date to around six or seven hundred years before Christ.

968. Nude (male)—first "realistic" portrayal in Greek sculpture

The first Greek Apollos (superlative 967) are stiff fellows, lacking the human warmth and contour of later Greek sculpture. The "stiff Apollo" phase may be regarded as lasting two or three hundred years. Then, in about 480 B.C., there "appears before us the perfect human body, the marble figure from the Acropolis known as the Ephebe of Kritios. Whether Kritios was the first or not to do work of this sort is hardly known today. Pythagoras of Rhegium has been cited as the sculptor who "first gave rhythm and proportion to his statues." It is suggested that the new concepts would have been expressed first in bronze rather than in marble.

969. Phalli—earliest found in Greece

Phalli—representations of the male genital organ—were found in Greece decades ago, and were dated to the early Stone Age. Plutarch wrote of *hermas* of ancient times, figures with heads of old men and erect genitalia. The *hermas* had religious significance and were assumed to have the capacity to ward off evil influences. In 415 B.C., some sacred *hermas* in Athens were found in a mutilated state. This was taken as an evil omen for the impending expedition against Sicily. In fact Alcibiades was accused of carrying out the mutilation and, in consequence, was exiled (578).

970. Phallic replica—largest

Various vast phallic monuments survive from ancient times. For example there is the neolithic Longstone or pillar at Clach-an-Truisel in the Island of Lewis: it is nineteen feet high and is surrounded by 39 other standing stones. Such longstones are common in Cornwall. And the mighty Men-er-Hroech in Brittany stands 67 ft. high and weighs 347 tons (579). And in various parts of the East, gigantic phallic models, up to 360 ft. high, of the erect male organ, were carried in procession (580).

971. Postcard bathing beauties—earliest

The earliest postcards of bathing beauties came from France around 1900, and soon after that such cards were made available in England. The first bathing scenes were created by artists. Later, when a camera was used the model was usually posed against a hand-drawn beach background. Postcards in the early 1900s featured "French Actresses," "Japanese Beauties" dressed in traditional costume, "Actresses" in color, and ballet dancers and bathers posing in tights. Some card manufacturers glued silk, oilcloth, or spangles on their pin-up cards (581).

972. Calendar (female)—first

Brown and Bigelow of Saint Paul, Minnesota, is the world's oldest calendar company. Around 1903 the firm produced its first calendar with a female subject— "Colette" (from a painting from Angelo Asti), a "charming but conservative portrait of a young beauty (582). In the years that followed, "Colette" helped to sell more than 1.5 million calendars. In 1904 the first pin-up calendar indicated that the manufacture of "girlie" calendars could be a lucrative business.

973. Calendar (nude)—first

In 1913, the first-known calendar nude appeared, called *September Morn*, a reproduction of an oil painting, *Matinée Septembre*, by a French artist, Paul Chabas (1869–1937). The painting might have gone unnoticed if Comstock, of the Society for the Suppression of Vice, had not demanded the removal of the painting from the window of a New York art gallery. A salesman explained that the painting had recently won a Medal of Honor from the French Academy, but, we may presume, Comstock was not impressed (582).

974. Pin-up (female)—first universal

In 1887, Charles Dana Gibson—then twenty years of age—began a long-term contract with *Life*. As a young man, Gibson "dipped his pen in the cosmic urge and tried to draw a girl so alluring that other young men would want to climb into the picture and sit beside her (583)." By the time of the 1890s the Gibson girl was well established, and she was a front-runner for twenty years. In 1903, Gibson signed a hundred thousand dollar contract with *Collier's* (1886–1957) to render a series of double-page "cartoons" over four years' time. "The Gibson Girl was not simply a model but represented a way of life (584)."

975. Pin-up (male)—first in women's magazine (UK)
Paul de Feu, reclining in a suitably modest position, was
photographed nude for a full-color, double-page spread in
Cosmopolitan (London), April 1972. It was of some interest that Mr. de Feu, aged 36, was married to, but separated from, Germaine Greer, the keen champion of
Women's Lib. A construction worker and college gradu-
ate, Mr. de Feu described his posing as "striking a blow
for male servitude." He was quoted in *Time* (14/2/72) as
saying "I'm a guy who likes birds. Normally I'd spend a
lot of time, chat, and money taking a girl out in the hopes
of getting somewhere with her. This way—being a pin-
up—I've got to the clothes-off stage with thousands of
birds straightaway." During the same month *Cosmopolitan*
(New York) printed a centerfold nude photograph of the
American actor Burt Reynolds (585).

976. Nudes (photography)—first
It has been claimed that the French photographer Lere-
bours photographed some nudes as early as 1840, only one
year after the historic introduction of Daguerre's process
(586). It was suggested that the interest in the nude at
this period was not only aesthetic—professional models
were among the first live subjects capable of holding a
pose for the required five to ten minutes. The Parisian
photographers, Nadar and Durieu, were among the first in
the world to photograph nudes.

977. Nudes (photography)—first magazine
The first nude photography magazine was *Camera Work*,
founded in 1902 by Alfred Stieglitz. Not all the pictures
were of nudes, but nude photographs were frequent, usually in portfolios by such photographers as Annie Brig-
man, Clarence Whitehead, Robert Demarchy, Renée Le
Begue and Frank Eugene. The treatment was such as to
suggest "feelings and associations beyond the actual subject." In particular, *Camera Work* included studies by the
Photo-Secessionists.

978. Nudes (photography)—first to aid painter

The painter Eugène Delacroix (1798–1863) studied photographs of the nude, from which he learned "far more by looking than the inventions of any scribbler could teach me." As with other artists, Delacroix also began to send models to pose for photographs from which he could make drawings and studies for paintings. One photographer who did such work for Delacroix was Eugène Durieu, a president of the Société Francaise de Photographie and particularly active in the 1850s.

979. Nude photographer—most famous woman

There have been a number of distinguished female photographers of the nude in the twentieth-century, including Emy Andriesse of Holland, and Nell Dorr and Ruth Bernhard of the United States. Miss Bernhard's work is the best known, having appeared regularly in magazines and books over the last three decades. She has been quoted as saying—"If I have chosen the female form in particular, it is because beauty has been debased and exploited in our sensual twentieth-century. We seem to have a need to turn innocent nature into evil ugliness by the twist of the mind. Woman has been the target of much that is sordid and cheap, especially in photography. To raise, to elevate, to endorse with timeless reverence the image of woman, has been my mission—the reason for my work which you see here (587)."

980. Breast exposure (film)—first (modern)

In the silent film days there was nothing to a bit of breast exposure. It was a commonplace of epic and small-scale production alike. In modern times, after a lapse lasting a decade or two, the battle had to be fought all over again, until the breast and other anatomical bits and pieces eventually won through! On 29 March 1965, a Negress in *The Pawnbroker*, also starring Rod Steiger, exposed both her breasts to the full, thereby breaking Section Seven, Subsection Two of the Motion Picture Production Code—"Indecent or undue exposure is forbidden." A commentator wrote—"For the first time in the history of the Hollywood Production Code, official recognition has been given to the good taste and artistic merit with which a subject is treated, not only to whether it hews to the current standards by which the Code is interpreted." A headline in *Variety* noted, more succinctly, "FILM ART REQUIRES NO BRA." *The Pawnbroker* later became the official United States entry in the 1964 Berlin Film Festival (588).

981. Pubic hair exposure (film)—first (modern)

This is another tricky one. Avid researchers into such matters have scrutinized films frame by frame. Was it hair or was it shadow? Not that it matters all that much, but some people find it nice to know the truth. Some connoisseurs opt for *Blow-Up*: there is a sexy scene in which David Hemmings romps with a couple of naked teenagers. The Catholic Office gave *Blow-Up* a Condemned rating (589).

982. Sex film club—first (UK)

The first sex film club was the Compton in Old Compton Street; it opened in 1961 and was run by the former managers of a striptease club and a local cinema. The first films to be shown were based on nudist camps as locations—"The hero and heroine ended up holding hands and the sun set on yet another game of volleyball (590)." The firm was eventually taken over by a large company and the name of the cinema was changed to Cinecenta.

983. Nudist film—first (UK)

There are those people who assert—and we know what they mean—that the nudist films have nothing to do with sex. Well, it may be so for some, but not for others. *The Garden of Eden*, appropriately enough, was the first of the nudist pictures in Britain. It appeared in January 1957 and featured Jamie O'Hara. The film was sent around to the local authorities—"They didn't object, and there was considerable public acceptance of the picture, which opened the screens to nudity (591)."

984. Nude film actress—youngest

Naked female babies have appeared in films, but perhaps that doesn't count. Apart from such stars the youngest woman (?) I have come across in a modern film is the 13-year-old Babra Grandhi. She appeared naked with full parental permission ("Mamma was always on the set") in the tale of a girl trapped between "the Devil and her deep blue sea lover (592)."

985. Film star (woman)—first sex symbol

Theda Bara was the first screen vamp. She was also the first star to have a screen personality specially created for her. Bara wore erotic costumes which often scarcely concealed her breasts or buttocks. "A couple of loosely spun spider's webs did duty for a bra, or else an asp curved snugly around the contours of each breast, while a few bead whorls appliquéd on her hip bone by gum arabic looked like some satyr's erotic doodling." She also had a liking for wearing metal chains against the naked flesh "in a way that carried an undertone of perversion (593). Theda Bara began her epic career before the First World War.

986. Film star (woman)—oldest sex symbol at start of career

Mae West has been portrayed as one of the very few stars who was "self-made and self-sustaining," owing her success to herself alone, not to a director, scriptwriter, make-up artist, or photographer. What is perhaps most remarkable about her is that she first arrived at Hollywood when she was forty years of age—"grotesquely late to begin a film career (594)." The extra ordinary vitality of Mae West is nicely revealed in an interview recently published in *Men Only* (Vol. 38, No. 12).

987. Film star (woman)—first to emphasize breasts

The eroticism of Theda Bara (superlative 985) was *generalized*, with no particular item or mode of behavior coming in for particular emphasis. In any event her breasts were not vast, so there was little scope for concentration on them! Not so with Jean Harlow. This latter actress usually gets the credit for focussing the erotic interest, for the first time on the screen, on a woman's breasts. At the end of the nineteen-twenties it was the flat-chested flappers who symbolized screen sex. Harlow's breasts were only large (34-inch bust) compared to the boyish females who had appeared on the screen before her—but she heaved up her breasts and used them to advantage. Harlow was said to be a compulsive exhibitionist, a "sexual provocatrice who knew the effect her body made on men." Her nipples were supposed to expand as the room temperature went up; and before a Press conference she would rub them with ice.

988. Film star (woman)—most famous sex symbol

This must be Marilyn Monroe. She featured on the most publicized calendar in history, published in 1951 by John Baumgarth Co. The original nude picture was taken in May 1949 by Tom Kelly, a California photographer. Kelly is supposed to have remarked at the time—"This wasn't just another girl. This was a girl with instinct for drama and showmanship. Her lips parted provocatively, her body was arched and magnificent. There was a natural grace about her." A series of later films made Monroe the leading American sex-symbol. Her mysterious death, following rumors of possible liaisons with eminent Americans, added something to her already vast legend. It was a simple matter to declare that she committed suicide. According to one report, however, no chemical "sludge" was found in her stomach after death. This has been held as evidence that she did not, in fact, commit suicide.

989. Film star (woman)—most famous European sex symbol

Brigitte Bardot has enjoyed the reputation as the most famous European pin-up girl of the mid-twentieth-century. She has been depicted as "moodier, tougher, more independent, and adventurous than Marilyn Monroe . . . (595)." Like Monroe she has had a checkered life in private and public. Bardot, however, has proved the more durable.

990. Film star (woman)—highest paid
The film *Cleopatra* (1963) cost around forty million dollars to make, of which a proportion was paid to Elizabeth Taylor. The auditors found a nice statement—"To Elizabeth Taylor, star: one million dollars." No other woman could command such a sum for playing a part in a film; and the earning power of Elizabeth Taylor has hardly diminished. For every film since *Cleopatra*, Miss Taylor has been paid at least the nominal million dollars. Her agent has been reported as saying—"Elizabeth has never lost money with any film ... So when they planned a big film like *Cleopatra*, they had to have [her] as security ... (596)."

991. Film star (man)—most famous lover
Rudolph Valentino began his career as a dancer, then rose to stardom as a dark passionate lover in *The Four Horsemen of the Apocalypse* (1921), *The Sheik*, and *Blood and Sand* (1922). When he died in hospital in 1926, thousands of people stopped the traffic (597). In addition several women committed suicide, 100,000 condolence telegrams were sent, and a monument erected to his memory was set up in Hollywood.

922. Film star (man)—longest lasting romantic lead
Cary Grant has been an immensely successful romantic lead in Hollywood for more than thirty years. No other male actor can compete with this record. One of his best known films—*Holiday*—appeared in 1938; yet still Cary Grant plays successful romantic leads.

993. Censorship (film)—most notorious U.S. Code
In 1921 the U.S. Motion Picture Producers and Distributors of America Inc. asked W. H. Hays, a prominent Republican, to be their president in an effort to ward off plans for government censorship. One of the first Hays initiatives was to insert a "morality clause" into all actors' contracts forcing them to maintain at least a façade of

clean living. In 1930 his Production Code was adopted by the industry; in 1934 it was made mandatory, with fines and sanctions on any film-maker who ignored it. The Code had a statement of general aims followed by twelve sections of "Particular Applications." These latter included such declarations as "The treatment of bedrooms must be governed by good taste and delicacy" and "Suicide, as a solution of problems occurring in the development of screen drama, is to be discouraged as morally questionable." Inevitably, all sex organs—even those of children—were forbidden for screen representation, as were all forms of "perversion." The critic George Jean Nathan has commented that the effect of the Hays Office Code on Hollywood film-making was "to picture most characters in their amorous reactions to each other as practically indistinguishable from little children dressed up in their parents' clothes and playing house (598)."

994. Censorship (film)—British Board first established

The British Board of Film Censors was created in 1912. The first President, George Redford, aimed to keep the cinema "clean and free of any stigma, even of vulgarity." Banned topics included—cremations, tear-impelling scenes at funerals, murder and suicide, mixed bathing, "compromising situations," ridiculing of Sovereigns, Judges, Ministers, etc. (599).

995. Censor (film)—most liberal in U.K.

John Trevelyan, while working for the British Board of Film Censors, evidently became more and more unhappy with the principle of censorship. He not only stirred up prudish wrath by allowing certain film sequences that would have amazed his predecessors in office, but was also prepared to write articles urging that pornography should be allowed to adults and that obscenity legislation was open to serious question. His recent book *What the Censor Saw* (600) charts the vicissitudes of film censorship over recent years in Britain. John Trevelyan has been portrayed as the most liberal of modern censors in this area.

996. Censorship—most vigorous campaign

We have already cited Comstock as the most active of prudes (see superlative 283), and his campaign for the Morally Proper may well be the most significant in history. There are, however, one or two precedents that deserve quoting. One we have mentioned—the Nazi obscurantism that resulted in the destruction of the Hirschfeld Sex Institute in Berlin. Another campaign worthy of note—and perhaps the earliest of them all—was one conducted in ancient China (601). Many censored books were published in the Ming and early Ch'ing periods. Novels were sometimes suppressed in the supposed interest of scholarship. A novel by Shu Hung-hsün was burned because it was "unclear and confused;" and a work by Yang Ming-lun was consigned to the flames for "vulgarity of language and a common style." In some instances the offenses of the authors resulted in torture and death, not only to themselves, but often to all the males in the family, and the deporting into slavery of all the womenfolk. Ch'ien Lung is said to have suppressed around three thousand volumes—"though the list of writers suffering the same fate was not recorded with the same diligence."

997. Erotic movie star—most famous

This is Linda Lovelace, renowned for her performance in *Deep Throat,* the most successful "pornographic" film to be shown in America. The film has been the subject of an obscenity charge in New York, a circumstance which may have helped it to gross some three and a half million dollars. The film focuses on the discovery by a sex-conscious young woman that oral sex can be fun, and the plot hinges on her singular capacities in this direction (602). The career of the 22-year-old Linda is blossoming; more films are planned; talk-shows want her as their guest; *Esquire* put her on the cover; it was reported in 1973 that she would be a *Playboy* pin-up; *Women's Wear Daily* asked the appropriate question whether she had had her tonsils out; and *Screw* wanted to know everything else that no one else would be prepared to print. And she even wrote a book (603)!

998. Erotic gravures—most famous

A special issue of *Avant-Garde* (604) was devoted to the erotic gravures (or engravings) of Picasso. In 1968, Picasso created 347 erotic engravings, of which "the most significant" are shown in this issue of *Avant-Garde*. Picasso has been quoted as saying that "Art is never chaste." And it has been suggested that *all* Picasso's work is in some sense erotic.

999. Erotic art exhibition—first international

The First International Exhibition of Erotic Art took place in public museums in the cities of Lund (Sweden) and Aarhus (Denmark) in 1968. The exhibition was based on the private collection of Drs. Eberhard and Phyllis Kronhausen, and was supplemented by loans from museums, galleries, and private collections. The exhibition included more than one thousand examples of erotic pictures and statuary from ancient and modern times and from the cultures of India, China, Japan, Africa, Europe, and the United States. More than 100,000 visitors attended the exhibition in two countries. A book was later published to commemorate the event (605).

1000. Sex fair—first in the world

The first Sex Fair was held in Copenhagen in October 1969. It showed erotic art, films, sex aids, strip-tease, etc., and by all accounts was an immense success. Many leading Scandinacian manufacturers were represented. A second Sex Fair followed in Odense in March 1970. As with the Kronhausen erotic art exhibition a book was published to describe the fairs (606).

REFERENCES

Chapter One

1. J. M. Coulter, *The Evolution of Sex in Plants*, Hafner Press, 1973 (reprint of 1914 edition), pp. 19-22.

2. M. Burton, *Animal Courtship*, Hutchinson, 1953, p. 83.

3. R. S. De Ropp, *Sex Energy*, Jonathan Cape, 1970, pp. 12-13.

4. M. Burton, *ibid.*, pp. 83-5.

5. R. Buchsbaum, *Animals Without Backbones*, Pelican, 1973, pp. 37-8; S. Lilar, *Aspects of Love in Western Society*, Panther, 1965, pp. 157-8.

6. E. L. Oginsky, W. W. Umbreit, *An Introduction to Bacterial Physiology*, W.H. Freeman & Co., 1959, p. 51.

7. H. Wendt, *The Sex Life of the Animals*, Arthur Barker, 1965, p. 80.

8. R. Buchsbaum, *ibid.*, pp. 51-2.

9. Cited by C. Darwin, *The Descent of Man*, John Murray, 1909, p. 409.

10. D. E. Carr, *The Sexes*, Heinemann, 1971, p. 14.

11. *Marshall's Physiology of Reproduction*, Vol. 1, Part One, Ed: A. S. Parkes, Longman's, Green and Company, 1956, pp. 105-6.

12. C. S. Ford, F. A. Beach, *Patterns of Sexual Behavior*, Eyre & Spottiswood, 1952.

13. D. Morris, "Homosexuality in the Ten-Spined Stickleback", *Patterns of Reproductive Behavior*, Panther, 1972, pp. 15-50.

14. A. C. Kinsey *et al.*, *Sexual Behavior in the Human Female*, Saunders, 1953, p. 449 (note).

15. Quoted by Wendt, *ibid.*, p. 89.

16. A. D. Jost, "Development of Sexual Characteristics" *Science Journal*, Vol. 6, No. 6, June 1970, p. 70.

17. F. A. E. Crew, *Sex Determination*, Methuen Monograph, 1965.

18. R. Robertson, "Sex Changes under the Waves" *New Scientist*, Vol. 58, No. 848, 31/5/73, pp. 538-40.

19. R. Buchsbaum, *ibid.*, pp.162-3.

20. D. E. Carr, *ibid.*, p.40.

21. D. E. Carr, *ibid.*, p.21.

22. H. Wendt, *ibid.*, pp. 110.

23. *Marshall's Physiology of Reproduction*, *ibid.*, 1956, p. 63.

24. *Marshall's Physiology of Reproduction*, *ibid.*, 1956, p. 81.

25. E. J. Slijper, *Whales*, Hutchinson, 1962, p. 351.

26. B. Messier, R. Gagnon, "Complete Diphallus in a Rat", *Rev. Canad. Biol.* April 26, 1967, pp. 317-21.

27. E. J. Slijper, *ibid.*

28. *Marshall's Physiology of Reproduction*, *ibid.*, 1956, p. 49-50.

29. J. Rostand, A. Tétry, *Larousse Science of Life*, Hamlyn, 1971, p. 138.

30. *Marshall's Physiology of Reproduction*, Vol. 1, Part 2, Ed: A. S. Parkes, Longmans, Green and Company, 1960, p. 6.

31. K. G. Davey, *Reproduction in the Insects*, Oliver & Boyd, 1965, p. 6.

32. *Marshall's Physiology of Reproduction*, ibid., 1960, p.6.

33. M. T. D. White, "The Chromosome Cycle and Spermatogenesis of *Miaster; J. Morph*, 1946, Vol. 79, pp. 323-69.

34. *Marshall's Physiology of Reproduction*, ibid., 1960, pp. 226 (table).

35. *Marshall's Physiology of Reproduction*, ibid., 1960, pp. 223-4.

36. S. Taber, M. S. Blum, "Preservation of Honeybee Semen", *Science*, 1960, Vol. 131, pp. 1734-5.

37. Russell Peterson, *Silently by Night*, Longmans, 1966, 166-7.

38. *Reproduction in the Female Mammal*, Butterworths, London, 1967, p. 254.

39. W. A. Wimsatt, *Anat. Rec, 83*, pp. 299-305.

39A. *Marshall's Physiology of Reproduction*, ibid., 1956, p. 82.

40. *Marshall's Physiology of Reproduction*, ibid., 1956, p. 57.

41. D. E. Carr, *ibid.*, p. 95.

42. J. Z. Young, *ibid.*, p. 114.

43. *Marshall's Physiology of Reproduction*, ibid., 1956, p. 229.

44. *Marshall's Physiology of Reproduction*, ibid., Vol. 11, 1910, p. 2.

45. C. R. Austin, *The Mammalian Egg*, Blackwell, 1961, p. 15.

46. P. Pesson, *The World of Insects*, Harrap, 1959, p. 109.

47. R. F. Chapman, *ibid.*, p. 335.

48. P. Pesson, *ibid.*, p. 109.

49. R. F. Chapman, *ibid.*, p. 336.

50. *Marshall's Physiology of Reproduction, ibid.*, 1910, p. 2.

51. J. Z. Young, *ibid.*, pp. 265-6.

52. *Marshall's Physiology of Reproduction, ibid.*, 1956,

53. E. J. Slijper, *ibid.*, 359.

54. N. A. Mackintosh, J. G. F. Wheeler, *Discovery Reports*, 1929, p. 384.

55. R. M. Laws, *Giant Ovaries of a Blue Whale, Nature*, No. 4412, 22 May 1954, p. 1003.

56. *Marshall's Physiology of Reproduction, ibid.*, 1956, pp. 46, 48-49, 420.

57. E. J. Slijper, *ibid.*, p. 380.

58. D. Raphael, *The Tender Gift: Breast Feeding*, Prentice Hall, 1973, pp. 59-61.

59. *Marshall's Physiology of Reproduction, ibid.*, 1956, p.58.

60. R. & D. Morris, *Men and Snakes*, Sphere, 1965, p. 141.

61. C. S. Ford, F. A. Beach, *ibid.*, p. 37.

62. *Marshall's Physiology of Reproduction, ibid.*, 1956, p. 296.

63. R. F. Chapman, *ibid.*, p. 313.

64. E. J. Slijper, *ibid.*, pp. 351-2.

65. A. N. Clements, *The Physiology of Mosquitoes*, Pergamon Press, 1963.

66. R. F. Chapman, *ibid.*, p. 321.

67. J. C. Jones, R. E. Wheeler, "Studies on Spermathecal Filling in *Aedes Aegypti* (Linnaeus). 1. Description: *Biol. Bull. mar. biol. Lab., Woods Hole*, 1965, Vol. 129, pp. 134-50.

68. A. Khalifa, "Spermatophore production in *Galleria Mellonella* L. (Lepidoptera)", *Proc. R. ent, Soc.* Lond. A. Vol. 25, pp. 33-42.

69. W. Loher, F. Huber, "Nervous and Endocrine Control of Sexual Behavior in a Grasshopper (*Gomphocerus rufus* L. Acridinae) *Symp. Soc. exp. Biol.* Vol. 20, pp. 381-400.

70. J. C. Jones, "The Sexual Life of a Mosquito", *Scientific American*, Vol. 218, No. 4, April 1968, pp. 108-11.

71. H. Wendt, *ibid.*, p. 166.

72. P. Pesson, *ibid.*, p. 100.

73. C. S. Ford, F. A. Beach, *ibid.*, quote F. F. Darling, *A Herd of Red Deer*, Oxford University Press, 1937.

74. W. B. Pomeroy, *Dr. Kinsey, and the Institute for Sex Research*, Nelson, 1972, pp. 184-7.

75. H. Wendt, *ibid.*, p. 105.

76. A. C. Perdeck, "The Isolating Value of Specific Song Patterns in two Sibling Species of Grasshoppers (*Chorthippus brunneus* Thumb. and C. biguttulus L.)," *Behavior*, Vol. 12, pp. 1-75.

Chapter Two

77. Discussion in E. & P. Kronhausen, *Walter the English Casanova*, Polybooks, 1967, pp. 244-5.

78. W. B. Pomeroy, *ibid.*, p. 467.

79. *Forum*, Vol. 3, No. 5, pp. 34-41.

80. Dr. Jacobus (nom de plume) *L'Ethnologie du Sens Génitale*, 5 Vols., Paris, 1935, Discussed and quoted in A. Edwardes and R. E. L. Masters, *The Cradle of Erotica*, Odyssey Press, 1970 (see in particular, p. 36).

81. D. Reuben, *Everything You Always Wanted to Know About Sex*, Pan, 1969, p. 7.

82. D. A. Sekellaropoules, "A Case of Congenital Hypoplasia of the Penis", *Hellen. Armed Forces Med. Rev.*, Vol. 214, 1968, pp. 461-3.

83. P. H. Gebhard, et al., *Sex Offenders: An Analysis of Types*, Heinemann, 1965, p. 480.

84. C. Wilson, *Origins of the Sexual Impulse*, Panther, 1963, p. 140.

85. *Clinical Surgery (Tropical Surgery)*, Vol. 8, Butterworths, 1965, p. 92.

86. There are many medical papers on "human diphallus". I quote three from those in my possession: C. Donald, "A Case of Human Diphallus", *J. Anat*, Vol. 64, 1930, p. 523; R. M. Nesbit, W. Bromme, "Double Penis and Double Bladder", *Amer. J. Roentgenol*, Vol. 30, 1933, p. 497; E. Kirsck, "Total Duplication of the Penis", *Zschr. Urol.*, Vol. 48, 1955, p. 711.

87. G. H. Seward, *Sex and the Social Order*, Pelican, 1954, p. 199.

88. F. Henriques, *Love in Action*, Panther, 1965, p. 19-20.

89. F. Henriques, *ibid.*, 1965, p. 21.

90. T. H. Van de Velde, *Ideal Marriage*, Heinemann, 1965, p. 86.

91. A. C. Kinsey *et al, ibid.*, 1953, p. 623.

92. H. Jolly, "Sexual Precocity", *Proc. Royal Soc. Med.*, 44, 1951, p. 459.

93. D. Davies, "A Shangri-La in Ecuador", *New Scientist*, Vol. 57, Number 831, February 1, 1973, pp. 236-8.

94. H. Ellis, *Physiology of Sex*, Heinemann, 1933, p. 273.

95. D. & H. Wolfers, *Vasectomy and Vasectomania*, Mayflower, 1974 p. 245.

96. G. I. M. Swyer, *ibid.*, p. 73.

97. A. Duhrssen, *Zschr f. Geburtsh Gynak*, Vol. 27, 1893, p. 216.

98. J. H. Van de Velde, *ibid.*, p. 95.

99. G. I. M. Swyer, *ibid.*, p. 25.

100. E. & P. Kronhausen, *ibid.*, 1967, p. 747.

101. J. H. Van de Velde, *ibid.*, p. 93.

102. P. Vaughan, *The Pill on Trial*, Pelican, 1972, p. 233.

103. C. S. Ford, F. A. Beach, *ibid.*, p. 88.

104. W. F. Benedict, *The Sexual Anatomy of Woman*, Polybooks, 1971, p. 78.

105. P. Mantegazza, *The Sexual Relations of Mankind*, Brandon, 1966, pl. 54.

106. W. Durstan, "Sudden and Excessive Swelling of a Woman's Breasts," *Phil. Trans*, 4th ed. 1731, p. 78.

107. H. Jolly, *ibid.*, p. 461.

108. W. F. Benedict, *ibid.*, p. 23.

109. Quoted by A. Edwardes and R. E. L. Masters, *The Cradle of Erotica*, Odyssey Press, 1970, pl. 47.

110. P. Mantegazza, *ibid.*, pp. 116-17.

111. F. W. Lynch, A. Maxwell, *Pelvic Neoplasm*, D. Appleton & Co, New York, 1927. Also in *Novak's Textbook of Gynecology*, Livingstone, 1965, p. 176.

112. *Novak's Textbook of Gynecology*, *ibid.*, pp. 131-4.

113. E. & P. Kronhausen, *ibid.*, 1967, p. 238.

114. G. I. M. Swyer, *ibid.*, p. 69.

115. J. C. Lauret, *The Danish Sex Fairs*, Jasmine Press, 1970, p. 6.

116. E. Chou, *The Dragon and the Phoenix*, Corgi, 1973, p. 150.

117. *Clinical Surgery, Vol. 15*, (Gynaecology & Obstetrics), D. W. T. Roberts, Butterworths, 1967, p. 58.

118. J. B. Banister, A. H. McIndoe, "Operation for the Cure of Congenital absence of the Vagina", *J. Obstek, Gynaec. Brit. Emp. 45*, 1938, p. 490. Also Discussed in *Clinical Surgery, Vol. IV (Plastic Surgery)*, R. J. V. Beattie, Butterworth's 1965, p. 80.

119. Theo Lang, *The Difference Between a Man and a Woman*, Sphere, 1973, p. 38.

120. W. P. Pomeroy, *ibid.*, p. 317.

121. H. Benjamin, R. E. L. Masters, *The Prostitute in Society*, Mayflower, 1966, p. 126.

122. B. J. Hurwood, *The Golden Age of Erotica*, Tandem, 1968, p. 193.

123. Quoted without comment by W. Francis Benedict, *ibid.*, p. 66. Quoted with some discussion by J. Davenport, *Aphrodisiacs and Love Stimulants*, Luxor Press, 1965, pp. 104-5.

124. W. F. Benedict, *ibid.*, p. 64.

125. H. Jolly, *ibid.*, p. 22.

126. E. Novak, *Menstruation and its Disorder*, D. Appleton & Co, New York, 1921.

127. G. I. M. Swyer, *ibid.*, p. 59.

128. P. Cauthery, M. Cole, *ibid.*, p. 108.

129. A. S. Parker, *ibid.*, pp. 195-204.

130. C. Faulder, "In the Search for Self Knowledge How Much of Yourself are You Prepared to See?" *Nova*, August 1973, p. 25.

131. T. H. Van de Velde, *ibid.*, p. 70.

132. H. Jolly, *ibid.*, p. 24.

133. A. C. Kinsey *et al.*, *ibid.*, 1953, p. 123.

134. H. Jolly, *ibid.*, p. 22.

135. R. Pearsall, *ibid.*, p. 236.

136. P. Mantegazza, *ibid.*, pl. 78, 84, p. 463.

137. G. I. M. Swyer, *ibid.*, pp. 67-8.

138. R. Green *et al.*, "A Case of True Hermaphroditism", *Brit. J. Surg.*, Vol. 40, 1952, p. 263.

139. E. Chesser, *"The Human Aspects of Sexual Deviation,* Arrow Books, 1940, pp. 107-9.

Chapter Three

140. C. Humana, W. Lu, *The Ying Yang,* Wingate, 1971, p. 68.

141. *Eustathii Commentarii ad Homerum,* Vol. 1, Editio Lipsiae, 1827, pp. 325, 403-9.

142. E. S. Gifford, *ibid.*, pp. 53, 57-8.

143. A. C. Kinsey *et al.*, *ibid.*, 1953, p. 541.

144. A. C. Kinsey *et al.*, *ibid.*, 1948, p. 177.

145. A. C. Kinsey *et al.*, *ibid.*, 1953, pp. 104-5.

146. A. C. Kinsey *et al.*, *ibid.*, 1953, p. 613.

147. A. C. Kinsey *et al.*, *ibid.*, 1948, p. 178.

148. Discussed in I. Singer, *The Goals of Human Sexuality,* Wildwood House, 1973, p. 128.

149. Discussed in I. Singer, *ibid.*, p. 129.

150. E. M. Brecher, *ibid.*, p. 137.

151. A. C. Kinsey *et al.*, *ibid.*, 1948, p. 216.

152. L. M. Terman, *Psychological Factors in Marital Happiness,* New York, McGraw-Hill, 1938.

153. L. M. Terman, "Correlates of Orgasm Adequacy in 556 wives", *Journal of Psychology*, 1951, pp. 115-72.

154. S. Fisher, *The Female Orgasm*, Allen Lane, 1973, pp. 39-43.

155. S. Fisher, *ibid.*, p. 212.

156. A. Edwardes, R. E. L. Masters, *ibid.*, p. 145.

157. Nicely discussed by S. Marcus, *The Other Victorians*, Weidenfeld & Nicholson, 1966, Chapter 1.

158. I. & S. Hegeler, *An ABZ of Love*, New English Library, 1969, p. 140.

159. References in R. & E. Brecher, *An Analysis of Human Sexual Response*, André Deutsch, 1967, p. 135.

160. S. Fisher, *ibid.*, p. 191.

161. M. Brecher, *ibid.*, p. 196.

162. W. B. Pomeroy, *ibid.*, p. 179.

163. P. Cauthery, M. Cole, *ibid.*, p. 143.

164. S. Fisher, *ibid.*, p. 189.

165. S. Fisher, *ibid.*, p. 181.

166. Quoted by R. E. L. Masters, *The Hidden World of Erotica*, Lyrebird Press, 1973, p. 224.

167. A. C. Kinsey *et al.*, *ibid.*, 1948, p. 316.

168. C. S. Ford, F. A. Beach, *ibid.*,

169. E. Marchand, *"Voyage Autour due Monde Pendant Les Annees, 1790, 1791, et 1792"*, Paris, 1797.

170. A. C. Kinsey *et al.*, *ibid.*, 1953, p. 113.

171. A. Edwardes, R. E. L. Masters, *ibid.*, p. 78.

172. A. C. Kinsey *et al.*, *ibid.*, 1948, p. 237.

173. A. C. Kinsey *et al.*, *ibid.*, 1948, p. 234.

174. A. C. Kinsey *et al.*, *ibid.*, 1953, p. 352.

175. P. Vaughan, *The Pill on Trial*, Pelican, 1972, p. 58.

176. C. S. Ford, F. A. Beach, *ibid.*, p. 79.

177. Discussed in P. Fryer, *The Birth Controllers* Corgi, 1967, pp. 149-55.

178. C. Humana, W. Wu, *ibid.*, pp. 164-5.

179. T. H. Van De Velde, *ibid.*, p. 107.

180. A. Edwardes, R. E. L. Masters, *ibid.*, p. 50.

181. A. Edwardes, R. E. L. Masters, *ibid.*, p. 69.

182. C. S. Ford, F. A. Beach, *ibid.*, p. 78.

183. A. Edwardes, R. E. L. Masters, *ibid.*, p. 65.

184. A. C. Kinsey *et al.*, *ibid.*, 1948, p. 217.

185. A. C. Kinsey *et al.*, *ibid.*, 1948, p. 235.

186. A. C. Kinsey *et al.*, *ibid.*, 1948, pp. 185-6.

187. A. C. Kinsey *et al.*, *ibid.*, 1948, p. 231.

188. A. C. Kinsey *et al.*, *ibid.*, 1948, p. 231.

189. A. C. Kinsey *et al.*, *ibid.*, 1953, p. 605.

190. I. Bloch, *Sexual Life in England*, Corgi, 1965, p. 260.

191. E. Chou, *ibid.*, pp. 210-11.

192. F. Henriques, *ibid.*, 1965, p. 128.

193. Norman Haire, *The Encyclopedia of Sex Practice*, Encyclopaedic Press, London, 1953, p. 42.

194. *British Medical Journal*, June 30, 1974, p. 780.

195. Cited by F. Henriques, *ibid.*, 1965, p. 326.

196. H. Montgomery Hyde, *A History Of Pornography*, Four Square, 1966, p. 53.

197. *The Koka Shastra, Being the Ratirahasya of Kokkoka*, Trans, A. Comfort, Allen & Unwin, 1964.

198. M. Brecher, *ibid.*, p. 83.

199. A. Comfort, *The Joy of Sex*, Quartet Books, 1974.

200. L. Kennedy, *The Trial of Stephen Ward*, Gollancz, 1974.

201. E. & P. Kronhausen, *ibid.*, 1967, jacket blurb.

202. M. Brecher, *ibid.*, p. 320.

203. J. Atkins, *Sex in Literature*, Panther, 1972, p. 137.

204. A. C. Kinsey *et al.*, *ibid.*, 1953, p. 683.

205. Quoted in J. Atkins, *ibid.*, p. 89.

206. Quoted in A. Edwardes, R. E. L. Masters, *ibid.*, p. 55.

207. E. Chou, *ibid.*, pp. 29-30.

208. B. J. Hurwood, *ibid.*, p. 190.

209. Suetonius, *The Twelve Caesars*, Penguin, 1960, p. 131.

210. G. R. Taylor, *ibid.*, pp. 39-40, 135. See also The National Secular Society Pamphlet, *The Crimes of the Popes*, by G. W. Foote and J. M. Wheeler.

211. B. Walker, *Sex and the Supernatural*, Macdonald Unit 75, 1970, p. 26.

212. 1 Kings i, 1-4.

213. *Economist*, March 16, 1974.

Chapter Four

214. R. V. Krafft-Ebing, *The Psychopathia Sexualis*, Panther, 1965.

215. I. Bloch, *ibid.*, p. 91.

216. R. C. Suggs, *Marquesan Sexual Behavior*, Constable, 1966, p. 45.

217. C. S. Ford, F. A. Beach, *ibid.*, pp. 188-9, 191.

218. E. Chesser, *ibid.*, pp. 47-48.

219. Much of it quoted by A. C. Kinsey *et al.*, *ibid.*, 1953, p. 141.

220. A. Comfort, *ibid.*, 1968, pp. 77-8.

221. P. Cauthery, M. Cole, *ibid.*, pp. 95-6.

222. P. Mantegazza, *ibid.*, p. 77.

223. A. Edwardes, R. E. L. Masters *ibid.*, pp. 163-4.

224. A. Edwardes, R. E. L. Masters, *ibid.*, p. 153.

225. Cited in A. Edwardes, R. E. L. Masters, *ibid.*, p. 155.

226. J. Atkins, *ibid.*, p. 314.

227. E. Chou, *ibid.*, pp. 27-8.

228. A. Edwardes, R. E. L. Masters, *ibid.*, p. 92.

229. G. Allgrove, *Love in the East*, Anthony Gibbs & Phillips, 1962, p. 63.

230. W. & J. Breedlove, *Swap Clubs*, Los Angeles, 1964.

231. E. M. Brecher, *ibid.*, p. 251.

232. H. M. Hyde, *The Other Love*, Heinemann, London, 1970, p. 1.

233. H. Licht, *Sexual Life in Ancient Greece*, Abbey Library, 1971, pp. 318-28.

234. A. Karlen, *Sexuality and Homosexuality*, Macdonald, 1971, pp. 19-20.

235. J. Cleugh, *ibid.*, pp. 24-25.

236. H. M. Hyde, *ibid.*, 1970, pp. 283-4.

237. H. M. Hyde, *ibid.*, 1970, pp. 182-3.

238. *Memories of Chevalier d'Eon*, Anthony Blond, 1970.

239. E. Chesser, *ibid.*, p. 119.

240. References in *Sexual Behavior: Social, Clinical, and Legal Aspects*, Eds: H. L. P. Resnik, M. E. Wolfgang, 1972, "*Incest between father and daughter*", pp. 169-83.

241. W. G. Sumner, *Folkways*, New York, 1960.

242. Maisch presents a number of examples of favored incest in primitive societies (*Incest*, p. 35).

243. G. R. Taylor, *ibid.*, p. 49.

244. O. Volta, *The Vampire*, Tandem, 1965, pp. 140-1.

245. O. Volta, *ibid.*, pp. 64-5.

246. Quoted by O. Volta, *ibid.*, p. 46.

247. R. E. L. Masters, *ibid.*, p. 23.

248. B. Malinowski, *The Sexual Life of Savages*, Routledge, 1939, p. 399.

249. Quoted in A. Edwardes, R. E. L. Masters, *ibid.*, p. 9.

250. H. Licht, *ibid.*, p. 504.

251. Allen Edwardes, *The Jewel in the Lotus*, Anthony Blond, 1961, p. 257.

252. R. E. L. Masters, *ibid.*, pp. 7, 17-18.

253. R. E. L. Masters, *ibid.*, p. 7.

254. Some reasons are suggested in the *British Journal of Sexual Medicine*, Jan./Feb. 1974, p. 43.

255. C. S. Ford, F. A. Beach, *ibid.*, p. 148.

256. K. Rasmussen, "Intellectual Culture of the Copper Eskimos", *Report of the Fifth Thule Expedition*, Copenhagen; Gyldendalske Boghandel, Nordisk Forlag, Vol. IX, 1932, pp. 1-350.

257. J. Cleugh, *ibid.*, 1968, pp. 62-3.

258. J. Cleugh, *The First Masochist*, Blond, 1967.

259. B. J. Hurwood, *ibid.*, p. 105.

260. I. Bloch, *ibid.*, p. 270.

261. F. Henriques, *ibid.*, 1963, p. 69.

262. Quoted by B. J. Hurwood, *ibid.*, p. 108.

263. O. Volta, *ibid.*, pp. 117-18.

264. O. Volta, *ibid.*, pp. 38-44.

265. E. Chou, *ibid.*, p. 216.

266. A. Edwardes, R. E. L. Masters, *ibid.*, p. 85.

267. Quoted in *Sexual Behavior: Social, Clinical and Legal Aspects, ibid.*, pp. 145-6.

268. All cited in J. M. Macdonald, *Rape, Offenders, and their Victims*, C. H. Thomas, 1971, pp. 28-30.

269. John Johnson, *Disorders of Sexual Potency in the Male*, Pergamon, 1968, p. 22.

270. J. Johnson, *ibid.*, pp. 22-3.

271. E. S. Gifford, *ibid.*, p. 232.

272. Albert Ellis, Edward Sagarin, *Nymphomania*, Mayflower, 1973, pp. 21-2.

273. A. Ellis, E. Sagarin, *ibid.*, p. 117.

274. H. Benjamin, R. E. L. Masters, *ibid.*, p. 132.

275. H. M. Hyde, *ibid.*, 1970, pp. 123-4.

276. L. Bassermann, *The Oldest Profession*, New English Library, 1969, p. 147.

277. J. Atkins, *ibid.*, p. 90.

278. L. Bassermann, *ibid.*, p. 26.

279. F. Henriques, *ibid.*, 1963, pp. 108-12.

280. B. J. Hurwood, *ibid.*, pp. 109-10.

281. R. Pearsall, *ibid.*, 1969, pp. 248-9; M. Harrison, *Fanfare of Strumpets*, W. H. Allen, 1971, p. 20.

282. H. Benjamin, R. E. L. Masters, *ibid.*, pp. 112, 211.

283. H. Benjamin, R. E. L. Masters, *ibid.*, pp. 117, 125-7, 133-4.

284. H. Benjamin, R. S. L. Masters, *ibid.*, pp. 45, 129, 225.

285. G. R. Scott, *Phallic Worship*, Panther, 1970, p. 78.

286. S. Barley, *Sex Slavery*, Heinemann, 1968, pp. 112-16.

Chapter Five

287. AL (1936 edn), p. 303, C. F. Webster, *Holy Bible* (1833), *passim*, and p. XVI: "Many words and phrases are so offensive, especially to females, as to create a reluctance in young persons to attend Bible classes and schools in which they are required to read passages which cannot be repeated without a blush". Cf also Webster, *Mistakes and Corrections* (1837), pp. 3-6. Quoted by Peter Fryer, *Mrs. Grundy*, Corgi, 1965, p. 30.

288. A. Comfort, *ibid.*, 1968, p. 72.

289. P. Fryer, *The Birth Controllers*, Corgi, 1967, pp. 213-21.

290. P. Fryer, *ibid.*, 1965, p. 184.

291. P. Fryer, *ibid.*, 1965, p. 20.

292. P. Fryer. *ibid.*, 1965, p. 58.

293. B. Walker, *ibid.*, pp. 45-6.

294. A. C. Kinsey, *et al.*, *ibid.*, p. 168.

295. G. R. Taylor, *ibid.*, p. 211.

296. A. Comfort, *ibid.*, 1968, pp. 81-2.

297. R. D. Potts, *Texas Medical Practitioner*, 1897-8, Vol. 2, pp. 7-9, Quoted by Comfort, *ibid.*, 1968, p. 118.

298. Quoted by E. Brecher, *ibid.*, p. 59.

299. A. Eyer, "Clitoridectomy for the Cure of Certain Cases of Masturbation in Young Girls," International Medical Magazine (Philadelphia), 1894-5, Vol. 3, pp. 259-62. Quoted by Comfort, *ibid.*, 1968, p. 111.

300. O. Nemecek, *Virginity, Pre-Nuptial Rites and Rituals*, Neville Spearman, 1961, p. 27.

301. E. Crawley, *The Mystic Rose*, Spring Books, 1965, pp. 76-7.

302. F. Henriques, *ibid.*, 1965, p. 73.

303. A. Smith, *The Body*, Allen & Unwin, 1968, pp. 95-6.

304. E. J. Dingwall, *The Girdle of Chastity*, Clarion Press, 1959, pp. 82-3.

305. *Guardian*, February 22, 1974.

306. See *Verzeichniss der Handschriften im preussischen Staate, Hanover*, (3 vols. Berlin, 1893-4), 63, Vol. i, p. 164. The girdle is in the tenth book. This reference is cited by Dingwall, *ibid.*, p. 33.

307. E. J. Dingwall, *ibid.*, pp. 51-4.

308. E. J. Dingwall, *ibid.*, pp. 14-20.

309. *Vierte Beilage zum Deutschen Reichsanzeiger und Königlich Preussischen Staatsanzeiger*, Montag, August 3, 1903, No. 180, p. 2. Cited, with other references, in Dingwall, *ibid.*, p. 122.

310. J. Cleugh, *ibid.*, 1963, pp. 37-8.

311. Quoted in R. H. Robbins, *The Encyclopedia of Witchcraft and Demonology*, Spring Books, 1968, pp. 490-1.

312. H. C. Lea, *History of Sacerdotal Celibacy in the Christian Church*, Watts, 1932, pp. 71-2.

313. J. Cleugh, *ibid.*, 1963, p. 272.

314. H. C. Lea, *ibid.*, pp. 29-30.

315. Pope Pius XII, *Holy Virginity*, 1954, Catholic Truth Society.

316. Saint Jerome, *Against Jovinian*; quoted by I. Singer *ibid.*, p. 45.

317. J. Cleugh, *ibid.*, 1963 pp. 175-83.

318. C. Wood, B. Suitters, *The Fight for Acceptance*, MTP, 1970, pp. 63-5.

319. G. R. Scott, *ibid.*, Panther, 1970, pp. 134-6.

320. T. Vanggaard, *Phallos: A Symbol and its History in the Male World*, Jonathan Cape, 1972, p. 82.

321. T. C. Longworth, *The Worship of Love*, Torchstream Books, 1954, pp. 50-2.

322. G. R. Scott, *ibid.*, pp. 125-6.

323. O. Keifer, *Sexual Life in Ancient Rome*, Abbey Library, 1971, pp. 112-14.

324. O. Kiefer, *ibid.*, pp. 108-10, 114-18.

325. E. Chou, *ibid.*, pp. 175-6, 181.

326. C. Wolfe, *The Castration*, Basel: Benno Schwabe, 1934. p. 16.

327. P. Fryer, *ibid.*, 1967, pp. 20-1.

328. H. Licht, *ibid.*, pp. 363-76.

329. The Perfumed Garden of the Shaykh Nefzawi, trans. Sir R. Burton, Neville Spearman, 1963.

330. B. Malinowski, *ibid.*, pp. 143-44.

331. R. C. Suggs, *ibid.*, p. 20.

332. G. L. Simons, *Sex and Superstition*, Abelard, 1973, Chapter 5, pp. 130-65.

333. D. M. Rorvik, L. B. Shettles, *ibid.*, pp. 30-1.

334. C. Wood, B. Suitters, *ibid.*, pp. 34-5.

335. In a letter to me (May 10, 1972), for which I am grateful.

336. R. H. Robbins, *ibid.*, p. 466.

337. R. H. Robbins, *ibid.*, p. 465.

338. G. R. Taylor, *ibid.*, pp. 34-6.

339. R. H. Robbins, *ibid.*, p. 464.

340. J. Atkins, *ibid.*, p. 71.

341. T. Lang, *ibid.*, p. 349.

342. V. Solanas, *S.C.U.M.* (*Society for Cutting up Men*) *Manifesto*, Olympia Press, 1971.

343. G. R. Taylor, *ibid.*, p. 147.

344. E. G. Davis, *The First Sex*, Dent, 1973.

345. O. Kiefer, *ibid.*, p. 15.

346. W. J. Fielding, *Strange Customs of Courtship and Marriage*, Four Square, 1964, p. 80.

347. E. Chou, *ibid.*, p. 15.

348. W. J. Fielding, *ibid.*, p.138.

349. J. Braddock, *The Bridal Bed*, Robert Hale, 1960, p. 35.

350. C. S. Ford, F. A. Beach, *ibid.*, p. 177.

351. C. S. Ford, F. A. Beach, *ibid.*, p 176.

352. W. Goldschmidt, "The Brideprice of the Sebei", *Scientific American*, Vol. 229, No. 1, July 1973.

353. I. Bloch, *ibid.*, p. 62.

354. A. C. Kinsey *et al.*, *ibid.*, 1953, p. 428.

355. J. Hawkes, Sir L. Woolley, *The Beginnings of Civilization*, Allen & Unwin, 1963, p. 492.

356. W. E. H. Lecky, *History of European Morals from Augustus to Charlemagne*, Vol. ii (London), 1890, p. 316.

357. *Codex Theodosianus*, Vol. IX, No. 24, p. 1.

358. Quoted by J. Cleugh, *ibid.*, 1963, p. 277.

359. A. C. Kinsey *et al.*, *ibid.*, 1953, p. 168.

360. O. Kiefer, *ibid.*, p. 84.

361. H. C. Lea, *ibid.*, p. 79.

362. C. Humana, W. Wu, *ibid.*, p. 59.

363. *Sexual Offences; A Report of the Cambridge Department of Criminal Science*, ed. L. Radzinowicz, Macmillan, 1957, p. 136.

364. N. Morland, *An Outline of Sexual Criminology*, Tallis Press, 1966, p. 123.

365. N. Morland, *ibid.*, pp. 135-8.

366. O. Volta, *ibid.*, pp. 130-1.

367. J. H. Gagnon, "Female Child Victims of Sex Offences" *Soc. Prob.* Vol. 13, 1965, p. 176.

368. S. Chaneles, "Child Victims of Sexual Offences", *Fed. Probation*, Vol. 31, 1967, p. 52.

369. E. Chesser, *ibid.*, Arrow, 1971, p. 101.

370. F. S. Caprio, D. R. Brenner, *Sexual Behavior,* Paperback Library, 1966, p. 49.

371. O. Volta, *ibid.,* p. 128.

372. P. H. Gebhard *et al., ibid.,* p. 479.

373. H. Bloch, G. Geis, *Man, Crime and Society,* New York, Random House, 1963, p. 290.

374. G. Geis, "Group Sexual Assaults" *Medical Aspects of Human Sexuality,* Vol. 5, (5), May 1971, pp. 100-13.

375. R. E. L. Masters, *ibid.,* p. 139.

376. E. G. Davis, *ibid,* p. 98.

377. A. C. Kinsey *et al., ibid.,* 1953, p. 370.

378. R. E. L. Masters, *ibid.,* p. 45.

379. J. Robitscher, "Statutes, Law Enforcement and the Judicial Process", In *Sexual Behaviors: Social, Clinical and Legal Aspects,* ed. H. L. P. Pesnik, M. E. Wolfgang, Little, Brown & Co., 1972, p. 14.

380. D. J. West, *Homosexuality,* Duckworth, 1955, p. 38.

381. H. M. Hyde, *ibid.,* Heinemann.

382. H. M. Hyde, *ibid.,* pp. 176-182.

383. H. V. H. Wullen, *J. Heredity,* 28, 1937, pp. 169-75.

384. D. & H. Wolfers, *ibid.,* p. 35.

385. G. K. Sturup, "Castration, The Total Treatment" in *Sexual Behaviors . . . . , ibid.,* pp. 361-82.

386. D. & H. Wolfers *ibid.,* p. 32.

387. A. Langelüddeke, *Castration of Sexual Criminals,* Berlin: W. de Gruyter, 1963, pp. 7-8.

388. D. & H. Wolfers, *ibid.,* p. 37.

389. H. Ellis, *ibid.*, p. 168.

390. *The Trial of Lady Chatterley*, ed. C. H. Rolph, Penguin Special, 1961.

391. For instance, see G. L. Simons, *Pornography Without Prejudice*, Abelard-Schuman, 1972.

392. G. R. Taylor, *ibid.*, p. 12.

393. See T. Palmer, *The Trials of Oz*, Blond & Briggs, 1971 and *ABZ of Pornography*, pp. 115-18.

394. G. L. Simons, *ibid.*, 1972, pp. 106-7.

395. G. L. Simons, *ibid.*, 1972, pp. 127-9.

396. H. Benjamin, R. E. L. Masters, *ibid.*, p. 46.

397. P. Tabori, *Dress and Undress*, New English Library, 1969, p. 71.

398. S. Barley, *ibid.*, p. 6.

399. S. Barley, *ibid.*, p. 63.

Chapter Six

400. I. Singer, *ibid.*, p. 13.

401. E. M. Brecher, *ibid.*, p. 3.

402. See for instance, W. P. Pomeroy, *ibid.*

403. A. C. Kinsey *et al.*, *ibid.*, 1948.

404. A. C. Kinsey *et al.*, *ibid.*, 1953.

405. K. B. Davis, *Factors in the Sex Life of Twenty-two Hundred Women*, New York and London, Harper and Brothers, pp. XX and 430.

406. A. C. Kinsey *et al.*, *ibid.*, 1948, p. 24.

407. P. H. Gebhard, "Human Sex Behavior Research", in *Reproduction and Sexual Behavior*, Indiana University Press, 1968, pp. 403-4.

408. P. H. Gebhard, *ibid.*, pp. 399-400.

409. A. C. Kinsey *et al.*, *ibid.*, 1948, pp. 27, 219, 221.

410. E. Brecher, *ibid.*, p. 287.

411. E. Brecher, *ibid.*, pp. 289-90.

412. S. Fisher, *ibid.*,

413. P. S. Achilles, *The Effectiveness of certain social hygiene Literature.* New York, Amer. Soc. Hyg. Assoc. pp. 116.

414. E. Brecher, *ibid.*, p. 105.

415. M. Schofield, *The Sexual Behavior of Young People*, Pelican, 1968, p. 29.

416. B. Malinowski, *ibid.*, 1939.

417. C. S. Ford, F. A. Beach, *ibid.*

418. E. Brecher, *ibid.*, p. 290-2.

419. E. Brecher, *ibid.*, pp. 207-8.

420. M. W. Barr, "Some notes on asexualization, with a report of eighteen cases", *J. Nerv. & Ment. Dis.*, Vol. 51, 1920, pp. 231-41.

421. A. Karlen, *Sexuality and Homosexuality*, Macdonald, 1971, p. 376.

422. Quoted by E. Brecher, *ibid.*, pp. 12-13.

423. H. Ellis, *ibid.*, p. 28.

424. *The Report of the Commission on Obscenity, and Pornography*, Bantam Books, 1970.

425. J. Cleugh, *ibid.*, 1963, p. 186.

426. G. R. Raylor, *ibid.*, p. 150.

427. J. Cleugh, *ibid.*, 1963, pp. 190-1.

428. W. Young, *Eros Denied*, Corgi, 1969, p. 231.

429. J. S. Horn, *Away with all Pests*, Paul Hamlyn, 1969, pp. 89-93.

430. F. Green, *China, the Country Americans are Not Allowed to Know*, New York, Ballantine Books, 1962.

431. T. Rosebury, *Microbes and Morals*, Secker & Warburg, 1971, Chapter 13.

432. Quoted by H. Wendt, *ibid.*, p. 57.

433. C. Wood, B. Suitters, *ibid.*, 1970, p. 100.

434. G. Leach, *ibid.*, p. 86.

435. G. Chedd, "Test-tube Genesis," *New Scientist*, Vol. 40, No. 623, November 14, 1968.

436. R. E. Brecher, *ibid.*, pp. 61-8.

437. S. Marcus, *ibid.*, p. 13.

438. H. Wendt, *ibid.*, p. 40.

439. E. Brecher, *ibid.*, p. 199.

440. R. L. Gardner, R. Edwards, *Nature*, Vol. 218, (1968), p. 346.

441. H. Wendt, *ibid.*, pp. 90-2.

442. Quoted by H. Wendt, *ibid.*, p. 204.

443. H. Wendt, *ibid.*, pp. 73-7.

444. John Burton, "Virgin Birth in Vertebrates", *New Scientist*, Vol. 59. No. 858, August 9, 1973, p. 334.

445. G. R. Taylor, *ibid.*, 1968, p. 30.

446. *Journal of the Ohio Herpetological Society*, Vol. 5. p. 115.

447. Cited in *Marshall's the Physiology of Reproduction*, *ibid.*, 1956, p. 351.

448. F. R. Lillie (1917) *J. Exptl. Zool*, *23*, pp. 271.

449. H. Wendt, *ibid.*, p. 305.

450. C. R. Austin, *Aust. J. Sci. Res*, Vol 134, 1951, pp. 581-96. M. C. Chang, *Nature*, Lond, Vol. 168, 1951, pp. 697-699.

451. *Reproduction in Female Mammal*, *ibid.*, pp. 464-5.

452. M. Barry (1843), "Spermatozoa observed within the mummiferous ovum", *Phil. Trans. Roy. Soc.*, Vol 133, p. 33.

453. H. Wendt, *ibid.*, p. 69.

454. G. R. Taylor, *ibid.*, 1968, p. 31.

455. J. M. Valentine, *J. Exptl. Zool.*, 58. 1931, pp. 165-227, cited in *The Hormones, Physiology, Chemistry and Applications*, Vol. IV, 1964, Academic Press, p. 119.

456. Jacobson *et al.*, *Science*, *132*, 1960, p. 1011.

457. T. Lang, *ibid.*, pp. 43-4.

458. J. Needham, Lu Gwei—Djen, *Endeavour*, Vol. 25, September 1968.

459. F. Neumann *et al.*, Antiandrogens in *Das Testosteron, Die, Struma. Symposion der Deutschen Gesellschaft für Endokrinologie*. Berlin, Springer, 1968, pp. 78-101.

460. H. Montgomery Hyde, *ibid.*, 1966, pp. 189-90.

461. Quoted by S. Marcus, *ibid.*, p. 56.

462. A. Comfort, *ibid.*, 1968, p. 28.

Chapter Seven

463. P. Fryer, *ibid.*, 1967, p. 19.

464. Quoted by S. Green, *The Curious History of Contraception*, Ebury Press, 1971, p. 45.

465. W. Godwin, *Thoughts Occasioned by the Perusal of Dr. Parr's Spital Sermon*, 1801, pp. 64-5.

466. P. Fryer, *ibid.*, 1967, pp. 147-56.

467. C. Wood, B. Suitters, *ibid.*, p. 37.

468. C. Wood, B. Suitters, *ibid.*, pp. 39-42.

469. S. Astwell, *A Practical Treatise on the Diseases Peculiar to Women*, London, Highley, 1845.

470. T. G. Thoman, *Diseases of Women*, London, Churchill, 1891.

471. This, with Astwell, quoted by C. Wood, *ibid.*, p. 11.

472. C. Wood, *ibid.*, pp. 20-1.

473. C. Wood, B. Suitters, *ibid.*, p. 129.

474. P. Fryer, *ibid.*, 1967, pp. 11-12.

475. C. Wood, B. Suitters, *ibid.*, p. 91.

476. S. Green, *ibid.*, p. 78.

477. P. Fryer, *ibid.*, 1967, pp. 26-7.

478. C. Wood, B. Suitters, *ibid.*, pp. 180-94.

479. B. Suitters, *ibid.*, p. 1.

480. *Population Control, ibid.*, pp. 204-6.

481. B. Suitters, *ibid.*, pp. 8, 202.

482. *Population Control. ibid.*, pp. 203-8.

483. IPPF Europe, *A Survey of the Legal Status of Contraception, Sterilization and Abortion, in European Countries*, 1973.

484. S. Stall, *What A Young Husband Ought to Know*, Philadelphia, 1900, quoted by A. Comfort, *ibid.*, p. 72.

485. P. Vaughan, *ibid.*, p. 236.

486. IPPF Europe, *A Survey of the Legal Status of Contraception, Sterilization and Abortion in European Countries*, Appendix 2, 1973.

487. C. Wood, *ibid.*, p. 44.

488. I. Schapera, *Married Life in African Tribe*, New York, 1941.

489. C. Wood, B. Suitters, *ibid.*, pp. 202-8.

490. P. Vaughan, *ibid.*, pp. 90-1, see also, B. Seaman, *The Doctors' Case Against the Pill*, Michael Joseph, 1970.

491. P. Vaughan, *ibid.*, pp. 68-9, 98-9.

492. E. A. Drake, *What a Woman of Forty-Five Ought to Know*, Philadelphia, 1902. Quoted by Comfort, *ibid.*, 1968, p. 70.

493. "Dr. Kendall: From Scicon to Fertility", *Computing*, 10 January 1974, pp. 10-1.

494. Population Report, *Sterilization*, Series, C-D, No. 2, George Washington University Medical Center, April 1973.

495. C. Wood, B. Suitters, *ibid.*, p. 23.

496. A. Cooper, *Observations on the Structure of Diseases of the Testis*, Longman, 1830: quoted by D. & H. Wolfers, *ibid.*, 1974, pp. 12-3.

497. M. Mettzer, *New York State J. of Med.*, Vol. 28, 1928, pp. 1290-2.

498. References in D. & H. Wolfers, *ibid.*, p. 16.

499. D. & H. Wolfers, *ibid.*, p. 41.

500. H. C. Rolnick, *Journal of Urology*, 1954, Vol. 72, p. 911.

501. S. Marshall, R. P. Lyon, *Journal of the American Medical Association*, Vol. 219, 1972, p. 1753.

502. D. J. Dodds, *Journal of the American Medical Association*, Vol. 220, 1972, p. 1498.

503. "One Thousand Vasectomies," *BMJ*, *ibid.*,

504. References in D. & H. Wolfers, *ibid.*, p. 190.

505. *Science,* Vol. 179, p. 293. Clive Wood, "The Hazards of Vasectomy", *New Scientist,* Vol. 58, No. 844, May 3, 1973, p. 268.

506. D. & H. Wolfers, *ibid.,* pp. 182-4.

507. A. C. Kinsey *et al., ibid.,* 1953, p. 719.

508. S. Kardiman, "Artificial Insemination in the Talmud", *Harofe Hawri, Hebrew Med. J.* 2., 1950.

509. *Marshall's Physiology of Reproduction, ibid.,* 1910, pp. 680-90.

510. A. M. C. M. Schellen, *Artificial Insemination in the Human,* Elsevier, 1957, p. 10.

511. G. Leach, *ibid.,* p. 74.

Chapter Eight

512. L. Legrain, (1936), *Ur Excavations, Vol. 111: Archaic Seal-Impressions.* Publ. Brit. Mus. and Univ. Pa. Mus. pp. viii †51†58 pl.

513. F. Henriques, *ibid.,* 1965, p. 324.

514. H. Ellis, *ibid.,* p. 297.

515. C. G. Brunius, *Forsok till Forklaringar ofver Hallis-tringar Lund,* 1868, Taf. V.

516. A. C. Kinsey *et al., ibid.,* 1948, p. 374.

517. H. Wendt, *ibid.,* p. 40.

518. P. Rawson, *Tantra,* Thames and Hudson, 1973, p. 7.

519. P. Rawson, "Early History of Sexual Art", *Primitive Erotic Art,* Weidenfeld and Nicholson, 1973, pp. 19-20.

520. E. Lucie-Smith, *Eroticism in Western Art,* Thames & Hudson, 1972, pp. 11-13.

521. G. S. Whittet, *Lovers in Art,* Studio Vista, 1972, p. 9.

522. P. Rawson, *Erotic Art of the East*, Weidenfeld & Nicholson, 1973, p. 86.

523. Cited in J. Atkins, *ibid.*, pp. 25, 200-1.

524. C. Humana, W. Wu, *ibid.*, p. 26.

525. A. Edwardes, R. E. L. Masters, *ibid.*, p. 97.

526. Cited in C. Humana, W. Wu, *ibid.*, p. 97.

527. Cited by R. H. Robbins, *ibid.*, p. 464.

528. "The Tale of Kamar al Zaman and Princess Budur," 182nd night (*Arabian Nights*) Cited by J. Atkins, *ibid.*, p. 203.

529. A. Edwardes, R. E. L. Masters, *ibid.*, p. 50.

530. C. Humana, W. Wu, *ibid.*, p. 26.

531. "Tale of Pomegranate-Flower and Badr Basim" (540th night, trs. Mathers).

532. J. Atkins, *ibid.*, p. 210.

533. Cited by J. Atkins, *ibid.*, pp. 325-30.

534. *Arabian Nights*, trans. Mardrus, London, 1923, pp. 148-50.

535. E. Chou, *ibid.*, p. 205.

536. E. S. Gifford, *ibid.*, p. 197.

537. Cited by J. Atkins, *ibid.*, p. 27.

538. G. Greer, *The Female Eunuch*, Paladin, 1970, p. 39.

539. Eskimo myth gathered by Holm in Eastern Greenland in 1884. Quoted by R. Caillois in *Le Myth et l'homme*, Paris, 1938.

540. J. Swift, *Gulliver's Travels*, Dent, 1961, pp. 124-5.

541. P. Mantegegazza, *ibid.*, 1966.

542. Quoted by E. Chou, *ibid.*, pp. 244-5.

543. E. Chou, *ibid.*, pp. 237-38.

544. F. Carr, *European Erotic Art*, Luxor Press, 1972, p. 50.

545. H. M. Hyde, *ibid.*, 1966, p. 116.

546. O. Kiefer, *ibid.*, pp. 185-92.

547. J. Atkins, *ibid.*, pp. 160-2. Quote from Schonfield.

548. A. C. Kinsey *et al.*, *ibid.*, 1953, pp. 673-4.

549. Some of his songs are performed in a three-record set by EMI, *The Art of Courtly Love*, Munrow SLS 863.

550. F. M. Brodie, *The Devil Drives*, Penguin, 1971, pp. 421-2.

551. J. Atkins, *ibid.*, pp. 48-9.

552. A. Brien, *Spectator*, November 15, 1963.

553. B. J. Hurwood, *ibid.*, pp. 19-20.

554. I. Bloch, *ibid.*, p. 53.

555. J. Scherr, *General History of Literature*, ninth edition, Stuttgart, 1895, Vol. 11, p. 47.

556. Pisanus Fraxi, *Catena Librorum Tacendorum*, London, 1885, p. 86.

557. E. & P. Kronhausen, *ibid.*, 1967, p. 1.

558. B. J. Hurwood, *ibid.*, p. 61.

559. *Wicked Victorians*, Odyssey Press, London, (Anthology), 1970, pp. 15-16.

560. M. Gabor, *The Pin-Up*, André Deutsch, 1972, pp. 76-7.

561. M. Gabor, *ibid.*, p. 31.

562. B. J. Hurwood, *ibid*, pp. 170-2.

563. *"To Deprave and Corrupt"*, edited by John Chandos, Souvenir Press, 1962.

564. "Erotic Dolphins Help Raymond Grow Richer", *Sunday Times*, February 26, 1974, p. 3.

565. *Wicked Victorians*, *ibid.*, p. 171.

566. J. Graham-Murray, *A History of Morals*, Library 33 Ltd., p. 150.

567. *The ABZ of Pornography*, *ibid.*, pp. 65-9.

568. Pornography, *The Longford Report*, Coronet, 1972.

569. G. L. Simons, *ibid.*, 1973, p. 190.

570. Cited by P. Fryer, *ibid.*, 1965, p. 79.

571. Quoted in B. J. Hurwood, *ibid.*, p. 33.

572. J. Cleugh, *ibid.*, 1963, p. 250.

573. J. Chastenet, *La Belle Époche*, (Paris 1951), p. 51.

574. R. Findlater, *Banned, Theatrical Censorship in Britain*, Panther, 1968, p. 5.

575. M. Gabor, *ibid.*, p. 33.

576. J. Cleugh, *ibid.*, 1963, p. 30.

577. H. Licht, *ibid.*, p. 88.

578. J. Vanggaard, *ibid.*, pp. 59-61.

579. T. C. Longworth, *ibid.*, p.41.

580. J. Cleugh, *ibid.*, 1968, p. 25.

581. M. Gabor, *ibid.*, p. 52.

582. M. Gabor, *ibid.*, p. 177.

583. F. Downey, *Portrait of an Era as Drawn by C. D. Gibson, A Biography*, (New York) and London 1936, p. 184.

584. M. Gabor, *ibid.*, p. 47.

585. M. Gabor, *ibid.*, p. 254.

586. P. Lacey, *The History of the Nude in Photography*, Bantam Books, April 1964, p. 14.

587. P. Lacey, *ibid.*, p. 130.

588. A. Walker, *Sex in the Movies*, Pelican, 1968, pp. 185-6.

589. A. Walker, *ibid.*, p. 262.

590. *The ABZ of Pornography*, *ibid.*, p. 36.

591. *The ABZ of Pornography*, *ibid.*, p. 36.

592. *Cinema X*, Vol. 5, No. 12, pp. 54-5.

593. A. Walker, *ibid.*, p. 25.

594. A. Walker, *ibid.*, p. 80.

595. M. Gabor, *ibid.*, p. 156.

596. A. Walker, *ibid.*, p. 141.

597. J. P. Chaplin, *Rumor, Fear and the Madness of Crowds*, Ballantine, 1959, Chapter 5.

598. *Penthouse*, Vol. 8, No. 1, p. 93.

599. R. Findlater, *The History of British Film*, Vol. 1, Rachæl Low (Allen and Unwin, 1948).

600. J. Trevelyan, *What the Censor Saw*, 1974.

601. C. Humana, W. Wu, *ibid.*, pp. 222-3.

602. *Sunday Times Magazine*, March 11, 1973.

603. L. Lovelace, *Inside Linda Lovelace*, Pinnacle, 1973.

604. *Avant-Garde*, September 1969.

605. E. & P. Kronhausen, *ibid.*, 1971.

606. J. C. Lauret, *ibid.*,